The Micro-Macro Link

The Micro-Macro Link

Edited by

Jeffrey C. Alexander

Bernhard Giesen

Richard Münch

Neil J. Smelser

UNIVERSITY OF CALIFORNIA PRESS

Berkeley · Los Angeles · London

1987

University of California Press
Berkeley and Los Angeles, California

University of California Press, Ltd.
London, England

Printed in the United States of America

2 3 4 5 6 7 8 9

LIBRARY OF CONGRESS CATALOGING IN PUBLICATION DATA

The Micro-macro link.

Based on papers given at a conference sponsored by the theory sections of the German and American sociological associations held June 21–24 in Giessen, West Germany.

Includes index.

1. Sociology—Methodology—Congresses. 2. Macrosociology—Congresses. 3. Microsociology—Congresses. I. Alexander, Jeffrey C.

HM13.M53 1987 301.01'8 86–11309
ISBN 0–520–05786–4 (alk. paper)
ISBN 0–520–06068–7 (pbk)

Contents

Preface and Acknowledgments

This volume is based on a conference sponsored by the theory sections of the German and American Sociological Association. The idea for such a meeting was conceived in Mexico City in the summer of 1982 at the 10th World Congress of the International Sociological Association, when officers of the German section approached their counterparts on the American side. Both sections were enthusiastic about the idea, and planning was begun.

The meeting was held June 21–24, 1984, at Schloss Rauischholzhausen in Giessen, West Germany . Our local host was Professor Bernhard Giesen of the University of Giessen. Raymond Boudon was invited as a European participant from outside Germany, and although he did not attend we are pleased to include his essay here. Jürgen Habermas participated in the conference but was unable to contribute a final paper for the volume.

Expenses for the meeting, including transportation for all concerned, were covered by the Stiftung Volkswagenwerk, for whose generosity we would like to express our sincere appreciation.

After the conference the essays were submitted for an initial reading at University of California Press, and the anonymous reviewer's comments initiated an extended period of reworking and rewriting. Introductions and conclusions were facilitated by trips made by Professors Giesen and Münch to the United States.

The Editors

INTRODUCTION

From Reduction to Linkage: The Long View of the Micro-Macro Debate

Jeffrey C. Alexander and Bernhard Giesen

Our aim in this introduction is to take the long view on the micro-macro debate. Rather than paraphrase the essays that follow, which are powerful statements in their own right, we will provide a historical and theoretical framework within which they might be read. By providing such a framework we hope to draw attention to the unusual significance of the efforts that follow. In their conclusion to this book our fellow editors, Smelser and Münch, look back on the arguments that have been offered in a more concrete and comparative way.

The following essays contribute to a debate that has emerged as a key issue in contemporary sociological theory. The micro-macro problem transcends paradigmatic boundaries and in doing so fosters communication between different theory traditions and disciplinary integration. Although the micro-macro theme has entered sociological theorizing as a distinct and firmly established issue only in recent decades, its prehistory can be traced from late medieval thinking through postwar metamethodological debates over science, epistemology, and political philosophy.

We will argue that the micro-macro dichotomy should be viewed as an analytic distinction and that all attempts to link it to concrete dichotomies—such as "individual versus society" or "action versus order"—are fundamentally misplaced. Only if it is viewed analytically, moreover, can the linkage between micro and macro be achieved. During its intellectual prehistory, however, the very distinction between micro and macro was superseded by other conceptual oppositions. Powerful philosophical dichotomies conflated this more analytically differentiated notion with deeply entrenched disputes that were often supported by political and social conflicts. This overlapping of the micro-macro theme with epistemological, ontological, and political distinctions gave rise to fierce disputes that demanded that decisions be made between incompatible alternatives. Such an all-or-nothing choice precluded any attempt at reconciliation.

Transmitting the micro-macro theme from general, all-encompassing philosophical and political debates into the disciplinary realm of social science, we believe, gradually qualified the oppositions and conflicts that were implied in presociological statements of the problem. The effort to constitute sociology as a scientific discipline helped to close the border to ontological and metaphysical issues. The result was that for the first time the problem could be treated in a distinctly sociological rather than philosophical or political manner. We will show that in its initial, classical phase, sociological theory recast the conflated dichotomies into arguments about the general character of empirical processes. The questions came to focus on whether action was rational or interpretive and whether social order was negotiated between individuals or imposed by collective, or emergent, forces.

Translation into sociological theory did not, however, fully "secularize" the micro-macro debate. Although the imposition of empirical discipline closed off certain philosophical extremes and pointed to certain synthetic possibilities, in the main the controversy was simply shifted to another level. Indeed, the postclassical period witnessed a resurgence of philosophical debate which polarized the issue anew. Political and explanatory issues were once again conflated, the very possibility of emergent properties was sharply challenged, and metamethodological controversy erupted concerning the boundaries of sociology as a scientific discipline.

This philosophical debate was followed by a new round of dichotomizing argument in sociology. The response to this phase, in turn, depended upon the attempt to conceptualize the micro-macro theme as a distinction between different levels of empirical reality. This, we believe, has been the distinctive accomplishment of sociological debate in its most recent phase. Rather than confronting incompatible conceptions about the constitution of social reality, the theoretical arguments presented in this volume seek to discover empirical relations among different levels of social reality. This analytical differentiation of the micro-macro relation has generated a new level of interparadigmatic discourse and a new statement of the problem: The conflict over reduction is replaced by the search for linkage.

The path toward linkage and the implied possibilities for theoretical synthesis were prepared by the earlier theorizing of Max Weber and Talcott Parsons. Their theories resist classification as either micro or macro. The current movement from reduction to linkage is inspired by the example set by these first great attempts at micro-macro synthesis, even when they do not follow the theories themselves.

1. PHILOSOPHICAL BACKGROUND

Despite the current effort to overcome the rigorous opposition between micro- and macroapproaches through analytical differentiation and theoretical synthesis, it is impossible to overlook the fact that current debate bears the unmistakable imprint of earlier controversies. In our view this does not represent a weakness of contemporary theorizing; it suggests, rather, its strength and vigor in the face of demands for reasoning of a purely inductive kind.

Although superseded and, to some extent, transformed by classical sociological ideas, the micro-macro distinction ranks with the core oppositions in Occidental thinking, at least since the late medieval differentiation between the individual and the state. Entering academic discourse and political debate as part of the nominalism versus realism dispute, it helped form the background for such enduring controversies as whether the whole is more than the sum of its parts, whether state and society can claim ontological and moral primacy over individuals, and whether the meaning of concepts can be reduced to their empirical referent or involves some transcendental ideal.

Although connected to one another by reference to a common ontology and frequently intertwined during the history of modern thought, the epistemological dimension of this dichotomy can be distinguished from the political and constitutional one. After the turn of the century neopositivism, and the growing pressure on antipositivist philosophy to cope with epistemological presuppositions, generated new formulations of the old theme. Vitalism in biology and Gestalt theory in psychology defended the macro position against radical psychological behaviorism and rigorous scientific physicalism. The philosophical background for the latter, micro position was provided by the neopositivist postulation of a unified science based on the atomistic ontology and experimental methodology of modern physics. The repercussions of these early epistemological and ontological disputes, as we will show at a later point, continued to be felt in postwar metamethodological debates and in confrontations over the mind-body problem in contemporary philosophy of social science.

The political branch of the micro-macro dichotomy dates from the controversy over constitutions versus divine rights of kings. It was also related to arguments that the newly emerging nation should be the prime basis for political loyalty as compared to the societal community composed of individuals. The contractual thinking of the Scottish moralists, as well as John Stuart Mill's liberalism, established the individualist tradition in political philosophy. This so-called Anglo-Saxon tradition has formed the background for the microorientation in classical and contemporary sociological debate. That it took shape against the mainstream of continental political thinking must not be forgotten. The German idealism of Fichte, Hegel, and Herder, and the French revolutionary naturalism of such thinkers as Rousseau, provided the holistic orientations upon which classical and contemporary macroformulations arose. Although the development of sociological thinking in the past 100 years has tended to undermine this relation among geographical, cultural, and theoretical concerns, the history of such conflicts between national styles certainly formed one impetus for the German-American theory conference from which the essays in this volume are drawn.

2. THE MICRO-MACRO SPLIT IN CLASSICAL SOCIOLOGICAL THEORY

In the latter part of the nineteenth century and the early years of the twentieth, these philosophical dichotomies came to be reproduced in the founding statements of a new, more empirical mode of discourse: sociological theory. Although general and abstract, sociological theory differs from philosophy in its explicit commitment to empirical science. In sociological theory nonempirical concerns such as metaphysics and morals become implicit parts of discourse; they rarely define its explicit character. They become the "presuppositions" of sociological argument. It is onto this general, presupppositional level that the philosophical debate about individual and society comes to be translated, and even this presuppositional debate is often conducted in terms of the nature of concrete, empirical facts.

Although Marx eventually produced the most influential argument for a purely macro perspective in sociology, the emphasis in his early writings was on consciousness and action. Bringing Hegel's transcendental idealism "down to earth" via Feuerbach's critical materialism, Marx brought the force of critical rationality into play by insisting on the centrality of human activity (*praxis*) over objective force. He argued in "Theses on Feuerbach" (Marx [1845] 1965) against "the materialist doctrine that men are products of circumstances" and that "changed men are products of other circumstances." Such a doctrine forgets, he insists, "that it is men who change circumstances." This radical emphasis on the activist changing of circumstances clearly gives to the micro level pride of place. When Marx goes on to argue against "the materialist doctrine" on the grounds that it "necessarily arrives at dividing society into two parts," one begins to wonder just how radical this early sociological call for microanalysis might be. Does the critique of materialism mean that we must conceive of individuals and consciousness alone, without any reference to supraindividual structures?

This, of course, was not at all the case. Why it was not, moreover, can tell us something important about how the micro-macro link can be conceived sociologically. From the very beginnings of Marx's sociological writings it is clear that he never conceived of the actor in an individualistic way, and because he did not do so he would never suggest a purely micro focus. The *praxis* that changes circumstances in Marx's early writings is a form of interpersonal communication that achieves its critical leverage by appealing to deeply held, universalistic systems of belief—that is, beliefs that unite isolated individuals. As Marx ([1842] 1967:135) explains in one of his earliest essays from this period, "Ideas, which have conquered our intelligence and our minds, ideas that reason has forged in our conscience, are chains from which we cannot tear ourselves away without breaking our hearts." Focusing on individual consciousness—in either a cognitive, moral, or affective sense—and the micro level, in other words, does not necessarily imply an individual*istic* position that sees this individual consciousness as unrelated to any distinctively social, or collective, process. What it does mean, however, is that such collective force must be subjectively conceptualized.

The kind of empirical microanalysis to which such subjective formulations of collective order might lead is suggested by Marx's focus on alienation in the *Economic and Philosophical Manuscripts*. In contrast to purely philosophical writing—for example, earlier idealist and later existentialist traditions—alienation is not viewed here as an ontological condition, a conception that guarantees the irredeemable dichotomy of individual (micro) and society (macro). Marx describes alienation, rather, as a contingent empirical fact. This allows him the possibility of thinking in terms of interrelated levels. Arguing that alienation is, indeed, an individual experience of estrangement, he suggests that it can be seen simultaneously as a "translation" on the individual level of interpersonal, structural conditions. In these early writings, however, Marx does not insist on complete homology, on the replication of macro in micro conditions. He has vigorously called our attention to the micro level of alienation for a reason. He believes that it reveals a relatively autonomous mediation of collective order that must be studied in its own right. When Marx ([1844] 1963:131) insists that it is alienation which creates private property, not private property which creates alienation, he is arguing that individual experience can be a significant independent variable in macrosociological analysis even when it is not considered to be the source of social order in a presuppositional way.

Marx moves in his later theorizing to a more exclusively macro focus, but he does not do so because he has moved from an individualistic to a collectivist philosophical position. His focus earlier was on emergent properties located at the empirical level of the individual; his focus later is on emergent properties located at the empirical level of the group, collectivity, and system. He continues, in other words, to recognize emergent properties, and this means that his presuppositions about order—whether order is "individualistic" or "collectivist" (see Alexander 1982*a*)—remain the same. What has changed is not his approach to order but his understanding of action. As we will argue more systematically later in this essay, however, this kind of shift can have significant consequences for the micro-macro link. Because he has shifted from an expressive conception of action to an instrumental one in the writings after 1845, Marx uses alienation neither to underline emotional estrangement nor to establish, on this basis, the necessity for a microfocus. He uses it, rather, to emphasize the objectified, antiemotional quality of action in capitalist society and to establish, on these grounds, the irrelevance of the micro, "motivational question" to sociological analysis (see Alexander 1982*b*:48–53).

Because commodification is "in the saddle" and exchange value rules, the concrete, particular sensibility that Marx believes underlies human interpretation in noncapitalist societies is impossible. Because actors are reduced to beings that calculate their external environment mechanically, theoretical attention shifts entirely away from the microanalysis of consciousness, motive, and intention. Capitalists and workers are ruled by the naturalistic laws of social life. It is the inevitable movement from absolute to relative surplus value that propels them to socialist revolution. Objective circumstances now change people.

Marx's brilliant empirical elaboration of instrumental action and of the way it is restricted by macrostructures made late Marxism paradigmatic for every sociological theory that sought to privilege macro- over microanalysis. This structural emphasis in turn has created fundamental problems for Western neo-Marxism, which has tried to reinstate the centrality of consciousness to critical theory.

The classical alternative to such a structuralist approach to collective order was established by Durkheim, who, from the beginning of his career, searched for a way to combine awareness of society with commitment to the individual. Durkheim's connection to the philosophical traditions of holism and realism is abundantly clear, as in his famous declaration in *The Rules of Sociological Method* (Durkheim [1895] 1938) that "social facts are things" that have a "coercive" relation to the individual. Yet the same cautionary statement must be made about Durkheimian structuralism as was made about Marxian and for the same reason. Even in his most dramatically macro vein, Durkheim's commitment to sociological as opposed to philosophical realism led him to root society in interaction, an effort that allowed him to avoid the maximal anti-individualist extreme. In *The Division of Labor in Society* (Durkheim [1893] 1933), for example, he locates the macro, social force in the "non-contractual elements of contract," and he sees these as emerging from the functional interventions of an order-seeking state. The historical origins of modern social structure are similarly linked, in Book Two of that early work, to concrete interaction, in this case to the increasing density of population and the resulting struggle for survival. In *Suicide* ([1897] 1951) Durkheim links reified "suicidogenic currents," which he treats as fields of force in a purely macro sense, to patterns of interaction in different kinds of solidary groups.

Although Durkheim's commitments to empirical reasoning may have prevented him from the realist excesses of philosophical theorizing, it is nonetheless true that in these earlier writings he conceptualized emergent properties as exclusively macro. Only as his thinking developed in the 1890s did Durkheim find a way to avoid Marx's antithesis between individual (micro) and social (macro) determination. In a sense he rediscovered the insight of the early Marx. He came to understand that if action were conceptualized as symbolic and emotional, then collective order could be seen as exercising constraints by its ability to inform the exercise of these voluntary capacities. This led Durkheim to acknowledge, in principle, that a social theory premised on emergentism could have an empirically micro focus.

Thus as Durkheim moved toward a fundamentally "religious" theory of society, he insisted that the most powerful elements of symbol systems depended upon sacredness, that they were effective only because they drew the most protective feelings from individual personalities (see Alexander 1982*b*:259–298). When Durkheim ([1912] 1965) described how Aborigines, in their ritual ceremony, transformed themselves into figures of the totem animal, this was theoretical, not merely ethnographic, description. He had discovered how individual action reproduced social control. Action consisted of unending representations, symbolic activity that conceptualized collective representations in an appropriately individual way.

Microanalysis was certainly justified by this later mode of Durkheim's theorizing, for the illumination of perceptual processes and emotional and symbolic exchanges was believed to be at the heart of collective life. Durkheim, however, never developed even the rudiments of a social psychology that could explain such microprocess satisfactorily. This failure, combined with his positivist commitment to observable, "lawful" regularities and his missionary zeal to defend the autonomy of the sociological discipline, meant that the strikingly micro qualities of his later theorizing were never brought systematically to light, either by Durkheim, his followers, or his interpreters on the contemporary scene. Just as Marx's later writings became paradigmatic for macrotheorists writing within a rationalistic and materialistic tradition, Durkheim's later theory became the "classical" referent for sociologists who believed in the subjectivity of action but considered it to be ordered in a strictly macro, antivoluntaristic way.

Durkheim and Marx, then, for all the complexities and possibilities of their work, produced strongly polemical arguments for a one-sidedly macro emphasis (Alexander 1984*a*). Given the range of philosophical discourse that lay in the background of this classical debate, it was inevitable that their positions would be challenged by theories that polemicized just as strongly in a micro, antistructural way. Just as Durkheim and Marx conflated the presuppositional defense of the collective, or emergentist, approach with extratheoretical issues such as ideology, so would the individualism of these "anticollectivist" approaches be underlined by latent political points.

American pragmatism developed in direct antagonism to transcendental idealism in both its Kantian and Hegelian forms and, at least in its Jamesian mode (Lewis and Smith 1980), presented as strong a reaction to realism of any kind. Individual experience, in the pragmatist perspective, is the source of ideas, and meaning arises from interaction rather than vice versa. Mead's work represents the most significant translation of pragmatic philosophy into sociological theory. Inspired by American ideology, which insisted on the fluid and malleable character of its democratic society, Mead ([1934] 1964) likened society to a game. The move by any given actor is drawn forth in response to the action of another; it cannot be seen as the product of some a priori collective force. The reaction of another player, moreover, defines in significant ways the very meaning of the action to which that player responds. In the contingency of such game situations, actions and responses become the critical source for patterning social order. So conceived, Meadian theory leads to a microsociology devoid of macroreference. Mead wrote, in fact, almost nothing about institutional processes or the internal constitution of cultural systems.

To present Mead in this way, however, is to emphasize only one side of his work, albeit the side that has been picked up and emphasized by his successors in the interactionist tradition. Although meaning can grow only out of interaction with others, Mead believed, actors' perceptions of these others gradually become so generalized that they carry a "slice" of society around in their heads. He was convinced, moreover, that the very spontaneity and randomness of interaction guarantee that this generalized other will not differ radically from one actor to another. Thus although games are contingent and proceed through responses, every intention and every understanding is filtered through the layered expectations that constitute rules. Mead's actors interpret reality by referring to social standards, and the very idea of standards implies some interpersonal regularities.

Mead's work, then, presents a microanalysis that is open to more collectivist concerns (Alexander 1985*a*), much as Durkheim's theory presented a macroperspective that opened to the individual. Mead's theory, moreover, promised to get beyond the "homology" or "reproduction" position that limited the scope of microtheory of a Durkheimian kind. Just as Durkheim completely lacked a social psychology, however, Mead lacked an institutional theory. For Durkheim this meant that the possibilities for macro-micro linkage went unnoticed; for Mead it meant exactly the same thing. None of Mead's followers was able to discern in his microanalysis a collective link; it was experience, not individually mediated structure, that became the hallmark of interactionist microanalysis.

Similar problems affected the other major development in microanalysis that viewed action in a subjectivist manner. Although Freud was certainly not a philosopher, his focus on the individual reflected broader intellectual movements, such as Darwinism and vitalism, that were significant challengers to realism in his day. The explicitly sociological theories of early psychoanalysis, as articulated, for example, in *Group Psychology and the Analysis of the Ego* (Freud [1921] 1959), *Future of an Illusion* (Freud [1927] 1928), and *Civilization and Its Discontents* (Freud [1930] 1961), described extraindividual group processes as threats to individual action that should be neutralized whenever possible. Not only did the psychoanalytic theory of society deny that any necessary function was served by groups and collectivities, but it linked the very existence of the latter to individual fantasy and pathology. It conceived of them as distortions of reality that could be eliminated if individuals became more rational. From this theoretical foundation there followed the dictum that all collective phenomena—wars, revolutions, institutions, cultural life—must be explained as manifestations of individual personalities. This reductionist epiphenomenalism has been responsible for the radically micro focus of most psychoanalytically informed social science to the present day.

In dramatic opposition to this reduction stands Freud's more fully developed and more empirically substantiated clinical theory of the personality (e.g., [1923] 1961). Starting from the primordial fact of an actor's need to cathect external objects, Freud described an unending series of object internalizations. As cathexis spreads to objects that are further away from the nurturant, primary ones, personality growth is propelled by successive internalizations. On the one hand Freud sees the subject as constituted through such introjections; on the other he sees socialized actors as independent inputs to the structure of the very objects they encounter in turn.

Freud's clinical theory, then, by giving both extraindividual and individual-contingent elements their due, laid the basis for a systematic reconstruction of the micro-macro link. But this theoretical possibility was never pursued within the orthodox psychoanalytic tradition itself. The problem was not so much the absence of an institutional theory—the problem for pragmatism—but the presence of an institutional theory whose presuppositions were in radical opposition to those which informed the clinical work.

Mead and Freud outlined the "other side" of Durkheim's macrotheory, portraying microsubjective processes that could be orderly without coercive constraint. There also developed a "micro mirror image" for the other classical macrotradition, the theory of constraint without subjectivity produced by Marx. Rather than emphasizing interpretation or emotion, this microtheory portrays action as objective, mechanistic, and rational. The Marxian image of action as exchange is maintained, but the ideological critique that bound this theory to the capitalist period is discarded. The point is not that actors do not engage in social life but that when they do so they are not conceived as being socialized prior to that interaction. As a result, they calculate their relation to external reality rather than interpret the nature of their attachment to it. Because calculation is assumed to be an inherent, natural capacity, actors do not need to be supplied by society with interpretive standards. This assumed rationality, moreover, undermines the possible emotionality of action, for the latter is thought to have irrational, hence uncalculable, implications. For rational action theory is committed to the notion that behavior can be predicted in standardized, objective ways.

This rational action approach, though just as instrumentalist as Marx's, differs by being aggressively individualistic. Indeed, Marx conceived of his own theory as a "critique of political economy" because while accepting its presuppositions about action he rejected its individualism. Rational action theory brings the argument full circle; its proponents often conceive it as a response not only to subjectivist thinking but to the coercive implications of theories such as Marx's, which insist on encasing the rational actor in a collective frame.

This rationalistic version of microtheory did not present itself in nearly as cohesive a manner as interactionism or psychoanalysis, nor can it be related to intellectual developments so central to the twentieth century. At least three different traditions fed into it. The most important development for its contemporary form has been behaviorism, the "psychology without consciousness" developed by Watson and reinforced by the experiments of Pavlov. Behaviorism follows the Darwinian emphasis on adaptation and experience but excludes the pragmatic emphasis on interpretation. It portrays action as stimulus and response and views learning as the agglomeration of material experiences through physical reinforcement. That these stimuli and reinforcements were often orderly, and produced orderly behavior in turn, was viewed by behaviorism as the happy but unintended consequence of an endless chain of individual interactions.

The same emphasis on the unintended order of rational actions was, of course, at the heart of the rational choice theory articulated by classical economics. Beginning with the work of Adam Smith (1776) and extending into neoclassical thinking in the twentieth century, economic theory has developed a simple yet powerful calculus for predicting individual action. Once again, motivational rationality and significant environmental parameters are assumed as givens. Prices play the role of stimulus; purchases and investments, the role of response. Social order emerges from actions that have an entirely individual, self-interested bent. Markets structure opportunities so that transactions can be mutually profitable and reciprocity established. Because of this "invisible hand," the microfocus of rational choice is considered sufficient unto itself.

In the history of sociology, the microemphasis fostered by behaviorism and rational choice theory was given powerful support by Simmel's sociology (e.g., Homans 1958). This is ironic given that Simmel's philosophical position was antinominalist and that he sharply rejected any antisubjective understanding of action. The peculiarities of Simmel's reception can be traced to the artificial divisions he established between different dimensions of his theorizing, particularly the distinction between formal sociology and metaphysics or cultural sociology (Simmel 1950). Whereas metaphysics deals with subjectivity and speculates about generalities, sociology properly so called must abstract away from the particular content of experience and speak only about forms. Formal relationships such as conflict or exchange must, Simmel insisted, be looked at purely in terms of their quantitative characteristics—for example, the number of people involved and the number and rate of interactions. Within the confines of such objective parameters, then, the structure of social order can be portrayed as emerging from individual action and choice.

Although Simmel acknowledged that general concepts such as "the individual" exist and may even be significant regulators of interaction (Simmel 1977), he portrayed them as standing outside and above the heads of individual actors. As a result, he often portrayed interaction as if it proceeded without any reference to "concepts" at all (e.g., Simmel 1955). It is not surprising, then, that significant aspects of his formal sociology could be taken up by behaviorists and exchange theorists as justifications for pursuing a purely micro sociology.

This discussion of the classical sociological translations of philosophical debates about individual and society, brief and schematic as it has been, suggests that from the very beginning sociological thinking offered the promise of more synthetic, less resolutely antagonistic conceptualizations of the relationship between the two. On the one hand the explicit disciplinary commitment to "society" created an inherent interest in the connection between individual and collective behavior even among such reductive sociological theorists as the behaviorists. On the other hand, the explicitly empirical emphasis of the new discipline forced even such macrotheorists as Marx and Durkheim to seek to ground their references to collective forces in the activities of observable, acting individuals. If a sociologist, for disciplinary *cum* presuppositional reasons, emphasized the significance of collective or group forces, this did not mean that he or she denied the existence of acting individuals in an ontological sense. In fact, this did not even mean that he or she would deny that individual, micro process had a critical role to play in the maintenance of macro order. Because the collective forces Durkheim conceptualized were "ideal" but also empirical, they had to reside, in ontological terms, in the internal states of human individuals.

As this suggests, sociological theorists separated questions of ontology from questions of epistemology and reformulated both issues in more strictly sociological terms (Alexander 1982*a*:64–112). For sociological theory, epistemology becomes "the problem of action": Is the knowing actor rational or interpretive? Yet however action is postulated, the ultimate source of this knowledge remains to be decided. It may be located inside or outside the knowing individual. This is the problem of order, and it indicates the sociological recasting of the ontological question. The question of order for sociology concerns the ultimate source of social patterns; it does not concern the ontological question of whether these patterns or the individuals who may or may not support them are real. The origin of patterns may be conceived individualistically, in which case the "credit" for social patterns, the role of independent variable, is given to microprocess in a contingent way. Conversely, the origin of patterns may be conceived as emanating from some source outside any particular individual, in which case the individual actor, whose existence per se is still acknowledged, may be conceived as the victim of collective circumstances or their more or less willing (because socialized) medium.

The emergence of sociological theory from philosophy, then, makes the micro-macro issue significantly more complex. For sociological theory, the micro may be conceived as a level of analysis that deserves independent consideration even though the individual may not be considered, either ontologically or metaphysically, as the source of order in his or her own right. Because sociology insists on an empirical focus, and because its disciplinary vocation is directed to society, the issues of contingency and freedom are not inherently connected to a focus on the individual per se. It is for this reason that empirical dispute ranges so widely.

Because of such presuppositional complexity, at least five major approaches to the micro-macro relation have been taken up. Sociological theory has maintained that (1) rational, purposeful individuals create society through contingent acts of freedom; (2) interpretive individuals create society through contingent acts of freedom; (3) socialized individuals re-create society as a collective force through contingent acts of freedom; (4) socialized individuals reproduce society by translating existing social environment into the microrealm; and (5) rational, purposeful individuals acquiesce to society because they are forced to by external, social control.

To explain this range of possibilities, it is vital to understand that in sociological theory the question of action is separated from the question of order. A collective position may be adopted which denies the primary responsibility of individuals and therefore negates a primarily micro focus. This position on order, however, may be associated with either of two different understandings of action: the instrumental-objective or the interpretive-subjective. The collective theory that takes an objectivist approach to action denies to subjective perceptions of order any empirical role at all, militating against any particular focus on the micro or individual level itself. This is option 5. The collective theory that takes an interpretive approach, in contrast, makes subjective perception central, although it insists that the contents of this perception lie beyond the contingency of individual acts. In this theoretical tradition microprocesses may well become central points of empirical interest, if only because phenomena such as personalities and interaction are conceived as central "conveyor belts" for collective facts. If individual subjectivity is so conceived as mere reproduction, we have option 4. If, however, subjective collectivist theory gives to the micro level analytical autonomy—if, that is, it recognizes that the socialized individual re-creates in the process of reproducing—then we have option 3.

For theoretical positions that stress the complete contingency of social action, moreover, even analytical autonomy is not enough. The micro is equated with the individual, and the latter is viewed as the primary source of order itself. To understand the relevance of even this latter tradition to the micro-macro debate, however, it is not sufficient to focus on the issue of individualism alone. Individualistic conceptions of order, just like collectivist ones, are always informed by different understandings of action. Individualistic theories may stress the rational and objective character of action, in which case microanalysis focuses on empirical phenomena such as costs, investments, and opportunities (option 1). If, in contrast, the subjectivity of individualistic order is stressed, the microfocus is shifted to the processes of interpretation and to how they are conducted in a contingent manner. This marks option 2.

In our discussion in this section we have suggested that classical political economy and behaviorism pursued the first option, whereas pragmatism and psychoanalysis embraced the second. Durkheim largely embraced the fourth possibility, and in his later and most influential writings Marx pursued the fifth. Contained in the theorizing of almost all of these figures, we have tried to indicate, there exists the outline of a more synthetic link. Depending on the theorist, this link points to combining several options, embracing option 3, or both.

3. THE FIRST SYNTHETIC FORMULATION: MAX WEBER

Although each of the positions we have described took up the relationship between micro and macro dimensions in its own particular way, and some made genuine contributions to outlining their actual interpenetration, all remained burdened by overcommitments to one side or the other. Of all the classical sociologists, only Weber seemed to see a clear way out of this traditional dilemma. Although in the end Weber's formulations are still not entirely satisfactory—and even their precise nature is subject to dispute—his contributions have remained central for every subsequent effort at establishing a micro-macro link.

As a German progressive strongly influenced by the Enlightenment and liberal traditions, Weber was particularly forceful in his rejection of organicist formulations. Because of this heightened sensitivity, which contrasts, for example, with the relatively complacent attitude of Durkheim, one finds no trace of an ontologically collectivist position in Weber's work. He insists over and over again that all that "really" exists is social action. This insistence, however, has often misled his interpreters to portray his theory as nominalistic. For this reason the rubric "action theory" is often applied to his work. To interpret Weber in this way, however, is to ignore not only the empirical mediation of ontology that is at the foundation of sociological theory but the specifically anti-individualistic thrust of Weber's own work.

Collective order was still Weber's point of departure. What he managed to avoid was conceptualizing this order in a manner that would imply the insignificance of acting individuals. Rather than speaking about "forces," Weber was careful to talk about "uniformities of action." A uniformity is not something that happens to an actor but a shorthand way of talking about what is actually a series of actions. "Within the realm of social action," he wrote in *Economy and Society* (Weber 1978:29), "certain empirical uniformities can be observed, that is, courses of action that are repeated by the actor or (simultaneously) occur among numerous actors." What sociology is concerned with is "typical modes of action," not individual actions as such.

Although empirical and action-related, uniformities are "orders" in the sense that they are not reducible to free and contingent acts. "Orders" refers to arrangements that are not contingent in the framework of any given act. Such arrangements can also be called structures, and structures, in all their historical and comparative variation, are what Weber's sociology is all about. Weber wrote about religious systems, legal institutions, political frameworks, modes of production, and urban associations. He devoted himself to exposing the structural patterns that are internal to each of these institutional spheres—the internal logic of theodicies, for example, and the inherent contradictions of patrimonialism.

Weber never assumed that such a system emphasis excluded the individual. His theorizing moves back and forth, naturally and fluidly, between the macroanalysis of ideational complexes and institutional systems and the microanalysis of how individuals within such situations make interpretations and purposefully act. Theodicies develop only because the human concern with death makes intellectual speculation about salvation a fundamental form of social activity (e.g., Weber [1916] 1946). Religious rationalization is possible only because the cognitive, affective, and moral constitutions of individuals lead them to respond to typical situational exigencies in an abstracting and systematizing way. Patrimonial systems can be contradictory because motives for status and power are omnipresent and because individuals' sense of their ideal interest emerges only within the context of local and concrete interactions.

Still, the recognition of individuals in societies is not, as we have seen, sufficient by itself to define a sociological position on the micro-macro dispute. Durkheim and Marx, although in much less sophisticated ways than Weber, held views on this issue which were not fundamentally different from Weber's. How does Weber differ from them? Where does Weber stand in terms of the five ideal-typical positions outlined above? To find out, it is necessary to explore his understanding of action separately from his understanding of order and to see whether this understanding blocks or facilitates an appreciation of contingency.

We argued earlier that the micro level can be forcefully brought into more collective theorizing only if subjective interpretation is considered a major characteristic of action. In much of his work Weber does, in fact, make interpretation central to his understanding of action. In *Economy and Society* (1978:4) he wrote that sociology is "a science which attempts the interpretive understanding of social action in order thereby to arrive at a causal explanation of its course and effects." In an earlier essay, *Roscher and Knies*, he insisted that to "understand" an action one must "identify a concrete 'motive' or complex of motives 'reproducible in inner experience,' a motive to which we can attribute the conduct in question with a degree of precision" (Weber [1903–1906] 1975:25).

When these statements are juxtaposed, it is clear that Weber was making two central and interrelated points. First, subjective motivation is central to conduct. Second, because of this centrality sociology must involve a microanalysis of the course of concrete, individual interaction. Such an analysis may not necessarily reveal the unique contingency of individual action. If the motives discovered through microanalysis are typical or "uniform," then the microanalysis will illuminate how individual action is crucial for the reproduction of ideational structures (option 4), not for their re-creation (option 3).

Weber devoted a major portion of his sociological energy to a historical and comparative analysis of the social requisites of individuality, to demonstrating that social reproduction increasingly comes to focus on the autonomous individual. Analyzing the transition from sib societies to entrepreneurial capitalism, he demonstrated how collective structures—from religion to law to family—affect the individual actor's capacities for individuality. He showed that individual autonomy is neither ontologically given nor the product of material sanctions and rewards but, rather, dependent upon the socially given perceptions of self and on socially structured motivation. The very fact that a reductionistic microsociology can be proposed in modern social theory, Weberian analysis suggests, may itself be evidence of this millennia-long social reconstruction of the individual. If the modern individual is indeed capable of resistance to social pressure, it is because of an inner strength that is historically and socially derived.

Weber, then, clearly articulated the fourth theoretical position on the micro-macro link presented earlier: He showed that the social environment relies upon its reproduction via socialized individual action. Weber did not merely render a theoretically sophisticated, historically amplified demonstration of this essentially Durkheimian point, however; he went beyond it in a significant way. His insistence on the centrality of action made him extraordinarily sensitive to contingency. This pushed him toward option 3, to the recognition that socialized individuals re-create society through their contingent action.

Historiographically, this insistence comes through in Weber's insistence on developmental as opposed to evolutionary history. He stresses the role of historical accident (e.g., Weber 1949 [1905]) and how the inherent temporality of action makes every general pattern dependent on specific, open-ended, individual decisions. Sociologically, the emphasis on contingency comes through in Weber's insistence on the role of leadership in politics and charismatic innovation in religion. What each of these emphases—accident, leadership, and charisma—entails is not simply empirical recognition of the micro level but an acceptance of its relative autonomy. Events, not just situations, become subjects of sociological analysis.

Given the power of Weber's insight, it is strange that so little microanalysis actually appears in his work. We find little in Weber about the processes of individual socialization, the dynamics of family interaction, the phenomenon of political persuasion, the emotional and moral underpinnings of social movements. Indeed, Weber's systematic sociology of modern twentieth-century society depicts a structural "iron cage" that produces adherence regardless of individual motive or inclination. In terms of the micro-macro link, this later sociology of modern society is not much different from that of Marx. Both are organized around theoretical option 5: Autonomous individuals acquiesce to society because they are forced to do so by coercive social control. This perspective makes reference to the micro level irrelevant, although it does not, of course, imply any ontological collectivism in the philosophical sense.

How has Weber arrived at such a position, a position that denies the very linkage between micro and macro he devoted so much of his work to sustain? He does so, we suggest, because of presuppositional tendencies (Alexander 1983*a*) in his work which counteract his interpretive understanding of action. There are strains of *Realpolitik* and liberal utilitarianism in Weber, strains that often lead him to presuppose action in a materialistic, objective, and instrumental manner. If action is so conceived, motive becomes irrelevant. What matters is the external environment of action and the pressures it mounts. Even in Weber's sociology of traditional life, clear manifestations of such an antisubjectivist theory occurred. In his analysis of contemporary rationalization, these tendencies came to dominate his work. This is the source of Weber's ambiguous legacy to general sociology. It is also the reason that Weberian sociology has done so little since Weber to link the levels of micro and macro debate.

4. THE RENEWAL OF PHILOSOPHICAL DICHOTOMIES IN THE POSTWAR PERIOD

Although we have argued that sociological theory made significant advances over earlier philosophical considerations of the micro-macro problem, it certainly did not put an end to philosophical attempts to consider it anew. For one thing, there is an inherent link between sociological theory and philosophy. For another, the efforts of classical sociology in no sense could be seen as having resolved the micro-macro polarization. To the contrary, we have shown that in crucial respects the classical efforts can be seen as reproducing this polarization on another plane.

It should not be surprising, then, that after World War II there emerged a new round of philosophical argument that reinstated the links among ontological, metaphysical, and presuppositional issues and, in so doing, sought to frame the micro-macro argument in the most rigorous either-or terms. The focus has been on the problem of emergence. Individualists such as Hayek (1952), Popper (1958, 1961), Berlin (1954), and Watkins (1952, 1959) claimed that the concept of emergence should be reserved for the relation between mind and body. It serves to demarcate the realm of autonomy, free will, and deliberation from the realm of material nature and determinism. To speak of emergence as referring to the relation between individuals and collectivities, they argued, is to deny individual autonomy and to subject human beings to the will of supraindividual powers. Social entities such as institutions and collectivities cannot exist without the individuals who create and support them. They must therefore be regarded as ontologically dependent on the actions and cannot, for this reason, exhibit emergent properties. Any conception of supraindividual entities transcending the scope of individual actions is a mistaken category. There was a metaphysical dimension to the individualists' argument as well. They regarded collectivist ontology as implying antiliberal ideology. As political liberals, they condemned emergentism as a menace to Western ideas of democratic and economic freedom.

The opposition to these arguments for microreduction, developed by philosophers such as Mandlebaum (1955, 1957) and Goldstein (1956, 1958) insisted on differentiating metaphysical from ontological issues (see also Giesen and Schmid 1977). Even if we concede the existence of supraindividual entities, our position with respect to them is by no means fixed. Just as faith in the existence of God need not automatically entail obedience to His will, the conception of supraindividual entities does not involve submission to them. We can admit that only individuals are capable of autonomous actions yet argue simultaneously that the products of human actions exhibit emergent properties (Mandlebaum 1955).

This defense of emergentism against the suspicion of metaphysical collectivism, though in no sense ending the debate, set the stage for a more delimited, methodological version of the philosophical dispute. Methodological individualists such as Nagel (1961), Opp (1972), and Malewski (1967) argued that microtheories are superior because the attributes of individuals are more directly observable than complex, theoretical attributes such as "stratification," "legal authority," or "class." On these grounds they argued that sociological terms must be translated into observable attributes of individual actors. This neopositivist design for the social sciences wished to follow the reductionist program of modern physics; for example, the successful reduction of chemical theories to physical laws. It was hoped that on the basis of a universal observational language, sociological terms could be translated into psychological terms and that on this basis a unified science of human behavior would emerge.

Methodological holists attacked these arguments for their naive empiricism. Without questioning the attraction of observability and reduction in principle, they nevertheless doubted the possibility of reducing existing sociological theories to psychological ones. Terms referring to social structures or institutions, they argued, can never be defined by individual behavior without enclosing other macroterms inside of these new definitions (Mandelbaum 1955; Giesen and Schmid 1977). Even if this translation could be achieved, moreover, it would certainly not support the case for methodological individualism in an unambiguous way. Translations and definitions establish only a relation of equivalence; such a relation could just as well be used to reduce micro- to macrotheories. Even the requirement of observability does not unequivocally justify microtheorizing. Attributes such as motive, personality, and biography can by no means be regarded as plainly observable; they are themselves informed by theoretical concepts. By the same token, in societies that have developed specialized institutional records and accounting procedures macrostructural properties such as legal systems or income distribution can, in fact, be observed.

This defense of the autonomy of sociology and the integrity of its subject matter, however, provided new grounds upon which individualistic philosophy sought to make its case. It was argued that even if we accept the notion that sociologists, and actors more generally, do use holistic notions about institutions and collectivities in their everyday practice, we cannot understand the meaning of such notions unless we recognize that they are merely the aggregate of individual actions. A satisfactory sociological explanation, then, must refer to the actions of individuals, to their intentions and to their definitions of the situation. Indeed, Popper, Hayek, and Watkins went so far as to contend that the centrality of human action in the social sciences limited theoretical options much more sharply than in the natural sciences. They maintained that the only viable framework for social science is the paradigm of rational action, in which "rational" and "action" are viewed as inherent properties of the autonomous individual.

This justification of microreduction through action theory leads us naturally to the sociological theory of Talcott Parsons. His work emerged at virtually the same time as this revival of postwar philosophical debate and, we believe, represented its most sophisticated sociological rejoinder.

5. THE SECOND SYNTHETIC FORMULATION: TALCOTT PARSONS

Although this philosophical argumentation certainly affected sociological thinking about the micro-macro relation—and clearly played a major role in bringing the problem itself to theoretical center stage—its tendency to resuscitate conflationary and dichotomous modes of thinking about the problem did not necessarily reflect the level of sociological debate. For in the midst of this renewed controversy about the possibility of emergence, Talcott Parsons was elaborating a theory that went beyond even Weber in showing exactly how such emergence proceeds.

A sophisticated commitment to emergence—to the empirical and naturalistic quality of "collective" control—marked Parsons's theory from the outset. In this respect he benefited from Weber's remarkable sensitivity to this issue and from Durkheim's manifest mistakes. In *The Structure of Social Action*, Parsons (1937) called for a voluntaristic theory of action. He defined voluntarism only conditionally in an individualistic way. On one hand he insisted on the centrality of action in the liberal and utilitarian sense. This marked the "micro" aspect of his analysis. Throughout the book, for example, Parsons conceptualizes collective order in terms of "means/ends chains." On the other hand Parsons insisted on distinguishing between what he called the "analytical" and the "concrete" individual. When he wrote about the "actor" in his concept of the "unit act"—the theoretical model of actor-means-ends-situation to which Parsons refers throughout the book—he meant to refer only to the analytical individual, not to a real individual in his or her concrete empirical form. What defines the analytical individual is the utter contingency of his or her acts, a quality Parsons identifies as effort. What defines the concrete individual, however, is not only effort but all manner of social constraints. Parsons believed that the concrete empirical individual must be made a significant part of social theory if the latter is to be voluntaristic. This voluntarism, like the concrete individual, combines contingency and control and implies the need for a micro-macro link.

Parsons's sophistication about collective control was evident throughout his early work, but his focus was not on the structure of collective systems as such. He focused, rather, on the boundary between action and order. He wanted to know the precise mechanism that links micro, individual action to macro, collective context. He discovered this mechanism in the phenomenon of internalization, a process he believed lay at the heart of the most important accomplishments of Durkheim and Weber. It is through recognizing internalization that a collective theory becomes voluntaristic.

Although Parsons discovered internalization in this early period, there is no discussion in *The Structure of Social Action* of the actual mechanisms by which such a process might be carried out. This was, in fact, the principal objection Parsons lodged against Durkheim: that he lacked a social psychology—in our terms, a microtheory—that could operationalize his subjectivist theory of order in a plausibly voluntaristic way. The need to supply such a mechanism defined the middle period of Parsons's career.

In the period that extended from the mid-1940s to the mid-1950s,

Parsons developed the most important formulation of the micro-macro link since Weber. He did so by finding a way to combine two of the most important representatives of the micro/macro split: Freud and Durkheim. Durkheim had developed a theory of collective order which implied that this order would be carried in the heads of individuals; his theory faltered, however, because he was unable to describe these interpreting individuals convincingly. Freud had demonstrated that interpretive, feeling individuals are formed from object internalizations of the external world; in his explicitly sociological work, however, he tried to explain this external world as if it were only the projection of personality.

Parsons sociologized the psychoanalytic theory of the personality and used these insights to psychologize fundamental macroprocesses in turn. In key chapters of his *Essays in Sociological Theory* (1954:89–102, 177–196, 298–322), *Family, Socialization, and Interaction Process* (and Bales 1955:3–186), and *Social Structure and Personality* (1963:passim), Parsons demonstrated in systematic empirical detail how the affective, cognitive, and moral development of the personality depends on the existence of group structures. The ecology and culture of an actor's environment structure the responses that can be made to his or her unfolding psychological needs. These responses, which are macro from the perspective of the personality, enter the actor's perceptual world, or microenvironment. After being mediated by preexisting personality structures, they become new parts of the personality. The macro has thus become the micro. This dialectic continues in subsequent interactions. Because projections of the socialized personality affect the social world in strategic ways, the micro will almost immediately become macro again.

Parsons demonstrated this micro-macro dialectic for "pathological" and "normal" development alike. He showed, for example (e.g., Parsons 1954:298–322), that the distance between work and home in modern society, a macro fact, made the young male child overly dependent on his mother. One result of this is an exaggerated Oedipal complex, a microdevelopment that makes it more difficult for adult males to control their dependency needs. Uncontrolled dependency produces frustration, and the anxiety is often displaced through aggression. The path of this displacement, however, can never be decided by this microdevelopment alone. It is affected by the nature of group conflict in any particular society. Depending on the particular macroenvironment, it can be channeled into individual competition, into racial or class conflict, or into war between national units. Although this macro side is independent of psychological conditions, through the social channeling of aggression these conditions enter and transform the macroenvironment in turn.

In terms of normal development, Parsons showed that social differentiation makes individual autonomy possible. The separation of father from teacher, for example (Parsons 1963:129–154), makes rebellion against authority more possible and more controllable, which encourages decathexis from the parent and a full resolution of the Oedipal stage. Because successful resolution of this stage makes control of emotions and dependency more likely, it constitutes a micro basis for the development of universalistic culture. The original differentiation of teacher from parent, however, is itself dependent upon the existence of some overarching universalistic culture and some opportunities for mobility based on achievement rather than ascription. Microstructures are built on internalizations; macrostructures depend on externalizations in turn.

It was as a result of his insight into the micro-macro link that Parsons elaborated the concept of "role." Roles are translations of macro, environmental demands onto the level of individual behavior. Roles are not collective in the ontological sense; they consist of internalizations, expectations, and resources that enter the contingent situation from some preexisting environment. The invisibility of roles allowed Parsons to insist that the apparently "purely micro" nature of individual interaction actually occurs within collective constraints.

In the sociological work that unfolded under the Parsonian rubric, the linkage between micro and macro was a central theme. Merton made the "role set" pivotal to a whole range of macrosociological processes (Merton 1968: 422–440), and Goode (1960) demonstrated how systemic contradictions often made themselves felt only insofar as they created role strain. Family structures were investigated and systematically linked to social structure (Slater 1968; Levy 1949; Bellah 1970); the dynamics of group interaction processes were mapped (Bales 1951; Slater 1966), and this map was used as the basis for the "interchange" model of social systems at large (Parsons and Bales 1955). Models developed to explain sequences of family socializations were used for studying social change (Smelser 1959) and collective behavior (Smelser 1962), and the differentiation of familial roles was connected to differentiation between systems such as economies and polities (e.g., Parsons and Smelser 1956).

Although Parsons conceptualized the micro-macro link in a more sophisticated manner than ever before, he did so in what remained a limited way. The problem was that despite his concern with the individual, he ignored contingency. Durkheim was interested in nesting individual action within social constraints. Freud was intent on reducing individual action to organized personalities. Both of the thinkers upon whom Parsons drew for his own conception of the micro-macro link, in other words, were intent on exploding the myth of the autonomous individual. For Parsons this meant pursuing, as Durkheim did, micro-macro option 4,[1] since he denied Freud's claim that organized personalities were not themselves reflections of social structure. Following both Freud and Durkheim, however, Parsons ignored the strands of the classical tradition that were concerned with contingency, either pragmatic or utilitarian. Both pragmatists and utilitarians recognized a space between actors and their environments, the former because interpretation intervened between every new moment and what was given before it (option 2); the latter because rational motivation objectified the environment of action in a manner that made it seem outside of the acting individual (option 1).

Parsons was correct that sociology could not exist if the analytical individual were taken as the topic of microanalysis. He was incorrect, however, to think the very concept of contingency could be replaced by the relatively socialized, concrete individual alone. True, he had discovered the social psychology that Durkheim lacked, but he used this microanalysis only to root the social firmly in the individual. Although the concept of contingent "effort" existed in his earliest formulations of action, his neo-Durkheimian position left him unconcerned with action-as-effort—and therefore unable to conceptualize option 3—in all but a few segments of his subsequent work. Furthermore, his tendency to normativize action made it impossible to consider the possibility that order could be objectified and exert coercive control over action (option 5).

6. THE RENEWAL OF MULTIPARADIGMATIC DEBATE

In the phase of sociological theorizing that followed this second major effort at synthesis, the controversies that had been rekindled earlier in philosophical discussion found their way back into sociological theory itself. In part this represented dissatisfaction with the limits of Parsons's understanding of linkage, both because of its idealist bias and because of its anticontingent stance. This motive represented, as it were, the "progressive" reason for the revival of the micro versus macro debate. From the perspective of the contemporary period (see, e.g., Alexander 1987), however, it is clear that these post-Parsonian debates can be considered regressive as well. Influenced by the revival of philosophical calls for dichotomization and by theoretical confusion about the meaning of Parsons's work, this new round of theorizing often failed to come to grips with the sophistication of Parsons's argument—and Weber's before him —that the interpenetration of micro and macro can be made.

6.1. RECONSTITUTING THE DICHOTOMIES IN AMERICAN SOCIOLOGY

In the period that extended roughly from the early 1960s to the early 1980s, sociological theorizing in the United States gradually severed the link that Parsons had laboriously constructed between microanalysis and macroanalysis. On the one hand there developed the most vigorous and creative renewal of microtheorizing in the history of sociology. On the other hand there emerged a form of "structural analysis" that emphasized macro constraints at the expense of action. Because of historical circumstances such as the renewal of social conflict; because of American ideology, with its emphasis on freedom; and because of autonomous theoretical considerations, it became difficult for American theorists to accept Parsons's emphasis on the socialized individual. They demanded new conceptualizations of action, new models of order, and new formulations of contingency.

When Homans (1958, 1961) introduced exchange theory, he was renewing the very utilitarian theory that had constituted the basis of Parsons's influential early critique. He rejected the collective, emergentist tradition in classical sociology entirely, as well as the interpretive strand of the microtradition. Drawing upon Simmel and Smithian political economy, he developed a sociological form of behaviorism in Skinnerian terms. Homans insisted that the "elementary forms" of social life were not extraindividual elements such as symbol systems, as Durkheim had argued in his later work, but individual actors of a decidedly rationalist bent. Rejecting the notion of emergentism, he focused on what he called "subinstitutional" behavior, and he considered the behavior of "actual individuals" to be entirely separated from the stipulations of norms. Intention and individual decision became the focus of analysis, first because individuals were considered to be encased in contingency and second because the assumption of absolute rationality meant that the social forces impinging on them were viewed, by both actor and analyst, as objectified and external to any act. This, of course, represents option 1.

Exchange theory became enormously influential in reviving the case for an interactionally based microsociology. Its simple and elegant model facilitated predictions; its focus on individuals made it empirically operational. It also caught hold of a fundamental insight that Parsons had ignored: Contingent participation in exchange decisions is the path by which "objective conditions" become translated into the terms of everyday life. The price for such insights was high, however, even for theorists inside the paradigm itself. Theorists such as Blau and Coleman have since tried to introduce significant revisions (for the sometimes surprising extent of these revisions, see their essays in this book), and such efforts are continued in the contemporary German scene.

The other strands of the micro revival have taken up the interpretive side of action. Blumer (1969) is the general theorist most responsible for the revival of Meadian work, although the tradition he called "symbolic interactionism" took up pragmatism only in its radically contingent form. Blumer insisted, in opposition to macroanalysis of the interpretive type, that meaning must be seen to be simply the result of individual negotiation. It is determined by others' reactions as much as by the individual act. The actor, moreover, is not viewed as bringing some previous collective order into this contingent situation. Situational relevance, not previous socialization, decides what the actor brings into play. "Self-indication" is the concept Blumer developed to describe actors' Promethean ability to make an object out of themselves. It is the actors' temporally rooted "I" which determines what elements of their past will be brought into play from moment to moment.

Blumer's call for getting into actors' heads, for a methodology of direct observation, became a second significant focus for the revival of sociological theory in an entirely micro mode. The most important empirical theorist in this movement, Erving Goffman, seemed to most observers of the time merely to point interactionist theory in a more problem-specific and dramaturgical direction. Indeed, in his early work Goffman (1959) emphasized the "presentation of self" as opposed to the significance of social roles and tried to explain institutional behavior as emergent from the direct face-to-face behavior of concrete actors. Goffman's later work turned more to the micro-macro link, but his greatest impact was to revivify an anticollective microsociology.

Ethnomethodology, the American version of phenomenology, makes a more complicated story. Garfinkel was a student not only of Schutz but also of Parsons, and his earliest work (1963) begins where Parsons's left off. He accepts Parsons's equation of internalization and institutionalization, and he made the autonomy of the macro level of social order the starting point of his microsociology. What Garfinkel explored in his early work, then, were the methods by which actors made social norms their own—their "ethno" methodology. From phenomenology he accepted, in a way that Parsons never had, the utter contingency of action, and he described cognitive techniques such as indexicality and "ad hocing" (Garfinkel 1967) by which binding rules were specified situationally and modified in turn. He pursued, in other words, the relatively unexplored theoretical option 3.

As ethnomethodology became a major theoretical movement, however, its dichotomous rather than synthetic approach to the micro-macro link became increasingly predominant (Alexander 1985). The mandate came to be seen as a call for producing an alternative to sociology, one that would raise "members' own practices" to the level of governing focus. The omnipresence of such practices as indexicality and ad hocing were now seen as evidence for the utter contingency of order. The practice of orderly activity came to be identified with order itself (Garfinkel et al. 1981). Microanalysis now assumed center stage, the macro perceived not as a level of empirical analysis but as an antagonistic presuppositional position. "Conversational analysis," the offshoot of ethnomethodology developed by Sacks and Schegloff (see the essay by Schegloff, chapter 9), conceptualized speech in quite a different manner, as interpretation governed by constraining interactional rules. Even though conversational analysts usually insisted that these rules emerge simply from the practice of speech, the openings between their perspective and macroanalysis were more distinct than developments in other late ethnomethodological work.

This revival of microsociology reintroduced the first and second theoretical possibilities outlined earlier: (1) the notion that free, rational individuals create order in a completely contingent way, and (2) the position that sees order as the contingent creation of free, interpretive individuals. This was the individualist direction taken by the post-Parsonian theorizing that challenged Parsons's limited version of the micro-macro link.

The other challenge attacked Parsons's synthesis from the opposite direction. Rather than claiming that Parsons was overly macro because he had ignored contingency, this development challenged him because he had overemphasized voluntarism and individuality; because, that is, he had been overly micro. This formula, too, had a significant element of truth, for in his insistence on the homology of subjective motive and social control Parsons had underplayed the manner in which instrumental motives allow social control to be objectified in an apparently coercive manner. Rational actors—albeit actors who are socialized to the capacity for objectification—are indeed often tied to macroenvironments mainly because of the external power of those environments.

This is a micro reworking of the fifth theoretical option. In emphasizing this option as the principal form of the individual-society relation, however, the post-Parsonian "structuralist" challenge broke the micro-macro link completely. It made an argument for an antimicro form of macrotheory.

The most important theoretical statements of this position have come from Europe, particularly from the French structuralist school of Althusser. We will discuss this theoretized structuralist position in our discussion of Germany in section 6.2. America, however, has provided the most influential macrostructuralist theories of the middle range. The mainly empirical reference of this American theory should not obscure its ambitious theoretical bent. No doubt the most imposing single work has been Skocpol's *States and Social Revolutions* (1979), which polemicized against all "subjective" and "voluntaristic" theories of revolutions in the name of a structuralist theory that focused exclusively on external environments. Wright's (1978) class analysis takes up the same antimicro theme, arguing that ambiguities in a group's class consciousness come from "contradictory class locations." Treiman (1977) similarly produced a "structural theory of prestige" that converted cultural into organizational control and denied any independent role to subjective volition. In still another influential work, Lieberson (1980) argued that racial inequality in the United States could be explained only by "structures of opportunity," and that the subjective inclinations of actors must not be given the status of independent variables.

6.2. THE STRUCTURALIST REVIVAL IN CONTINENTAL SOCIOLOGY

In Central European sociology, the reaction against the predominance of Parsonian functionalism during the 1950s took quite a different turn. The collectivist view of functionalism was maintained, but its attempt to link structural processes to patterns of consciousness was broken. The most influential formulation of this Marxist alternative was provided by Althusser and his students (Althusser and Balibar 1968; Godelier 1967). "Objective social structures" above and beyond subjective consciousness are postulated. Historical developments, social conflicts, and collective actions are analyzed as particular variations, transformations, and incarnations of fundamental structural principles. Rather than starting with the empirical and phenomenal diversity of social actions and life-worlds, as contemporary microtheorists advised, structuralists gave ontological and methodological primacy to the "totality": One starts with fundamental structures and relates phenomenal diversity to it. Although individual actions may deviate from structural imperatives, the objective consequences of these actions are determined by these structures, which exist beyond the actors' control.

The major effort to counter this disregard for the micro level also emerged from within the Marxian camp. Exegetically based on the philosophy of the young Marx (see section 2 of this introduction), "praxis philosophy" (e.g., Thompson 1978) and "critical theory" (e.g., Habermas 1970) stressed the revolutionary role of subjectivity, reflection, and dialectical fantasy in opposition to the "repressive structures of society." Because Parsons took the micro as homologous with social structures, he could reason from social consensus to system equilibrium. Structural Marxism took system conflict as its first principle, and its severing of the micro-macro link allowed it to disregard subjective consensus in turn. Critical, or praxis, theory agreed with functionalism that a system's structures might be temporally intact (Marcuse 1963), but the break it postulated between micro and macro allowed it to maintain the omnipresence of rebellion nonetheless.

Because of the scarcity of theoretical resources within Marxism, and because of ideological constraints as well, this micromovement within Marxism was eventually charged with being scarcely more than a critical methodology. Some of the key participants in the earlier subjectivist movement returned to orthodox structuralist assumptions and political economy (Offe [1972] 1984; Hirsch 1974). They focused on the function of the state in capitalist accumulation and tried to derive social problems and crises from "inevitable" state intervention. These interventions, it was maintained, uncoupled the antagonistic structure of capitalist societies from class conflicts and social movements.

Marxist theorizing in the 1960s and 1970s, then, seemed to have an inherent tilt toward the macro side. This persistent disregard for structures of consciousness, for contingency, and for patterns of concrete interaction eventually produced a reaction in German sociology. This occurred for disciplinary as well as scientific reasons. When the interest of sociology with respect to social action is reduced to discovering the traces and imprints of all-encompassing economic macrostructures, then sociology is on the verge of being reduced to a subdiscipline of economics. The effort to counteract the predominance of Marxist political economy has led to a renaissance of Weberian and Parsonian theorizing in German sociology on the one hand and to a growing interest in phenomenological and interactionist theories on the other. Both tendencies set the stage for the thrust for linkage that we believe has characterized the most recent phase of sociological debate.

7. TOWARD LINKAGE

Although the differences forcefully articulated by this multiparadigmatic debate continue to inform sociological theory today, it is our belief that the vital and creative phase of this movement has now come to an end. We suggest that in the present decade a quite different phase of theoretical debate has emerged, one marked by the serious ongoing effort within every theoretical tradition and from both sides of the great divide to link micro- and macroperspectives. We are under no illusion that this new development will replace theoretical disagreement with some Newtonian synthesis, but we are convinced that the scope and intensity of this search for linkage are without precedent in the history of sociology.

The continuity and originality of the present discussion are exemplified by the organization of the chapters that follow. The four essays in part I, "Micro and Macro: General Approaches," indicate that the micro-macro link often continues to be conceptualized in terms of one or the other side of the great divide. Boudon argues for beginning from an individualistic position; Blau insists that the beginning can be made only from the structural side. Luhmann argues that the micro-macro split corresponds to different empirical spheres that have emerged in an evolutionary way, and Gerstein argues that the difference is purely analytical. What is equally striking, however, and certainly what distinguishes such arguments from earlier ones, is that all four theorists (Blau being only a partial exception) argue that the link between micro and macro must be made.

The essays that follow part I have been organized in a manner to make much the same point. They manifest the new thrust toward linkage even while they reveal the continuing relevance of traditional theoretical divisions. Thus in part II Wippler and Lindenberg and Coleman attempt a micro-macro link from the perspective of rational action. In part III Haferkamp, Collins, and Schegloff draw the link in terms of interpretive action. In part IV, Kurzweil, Hondrich, and Smelser conceptualize linkage from affective action. Contrasting assumptions about order continue to be revealed as well, though these are more randomly distributed. No matter what conception of action or order, each of the essays tries to close the micro-macro gap.

The essays in the concluding part, "Synthetic Reconstructions," crystallize this underlying theme and attempt to systematize it. Alexander, Münch, and Giesen each argue in different ways that an analytical approach is the only basis for a full micro-macro link and suggest that on this basis each of the three different conceptions of action can be brought together.

There are social and institutional as well as intellectual reasons for this new phase in contemporary sociological theory. Certainly one important factor is the changing political climate in the United States and Europe. Most radical social movements have faded away, and in the eyes of many intellectuals Marxism has been morally delegitimated. The ideological thrust that fueled anti-Parsonianism in both its micro and macro form in the United States, and that stimulated Marxist structuralism on the Continent, has now been spent.

This political shift, in addition to the simple passage of time, has created new generational circumstances. In the United States and England there is a new generation of theorists for whom Parsons was never a dominant figure and who therefore feel no particular attraction to the polemic against him. By standing outside the fray, these younger theorists are committed to neither the micro nor the macro anti-Parsonian alternative, and, indeed, their new theorizing has often returned to Parsons's commitment to linkage, if not the substance of his theory. In Germany the younger, post-Marxist generation has been forced to look elsewhere for theoretical ideas. Many of these came, in fact, from the United States. When individualistic theories made the transoceanic transition, however, they were taken up in a less polemical way, and the migration of Parsonian ideas to Germany (see Alexander 1984*b*), rather than inspiring divisive debate, has been part of an effort at renewed theoretical integration.

There has been the passage of intellectual time as well. One-sided theories are provocative, and at various points they can be enormously functional in a scientific sense. Once the dust of theoretical battle has settled, however, the cognitive content of their theorizing is not particularly easy to maintain. The multiparadigmatic debate succeeded in eclipsing early efforts at theoretical synthesis. Moreover, the postwar philosophical revival of individualism that fueled this debate has now died out. The legacies of Weber and Parsons remain, however, presenting an enduring demand for linkage that calls sociological theory to task. For internal reasons of theoretical logic, as well as for external reasons of social and institutional life, a new and unprecedented thrust of contemporary debate toward linkage has begun.

In terms of macrotheories, the shift toward linkage can be seen in each of the major theoretical schools. Giddens's earliest work (1971) was continuous with the structuralist thrust of anti-Parsonian theory and neo-Marxism, but later in the 1970s his work fundamentally changed course. He became convinced of the need for a complementary theory of action. Building from, among other traditions, the ethnomethodological insistence on the reflexive, contingent nature of action, Giddens developed a theory of structuration that tries to interweave action and order (Giddens 1976, 1979). Collins's development shows a similar trajectory. Although more interested in ethnomethodology from the beginning of his career than Giddens, Collins, in his early work (1975), presented primarily a case for structuralistic conflict sociology. In recent years he has embraced radical microsociology, both phenomenological and Goffmanian, developing the notion of interaction ritual chains (see his essay, chapter 8) as a means of mediating the micro-macro link.

Habermas, too, began his career with a more typically macrostructuralist model of social dynamics (Habermas 1973). Although there are clear references to moral claims and to different types of action, these remained residual to his argument. In his recent work (Habermas 1984), however, he explicitly and systematically developed theories about the microprocesses that underlie and sometimes oppose the macrostructures of social systems. He has used individual moral and cognitive development to anchor his description of world-historical phases of "social learning," descriptions of speech acts to develop arguments about political legitimacy, and the conception of an interpersonally generated life-world to justify his empirical explanation of social strain and resistance.

Giddens and Collins have tended to bring theoretical options 1 and 2 (instrumental and interpretive individualism) into contact with option 5 (objective structuralism). By contrast, Habermas's sensitivity to cultural gestalts has led him to connect option 5 with linkage arguments that stress homology and socialization (option 4). As his critics have argued, although he has embraced the micro, his theory is not really open to contingency, particularly to historical processes such as individual and collective rebellion, which have been stressed by Marxism in its more historical and political forms. Eder (1983) developed a theory of "specific evolution" in order to push Habermasian theory in this direction;

that is, toward the more contingent options 1–3. A sharper departure from the determinism of macroevolutionism has been made by Schmid (1982) and Giesen (Giesen and Lau 1981; Giesen 1980; also see Giesen's essay, chapter 15). They have argued that progress, directional development, and societal growth must be seen as macroprocesses that are contingent on the microprocesses of variation and selective reproduction, although the latter are themselves subject to selective pressures exerted by macrostructures such as stratification.

In Habermas's efforts at linkage he has been influenced by new developments in Parsonian and Weberian theories. Although Luhmann (1979) has certainly raised the radically macro concept of "systems" with vigor, it must not be forgotten that he explains the very existence of systems by referring to fundamental microprocesses, which he identifies as existential needs to reduce complexity. His more recent work (see chapter 4) on autopoietic systems, moreover, makes the dialectic of micro and macro into the very essence of modern societies. Indeed, he wishes to argue that the micro-macro split properly understood is not a theoretical issue but an empirical reflection of the historical differentiation of interaction and society.

This emphasis has had a major influence on Münch's effort (1981–1982) to reshape Parsons's systematic theory. Unlike Luhmann, Münch has returned to Parsons's more analytical notion of systemic interpenetration, an interpenetration not only of norms and interests but of micro and macro. Indeed, Münch (1981) has extended and more systematically elaborated Parsons's notion that socialization lays the moral basis for social integration and control. Although he generally criticizes individualistic theory and thereby maintains theoretical option 4, however, Münch has incorporated contingency into his four-dimensional models in a way that Parsons never contemplated (see Münch's chapter in this volume).

Although Alexander's initial work (1982*a*, 1982*b*, 1983*a*, 1983*b*) argued that action and order, taken together, are the inescapable presuppositions of social thought, he did not identify these positions with micro and macro emphases, respectively. Indeed, he argued that only by presupposing collective, or emergent, order could theory encompass the mutuality of contingency and constraint in social life. At the same time, however, this early work did not entirely escape Durkheim's and Parsons's identification of action theory with the differentiation of homologous personalities and societies (option 4). Since that time he has tried to give action *qua* contingency a more systematic role, outlining syntheses between structural theory and ethnomethodology, symbolic interaction, and theories of exchange (Alexander 1984*a*, 1985; Alexander and Colomy 1985; and see chapter 13).

The mirror image of this development has been produced within Weberian theory by Schluchter (1979, 1981). He has insisted from the beginning of his work that the decoupling of individual action and society is at the heart of Weber's achievement, and that this Weberian understanding (reflecting options 2 and 3) is necessary to perceive the significance of individuality and responsibility in modern society. At the same time, however, Schluchter has relied heavily on Parsonian and, later, Habermasian formulations about moral and cultural evolution, and his notion of individual autonomy seems to rely implicitly on theoretical option 4 as well. This has set the stage for renewing the more synthetic position (option 3), whose initial formulation was such a singular contribution of Weber himself.

The same shift toward linkage marks recent developments in each of the major microtraditions. Striking developments have occurred, for example, in symbolic interactionism. Although Goffman (1959) began his career more or less within the radically contingent tradition of Blumer (option 2), in his later writings there emerged a dramatic shift toward the more structural concerns of positions 3 and 4. The creative strategies of actors were still Goffman's target, but he was now concerned with them insofar as they illustrated the instantiation of cultural and stratificational structures in everyday life (e.g., Goffman 1967, and see Collins's essay, chapter 8). Similarly, whereas Becker's (1963) early impact on deviance theory derived from his emphasis on contingency and action, his most recent work takes an emphatically systemic view of creativity and its effects (Becker 1984). Indeed, recently a spate of formal efforts by symbolic interactionists to systematize the links between actors and social systems has appeared. Haferkamp (1985) tried to add to Mead's individual construction of meaning an objective-material basis for action (combining options 2 and 5), and Lewis and Smith (1980) argued that Mead was actually an antinominalist who took what we have called the reproductionist position (4). Stryker (1980:52–54, 57–76) has gone so far as to present interactionism as if it were basically a modification of social systems theory itself. (See also, in this regard, Handel 1979; Maines 1977; Strauss 1978; and Haferkamp's essay, chapter 7).

Similar developments can be seen in the rational action model revived in Homans's exchange theory. The pressure to demonstrate that this polemically micro approach (option 1) could cope with macrosociological explanation (e.g., see Lindenberg 1983) gradually shifted the focus of analysis from individual actions to the transformation from individual actions to collective effects, and, by extension, to unintended rather purposive activity. Thus Lindenberg (1977; also see Wippler and Lindenberg, chapter 5) and Coleman (chapter 6) rejected the notion that the connection between individual actions and macrophenomena could be viewed as a causal relation between discrete empirical events. If there were only empirical simultaneity, then the linkage between micro and macro would have to be seen as an analytical one sustained by invisible processes in the larger system. Such an analytical linkage was achieved by the application of "transformation rules" (e.g., voting procedures) to individual actions.

Theorists were led by this focus on transformation to consider individual actions not as subjects for analysis in their own right but as initial conditions for the operation of structural mechanisms (combining options 1 and 5). In this way structural explanations—about the rules of constitutions, the dynamics of organizations, the system of prestige allocation—began to replace utility arguments within the rationalistic tradition (Coleman 1966; Goode 1979). There emerged extensive theorizing about the unintended effects of individual actions (Boudon 1977; Wippler 1978; and see Boudon, chapter 1) and even about the genesis of collective morality (Lindenberg 1983).

Although Garfinkel, the founder of ethnomethodology, continues to advocate a radically micro program (option 2) for the school (Garfinkel et al. 1981; also see Schegloff, chapter 9), and although the movement toward linkage is less developed here than within the other microtraditions, it seems impossible to deny that a similar crisis and a similar movement permeate phenomenological sociology as well. Cicourel, for example, certainly one of the key figures in the radical early phase, has recently sought a more interdependent approach (Knorr-Cetina and Cicourel 1981). A phenomenologically based "social studies in science" movement has emerged that, while arguing for a micro base to science studies, tries systematically to acknowledge the framing effects of social structure (Knorr-Cetina and Mulkay 1983; Pinch and Collins 1984). Although Smith (1984) and Molotch and Boden (1985) have insisted on the indispensable autonomy of ethnomethodological practice, they have produced significant studies detailing how this practice is structured by organizational context and the distribution of power (combining options 2 and 5). Oevermann (1979) has demonstrated how practical action is confined by cultural codes (combining options 2 and 4), and Luckmann (1984) has linked it to social evolution.

We are not suggesting here that the widespread acceptance of a new theory of micro-macro articulation is imminent. We have no doubt that sociological debate will continue to be organized around competing versions of action and order. In this sense the debates we have just recounted are more about the secondary and peripheral circles of theoretical traditions than about their central core. Notwithstanding Blau's dramatic switch from micro- to macrosociology (see his essay, chapter 2)—a switch that is actually more incremental than appearances would indicate—few of the recent advocates of linkage have ever "jumped ship."

Indeed, it is this very loyalty to initial starting points, we believe (Alexander 1985, 1987), which limits the success of most of these linkage proposals in fundamental ways. It is our view that only by establishing a radically different theoretical starting point can a genuinely inclusive micro-macro link be made. This inclusive model would not simply combine two or three of the theoretical options in an ad hoc manner. Rather, it would provide a systematic model in which all five of the options are included as analytical dimensions of empirical reality as such. This can be achieved on the basis of an emergentist, or collective, understanding of order, a multidimensional understanding of action, and an analytic understanding of the relations among different levels of empirical organization. We argue for such a basis in our own essays (see chapters 13 and 15).

Our purpose in this introduction, however, has not been to argue for or against any one of these proposals for linkage. Our purpose has been to draw a circle around all of them, to demarcate them as a new phenomenon in sociological discourse, and to commend this new discourse to the community at large. The essays that follow, we believe, open new windows onto the sociological imagination.

NOTE

1. See the earlier discussion of the five alternative ways of conceptualizing the micro-macro link.

REFERENCES

Alexander, Jeffrey C. 1982*a*. *Positivism, Presuppositions, and Current Controversies*. Vol. 1. *Theoretical Logic in Sociology*. Berkeley, Los Angeles, London: University of California Press.

———. 1982*b*. *The Antinomies of Classical Thought: Marx and Durkheim*. Vol. 2. *Theoretical Logic in Sociology*. Berkeley, Los Angeles, London: University of California Press.

———. 1983*a*. *The Classical Attempt at Synthesis: Max Weber*. Vol. 3. *Theoretical Logic in Sociology*. Berkeley, Los Angeles, London: University of California Press.
———. 1983*b*. *The Modern Reconstruction of Classical Thought: Talcott Parsons*. Vol. 4. *Theoretical Logic in Sociology*. Berkeley, Los Angeles, London: University of California Press.
———. 1984*a*. Structural Analysis: Some Notes on Its History and Prospects. *Sociological Quarterly* 25, 1:5–26.
———. 1984*b*. The Parsons Revival in Germany. *Sociological Theory* 2:394–412.
———. 1985. The Individualist Dilemma in Phenomenology and Interactionism: Towards a Synthesis with the Classical Tradition, in S. N. Eisenstadt and H. J. Helle, eds., *Perspectives on Sociological Theory*. Vol. 1. Beverly Hills, Calif.: Sage.
———. 1987. *Twenty Lectures: Sociological Theory Since World War II*. New York: Columbia University Press.
Alexander, Jeffrey, and Paul Colomy. 1985. Towards Neofunctionalism: Eisenstadt's Change Theory and Symbolic Interactionism. *Sociological Theory* 3, 2:11–23.
Althusser, Louis, and Etienne Balibar. 1970. *Reading Capital*. London: New Left Books.
Bales, Robert F. 1951. *Interaction Process Analysis*. New York: Free Press.
Becker, Howard S. 1963. *Outsiders: Studies in the Sociology of Deviance*. Glencoe, Ill.: Free Press.
———. 1984. *Art Worlds*. Berkeley, Los Angeles, London: University of California Press.
Bellah, Robert N. 1970. Father and Son in Confucianism and Christianity, pp. 76–97 in *Beyond Belief*. New York: Harper & Row.
Berlin, Isaiah. 1954. *Historical Inevitability*. New York: Oxford University Press.
Blumer, Herbert. 1969. *Symbolic Interactionism*. Englewood Cliffs, N.J.: Prentice-Hall.
Boudon, Raymond. 1977. *Effets pervers et ordre social*. Paris: Presses Universitaires de France.
Coleman, James S. 1966. Foundations for a Theory of Collective Decisions. *American Journal of Sociology* 71:615–627.
Collins, Randall. 1975. *Conflict Sociology*. New York: Academic Press.
Durkheim, Emile. 1933. *The Division of Labor in Society* (1893). New York: Free Press.
———. 1938. *The Rules of Sociological Method* (1895). New York: Free Press.
———. 1951. *Suicide* (1897). New York: Free Press.
———. 1965. *The Elementary Forms of Religious Life* (1912). New York: Free Press.
Eder, Klaus. 1983. "The New Social Movements in Historical Perspective, or: What Is New in the 'New' Social Movements?" Unpublished Paper. Munich.
Freud, Sigmund. 1928. *Future of an Illusion* (1927). New York: Norton.
———. 1959. *Group Psychology and the Analysis of the Ego* (1921). New York: Norton.

———. 1961. *The Ego and the Id* (1923). New York: Norton.
———. 1961. *Civilization and Its Discontents* (1930). New York: Norton.
Garfinkel, Harold. 1963. A Conception of and Experiments with "Trust" as a Condition of Concerted Stable Actions, pp. 187–238 in O. J. Harvey, ed., *Motivation and Social Interaction*. New York: Ronald Press.
———. 1967. *Studies in Ethnomethodology*. Englewood Cliffs, N.J.: Prentice-Hall.
Garfinkel, Harold, Michael Lynch, and Eric Livingston. 1981. The Work of a Discovering Science Construed with Materials from the Optically Discovered Pulsar. *Philosophy of Social Science* 11:131–158.
Giddens, Anthony. 1971. *Capitalism and Modern Social Theory*. London: Cambridge University Press.
———. 1976. *New Rules of Sociological Method*. London: Hutchinson.
———. 1979. *Central Problems in Social Theory*. London: Macmillan.
Giesen, Bernhard. 1980. *Makrosoziologie*. Hamburg: Hoffman and Campe.
Giesen, Bernhard, and C. Lau. 1981. Zur Anwendung darwinistischer Erklarungsstrategien in der Soziologie. *Kölner Zeitschrift für Soziologie und Sozialpsychologie* 33, 2:229–256.
Giesen, Bernhard, and Michael Schmid. 1977. Methodologischer Individualismus und Reduktionismus, pp. 24–47 in E. Eberlein and J. J. Kondratowitz, eds., *Psychologie statt Soziologie*. Frankfurt/New York: Campus.
Godelier, Maurice. 1967. System, Structure, and Contradiction in "Capital," in Ralph Miliband and John Saville, eds., *The Socialist Register*. New York: Monthly Review Press.
Goffman, Erving. 1959. *The Presentation of Self in Everyday Life*. New York: Doubleday.
———. 1967. *Interaction Ritual*. New York: Doubleday.
Goldstein, L. 1956. The Inadequacy of the Principle of Methodological Individualism. *Journal of Philosophy* 53:801–813.
———. 1958. The Theses of Methodological Individualism. *British Journal for the Philosophy of Science* 9:1–11.
Goode, William J. 1960. A Theory of Role Strain. *American Sociological Review* 25:483–496.
———. 1979. *The Celebration of Heroes: Prestige as a Social Control System*. Berkeley, Los Angeles, London: University of California Press.
Habermas, Jürgen. 1970. *Toward a Rational Society*. Boston: Beacon.
———. 1973. *Theory and Practice*. Boston: Beacon.
———. 1984. *Reason and the Rationalization of Society*. Vol. 1. *Theory of Communicative Action*. Boston: Beacon.
Handel, Warren. 1979. Normative Expectations and the Emergence of Meaning as Solutions to Problems: Convergence of Structural and Interactionist Views. *American Journal of Sociology* 84:855–881.
Hayek, Frederick. 1952. *The Counter-Revolution of Science: Studies on the Abuse of Reason*. Glencoe, Ill.: Free Press.
Hirsch, J. D. 1974. *Staatsapparat und Reproduktion des Kapitals*. Frankfurt: Suhrkamp.
Homans, George. 1958. Social Behavior as Exchange. *American Sociological Review* 63:597–606.

———. 1961. *Social Behavior: Its Elementary Forms.* New York: Harcourt, Brace, and World.
Knorr-Cetina, Karin, and Aaron Cicourel, eds. 1981. *Advances in Social Theory and Methodology: Towards an Integration of Micro and Macro-Sociology.* London: Routledge & Kegan Paul.
Knorr-Cetina, Karin, and Michael Mulkay, eds. 1983. *Science Observed: New Perspectives on the Social Study of Science.* Beverly Hills, Calif.: Sage.
Levy, Marion. 1949. *The Family Revolution in China.* Cambridge, Mass.: Harvard University Press.
Lewis, J. David, and Richard L. Smith. 1980. *American Sociology and Pragmatism.* Chicago: University of Chicago Press.
Lieberson, Stanley. 1980. *A Piece of the Pie.* Berkeley, Los Angeles, London: University of California Press.
Lindenberg, Siegward. 1977. Individuelle Effekte. Kollective Phänomene und das Problem der Transformation, pp. 46–84 in K. Eichner and W. Habermehl, eds., *Probleme der Erklarung sozialen Verhaltens.* Misenheim/Glan: Hain.
———. 1983. The New Political Economy: Its Potential and Limitations for the Social Sciences in General and for Sociology in Particular, pp. 7–66 in Wolfgang Sudeur, ed., *Ökonomische Erklarung sozialen Verhaltens.* Duisburg: Sozialwissenschaftliche Kooperative.
Luckmann, Thomas. 1984. Bemerkungen zu Gesellschaft Struktur Bewussteins Formen und Religion in der Modernen Gesellschaft. Paper presented to the Sozialen Tag. Dortenund.
Luhmann, Niklas. 1979. *Trust and Power.* New York: John Wiley.
Maines, David. 1977. Social Organization and Social Structure in Symbolic Interactionist Thought. *Annual Review of Sociology* 3:235–260.
Mandelbaum, M. 1955. Societal Facts. *British Journal of Sociology* 6:309–317.
———. 1957. Societal Laws. *British Journal for the Philosophy of Science* 8:211–224.
Malewski, A. 1967. *Verhalten und Interaktion.* Tübingen: Mohr.
Marcuse, Herbert. 1963. *One Dimensional Man.* Boston: Beacon.
Marx, Karl. 1963. Economic and Philosophical Manuscripts, in T. B. Bottomore, ed., *Karl Marx: Early Writings* (1844). New York: McGraw-Hill.
———. 1965. Theses on Feuerbach, in Nathan Rotenstreich, ed., *Basic Problems of Marx's Philosophy* (1845). Indianapolis: Bobbs-Merrill.
———. 1967. Communism and the Augsburg "*Allegemeine Zeitung*," in Lloyd D. Easton and Kurt H. Guddat, eds., *Writings of the Young Marx on Philosophy and Society.* New York: Doubleday.
Mead, George Herbert. 1964. Selections from *Mind, Self, and Society*, pp. 165–282 in Anselm Strauss, ed., *George Herbert Mead on Social Psychology* (1934). Chicago: University of Chicago Press.
Merton, Robert K. 1968. Continuities in the Theory of Reference Groups and Social Structure, pp. 334–440 in *Social Theory and Social Structure.* New York: Free Press.
Molotch, Harvey, and Deirdre Boden. 1985. Talking Social Structure: Discourse, Domination, and The Watergate Hearings. *American Sociological Review* 50:273–288.
Münch, Richard. 1981. Socialization and Personality Development from the

Point of View of Action Theory: The Legacy of Durkheim. *Sociological Inquiry* 51:311–354.
———. 1981–1982. Talcott Parsons and the Theory of Action. Parts I and II. *American Journal of Sociology* 86–87:709–739, 771–826.
Nagel, Ernest. 1961. *The Structure of Science*. London: Routledge & Kegan Paul.
Offe, Claus. 1984. *Contradictions of the Welfare State* (1972). Cambridge, Mass.: MIT Press.
Opp, K. D. 1972. *Verhaltenstheoretische Soziologie*. Stuttgart: Enke.
Oevermann, U. 1979. Die Methodologie einer objectiven Hermeneutik, pp. 353–434 in H. G. Soeffner, ed., *Interpretative Verfahren in den Sozial und Textwissenschaften*. Stuttgart.
Parsons, Talcott. 1937. *The Structure of Social Action*. New York: Free Press.
———. 1954. *Essays in Sociological Theory*. New York: Free Press.
———. 1963. *Social Structure and Personality*. New York: Free Press.
Parsons, Talcott, and Robert F. Bales, eds. 1955. *Family, Socialization, and Interaction Process*. New York: Free Press.
Parsons, Talcott, and N. J. Smelser. 1956. *Economy and Society*. New York: Free Press.
Pinch, T. J., and H. M. Collins. 1984. Private Science and Public Knowledge. *Social Studies in Science* 14:521–546.
Popper, Karl. 1958. *The Open Society and Its Enemies*. London: Routledge & Kegan Paul.
———. 1961. *The Poverty of Historicism*. London: Routledge & Kegan Paul.
Schluchter, Wolfgang. 1979. The Paradoxes of Rationalization, pp. 11–64 in Guenther Roth and W. Schluchter, eds., *Max Weber's Vision of History*. Berkeley, Los Angeles, London: University of California Press.
———. 1981. *The Rise of Western Rationalization*. Berkeley, Los Angeles, London: University of California Press.
Schmid, Michael. 1982. *Theorie sozialen Wandels*. Opladen: Westdeutscher Verlag.
Simmel, Georg. 1950. Fundamental Problems of Sociology, pp. 3–25 in Kurt H. Wolff, ed., *The Sociology of Georg Simmel*. New York: Free Press.
———. 1955. Conflict, pp. 11–123 in *Conflict and the Web of Group Affiliation*. New York: Free Press.
———. 1977. *Problems of the Philosophy of History*. New York: Free Press.
Skocpol, Theda. 1979. *States and Social Revolutions*. New York: Cambridge University Press.
Slater, Philip. 1961. Parental Role Differentiation. *American Journal of Sociology* 67:296–308.
———. 1966. *Microcosm*. New York: John Wiley.
———. 1968. *The Glory of Hera*. Boston: Beacon.
Smelser, Neil J. 1959. *Social Change in the Industrial Revolution*. Chicago: University of Chicago Press.
———. 1962. *Theory of Collective Behavior*. New York: Free Press.
Smith, Adam. 1776. *The Wealth of Nations*.
Smith, Dorothy. 1984. Textually Mediated Social Organization. *International Social Science Journal* 36:59–75.
Smith, J. David, and Richard L. Smith. 1980. *American Sociology and Pragma-*

tism: Mead, Chicago Sociology and Symbolic Interactionism. Chicago: University of Chicago Press.

Strauss, Anselm. 1978. *Negotiations: Varieties, Contexts, Processes and Social Order*. San Francisco: Jossey-Bass.

Stryker, Sheldon. 1980. *Symbolic Interactionism*. Menlo Park, Calif.: Benjamin Cummings.

Thompson, E. P. 1978. *The Poverty of Philosophy and Other Essays*. London: Merlin.

Treiman, Donald. 1977. *Occupational Prestige in Comparative Perspective*. New York: John Wiley.

Watkins, J. 1952. The Principle of Methodological Individualism. *British Journal for the Philosophy of Science* 3:186–189.

———. 1959. Historical Explanations in the Social Sciences, pp. 503–514 in P. Gardiner, ed., *Theories of History* (1957). New York: Free Press.

Weber, Max. 1946. Religious Rejections of the World and Their Directions, pp. 323–359 in Hans Gerth and C. Wright Mills, eds., *From Max Weber* (1916). New York: Oxford University Press.

———. 1949. A Critique of Eduard Meyer's Methodological Views, pp. 113–163, in *Methodology of the Social Sciences* (1905). New York: Free Press.

———. 1975. *Roscher and Knies* (1903–1906). London: Routledge & Kegan Paul.

———. 1978. *Economy and Society*. Berkeley, Los Angeles, London: University of California Press.

Wippler, Reinhard. 1978. Nicht-intendierte social Folgen individuelle Handlungen. *Soziale Welt* 29:155–179.

Wright, Erik Olin. 1978. *Class, Crisis, and the State*. London: New Left Books.

PART ONE

Micro and Macro: General Approaches

CHAPTER ONE

The Individualistic Tradition in Sociology

Raymond Boudon

The importance of the individualistic tradition in sociology often seems to be widely underestimated (Homans 1982). Epistemological works advocating methodological individualism in the social sciences often rest upon abstract examples or upon examples taken from economic theory (Popper 1963; O'Neill 1973). As for sociologists themselves, they generally accept that descending to the individual level is an adequate approach in organization or small group studies. Many of them, however, reject the idea that methodological individualism (MI) could be of any use in macroscopic studies, and they often perceive the proposal of using MI in such studies as leading to an inadequate imitation of a way of thinking borrowed from economic theory (Van Parijs 1981).

I will deal in this essay primarily with *macrosociology* and try to suggest, first, that if macrosociology currently uses several paradigms, MI also is a traditional paradigm in macrosociology. I will propose a tentative list of these paradigms in order to see more clearly the distinctive features of the latter paradigm. Second, I will consider in some detail two examples borrowed from classical sociology to illustrate the point that, either consciously or unconsciously, classical sociologists used the MI approach even when dealing with such macrosociological questions as the explanation of differences among societies. Third, I will try to suggest that the individualistic tradition is a more or less permanent tradition in macrosociological research. Finally, as this point is, in my opinion, often ill perceived, I will devote some attention to the differences between the economic and sociological version of the individualistic paradigm.

THE BASIC MACROSOCIOLOGICAL PARADIGMS

The individualistic paradigm can be defined in the following fashion: Suppose we want to explain any phenomenon of sociological interest—for instance, following Tocqueville in his *Old Regime*, why Britain and France differed in certain respects in the eighteenth century, or, following Sombart in his famous work, why there was no socialism in the United States in the nineteenth century. Such questions are obviously macrosociological. According to the MI paradigm, in order to explain such phenomena one has to make them the outcomes of individual actions or behaviors. Of course, it will be necessary to make these actions understandable. This is done by relating them to the social context within which the actors are located. Finally, the social context itself must be explained.

To summarize, suppose M is the phenomenon to be explained. In the individualistic paradigm, to explain M means making it the outcome of a set of actions m. In mathematical symbols, $M = M(m)$; in words, M is a function of the actions m. Then the actions m are made understandable, in the Weberian sense, by relating them to the social environment, the situation S, of the actors: $m = m(S)$. Finally, the situation itself has to be explained as the outcome of some macrosociological variables, or at least of variables located at a level higher than S. Let us call these higher-level variables P, so that $S = S(P)$. On the whole, $M = M\{m[S(P)]\}$. In words, M is the outcome of actions, which are the outcome of the social environment of the actors, the latter being the outcome of macrosociological variables.

I will try to show that classical sociologists such as Tocqueville or Weber, as well as many modern sociologists, implicitly or explicitly considered that the main task of sociology was to answer questions such as "why M?" Why do we observe a particular puzzling phenomenon? They considered also that the answer to the question had to take the form of the three-stage analysis sketchily described earlier.

This individualistic paradigm is not the only one that has been proposed and used in macrosociological research, however. Another, very important, paradigm can be called the *nomological paradigm*. Here the objective, rather than to answer questions of the type "why M?" is to discover macrosociological regularities, or lawlike statements. These "laws" can take the form of statements on trends, on conditional regularities of the form "if A, then B," on structural regularities of the form

"A, B, C, D always or most often go together." They can take other forms as well, but I will not detail them here.

When Comte states that social evolution has to go through three stages, he proposes a lawlike statement. So does Durkheim when he contends that, as we would say in our terms, industrialization, modernization, or the increase in the division of labor is necessarily accompanied by a laicization effect, or when he contends that with increasing anomie or increasing egoism rates of suicide increase.

Often lawlike statements are derived from an individualistic analysis, as in the case of Parsons's law on the effects of the increase in the division of labor on family structures. In spite of this possible overlap, however, the two paradigms should be distinguished, for the following reasons. First, in the individualistic paradigm the research of lawlike statements is only one possible objective of sociology. In this paradigm explaining singularities can be as valid an objective as looking for lawlike statements. Second, in the nomological paradigm relating the micro level to the macro level is not always considered an indispensable task. Durkheim considered, on the contrary, that such a task was to be dispensed with. To him, as the interpretation of actions is an uncontrollable operation, it should be evacuated as much as possible from any sociological analysis. Ideally, according to Durkheim and to many of his followers, Mill's rules of induction describe both the objective and the basic methodology of sociological research.

In addition, in the nomological paradigm the nature of the explanation is not conceived in the same way as in the individualistic paradigm. The formula $M = M\{m[S(P)]\}$ defines the nature of the explanation of M in the latter case; in the former, in order to explain M one would have to derive it from a "covering law" (Hempel 1965). Thus Durkheim explains the rates of suicide among Protestants through the covering law relating "egoism" and propensity to suicide. In other words, determining lawlike statements is an objective not only in the nomological paradigm; such statements are also the core of the explanation of any phenomenon M. As contained in the individualistic paradigm, lawlike statements are neither the exclusive or the main research objective nor the indispensable instrument of the explanation of a given phenomenon M.

A third paradigm I call the *interpretive paradigm.* The basic postulate in this case is that as soon as we leave the low levels illustrated by organization or small group studies and proceed to more complex levels, the individual actors can advantageously be forgotten. It is not assumed in this paradigm, however, that looking for lawlike statements should be the only or even the most interesting or urgent task of sociological research. It can be as interesting to try to characterize the differences between, say, two eras, between two societies, or between different types of culture.

Illustrations of this type of paradigm can be easily found. In his *Kultur der Renaisssance in Italien*, Burckhardt attempts to answer a major question: In what sense is it possible to see a new culture in the Italian Renaissance? Why do we have the impression that a new system of values was born in that time and place? As to Burckhardt's method, it is close to what Lazarsfeld called a matrix formulation (Barton and Lazarsfeld 1961). Burckhardt summarized the innumerable specificities that, when considered together, gave historians the feeling that something really new had happened. In that time and place, a new set of values, according to Burckhardt, was discovered. And this set could be characterized by one word: individualism. The typical Renaissance Italian would be guided by an individualistic worldview and by individualistic ethics. (Obviously "individualism" is not taken here in the methodological sense.)

Because I have used Lazarsfeld's notion of matrix formulation, I mention another well-known illustration of matrix formulation: the distinction proposed by R. Benedict between Apollonian and Dionysian cultures. Obviously it is difficult to give a satisfactory definition of the interpretive paradigm. Matrix formulation, in addition, is certainly not the exclusive methodological operation to be associated with this paradigm. These examples, however, sufficiently show that macrosociological research often follows a paradigm or program different from the individualistic paradigm and the nomological paradigm referred to earlier. An interesting line of methodological research would be to investigate the procedures used in this type of program. This is not my task in this essay, however.

A fourth paradigm or program can be described as the *critical paradigm*. Weber, who can be considered the main promoter of the individualistic paradigm, and Durkheim, the main advocate of the nomological paradigm, in many respects had opposite views as to the aims and procedures of sociology. They both considered, however, that sociology not only could but should attempt to be scientific and positive. As a positive discipline sociology should, according to both founding fathers, be concerned with explaining observable phenomena selected either because they are puzzling or because they point to social regularities. As a scientific discipline sociology should aim at proposing controllable theories;

that is, theories capable of being either confirmed or falsified by the observable data.

Needless to say, some sociologists consider that this axiological neutrality is impossible in the social sciences and that, moreover, it would give rise (were it possible) to worthless findings or at least to findings of questionable value. To them sociology should be critical. As in the case of the physician, positive knowledge can help the sociologist, but disinterested knowledge and its accumulation cannot be the main goal. It is only a means toward that goal. I hope that Habermas would agree with my definition of the critical paradigm in spite of its simplicity.

My objective in this essay is not to say that a particular paradigm is better than the others but merely to underline some distinctions. In fact, discussing whether the critical paradigm is better, for instance, than the Durkheimian or the Weberian paradigm is, in my opinion, as interesting as to discuss whether being a biologist is better than being a physician. What I want to suggest is that, at a conceptual level at least, four (and maybe more) distinct types of orientations, programs, or paradigms can be distinguished on the basis of actual macrosociological research. In the reality of research, of course, these conceptual distinctions can become less clear.

In the following I will leave the three other paradigms and concentrate on what I called the individualistic paradigm.

2. TWO CLASSICAL EXAMPLES USING THE INDIVIDUALISTIC PARADIGM

In order to prepare the further discussion on the nature and extension of the individualistic paradigm in sociology, I will consider in detail two classical examples. Although I could have selected more, two will be sufficient to reach a precise definition of the individualistic program in its sociological version.

2.1. TOCQUEVILLE'S OLD REGIME

In the first sentence of his well-known work, Tocqueville writes, "The book which I am now writing is not a history of the French Revolution." By so writing he had in mind that his work was a sociological rather than a historical book. For obvious reasons he probably had a weak propensity to use the word "sociology." In fact, Tocqueville's work can be properly considered a piece of comparative sociology, considering that a large part of it can be viewed as an attempt to explain a list of differences between French and British society in the eighteenth century. One difference was that the French agricultural system was underdeveloped at a time when British agriculture became modern. This is puzzling in light of the fact that the physiocrats had a great influence among French political elites at that time.

Tocqueville's explanation of the difference follows the typical individualistic paradigm I described earlier. Because of the high degree of "administrative centralization" (P), French landlords are not in the same situation (S) as the British. As a consequence of P, public offices are more numerous in France. In addition, because of this centralization every civil servant may consider himself or herself part of the central power. Consequently power, prestige, and influence are attached to the public offices to a larger extent in France than in Britain. Considering that the public offices are sold by the Crown and represent an important source of income, an inflationary spiral is created: Both the supply and demand of offices increase. On the whole landlords are strongly motivated to buy public offices: They have the resources to do so; public offices are available; and rewards are associated with them. So, as an outcome of the structure of the environment (S), they buy public offices, leave their land, and settle in the next city, leaving the tenants to take care of the land. Because landlords are not motivated to increase the productivity of their land, and because tenants lack the capacity to do so, as an aggregate outcome M(m), the French agricultural system remains underdeveloped in comparison to the British.

Another macroscopic factor, say P′, reinforces these effects: In the long historical process during which the Crown reinforced its power over society, the cities had long been poles of resistance. For this reason they had been able to retain a number of privileges—among others, tax privileges. There was no income tax in the cities in the eighteenth century. This circumstance reinforced the other factors generating landlord absenteeism.

Thus Tocqueville explains the macroscopic feature represented by the differential development of agriculture in Britain and France as the aggregate outcome of the behavior of the landlords. He makes this behavior understandable, in the Weberian sense, by relating it to what I called the structure of their situation; the structure of the situation is explained by such macroscopic factors as tax privileges of the cities or administrative centralization.

I will consider briefly the Tocquevillian analysis of another difference between Britain and France in the eighteenth century in order to suggest that the formula, $M = M\{m[S(P)]\}$ summarizes adequately not merely one but most of the explanations developed by Tocqueville. This difference deals with the style of French as compared to British political philosophy. The question is important because a great deal of the intellectual production at that time took the form of political philosophy. Whereas the British political philosophy, says Tocqueville, is more concrete, pragmatic, and reformist, the French tends to be abstract, utopian, and radical. Although the former insists on the spontaneous mechanisms of social control that develop within the society, the latter tends to locate this control almost exclusively at the level of the state. Why is that so?

Tocqueville's explanation of this phenomenon takes the same form as earlier: Because of the higher degree of administrative centralization in France, French political philosophers believe that everything in society is dependent on the state. Moreover, as the state is centralized, the *real* power is perceived as located, in the last instance, at the central level. The consequence of the state's visibility is that it is perceived by French political philosophers as the main, if not the only, collective actor endowed with power.

Of course, the structure of what we would call their *role* as they perceived it stimulated the political philosophers to present their ideas in a universal fashion, without reference to any concrete society. Although they wrote about the state or about the society in general, Tocqueville suggests, they had in mind the singular society within which they lived. Moreover, they could expect to draw an influence from their theories to the extent that these theories, although dealing with the eternal and universal problems of political philosophy, were perceived as related to the singular social and political contexts characteristic of this audience. By deriving their proposals of political change from universal theories, they could expect to give them greater strength and influence.

To these circumstances Tocqueville adds the fact, which is more controversial, that the French philosophers, less often than the British, generally had direct experience of public affairs, as the real decision centers were limited to narrow political circles surrounding the king. At any rate, all these circumstances led French philosophers to describe and conceive their society as regulated and dominated by the state and to promote the radical view of equal participation of all to the power of the state.

Again, in this piece of analysis belonging to what could be called the sociology of knowledge, Tocqueville explains a macroscopic difference by making it the outcome of actions. (In this case these actions take the form of the production of political theories.) These actions are interpreted as *understandable* given the social and political context surrounding the actors, given the structure of their role, and given the perception they had "naturally" of the relations between the state and the society.

In summary, what we have in Tocqueville's *Old Regime* is good methodological individualism: Various macroscopic features are explained as the outcome of actions. As with Weber, these actions of the ideal-typical actors (e.g., landlords, philosophers) are considered understandable given the context and in that sense, *rational*. Tocqueville, as does Weber, uses however implicitly a theory of rationality that is much broader than, say, the economic theory of rationality. I will return to this point later.

2.2. WEBER'S PROTESTANT SECTS

At the end of his life, in a letter to Rolf Liefmann (quoted in Mommsen 1965), a prominent member of the Austrian marginalist school of economics, Max Weber wrote, "Sociology too should use a strictly individualistic methodology" ("*Soziologie auch muss strikt individualistisch in der Methode betrieben werden*"). Probably Weber became progressively aware of the relevance to sociology of the individualistic methodology that had been used with success in economics. This relevance is clearly stressed at the beginning of *Wirtschaft und Gesellschaft*. Although it is not always explicitly used in Weber's empirical writings, it is implicitly used in many of his works. In some of these he uses postulates and procedures generally considered typical of economic theory: use of highly simplified models, methodological individualism, postulates of the rationality of action. To illustrate this point I will consider the case of his article on the Protestant sects in America (1958).

The topic of this short but brilliant paper is worthy of consideration. The sociologists attached to the nomological program—Comte and Durkheim, for instance—had claimed that with the increase in the division of labor, traditional religions would lose their power of attraction: Industrialization, or modernization, would produce a laicization effect. In general very skeptical about the validity of nomological statements in sociology, Weber might have been attracted by the case of the United States, partly because it was a vivid refutation of the commonsense law-like statement on the effects of modernization on laicization. In this highly modern, industrialized society, Protestantism appeared as lively as ever.

Thus in the selection of his topic, Weber shows that exploring singularities can be as interesting an objective for sociologists as looking for implausible regularities. In other words, to him, as to Tocqueville, the distinction between history and sociology does not derive from the fact that the latter would be essentially a nomological discipline. Rather, the distinction rests on the fact that sociologists, like economists, can choose to explore the questions that are suggested to them by the observation of social reality with the help of highly simplified and idealized models.

Parenthetically I will note, following Watkins, that in his later work Weber uses effectively his notion of ideal type in a sense very close to our modern notion of model. Thus he mentions Gresham's "law" as an example of an ideal type in *Wirtschaft und Gesellschaft*. It is significant that he puts the word "law" in quotation marks, indicating that to him this law was not a law in the sense of, for instance, Kepler's laws but rather a consequence of what we would call a model and what he calls an ideal type.

The explanation of the vitality of Protestantism in America effectively takes the form of a model, one using the IM principle. To begin with, Weber lists in a very simplified and abstract fashion some major macroscopic differences between American society and the two European societies he implicitly and, in many incidental remarks, explicitly compares to the latter throughout: German and French society. In the United States social and geographic mobility are greater; ethnic heterogeneity is greater; the stratification system is less rigid; and the stratification symbols are less visible and less marked than in France or Germany. The French have their *légion d'honneur*, and the Germans make great use of their academic titles, for instance. As far as the religious system is concerned, *churches* prevail in France or Germany, but American Protestantism takes the form of *sects*, for reasons historically easy to explain.

According to my symbols, this list of factors describes the explanatory macroscopic factors P. Whereas the United States is P with respect to these factors, Germany or France is, say, P′. The next stage in the analysis, as I reconstruct it here, is to show that P and P′ will respectively create distinct situations, say S(P) and S′(P′), for the categories of actors relevant with regard to the objective of the analysis. These categories are two from Weber's analysis: those in charge of the Protestant sects and those willing to make business with one another.

As far as the latter are concerned, the factors P have the consequence that in the United States it is more difficult for two persons, say A and B, who wish to conduct business to know whether they can have confidence in their potential partner. First, because of the greater mobility in the

United States, they are less likely to know each other; previous familiarity is less likely to provide indicators of the degree of trustworthiness of the partner. Second, because of the weaker visibility of status symbols, the latter will not be as easily usable as in France or Germany. In other words, P creates a demand for symbols, for signals whereby A and B would know whether they can have a sufficient degree of confidence in each other before embarking on a business relationship that will, given the complexity of the economic system, in many cases include effects delayed over time. Such a demand exists also in the European societies, but the factors P′ have the consequence that it is more likely satisfied, either by previous knowledge or by the use of stratification symbols.

This demand naturally will now be met on the supply side by the Protestant sects, first because the elites of the country are more than proportionally Protestant, so that "being Protestant" can easily work on many occasions as a positive *label* (this word is, of course, not Weber's), and second, competition among sects is a favorable factor. By imposing high entry costs, those in charge of a given sect can increase the resources of the sect, test the economic liability of their members, hope to increase the value of the certificate of honorability they grant to their members, and thus increase the influence of the sect. In other words, the general conditions P reinforce the competition between Protestant sects: The more influential are those who are able to deliver their certificates of honorability to a high cost. Weber noted with amusement that if the costs of entry in the Lutheran Church had been as high in Germany as in America, there might no longer be any Lutherans in Germany.

Thus P creates a situation S(P) that generates a demand m(S) from those who want to enter into a business relationship with others. This demand is met by a supply provided by actors who, given the conditions P, can be considered natural suppliers, those in charge of the Protestant sects. On the whole, P generates the macroscopic phenomenon that constitutes the object of the analysis; that is, the vitality of Protestantism in the United States.

In other words, this phenomenon is explained by making it a consequence of a deductive model. As with any model, this one rests on simplifying assumptions. Thus the differences between the United States on the one side and Germany or France on the other are reduced to a small number of features. In addition, few categories of actors are considered, and the motivations of these actors are reconstructed in a simple fashion, well in the style of economic analysis. They are given simple, a priori motivations. Finally, the explanation (the liveliness of the Protestant religion in the United States) is interpreted as the aggregate outcome of these individual motivations.

As in the case of Tocqueville, the structure of the explanation is very close to that currently used in economic analysis. At any rate, the explanation rests upon the MI principle.

2.3. THE INDIVIDUALISTIC PARADIGM

The two foregoing examples define a general paradigm, earlier referred to as the individualistic paradigm. As this paradigm corresponds to an important and continuous sociological tradition, it would be useful to summarize its main features, starting from our two classical examples.

1. As far as the objectives of sociology are concerned, they consist in explaining singularities as well as regularities, and also in explaining differences between social systems. By contrast with the nomological paradigm of the Durkheimian tradition, the search for lawlike statements is neither the exclusive nor even the main objective. As a lawlike statement is interpreted in this paradigm as the outcome of actions, it is always conceived as a provisional and fragile statement that can become false as soon as some of the conditions under which the statement is valid are altered. Thus industrialization often produces a laicization effect, but it can also *not* produce such an effect.

2. According to this paradigm explaining any phenomenon, say M, amounts to showing that it is the outcome of actions, that these actions can be made understandable given the social environment of the actors (i.e., the structure of the situation within which they move). As to the structure of the situation, it must be explained as the product of some variables defined at the system level.

3. The explanation takes the form of a model; that is, of a deductive system resting upon highly simplifying assumptions. Relevant categories of actors are defined, generally, in small number. These actors are provided with simple motivations. In the same way, the structure of the situation of action is characterized by a few features.

4. The social actors are supposed to be rational given the context within which they move, but this is only another way of saying that in principle any observer who would know the situation of the actor could conclude, "I could have easily done the same thing he did if I had been in the same situation." Rationality in this instance is entirely coextensive to Weber's notion of *Verstehen*. I will return to this notion of situation-bound rationality later.

5. Among the objections raised against the individualistic paradigm, one occurs frequently: that it cannot easily be used in macrosociological analysis. The examples show that this is not the case; both Tocqueville and Weber were concerned in these examples with macroscopic questions. The individualistic approach becomes compatible with macrosociological analysis as soon as it is perceived that it uses highly simplifying assumptions built into a model. The three main pieces of Weber's methodology—models (ideal types), rationality of action (*Verstehen*), and individualism—are organically related to one another.

6. Because of these simplifying assumptions, the question arises as to the validity of the model. This question is implicitly solved in the individualistic tradition in a fashion I would anachronistically qualify as Popperian: A model is considered valid if it succeeds in explaining a number of observational data. Tocqueville's analyses in the *Old Regime* are still considered important and valid possibly because, starting from the simple notion of "administrative centralization," he was able to explain a number of differences between France and Britain in a parsimonious fashion. In addition, his microsociological assumptions meet the Weberian *Verstehen* criterion. Thus assumptions about the motivations of the landlords or of the *philosophes* can easily be understood. In summary, a model is valid if it meets the Weberian *Verstehen* criterion and the Popperian criteria.

7. The individualistic paradigm is general. It can be applied, as already mentioned, to phenomena located on all scales: small groups, organizations, but also national societies. Moreover, as the two examples sufficiently suggest, it can be applied to any kind of phenomena. By some of their aspects Tocqueville's analyses belong to the sociology of knowledge; by others, to economic sociology. They can also be applied to any kind of society.

This latter point is important because it is often contended that the individualistic paradigm can be used in the case of "individualistic," modern societies but not in the case of "traditional" societies. This criticism rests on a confusion, however: a confusion between the methodological and the sociological-ethical meaning of the word "individualism." In a traditional society, in a *Gemeinschaft* in Tönnies's sense, individuals are generally more closely interdependent on one another than in a *Gesellschaft*. In this sense their autonomy is weaker. This does not imply, however, that the phenomena that occur in such social systems should not be analyzed as the outcome of individual behaviors. As I shall suggest in the next section, many studies can be mentioned which deal with traditional societies and which use the individualistic approach.

3. MODERN SOCIOLOGY AND THE INDIVIDUALISTIC PARADIGM

I could have presented many other examples drawn from classical sociology and using the individualistic paradigm. Elsewhere I have analyzed along earlier lines Sombart's *Why Is There No Socialism in the U.S.?* Generally the classical German and Italian sociological traditions, as well as the non-Durkheimian French tradition, have made great use of this paradigm, although it often remains implicit rather than explicit.

In this section I will suggest that the individualistic tradition remains very active in modern sociology in the most varied fields of interest. I will examine some of these fields, but only briefly. As in the previous section, I will use some typical examples.

3.1. DEVELOPMENT ANALYSIS

The case of the analysis of socioeconomic development or of modernization theory is particularly interesting because it deals with a problem that is intrinsically macrosociological. In this field the nomological program is widely used (Boudon 1983*a*, 1983*b*, 1984*a*). Many studies bear on the conditions of development, on the factors that inhibit development. Other studies investigate "stages of growth." Still others attempt to show that a given organization of the relations of production necessarily induces a particular change or, conversely, generates reproduction effects. As with other fields, this nomological program has provided interesting findings. It has helped to draw attention to certain factors, but it has also aroused some doubts. National societies are such complex systems that no two of them are comparable. As a result, some factor, A, can induce B in one context and not-B in another. Thus it is questionable whether any genuinely valid lawlike statement can be proposed in this field. In other words, the nomological program perhaps has essentially a heuristic value.

At any rate, beside the numerous studies conducted on the nomological program, many can be mentioned which belong to the individualistic program. Some of them take the form of theories or models explaining a singular phenomenon or process. Others take the form of general models. An example of a study belonging to the first category is Hirschman's work on the development of the Brazilian northeast (1963). Although the problem of the development of this region was perceived as a crucial political problem in the third part of the nineteenth century, and although many efforts were made to solve it, they were largely a failure.

Why? The failure is interpreted by Hirschman as the aggregate outcome of reasonable or understandable actions.

For reasons that can be explained, the problem of the northeast was interpreted very early as a *technical* problem: the region would develop if the consequences of the long and unforeseeable periods of dryness that characterize the climate could be limited. The building of dams and irrigation networks was the obvious solution to the problem of poverty in the northeast. Hirschman explains very well why this solution, which was not the only one, was perceived as "natural" in the nineteenth century and in the twentieth century until World War II.

At any rate, what happened is the following: The dams were built first. As they are more visible than the irrigation channels, it was *politically* advisable to spend public funds on dams rather than on irrigation networks. Therefore irrigation was postponed. *Economically*, this priority given to the dams was not unreasonable either; the dams and reservoirs were efficient remedies for the effects of dryness. The fact that, for understandable reasons, irrigation was postponed, however, generated a number of undesired effects that largely canceled the positive effects of the program. Plots in the neighborhood of the reservoirs were often bought by rich landlords who took advantage of the increased supply of water to develop commercial and industrial crops. As a result, the program contributed much less than expected to increase the overall production of subsistence crops, although this was one of its main objectives. Moreover, the development of commercial crops on the large farms near the reservoirs created job opportunities for the poor peasants, who otherwise would have emigrated to the coast in dry periods, as they had done during previous decades. Because they could use this cheap labor force, the landlords were weakly motivated to increase the productivity of their land. On the whole, the mass of poor peasants benefited little from the dams; poverty remained; and the agricultural system remained underdeveloped.

It is interesting to compare this "individualistic" analysis to the neo-Marxist nomological analysis that is currently given of similar processes, using the "covering law" according to which the dominant classes would always manage to keep up their position.

I will briefly consider a second example, selected almost at random in a wide set of possible examples. This example deals with a study in which a singular development process is analyzed in the framework of the individualistic paradigm as defined earlier.

During several decades at the end of the nineteenth century and at the beginning of the twentieth, Colombia enjoyed a high rate of development in comparison to similar countries. The phenomenon attracted the attention of many social scientists because all the "bottlenecks" which the nomological theories present as inhibiting development were more or less present in Colombia (little overhead capital, fragmented markets, weak overall saving capacities, etc.). The puzzle of the Colombian development was brilliantly solved by Hagen (1962). Because of a number of well-known historical factors, in the second part of the nineteenth century the elite of one province, Antioquia, was confronted with a structure of opportunities characterized by the following features: The members of this elite were not motivated to invest their resources in land because there were no landed gentry in the province. They were not motivated either to push their children toward the professions. Because of historical reasons, in Antioquia there were no institutions of higher education with minimum prestige. Nor were the gentry incited to push their children toward politics: As the province was considered a backwater by the rest of the country, they could not easily reach central political positions. These factors make up the negative side of the opportunity structure characteristic of the province.

On the positive side, the elite among the Antioqueños had accumulated experience in business techniques and business organization over time. As they had been active in mining and transportation, two activities characterized by a high degree of risk in the context, they had developed and used complex forms of organization with limited liability found in more advanced societies. On the whole, the structure of the situation, the structure of opportunities, pushed these elite toward business and prevented their engaging in other types of activities.

Curiously enough, Hagen did not present his analysis in the way I did. Rather, he tried to show that the role played by the Antioqueños in Colombian development was to be explained by a covering law: status loss among the Antioqueños resembled that among the Japanese samurai, the cause of their need for achievement. Evidently, to Hagen, the social sciences are to be defined by a nomological program.

Hagen's model explains very well why Colombia experienced this high rate of development at one time, but it also explains a considerable number of data: why the Antioqueños took a more than proportional part in the development process; why they were considered in the other provinces as "different" or peculiar; why they displayed a weak national feeling; and so on.

In my opinion the Hirschman and Hagen examples are of the same variety as the classical examples I evoked earlier. The two use an individualistic model to explain a puzzling singular phenomenon or process. As

I said earlier, individualistic models can have a *singular* orientation, as here, but they can also have a *general* orientation. Development theory has produced many models of the first type, that illustrated by the Hirschman and Hagen examples, but also many models of the second type. Such a model was proposed by Bhaduri (1976). Although it was inspired by singular data (on West Bengal), the model is general in the sense that, according to the way it is parametrized, it can generate various outcomes or consequences. This amounts to saying that the same model can be used to explore or explain a variety of contexts.

West Bengal is characterized by what Bhaduri calls "semifeudal" relations of production. This means that the tenants are formally (i.e., legally) free to sell their force of labor but still bound to their landlord because of their permanent indebtedness to him. Bhaduri's point is that such a system should often have the consequence of preventing landlords from increasing the productivity of their land, as this would reduce the tenants' indebtedness and consequently the part of their income the landlords draw from their loans.

The model explains well this author's point: why, in spite of the efforts of the administration, innovations are currently rejected in West Bengal and why agricultural productivity remains stagnant. At the same time the model has a general orientation in the sense that it could also explain, if it was parametrized otherwise, why in another context innovation could be accepted in spite of the semifeudal social organization. Thus the model supposes tacitly that the decision power with regard to the adoption of innovations is entirely in the hands of the landlords. Although this parametrization is relevant for certain types of innovation, it is less relevant for others. Or, to mention a second parameter, the model supposes that no landlord has an interest in being more competitive than his neighbor. This parameter need not be in this state.

My main point in presenting this example in brief was to draw to the reader's attention the fact that the individualistic paradigm gives rise to two types of models: those which are limited to the explanation of a singular process or phenomenon and those which, although they are often inspired by the analysis of a singular process or phenomenon, have a more general scope.

3.2. SOCIAL MOVEMENTS

In this other field, as in the case of development analysis, many examples can be cited of any of the four main paradigms listed in the first section. Thus many lawlike statements have been proposed about the conditions making the outbreak of revolutions more or less likely (Davies 1962). Many interpretive studies could also easily be mentioned, dealing, for instance, with the meaning of the French Revolution. Of course, the critical paradigm has also been used currently in this area of research.

The individualistic paradigm has also been widely used. Among the models that are part of this paradigm and also of the class of models with a general orientation, Olson's (1965) well-known theory of collective action can be mentioned. This model constitutes a general framework. Depending on the states of its parameters, it predicts either the development or the nondevelopment of collective action (but see Hirschman 1982).

Among the models with a singular orientation, Oberschall's (1973) work can be mentioned. In perhaps the most interesting part of his study, Oberschall explains very convincingly why the black movement in the United States in the 1960s generally took a nonviolent form in the South and a violent form in the North. According to the general formula describing the individualistic paradigm, the contrast between North and South is explained by (1) identifying some relevant conditions opposing the North and the South (e.g., the integrating role played by the black Protestant churches in the South), in my symbols, P and P'; (2) showing that P and P' created contrasted contexts S and S' for the black leaders; and (3) showing that although the southern context incited the leaders to a nonviolent strategy $m(S)$, the northern one had opposite effects $m'(S')$.

Many other examples following the same line of thought could be given. Trevor-Roper (1972) explains the success of Erasmism and later of Calvinism in Europe in the sixteenth century by making it the aggregate outcome of attitudes that naturally developed, notably among the economic elites. These reactions can be seen as natural, in the sense that they are *understandable*, reactions (in the Weberian sense) of these actors to their situation.

3.3. SOCIAL MOBILITY

To take a final example, the various paradigms distinguished earlier can be identified in the case of social mobility analysis. Studies belonging to the nomological paradigm attempt, for instance, to discover the factors influencing the overall rates of social mobility, or to identify and to measure the influence of factors such as social background, father's level of education, subject's level of education, making individual mobility, downward or upward, more or less likely (Soerensen 1976). In all those studies the units of analysis are not individuals but variables. Thus a typical finding of such studies will take this form: In a particular context the level of education influences mobility to a small or a large extent. Very often this influence will be presented in a quantified form. In most cases such findings will be considered final results. In other words, no effort will be made to relate the statistical relations between variables to their real causes; that is, the individual behaviors of which they are the outcome.

In other cases the individualistic paradigm is used; that is, an effort is made to build models incorporating a set of assumptions on the behavior of individuals with the expectation that once these behaviors are aggregated, the outcome will reproduce more or less correctly some observed data or some structural properties of the data. An example of a study belonging to this type of logical framework is provided by Lévy-Garboua (1976) on the demand for college degrees among French youth. He had at his disposal a set of data on college enrollments over time, on degrees prepared, on failure and success in the examinations, and on time spent on the preparation of degrees, leisure activities, part-time salaried occupations, stipends, the value of degrees in the labor market, and the evolution of this value over time, among other factors. In order to explain these data he built a behavioral model on the main assumption that students try to obtain as high a degree as possible because the value of all degrees remains positive throughout the period under consideration. Because the relative value of any degree also diminishes continuously in the period, Lévy-Garboua introduced the assumption that students would compensate for this loss by devoting more time to leisure and paid work and less to academic work. On the whole, this simple behavioral model reproduces and thus explains more or less correctly the main structural features of the quantitative data.

I have taken a similar path in my own works in the sociology of education and mobility (Boudon 1974). My analysis in *Education, Opportunity and Social Inequality* was motivated by a series of statistical findings that I perceived as puzzling: Why does the structure of social mobility—the structure of mobility tables—change so moderately over time? Why does the expansion and democratization of the educational system seem empirically to have such little effect on mobility? Other questions can be posed as well. In order to solve this puzzle, I built a model using simple behavioral assumptions. These assumptions led to a simulation model that reproduced more or less correctly the main structural features of a set of statistical data on educational demand and its evolution. In particular the model generated a decrease in the inequality of educational opportunities. Then I continued by supposing that once they had reached a given level of education, the fictitious individuals of the model would be exposed to a queueing process whereby those with a better education would be more likely to be given a better position in the status market. To my surprise, once this was done I noticed that the model generated little change in the structure of the mobility matrices for broad sets of acceptable (i.e., realistic) values of the parameters. I interpreted this stability as a counterintuitive aggregation effect.

I have considered briefly the fields of development of social movements and of social mobility. Examples could be cited from many other fields. In most cases I imagine it would be rather easy to find examples of studies belonging to the various paradigms described in the first section and particularly to the individualistic paradigm. The examples selected in the three fields confirm that the individualistic approach can be used very efficiently at the macrosociological level. This point, which had been well understood by Tocqueville, Weber, and others, appears to be confirmed as well by many modern sociological studies.

4. CONTEXT-BOUND RATIONALITY

In foregoing sections I have tried to suggest that the individualistic paradigm constitutes the backbone of an important sociological tradition, from the founding fathers to modern sociology. Stressing this point seems to me important given that sociology is often viewed as grounded in opposition among the individualistic methods commonly practiced, notably in economics. When some modern sociologists defend an individualistic approach to social phenomena, they are often considered in some sociological circles as breaking with the essential principles of *the* sociological tradition. For this reason it was important to stress that the individualistic tradition is ongoing and of long standing among the other sociological traditions.

It is also important, however, to see one main difference between the economic and the sociological individualistic traditions. Although these two traditions hold as a postulate that individual actions must be considered *rational*, the sociological individualistic tradition gives a much broader meaning to this notion. This point is well known, and every sociology student knows, for instance, that Weber introduced the notion of *Wertrationalität* beside what is called *Zweckrationalität*. It might be useful to introduce some remarks in order to clarify the meaning of the notion of rationality in sociology. In a thought-provoking paper on rationality, Lukes (1967) made the point that the very notion of *Wertrationalität* shows that Weber used the word "rationality" in a loose and indefensible fashion. I mention this paper not because I agree with Lukes on this point but because it suggests that the idea of rationality as used by sociologists requires clarification.

On the whole, if the various theoretical reflections of Weber, Pareto, and others on the theory of social action were systematized and combined with the implicit theory of action incorporated in the many studies using the individualistic paradigm, the main idea that would emerge from such an inventory might be the notion of *context-bound rationality*. In the individualistic sociological tradition individual action is considered rational, but this rationality can take various forms as a function of the context. The actions of the social actors are always in principle *understandable*, provided we are sufficiently informed about their situation. This context-relatedness of rationality can take many forms, and I cannot undertake a systematic inventory in this respect. Therefore I will make a few brief remarks.

There can be context-relatedness in the sense that collective values can have the consequence that action A will bring to the actor rewards that are a function of the collective values. Thus in Tocqueville's example, serving the state, becoming a civil servant, is rewarding to the French landlord; it brings him prestige because the state is collectively perceived as prestigious. At least according to Tocqueville, serving the state is considered a more desirable activity in France than in Britain, because in France this activity is collectively more valued with respect to others. This collective valuation can be explained in individualistic terms. Tocqueville suggests that the state was more respected in France because it was actually more powerful, more present in the everyday life of any citizen. In this example one might speak of a *collective value-related* rationality: the collective values contribute to making a particular end more desirable or rewarding to the actor.

There also can be context-related rationality in the sense that although the actor can be confronted with choice or decision situations in which the means-end classical scheme can be viewed as a plausible description of his or her behavior, in other cases it cannot. Such cases arise, for instance, when the actor is confronted with a problem of such complexity that one cannot assume that he or she will cope with it by exploring a set of means, ordering them according to some criteria. Even the "limited rationality" version of the classical means-end rationality model will be, given the complexity of the problem, an inaccurate description. In such a case what I call a *cognitive* type of rationality will likely come into play: The actor will choose not between *means* properly but between *interpretations* of the problem. I mentioned earlier an example of this type of situation generating a cognitive form of rationality when I discussed Hirschman's example of the development of the Brazilian northeast. The problem was interpreted as a technical one (limiting, by technical means, the effects of dryness) neither because this interpretation was the only possible one nor because it was judged better as alternative interpretations but because, for all kinds of reasons, it could be perceived as *natural*.

Other examples easily could be given. When, in the first years of the Third Republic, the French government was confronted with the problem of reorganizing the higher education system, it hesitated between two interpretations: reorganizing the system around the idea that universities should be treated as enterprises (though enterprises of a special kind) or as public service organizations. The two interpretations had their promoters. Those impressed by the achievements of the German university system tended to prefer the first, but others thought that the second interpretation was more congenial to French political traditions.

Not only those in charge of political decisions can be confronted with such complex decisions generating cognitive rationality. Downs (1957) suggested that common voters use such a rationality: They will not make up their minds by comparing the programs of candidates A and B; they do not know whether or not the programs will actually be worked out or exactly what consequences they would generate. Rather, voters will choose candidate A, for instance, because A is a "rightist" or a "leftist" and because rightists (or leftists) seem to have a more reasonable and acceptable conception of political action. Of course, for such notions as "left" or "right" to be used by the common voter, they have to exist—that is, to be perceived collectively as meaningful interpretations.

It must be stressed that the relative validity of alternative interpretations of a complex problem can be affected by social factors. Thus when Lenin reflected, in 1895, on the best way of organizing the Russian social-democratic party, he started from the interpretation that a worker party should follow the spontaneous worker movements, that the intelligentsia should only help and assist the masses. In 1902, in *What Is to Be Done?* he defended the opposite view that the party should incite and stimulate the workers, that the intelligentsia should be the prime movers, and that consequently the party should be active, effective, and organized in a centralized and authoritarian fashion.

This change in the interpretation of the relationship between the party and the masses was a result mainly of a drastic change in the social *conjoncture* in Russia (Brym 1980). In 1895, because of an impressive economic boom, the worker movements were very active and strikes numerous. Worker leaders held the intellectuals in relative suspicion because of the latter's earlier involvement in anarchism, terrorism, and populism. In 1902, the *conjoncture* completely changed. Because of the recession the strikes disappeared and the worker movements became lax. Because the unions and workers had not been able to accumulate resources in sufficient amounts, the workers were more concerned with protecting their resources than with taking part in collective action. At the same time a new activism developed among university students, and a violence-repression cycle was started between the czar and the students. Probably because of this variation in the *conjoncture*, the interpretation Lenin gave of the relation between the party and the workers changed in the meanwhile. This change need not be interpreted as the product of any opportunism. Rather, the situation was such in 1895 that it was difficult to believe that the spontaneous worker movements could be controlled from above, whereas this belief was well adapted to the *conjoncture* generated by the recession that started in the last years of the nineteenth century.

On the whole one can speak not only of a value-rationality (the Tocquevillian landlords were rational when they valued highly the position of civil servants) but of a belief-rationality. Lenin was rational when he believed one thing in 1895 and its contrary in 1902, as the two beliefs can be made understandable given the complexity of the problem of organizing a party and the social *conjoncture*.

Pareto is the classical author who seems to have developed most convincingly the idea that many situations cannot be handled by the social actors in the way described by the classical means-end model even in its relativized version (Boudon 1984*b*). He insisted that many situations imply that the actor has recourse to beliefs. Actions led by beliefs Pareto called *nonlogical*. But non-logical does not mean "irrational" in his language. These actions are *non-logical* in the sense that by contrast with the action of the engineer who builds a bridge, the means are not determined by scientific knowledge. The beliefs behind the non-logical actions can be made understandable, however, provided one sees that many problems (for instance, voting) cannot be handled by the actor in a *logical* way. Once this is seen, the beliefs of the actor can be related to the *conjoncture*, to the beliefs of others, to the actor's own resources, values, and so on and, by so doing, be made *understandable*—that is, rational in the Weberian sense.

A question usually raised about Pareto concerns whether or not his work in sociology is compatible with his work in economics. The answer seems very simple: To him, economics deals with actions of a particularly simple type, and these actions are often met in the phenomena generally considered by economists, whereas sociologists are often concerned with actions of a more complex type. For Pareto both economic and social phenomena should be considered outcomes of individual actions. Actors can be considered rational in the sense that their actions can be made understandable provided enough is known about the context within which they move. In other words, economics and sociology have much in common, although the latter needs and effectively uses a more general theory of rationality.

Well-accepted sociological ideas, as the notion of reference group, describe particular forms of the general idea of context-related rationality. What may be called "reference group rationality" will work naturally, for instance, in competitive situations. In my own work on mobility I have tried to show that the costs and benefits of an investment in education was subjectively perceived by individuals as related to their social origins. A lawyer's son will perceive a given degree as insurance against intergenerational demotion and will attach great importance to the degree. A worker's son will perceive the same degree as a kind of luxury giving him a chance to advance still further in the already likely promotion (Alker 1976).

Besides being *complex*, a choice situation can also be *ambiguous*, in the sense that all of the alternative courses of action entail costs and rewards between which the actor makes a clear-cut choice, usually with difficulty. In such a case beliefs can help the actor to reach a decision. An interesting example in this respect is provided by Dore (1959) in his book on the modernization of agriculture in Japan.

Following an old custom, Japanese landlords were not supposed to increase the rent in good years but to decrease it in bad years. The custom had the effect of putting the landlords in an ambiguous situation when they were confronted with the problem of whether they should adopt a particular innovation in order to increase the productivity of their land. If they did adopt the innovation they could draw benefit from it, but with difficulty, as the tenants would consider that there would be no more cause to increase the rent when the production increased because of the innovation than when it increased because of the weather. If the landlords did *not* adopt the innovation, they would lose the opportunity to not decrease the rent, as the effects of the innovation would cancel the effects of the bad weather conditions. Interestingly enough, Dore observed that those who adopted the proposed innovations were likely to have been exposed to the physiocratic ideology that had been imported into Japan by the Dutch at the end of the eighteenth century. Obviously, once an innovation was accepted by some landlords, the others were progressively motivated to adopt it for evident economic reasons. The interesting point of this example is that it shows that beliefs and ideology can help to reach a decision when a choice situation cannot, because of its ambiguity, be handled in a rational fashion, in the classical sense of the word.

More generally, again following Pareto, one can say that beliefs and ideologies are normal ingredients of social action, that they should be analyzed by individualistic methods and viewed as understandable (i.e., as rational in Weber's sense). To return to an example I briefly alluded to, the economic elites of the early sixteenth century were in an uncomfortable position. They were influential and powerful, but their status was not widely recognized, as the Catholic ideology had always considered worldly activities of little dignity in comparison with spiritual and clerical activities. The extraordinary success of Erasmus was a result of the fact that he cleverly mobilized the authority of the Gospel to suggest that the dignity of God could be served just as well through worldly activities. To the ideological demand he responded by offering an ideological supply. He felt the demand and, as a good strategist, saw that the dignity of the economic elites would be efficiently defended if it were derived from the message of the collectively accepted authority, the Gospel.

This analysis shows not only that ideologies can be analyzed in an individualistic fashion but also that they are often normal ingredients of rational action. The enthusiasm of the entrepreneurs of the sixteenth century for Erasmus is easily understandable given their environment, and the message of Erasmus can be interpreted as an answer to a rational ideological demand.

REFERENCES

Alker, H. 1976. Boudon's Educational Theses about the Replication of Social Inequality. *Social Science Information* 15, 1:33–46.

Barton, A. H., and P. F. Lazarsfeld. 1961. Some Functions of Qualitative Analysis in Social Research, in S. Lipset and N. Smelser, eds., *Sociology: The Progress of a Decade*. Englewood Cliffs, N.J.: Prentice-Hall.

Bhaduri, A. 1976. A Study of Agricultural Backwardness under Semi-Feudalism. *Economic Journal* 83:120–137.

Boudon, Raymond. 1974. *Education, Opportunity, and Social Inequality*. New York: John Wiley.

———.1983*a*. Individual Action and Social Change. *British Journal of Sociology* 34, 1:1–18.

———.1983*b*. Why the Theories of Social Change Fail. *Public Opinion Quarterly* 57:143–160.

———.1984*a*. *La place du désordre*. Paris: Presses Universitaires de France.

———.1984*b*. Le phénomène idéologique: en marge d'une lecture de Pareto. *L'Année Sociologique* 34:87–126.

Brym, R. 1980. *Intellectuals and Politics*. London: Allen & Unwin.

Davies, J. 1962. Toward a Theory of Revolution. *American Sociological Review* 27, 1:5–19.

Dore, R. P. 1959. *Land and Reform in Japan*. London: Oxford University Press.

Downs, A. 1957. *An Economic Theory of Democracy*. New York: Harper.

Hagen, E. 1962. *On the Theory of Social Change: How Economic Growth Begins*. Homewood, Ill.: Dorsey Press.

Hempel, C. 1965. *Aspects of Scientific Explanation and Other Essays in the Philosophy of Science*. New York: Free Press.

Hirschman, A. 1963. *Journeys toward Progress*. New York: 20th Century Fund.

———.1982. *Shifting Involvements*. Princeton. Princeton University Press.

Homans, George C. 1982. The Present State of Sociological Theory. *Sociological Quarterly* 23 (Summer):285–299.

Lévy-Garboua, L. 1976. Les demandes de l'étudiant ou les contradictions de l'Université de masse. *Revue Française de Sociologie* 17, 1:53–80.

Lukes, S. 1967. Some Problems about Rationality. *European Journal of Sociology* 8, 2:247–264.

Mommsen, W. 1965. Max Weber's Political Sociology and His Philosophy of World History. *International Social Science Journal* 17:35–45.

Oberschall, A. 1973. *Social Conflicts and Social Movements*. Englewood Cliffs, N.J.: Prentice-Hall.

Olson, Mancur. 1965. *The Logic of Collective Action*. Cambridge, Mass.: Harvard University Press.

O'Neill, J., ed. 1973. *Modes of Individualism and Collectivism*. London: Heinemann.

Popper, Karl R. 1963. *The Poverty of Historicism*. London: Routledge & Kegan Paul.

Soerensen, A. 1976. Models and Strategies in Research on Attainment and Opportunity. *Social Science Information* 15, 1:71–92.

Trevor-Roper, H. R. 1972. *Religion, the Reformation and Social Change, and Other Essays*. London: Macmillan.

Van Parijs, P. 1981. Sociology as General Economics. *Archives Européennes de Sociologie* 22:299–324.

Weber, Max. 1958. The Protestant Sects and the Spirit of Capitalism, pp. 302–322 in H. Gerth and C. W. Mills, eds., *From Max Weber*. New York: Oxford University Press.

CHAPTER TWO

Contrasting Theoretical Perspectives*

Peter M. Blau

Microsociology and macrosociology involve contrasting theoretical perspectives on social life and consequently explain it in different terms. The units of analysis are different—individuals in the first case and populations in the second—and so are the concepts and variables—attributes of human beings in microsociology, emergent properties of population structures in macrosociology. Individuals can be rich or poor, but only collectivities can exhibit more or less economic inequality. I consider the term "actor" for both individuals and collectivities misleading because the most relevant characteristics for analyzing the two are entirely different.

Thus microsociology and macrosociology employ different concepts and seek to formulate different theories to explain social relations and the more complex social patterns and phenomena based on social relations. Microsociology analyzes the underlying social processes that engender relations between persons. The focus is on social interaction and communication, and important concepts are reciprocity, significant symbols, obligations, exchange, and dependence. Macrosociology analyzes the structure of different positions in a population and their constraints on social relations. The focus is on the external limitations of the social environment on people's relations, and important concepts are differen-

*This is a somewhat altered version of a paper that appears in the Festschrift for Richard Emerson: Karen Cook (ed.) *Social Exchange Theory* (Beverly Hills, Calif.: Sage, in Press).

tiation, institutions, inequality, heterogeneity, and crosscutting circles. In short, microsociology dissects the internal dynamics of social relations, whereas macrosociology analyzes the influences on social relations exerted by external social constraints and opportunities—Durkheim's social facts.

There are many versions of microsociological and macrosociological theoretical schemes, but I shall deal only with one of each. After a few remarks about exchange theory, with which I assume the reader is familiar, I shall deal somewhat less briefly with the macrostructural theory I have advanced in recent years.

REFLECTIONS ON EXCHANGE THEORY

I hope readers will not object if I indulge in some autobiographical reflections on exchange theory. The idea of conceptualizing social interaction as an exchange process originally occurred to me more than a third of a century ago in a case study of government officials, largely based on direct observation at work, which I did for my Ph.D. dissertation. This idea was influenced by Whyte's (1943:256–258) principle of "mutual obligation," but at that time I was not aware (or did not remember) that conceptions of social exchange had been used by many others before, from Aristotle to Mauss. Early in my research while observing officials I noticed that colleagues often discussed cases with one another, although everyone was responsible for a different set of cases. In the office one nearly always saw two or a few agents deeply involved in a conversation about their work. Lunch times were filled with shoptalk about interesting or problematic cases.

This practice of consulting struck me immediately as something of interest, and my curiosity was particularly stimulated when the supervisor told me that agents are actually prohibited from consulting colleagues but are required to confer with him when they encounter problems. I interpreted these transactions as social exchanges in which one official receives help in his work, without having to expose his difficulties to the supervisor, in return for paying the consultant respect, which is implicit in acknowledging the need for another's advice by asking for it. Repeated exchanges of this kind raise the informal status of officials whom many colleagues often ask for advice, which is the ultimate price for help with difficult decisions.

The main reason for my interest in social exchange is that I consider it a strictly social phenomenon and thus particularly well suited for investigation by sociologists. This is not the case for most of the subjects studied in surveys. People's attitudes, votes in elections, education, career achievements, and work satisfaction, for example, are certainly socially conditioned and influenced, and many are oriented toward other people, but these factors themselves refer to the acting and thinking of individuals and not to a social process. Social exchange, in contrast, centers attention directly on the social process of give-and-take in people's relations and analyzes how ego's behavior depends not on ego's prior conditioning, experiences, or attributes but on alter's behavior, which in turn is contingent on ego's behavior. The behavior of each is, of course, psychologically motivated, but exchange theory does not seek to explain why each individual participates in the exchange in terms of these motives. Rather, it dissects the transaction process to explain the interdependent contingencies in which each response is dependent on the other's prior action and is simultaneously the stimulus evoking the other's further reaction. Thus the motivation of participants is taken as given, and concern is with the alternating reciprocities underlying the social interaction. My disagreement with Homans's theory stems from this conception of the distinctly social nature of exchange. To be sure, exchange can be analyzed in terms of the motives of the partners in the transactions, just as conflict can be analyzed in terms of the motives of the adversaries. Such psychological reductionism, however, ignores the social process presumably under investigation, the repeated reciprocities implicit in exchange, or the seemingly inevitable growth of conflict potential resulting from threats and counterthreats as illustrated by an arms race.

There are other reasons for sociologists to be concerned with the analysis of social exchange. It is one of the few subject matters, aside from mathematical sociology, that lends itself to the development of systematic axiomatic theory. Such concepts as marginal utility, borrowed from economics, can be adapted to explain noneconomic observations—for example, the declining significance of social approval has already been received—and hence can serve as building blocks for constructing rigorous, hypotheticodeductive theory. Indeed, Homans's exchange theory is one of the rare attempts in sociology to devise such a theory, and whereas I disagree with the psychological reductionism of this theory, I fully agree with Homans that it is important for sociology to develop more systematic deductive theories. Another advantage of exchange theory is that its basic ideas and concepts are so widely applicable and give new meaning to everyday observations; for example, why people do favors even for strangers or why they often fight over who pays the check in a restaurant. A final attraction of exchange theory is that I hoped that it could serve as a microsociological foundation on which to build a macrosociological theory of social structure. This is what I attempted to do in my book on the subject twenty years ago, but I was more successful in the microsociological analysis of exchange processes than in employing the microprinciples as the groundwork of a rigorous macrostructural theory. This is the main reason that my interests shifted away from social exchange to a different approach to macrosociological theorizing.

Before I returned to primarily theoretical analysis, however, I spent more than a decade conducting empirical research on bureaucratic organizations of various kinds. I had a long-standing interest in the organizational principles of Weber's analysis of bureaucracy, and this interest motivated my early case studies of government offices. I could deal with bureaucratic principles there only inferentially and not directly, however, because general principles of organizations require comparing many and cannot be based on case studies. Homans noted this in a book review of my early research, which, though generally favorable, indicated that the title (*The Dynamics of Bureaucracy*) is misleading because my book deals essentially with informal relations in work groups of officials and not with bureaucracy. To attack problems of organizational structure directly I carried out a series of studies, each of which involved the quantitative analysis of data collected from a large number of comparable organizations—for example, many government agencies, many academic institutions, or many factories. This research does address the macrosociological issues of bureaucratic structure with which Weber's theory is concerned. Although not devoid of theoretical inferences and implications, these studies concentrated on the analysis of empirical findings. I became increasingly eager to escape being submerged in empirical data and to try to develop a deductive macrosociological theory of social structure.

An important issue in constructing macrosociological theory is the linkage with microsociological theory. One approach is to start with microsociological principles and use these as the foundation for macrosociological theory. The alternative approach rests on the assumption that different perspectives and conceptual frameworks are necessary for micro- and macrotheories, primarily because the major terms of macrosociological theories refer to emergent properties of population structures that have no equivalent in microsociological analysis. I have come to the conclusion that the second approach is the more viable one, at least at this stage of sociological development.

MACROSTRUCTURAL CONCEPTUAL SCHEME

The macrosociological theory of social structure I have formulated is a deductive theory (Braithwaite 1953; Popper [1934] 1959) of the quantitative dimension of social life. The two classical sociologists who have most influenced my orientation are Durkheim ([1895] 1938) and Simmel (1908), particularly Durkheim's focus on social facts that exert external constraints on people and Simmel's emphasis on the quantitative dimension of social life and the significance of crosscutting social circles. The units under study are societies or communities or other large collectivities, not individuals or small groups. It is a structural theory in Marx's sense rather than in Lévi-Strauss's. That is, by "structure" I refer to a system of objective differences in social positions among people and their relations, not to cultural myths, symbols, or marriage rules. My theory differs from Marx's primary concentration on economic positions and relations because it is concerned with other social differences, such as racial or ethnic ones, as well as with economic differences. Following Parsons's distinction between culture and social structure—which makes him, as he himself notes (1966:13), "a cultural determinist"—my theory centers attention on the structural rather than the cultural effects on social life.

The theory's objective is to explain patterns of social relations in structural terms, not individual behavior in cultural or psychological ones. In short, both the explicandum and the explicans of the proposed theory are distinctly social. The explicanda are the configurations or networks of social relations in a collectivity, particularly the extent of social relations among persons in different social positions. An example is the prevalence of intermarriage between different ethnic groups or of friendships between persons in the middle class and those in the working class. Of course, all human relations involve behavior of the participants. The structural theory's objective, however, is not to account for this behavior on the basis of the motives inducing it but to account for the pattern of social relations on the basis of the external constraints and opportunities for various social relations created by the composition of the population—that is, the structure of different positions in the social environment. In a community composed mostly of Protestants, the religious structure limits opportunities to marry Catholics and expands opportunities to marry Protestants. The explicans is not the influence of internalized cultural values and norms; neither is it that of psychological preferences. Instead, it is the influence of the external limits on opportunities imposed by the social structure—that is, the differentiation in the population along various lines—and these limits restrict relations whatever the cultural values and psychological preferences.

In sum, social structure refers here to people's differences in social position along various lines, as illustrated by the ethnic differences in a population, their economic differences, or their differences in education. The specific criterion of a collectivity's differentiation in a given dimension is the distribution among different occupations or income levels. The concept of social position is broadly defined. Any difference in attributes among people that they themselves take into account in their social relations, whether intentionally or inadvertently, is considered to reflect social positions. Given that social positions are thus defined on the basis of their influence on social relations, any proposition that stipulates such an influence would be tautological. However, the theorems advanced do not specify the influences of an individual's social positions on her or his social relations but the influences of an entire population's differentiation along various lines on the patterns of social relations in this population. These two influences—that of a person's position and that of the distribution of persons in a given dimension—are not the same. Indeed, they are often opposed, as we shall see. Simmel's concern with the significance of size for social life is thus extended to the significance of size distributions. Since all individuals in one population have only a single size distribution on any one dimension, analysis of the macrostructural propositions requires the comparison of different populations, not merely the comparison of individuals in one population.

Every individual naturally occupies numerous social positions. A person lives in a neighborhood, belongs to an ethnic group, has a religion, is more or less educated, works in an industry, has an occupation, and earns an income. Even simple societies are differentiated along several lines, and complex ones exhibit many dimensions of differentiation. A population distribution exists for every dimension. Hence social structure can be defined as a multidimensional space of positions among which people are distributed. Social structure is an abstract theoretical term that cannot be operationally represented by a single variable. Rather, it encompasses many specific concepts that can be so represented: the specific dimensions of differentiation.

The degree of differentiation in one dimension, or in a combination of several, is called a *structural parameter*. Social structures are delineated by their parameters. In other words, structural parameters refer to the degree of variation among the members of a population in various respects. Illustrations are a nation's concentration of wealth, an economy's industrial diversity, an organization's division of labor, a city's income distribution, or a neighborhood's racial composition. Comparisons must be made of the same social units, of course—either different societies or different cities, for example. It is important to note that the various dimensions of differentiation are not necessarily orthogonal. Some differences in social positions, such as education and occupational status, tend to be closely related, whereas others, such as sex and religion, generally exhibit little relation. The extent of covariation of one social difference with others is also considered a structural parameter; for example, the degree to which people's ethnic differences are related to their educational, occupational, and economic differences.

Three generic forms of parameters can be distinguished which subsume the many specific lines of social differences among people. Two parameters refer to differentiation in a single dimension, whereas the third refers to covariation of several dimensions among the members of a collectivity. The criterion for distinguishing the first two is whether the social differences divide the population into unordered nominal categories with relatively distinct boundaries, such as religious denominations or ethnic groups, or whether they classify people on the basis of a status gradation without clear boundaries, such as income or power. The two unidimensional forms of differentiation are heterogeneity and inequality.

Heterogeneity is the extent of differentiation of the members of a collectivity into nominal groups. Society's division of labor illustrates heterogeneity; so does a community's linguistic diversity. The larger the number of subgroups into which a population can be divided in a given dimension and the more uneven people's distribution among these groups, the greater the heterogeneity. The criterion of heterogeneity is the chance expectation that two randomly chosen persons belong to different groups. To compare the heterogeneity of various societies or communities, it is necessary that the same classification into subunits be used for all; for instance, either detailed occupations or major occupational groups must be used for all cases to compare the division of labor. (A measure proposed by Gibbs and Martin [1962] represents this criterion operationally and can be used in research on all types of heterogeneity.)

Inequality is the extent of differentiation of a population in terms of resources or ranked status. The concentration of wealth is a form of inequality; so is the extent of differences in education. The criterion of a society's or community's inequality in a given dimension is the mean absolute difference in status or resources between any two persons proportionate to the mean status or resources for all persons. Thus the average absolute difference in income between all possible pairs divided by the mean income of the labor force indicates income inequality. (The Gini coefficient is the most direct operational measure of this criterion.) A paradox of inequality in resources is that great inequality in a society (for instance, in wealth or power) means that most of the resource is concentrated in few hands, yet it simultaneously implies that the large majority of people are nearly equal (in this example, that most have hardly any wealth or power).

The third type of parameter refers to the degree to which several kinds of differences among people are closely related rather than being more or less unrelated and thus *intersecting*. If differences in social positions along various lines are strongly correlated, they consolidate group boundaries and class distinctions and strengthen the barriers between ingroup and outgroup or between persons who differ in hierarchical status. Illustrations are the typically close connections among racial background, education, occupation, income, and power. The inverse of such consolidation of various dimensions of social positions is the intersection of various dimensions manifest in their weak relations, as exemplified by low correlations of religion, sex, and age. Such weak relations between social differences in various respects represent Simmel's concept of crosscutting social circles. Intersecting group boundaries and hierarchical differences diminish the significance of social distinctions and lessen the strength of ingroup affiliations. In this situation the difference between insiders and outsiders is no longer unequivocal because people's outgroup in one dimension contains many persons who are members of their ingroups in other dimensions. Complete intersection of all social differences is an impossible extreme, just as complete consolidation is, but the degree of intersection or consolidation of the same set of factors varies among societies and among communities of the same society. These variations have important implications for the structure of social relations and the social integration in large collectivities.

Social integration is often interpreted as resting on strong ingroup bonds, and the weakening of such bonds in modern times has frequently been deplored. This is a microsociological conception of social integration, however, appropriate for small groups and small tribes but not for the conditions in large and complex societies or communities. From the perspective of large populations, which are necessarily divided into many subunits along various lines, strong ingroup bonds, far from integrating the subunits, fragment society into antagonistic segments, as illustrated by the often violent conflicts between ethnic or religious groups in many countries. The social integration of a large population depends on prevalent intergroup relations—on extensive cordial and even intimate associations between members of different groups and persons occupying different positions—that cement the connections among diverse segments and unite them in a relatively integrated social structure and distinctive community. The theory centers attention on intergroup relations because these relations are considered essential for macrosocial integration.

MACROSTRUCTURAL THEORY

People's cultural values and psychological preferences affect their choices in social relations, particularly profound and lasting ones such as marriage. These values are not the only factors that affect social bonds, however. The social environment also limits our options; that is, the population composition of the place where we live. (I shall ignore migration in this short presentation, except to say that it merely alters but does not eliminate the constraints the population structure exerts on choices of associates.) The issue of free will is completely irrelevant for these external social influences. Whether our choices are fully determined by our constitution, background, and experiences or whether we are entirely free to marry anyone who is willing to marry us, we cannot marry Eskimos if there are none around. These limits on options are much more severe when large numbers, not merely single individuals, are under consideration. For example, it is impossible for most white Americans to have close friends who are blacks, as this would require that the average black American have about ten close friends who are whites.

A domain assumption, in Gouldner's (1970:31–35) phrase, implicit in the theory is that the structural constraints and opportunities created by the population composition in a place exert a dominant influence on social relations which counteracts the influences of social values, psychological dispositions, and ingroup preferences. These influences are the external constraints of social facts Durkheim emphasized, notably in his earlier works. The major theorems reflect this structural assumption, and empirical evidence corroborating them provides indirect evidence for the assumption. To illustrate the theory, three major theorems will be deduced from two higher-order premises, which are assumptions postulated as valid but for which there is also substantial empirical evidence from previous research.

The first assumption is that people tend to associate disproportionately with others proximate to them in social space—that is, with others who belong to the same group or whose social status is close to their own—whatever the dimension under consideration. There is much empirical support for this proposition that associations between persons in similar social positions exceed chance expectations. Thus disproportionate numbers of marriages involve spouses of the same race, religion, and national origin (Kennedy 1944; Hollingshead 1950; Carter and Glick 1970; Abramson 1973; Heer 1974; Alba 1976). Similarities in education, occupation, and social class have also been observed to enhance the likelihood of marriage (Centers 1949; Hollingshead 1950; Blau and Duncan 1967; Carter and Glick 1970; Tyree and Treas 1974). Friendships, too, have been found to be promoted by shared social positions. The second assumption postulates that the extent of social associations depends on opportunities for contact. Aside from the fact that this is virtually self-evident, it implies that physical propinquity, which engenders contact opportunities, is expected to increase the likelihood of marriages and friendships, and empirical studies found this to be the case (Abrams 1943; Festinger et al. 1950; Caplow and Forman 1950).

One major theorem stipulates that heterogeneity promotes intergroup relations. This seems paradoxical inasmuch as it appears to contradict the first assumption that people tend to associate with others of their own group. The theorem, nevertheless, is deducible from the two assumptions jointly with the definition of heterogeneity. Given that the defining criterion of heterogeneity is the chance expectation that two randomly chosen persons belong to different groups, and given the assumptions that people tend to select ingroup associates and that associations depend on contact opportunities, it follows that heterogeneity increases the chances that fortuitous encounters will involve members of different groups, which reduces opportunities for ingroup associations and increases probabilities of intergroup associations.

Another main theorem is that inequality fosters status-distant social relations. The originally published formulation of this theorem was incorrect (Blau 1977:55). My reasoning then was that if status distance inhibits social associations, by assumption, and if inequality refers to average status distance, it follows that inequality discourages status-distant associations. This argument, however, completely ignores the external constraints of the population composition, which acts as a counteracting influence in the case of inequality, just as it does in the case of heterogeneity. Since inequality, as defined, increases the likelihood that chance encounters will involve two persons relatively distant in status, it constrains individuals to modify their preferences for status-proximate associates and makes status-distant associations more likely.

The final theorem to be presented is that many intersecting social differences promote intergroup relations. This central proposition of my theory incorporates Simmel's concept of crosscutting circles. If people tend to associate with others in proximate positions in various dimensions, as is assumed, and if the various dimensions intersect, people's very tendencies to associate with others in their ingroup on any one dimension often involves many of them in intergroup associations with respect to other dimensions. The multiform heterogeneity generated by many crosscutting social circles creates compelling constraints to associate with persons outside one's own groups, because most of one's ingroup associates in any one dimension are outsiders belonging to different groups in several other dimensions. The greater our ingroup bias in some respects, the more we restrict our choices in others, increasing the constraints to maintain intergroup relations in these other respects. A corollary of this theorem is that consolidated social differences, which reinforce one another and strengthen the barriers between different social positions, discourage intergroup relations.

After the deductive theory was formulated, a research project was designed to test the three theorems outlined, as well as some others (Blau and Schwartz 1984). The research was based on data from the 1970 U.S. census on the 125 largest metropolitan areas in the United States, ranging in population from one-quarter million to eleven million. The objective was to ascertain whether the theorems correctly predict the influence of the structural parameters specified on rates of intermarriage. Data on intermarriage provide a severe test of the theory and its structural assumptions. The domain assumption is that structural conditions limit options and influence intergroup relations even in the face of opposite influences exerted by cultural values and psychological predispositions (which are reflected in the ingroup assumption). The observation of such opposite structural influences is most plausible for casual acquaintances in small places, inasmuch as one would expect opportunities for chance encounters to influence superficial associations in a neighborhood. Marriage, in contrast, is an enduring relation into which people do not enter lightly merely as the result of casual meetings but which is undoubtedly much affected by cultural values and personal attitudes, ranging from religious beliefs and racial bias to tastes in music and movies. Besides, in a metropolis with many thousands of people, it should be relatively easy to escape the constraints imposed by the population composition and find a spouse of one's own choosing. If marriage in large metropolitan areas is subject to the structural influences implied by the theorems, casual social relations in smaller places are still more likely to be so.

The theorem discussed first was tested with six forms of heterogeneity (using nine different measures), ranging from racial to occupational heterogeneity and intermarriage. The second was tested with inequality in education, occupational status, and earnings (using four measures). The theorem last described was tested with eight forms of the intersection of one kind of social difference with several others (using ten measures). The empirical findings corroborate the theorems; all conform to the predictions when proper controls are introduced, and most also do so without any controls (that is, employing simple correlations). In sum, macrostructural constraints apparently exert substantial influences on social relations and the integration of diverse segments in a large community.

CLOSING THE CIRCLE

This macrostructural theory seems to be far removed from microsociological exchange theory. Indeed, the two are fundamentally different because they look at social relations from opposite perspectives. One might say, speaking metaphorically, that exchange theory examines social relations from within whereas macrostructural theory examines them from without. The former dissects the exchange processes assumed to underlie all social relations and that govern their features and dynamics, whatever the broader social system in which they are embedded. It is a micro but a general theory, like microeconomics. Macrostructural theory analyzes the structural framework consisting of the population composition that limits the social relations that can develop, regardless of cultural norms and individual desires, and thereby shapes the patterns or structures of social relations in communities and other large collectivities. The contrasting perspectives yield quite different but not contradictory explanations. An analogy would be that the clotting of blood can be explained chemically by its contact with oxygen or biologically by its preventing loss of life from small wounds. There is no conflict between these explanations; they simply examine a phenomenon from different standpoints.

Exchange theory and macrostructural theory are complementary, not contradictory. Merton (1975) stresses the significance of pluralistic theories in a discipline for the advancement of knowledge. Different subject matters often require explanations by different theories, at least in the early stages of the development of a discipline, notwithstanding the ultimate goal of integrating the various theories, in accordance with the principle of Occam's razor. What I mean by saying that the two theories are complementary is that what the one takes as given and postulates as an assumption without trying to explain it the other treats as problematical and seeks to explain. The macrosociological focus is appropriate for the study of entire societies or other large collectivities because it is impossible to trace and dissect the interpersonal relations of many thousands or millions of people. In this case, the minutiae of daily social life must be neglected and the major regularities and patterns must be abstracted from them, which the macrostructural approach does by ignoring the social interaction between individuals and analyzing the rates of social interaction between social positions—that is, persons classified on the basis of various social dimensions.

We are also interested, however, in the social processes implicit in all human relations and essential for understanding them. The macrosociological approach, painting a large canvas in bold strokes, cannot explain these processes because it does not investigate interpersonal relations in depth. For example, the existence of ingroup tendencies is assumed by the macrostructural theory, but the processes producing them are not explained. Exchange theory seeks to explain these tendencies by noting how similarities in background, experience, and social position make it likely that people exchange mutual support for their opinions and conduct, furnishing incentives for social interaction. Moreover, ingroup preferences, like people's values generally, have two manifestations: they induce persons to associate with members of their own group themselves, and they motivate them to approve of others who choose ingroup associates and to disapprove of those who choose outsiders. These exchange processes sustain and reinforce the ingroup pressures assumed to exist by macrostructural theory. According to this theory, however, structural conditions may constrain persons to engage increasingly in intergroup relations, as we have seen. Such greater prevalence of intergroup relations implies that ingroup pressures are weakened, because when many persons are involved in intergroup relations these are no longer widely disapproved. Here again exchange theory can explain the diminished ingroup pressures by the lesser approval people earn for confining their relations to the ingroup.

Exchange theory is not concerned with the structure of social relations that develop in the larger social environment and with the significance of that structure for the nature of social exchange. Macrostructural theory directly addresses the first issue and has some implications for the second. An increase in intergroup relations, as the result of new and different structural conditions, alters the nature of the prevalent exchange transactions, because social exchange in intergroup relations tends to differ from that in ingroup relations. (Although most social relations are simultaneously ingroup and intergroup on different dimensions, social exchange usually centers either on the shared or on the different attributes of the dyad.) Exchange theory dissects the processes in different social relations but takes these differences as given, whereas macrostructural theory seeks to explain why some social relations are more prevalent than others.

Social exchange between members of the same ingroup, who tend to share views and opinions, often involves mutual support and approval. Exchange in intergroup relations, however, usually involves different benefits or services, owing to differences in experience and resources. Person A may advise person B about gardening, and person B discharges his or her obligation by helping person A to repair the family car. Social differences also create the possibility that person A can advise and help person B but that person B has nothing to return except respect, gratitude, and deference. In this way status differences are generated in intergroup relations. These informal differences in prestige and influence between associates, however, are quite different from formal authority or power, as in the case of managers over workers. The personal element in informal status differences resulting from unilateral exchange makes it less inescapable and oppressive than the formal authority of the boss or the coercive power of the police officer.

Exchange theory and macrostructural theory are two sociological viewpoints to which I have made some contributions, and in this essay I have attempted to establish a link between these two apparently unconnected theoretical orientations, thereby closing a circle by filling a gap. I do not claim to have integrated the two theories; in fact, I do not believe that this is possible as yet. Let me conclude with a plea for taking rigorous theorizing more seriously. Homans has made a start in this direction with exchange theory; network models have done so with microstructural theory; and I have tried to do so with macrostructural theory.

REFERENCES

Abrams, R. H. 1943. Residential Propinquity as a Factor in Marriage Selection. *American Sociological Review* 8:288–294.

Abramson, Harold J. 1973. *Ethnic Diversity in Catholic America*. New York: John Wiley.

Alba, Richard D. 1976. Social Assimilation among American Catholic Groups. *American Sociological Review* 41:1030–1046.

Blau, Peter M. 1977. *Inequality and Heterogeneity*. New York: Free Press.

Blau, Peter M., and Otis Dudley Duncan. 1967. *The American Occupational Structure*. New York: John Wiley.

Blau, Peter M., and Joseph E. Schwartz. 1984. *Crosscutting Social Circles*. Orlando, Fla.: Academic Press.

Braithwaite, R. B. 1953. *Scientific Explanation*. Cambridge: Cambridge University Press.

Caplow, Theodore, and Robert Forman. 1950. Neighborhood Interaction in a Homogeneous Community. *American Sociological Review* 15:357–366.

Carter, Hugh, and Paul C. Glick. 1970. *Marriage and Divorce*. Cambridge, Mass.: Harvard University Press.

Centers, Richard. 1949. Marital Selection and Occupational Strata. *American Journal of Sociology* 54:508–519.

Durkheim, Emile. 1938. *The Rules of Sociological Method* (1895). Chicago: University of Chicago Press.

Festinger, Leon, Stanley Schachter, and Kurt Back. 1950. *Social Pressures in Informal Groups*. New York: Harper.

Gibbs, Jack P., and Walter T. Martin. 1962. Urbanization, Technology, and the Division of Labor." *American Sociological Review* 26:667–677.

Gouldner, Alvin W. 1970. *The Coming Crisis of Western Sociology*. New York: Basic Books.

Heer, David M. 1974. The Prevalence of Black-White Marriage in the United States. *Journal of Marriage and the Family* 36:246–258.

Hollingshead, August B. 1950. Cultural Factors in the Selection of Marriage Mates. *American Sociological Review* 15:619–627.

Kennedy, Ruby J. 1944. Single or Triple Melting Pot? *American Journal of Sociology* 39:331–339.

Merton, Robert K. 1975. Structural Analysis in Sociology, pp. 21–52 in Peter M. Blau, ed., *Approaches to the Study of Social Structure*. New York: Free Press.

Parsons, Talcott. 1966. *Societies*. Englewood Cliffs, N.J.: Prentice-Hall.

Popper, Karl R. 1959. *The Logic of Scientific Discovery* (1934). New York: Basic Books.

Simmel, Georg. 1908. *Soziologie*. Leipzig: Duncker & Humblot.

Tyree, Andrea, and J. Treas. 1974. The Occupational and Marital Mobility of Women. *American Sociological Review* 39:293–302.

Whyte, William F. 1943. *Street Corner Society*. Chicago: University of Chicago Press.

CHAPTER THREE

To Unpack Micro and Macro: Link Small with Large and Part with Whole

Dean R. Gerstein

INTRODUCTION

The language of micro and macro has become quite prominent in sociological theory in recent years. One need only cite, for example, the collections edited by Knorr-Cetina and Cicourel (1981), Hechter (1983), and Eisenstadt and Helle (1985); the inaugural prize in sociological theory awarded by the theory section of the American Sociological Association to Collins (1981); and, of course, the theme selected for this volume. The problem of linkage between micro and macro has also been a matter of comparatively long standing but recently increasing prominence in economics (Schelling 1978; Nelson 1984).

The concepts of micro and macro, however, have not been systematically analyzed in sociology. They are taken to refer to two levels of analysis: individual mental processes, personal preferences, or primary interaction versus very large-scale social organization such as transnational corporate capitalism, modern occupational prestige hierarchies, the formation of nation-states (as in revolution), or technological rationality. The issue of linkage is how to create theoretical concepts that translate or map variables at the individual level into variables characterizing social systems, and vice versa.

This essay's objective is to "unpack" this micro-macro rubric and locate it within some broader and richer concepts of theory and action. A basic assumption here is that finding viable linkages between micro and macro levels is not merely an abstract issue in theory but a core problem of practical action. That is, live individual actors and durable collectivities (as well as more diffusely located cultural constructs), in order to act successfully and maintain themselves integrally, must find and enact solutions to the problem of linking micro and macro levels. The primary challenge of theory is to develop comprehensible and ultimately comprehensive models of such solutions as they vary among types and between failure and success. Although the span of this essay is inadequate to treat the issue comprehensively, it is possible to clarify the nature of such models and sketch some telling examples. The argument is as follows.

There are certain methodological principles within which reference to micro-macro linkage or any similar theoretical subjects should be treated. These principles concern the duality of social life as qualitative and quantitative, the nature of general analytical concepts, and the best ways to handle questions of causality and reification. Within this framework it is useful first to assess the main external stimulant for macro, micro, and associated linkage concepts in sociology—namely, economics. Although from a sociological perspective there are inherent limitations to the concepts used by economists, their central qualitative distinction, between analyses geared to general equilibrium as opposed to component rationality, is a valuable one.

A sociological approach to micro- and macroconcepts is based first on the original sense of these terms as quantitative antonyms for certain physical dimensions. This leads to the sociological contexts in which physical space and time are measured at the micro and macro level and, more particularly, how these fundamental scales are socially mediated through diversified concepts and methods of aggregation and disaggregation.

The fundamental social quality of membership and the mediating processes of identification and differentiation typify the second fundamental context for micro- and macroconcepts in sociology. Qualitative and quantitative linkages between micro and macro levels—mostly a matter of smaller parts fitting with larger wholes—operate in diverse forms of social action. Prominent examples are the social actions surrounding the production, diffusion, and uses of culturally encoded products such as motion pictures and computers, and the organization of relations between states and citizens, for example, in the control of instruments of coercion.

An expanded view of micro and macro enables one to return to economic action with a more satisfactory theoretical armory. The movements from elementary agriculture to small-scale factory production to large-scale, high-technology corporatism involve a complex set of linkage problems that call on the fuller array of micro-macro concepts and practices. Overall, sociological theorists should welcome the recognition of and inquiry into small/large and part/whole aspects of social action at all levels.

FOUR PRINCIPLES

Four methodological principles need to be made explicit prior to treating the substantive problem.

1. It is essential to recognize that social action is inherently and inseparably dual in nature. It is both quantitative and qualitative. It has scale as well as significance, and these do not necessarily work in the same way. In Weber's famous duofold, an account of social action must strive for interpretive adequacy at the level of statistics and the level of meaning. The need to take adequate account of this dual nature operates for the engaged actor as much as for the scientific observer; it is a practical as well as a scientific principle. The micro/macro distinction cuts across this quantitative and qualitative duality; it is not parallel but perpendicular to it.
2. A fundamental distinction such as that between micro and macro must be general and analytical, not tied to a fixed case. By this standard, the individual person, household, or firm cannot be treated as intrinsically micro or the society, nation, or economy as unalterably macro. Rather, designations of micro and macro are relative to each other and, in particular, to the analytic purpose at hand. The overall status or role of a given family member (ego) may be macro relative to ego's relation with a certain kin group member but micro relative to the status or role of ego's lineage in a marriage exchange system; the marriage system in turn may be micro relative to a mythic cycle. The job satisfaction of a worker may be macro relative to the psychological stress on his or her children but micro relative to the quality of his or her job. That in turn may be micro relative to the morale or efficiency of the factory or branch office, which is micro relative to the financial condition of the corporation, which is micro relative to the competitiveness of the industry or the business cycle of the national and international economy—which are, however, micro relative to the ideological spirit of the age. None of these is a rigid empirical relation but rather a state-

ment about analytical and practical strategies. An equally legitimate focus could take psychological stress on children as the macrophenomenon, asking how other partial causes, such as parental work life, make their continuations. This brings us to the third point.

3. The causal nature of micro-macro linkages should not be assumed to be known in advance or always and everywhere to be the same. Causal propositions about the direction of linkage are necessary to sharpen research investigations, but they are to be considered hypothetical and incomplete until proven otherwise. Certainly one may theorize that causes are inherently micro and that macro levels are simply nominal, epiphenomenal, or categorical glosses. Or the reverse view may be taken: that the macro is all-determining and the micro simply represents locally visible manifestations of global underlying causes. These are microreductionist and macroreductionist approaches. There is also a radically relativist alternative: that macro and micro have little bearing on each other, that the rhythms of daily life go on in war the same as in peace, that empires do not mark the comings and goings of mere generations.

   The most preferable course, in my view, is to assume that micro and macro have interactive potential, with the degree of linkage and the exact balance of causal priority shifting from time to time and under different conditions. This is a mediationist position; it gives license to diverging theoretical speculation but at the price of heavy empirical requirements.

4. Finally, we should acknowledge that the habitual and successful use of a particular subject or focus of analysis can lead quite naturally to the reification of the particular micro-macro distinction. Such reifications can become schools of thought, academic disciplines, or even national characteristics. One can further expect important micro-macro linkages to become matters of causal competition, with those who focus on a particular relation seeking to begin all lines of causation in their favored domain. A familiar example is the conflict between psychologistic and sociologistic reductionisms, or between "conflict" and "consensus" sociologies.

   Reification is not inherently evil. Competition between reified schemes is probably good for the production of knowledge, so long as it takes place under appropriate arrangements—namely, relatively egalitarian access to resources, recognition of common ethical and cognitive standards, and understanding that one scheme's winning a particular point does not disqualify the others' proponents from further competition.

In summary, (1) explicit attention to qualitative/quantitative duality is a necessary basis for analysis, and this distinction crosscuts the micro-macro dimension; (2) micro and macro are general, mutually correlative terms, which may be usefully instantiated in many different ways; (3) causality can operate any number of ways in micro-macro linkages and therefore diverse theoretical speculations are permissible but require empirical contests for confirmation; and (4) reifying a particular micro-macro linkage is reasonable so long as it opens rather than closes competitive opportunities.

THE ECONOMIC INTERPRETATION

Economic decision making is a major type of social action. Perhaps as important for present purposes, economics is a major social science, and the classical works of nineteenth- and early twentieth-century social theory were in large respect designed to respond to the challenges and perceived inadequacies of regnant utilitarian economics, principally by embedding economic action in a more expansive social context, a job that is clearly unfinished (Granovetter 1985). Given the importance of the economy in the social system and the stimulus of economic concepts for sociological theorizing, a good place to start an assessment of micro and macro in sociology is to review how microeconomics and macroeconomics are differentiated and how their linkage is currently being redefined.

Micro and macro seem to have been adopted first as standard terms in economics in the 1950s, largely in acknowledgment of innovative developments that began with the creation of national economic accounts in the 1930s along with theoretical work on the causes of the Great Depression. Macroeconomics came to be understood as the study of national aggregates (product, income, employment, savings, investment, interest rate, government spending, inflation) expressed in monetary or undimensioned index terms and the functional relations between these totals. An analysis is macroeconomic when it refers to the total movement of a whole economy, classically a national economy (although there is allowance for trade balances and intense interest in world economic models). In macroanalysis the object is to explain the scope and movement of general equilibria as a function of the major aggregate components of a system—that is, to identify and account for the overall balance reached between opposing forces, such as preferences for investment, consumption, and liquidity; supply and demand; use-values and exchange-values; and capital and labor.

A fundamental assumption of such analyses is interdependence between the actions of the components. There may be outside or "exogenous" inputs to the system, particularly the lagged effects of behavior in earlier periods, or inputs from parallel macroeconomies, but the principal action takes place between system components. Keynesian, monetarist, and "supply side" models of the national economy are textbook macroeconomics, as are project LINK-type world macroeconomic models, which forecast component national economic equilibria with special attention to international investment, currency flows, and trade (Klein 1986).

Every other kind of analysis is microeconomic, even though much of the same type of data, such as sectoral input-output tables, and many of the same conceptual tools, such as calculation of market-clearing prices to track behavior in particular markets, are also used to refine estimates of national aggregates. Microeconomic analysis is concerned with the decision-making behavior of economic units—consumers, producers, investors, managers, workers—facing contingent environments; in short, with the problem of rationality or, as usually assumed, of utility maximization. In microanalysis the object is to explain how the purposes and resources of individual units interact with the contingencies imposed by the immediately pertinent environment to produce particular actions or probabilities of action. In pure microeconomic analysis, one takes a single (usually a "typical") microunit making choices within a given set of contingencies. These choices and actions can be approached prescriptively, defining the "normative" economics of utility maximization theory or, descriptively, the "positive" economics of observed behavior, which generally diverges somewhat (or more than somewhat) from normative utilitarian standards.

In short, macroanalyses and microanalyses in economics distinguish between focusing on wholes as opposed to focusing on parts. The mode of analysis, not the absolute size of the aggregate, discriminates between macro and micro in this context; the national economies of many smaller nations are dwarfed not only by particular markets in larger national economies but by individual firms and even some individual investors. The perspective of the whole, the system, is balance, the achievement of general internal equilibrium between the actions of its parts; the concern of the part is to rationalize action in the context of an environment external to it.

The topics of greatest interest and controversy in economic theory currently bear on the mediation through organizational, contractual, and informational mechanisms of relations between the general equilibrium of the system and the decisions and resources of individuals within the system. Three major new linkages have developed between microeconomic and macroeconomic theory in recent years. The first, the school of rational expectations, predicates economic behavior on optimal statistical predictions about the future course of the economy rather than adaptation to imperfectly observed recent market forces (modified by irrational surges and failures of "confidence"). A second major line of work is the study of market efficiency as affected by the interaction between government policy and responses to (including anticipation of) policy-based sanctions and incentives in major durables and capital markets. A third area is experimental economics, the study of microeconomic postulates of rationality in individuals, using experimental incentives, assorted distributions of information, and measurements of performance to simulate practical market situations and behavior. A sociologically interesting example of positive microanalysis of decision behavior is the experimental study of "heuristics" (Kahneman et al. 1982), in which individuals are offered a series of risky choices, trades, and other calibrated transactions and the nature of systematic departures from normative principles of rationality is observed.

In general, the distinction between equilibrating macroeconomic wholes and more or less rationally economizing parts has proven very useful. The problem from a sociological perspective is that the aggregation of social action into monetary quantities is an incomplete part of what interests sociologists. Moreover, the utilitarian rationalist perspective works well only within contexts that do not arise universally or spontaneously but that require processes of institutional derivation and maintenance which are themselves not well explained by macroeconomics or microeconomics. Although theoretical arguments have been advanced and some empirical inquiries initiated about implicit financial calculations in human capital decisions (Becker 1981), many observable individual and collective decisions involve nonmonetary and probably nonmonetizable elements that compete, often successfully and in some areas without evident contest, for causal dominance. Institutional economists and economic historians have not missed these deficiencies, and work by Williamson (1975), Nelson and Winter (1982), and Olson (1965, 1982), for example, has attracted substantial attention among sociologists.

Regardless of the degree of subordination and recasting that seems necessary to make the monetary and rationalist foundations of micro- and macroeconomics more useful to sociology, there is a valuable lesson in the insight that a macroanalysis can look profitably at general equilibrium matters (balance or loss of balance from the point of view of an inward-looking totality). Microanalyses are concerned with more discrete actions from the perspective of a unit looking outward to maximize gains and minimize losses in a contingent environment.

The moment has come to step back from the economic frame of reference and to consider how we would have encountered the terms "micro" and "macro" if economics had not first appropriated them. In doing so we are led into sociology from a completely different direction.

MEASURING SOCIAL SPACE AND TIME

"Macro" and "micro" come to us etymologically by way of Latin from the Greek morphemes μακρός and μικρός. Unlike Greek qualitative morphemes, which generally derive from idealization of the characteristic qualities embodied by particular mythic personae or objects in traditional narratives, macro and micro are workaday terms of physical magnitude referring to extension in time and space. They are standards for quantitative measurement, the application of number to physical dimension.

Undimensioned numbers are, of course, the most abstract units of quantity. The extreme distinction is between infinity and zero or, somewhat more concretely, the scale from all to none. In less extreme or polarized terms one speaks of more (a larger number) and less (a smaller number). However, the Greek terms are material, not abstractly numerical. The best equivalent usages in plain English are the antonyms "long" and "short" and, secondarily, "large" and "small" (Liddell and Scott 1940); in German, *lang* and *kurz*, *gross* and *klein*. In this quantitative aspect, macro and micro clearly point to certain types of fundamental scalar relations that are pertinent in any analysis involving physical objects or events with extension in time or space.

The quantitative problem is to link small units (for example, of time or space) with large ones, and vice versa. Whenever a smaller social unit has to take account of or use information about a social unit of substantially larger extension or duration (or the reverse, from large to small), this problem appears. It is a problem virtually universal in historic human societies, as the spread of attentional requirements across time and space radically distinguishes enculturated human behavior from that of all other socializing animals.

The use of measurement devices to relate micro and macro begins with the spatial and temporal dimensions of objects. In the temporal domain we readily distinguish between long and short durations. The most extreme contrast is between the instant—the single moment in time—and eternity. In more continuous measure, one speaks of short versus long terms, periods, or waves. A microtemporal analysis distinguishes an ordering of events across small intervals of clock time: the layering of turns in a conversation, the order of finish in a timed competition, the sequence of discovery in a chain of questions, or the ordering of choice points in a decision tree. At medium range in calendar time are weeks, months, and seasonal differences. A macroanalysis bites off larger chunks: historical time—the cycles of election years, economic booms and busts, wartime and peacetime, before and after a revolution, demographic transitions, and, more grandly, the modern, medieval, and ancient ages.

These are useful kinds of distinctions in social research as well as in practical life (Zerubavel 1981, 1985; Schwartz 1975). In survey design, for example, there is the contrast between a cross-sectional survey designed to capture the state of things in a given brief period and a longitudinal panel designed to reveal how things get from one state to another over a course of years. In historical and calendrical terms we distinguish between the historic event punctuated by a single date (e.g., 1688, 1789, 1870) and the era (for example, A.D. 1600–1900). At the individual or small group level there is the problem of brief encounters, as between strangers, as opposed to the cycle of family roles across the life span.

Adopting a conventional zero point, one may also count time in terms of distance from the present: what is now versus the distant past or future. This in turn opens many issues of signification based on horizons of time: short-run calculation versus the long term, the valuation of expediency as against integrity, novelty as against tradition. Temporal measures are prominent in the social and cultural prestige ordering of persons, institutions, and ideas (by age, tenure, precedence), the importance of "timing" and being "on schedule," and the importance of doing things in a particular temporal order.

The statistical measurement of time in the medium term, calendrical time, is one of the oldest achievements (perhaps the hallmark) of so-called high civilization: temporal calculation based on observing the motional regularities of the sidereal, solar, and lunar "clockworks." The advent of modernity coincides, by no accident (Landes 1983), with the invention of more intricate time measurement by mechanical calculators (that is, clocks and watches), leading most recently to statistical dating techniques based on the physical and chemical measurement of isotopic decay or atomic oscillation. In cosmological astrophysics, the most esoteric (and therefore "highest") culture of our times, subtle mathematical GUTs (Grand Unified Theories) and enormously expensive orbital observatories and terrestrial accelerators are used to help estimate the structure and dynamics of the universe in the first 10^{-38} seconds after the "big bang" occurred ten to twenty billion years ago (Astronomy Survey Committee 1982).

On a more pedestrian and practical level, statistical linkage of time writ large and small gives practical force to Mills's (1959) location of sociology in the intersection of history and biography. A major example is the social significance of time-essential concepts such as the discount rate (the "time rate of money," mathematically equivalent to the decay rate of a radioisotope) in its particular applications to loans at interest, price inflation, and the like. Of similar importance are formal "labor time" constructs such as "man-hours," "work weeks," "part-time," and "full-time" jobs (or job-equivalents). These time-based measures are indispensable (though obviously not sufficient) for the operation and organization of modern financial and economic life.

In summary, durational measures have developed socially; they have become more precise and extensive in the course of modernization; and they have always been enfolded into vital criteria of precedence, sequence, schedule, and intertemporal calculation.

In the spatial domain the polar opposites are a single geometric point, a mere "locus" with no physical extension, in contrast to unbounded space spreading beyond limit (in short, the universe). In continuous terms the macro simply covers much more space than the micro. It is large scale rather than small scale, global rather than local. This immediately suggests a host of issues that arise in social measurement. In the familiar terms of statistical survey design, we ask what boundaries or spatial units a claim, a jurisdiction, or an investigation is meant to tap: the world, a particular international region, a nation, a metropolitan or urban area, a neighborhood or tract, and so forth down to a single dwelling unit and on to "personal space" and the parameters of the body. These are boundaries and concerns that researchers inherit from (as well as inject into) social and political processes, rather than issues of unfettered geography and biology. Indeed, the division of territory by governing lines rather than natural drainage patterns or other ecological boundaries is a common lament of environmental interests.

Geological, climatic, and biotic malleability guarantee the continuous alteration of the contours of the earth, but territoriality and its measure are inherently guided by religious and political economy, as surveyed through the lenses of sanctity, sovereignty, and property. The resultant images are very complex. For example, the sovereignty of political borders is modified by balances of power, zones of vital interest, spheres of influence, trade privileges, diplomatic immunity, extraterritoriality, treaty concessions, and so forth. As for property ideas, spatial notions have been powerfully driven by the legal evolution of real property concepts from use-based possession hallowed by longevity to absolute or eminent domain secured by royal writ or force of arms, to the modern bundle of limited and separable contractual obligations, privileges, uses, and agreements. Consider the separation of water, mineral, and air-space rights; easements, dedications, declarations, and covenants; liens, mortgages, deeds, leases, tenancies, and reversions. The maze of currently recognized (or contended) rights of personal privacy, security, and confidentiality allocate ownership in the informational as well as material domains. These rights descend from protection against arbitrary searches or seizures of goods or persons, from the extension of royal privy, from Hippocrates' ethics, the confessional, and the rule of sanctuary. The linkages between macro and micro—global and personal—levels of territorial security are nowhere more heavily stressed than in considerations bearing on the deployment and potential uses of nuclear weaponry.

Of course, it is common to have spatial-temporal modes of action (and, perforce, of research) that are relatively macro on one dimension and relatively micro on another. Contrast family genealogy, for example, or a multigenerational shift in land tenure patterns in a single village, with a stratified sample survey to reveal national labor force participation and the national unemployment rate during a single week in a year. The dimensions of social space and social time are independent but inevitably conjoined in some way in all social action. As fundamental components of social action, they find their way into the most systematic attempts to build a priori categories for social action. For example, patterning in time is the very kernel of the concept of contingency, whereas spatial patterning is the kernel of complexity (Baum 1976; Luhmann 1976, 1982; Münch 1982).

LINKING QUANTITIES: AGGREGATION AND DISAGGREGATION

As the foregoing discussion suggests, the movement from small to large is a common aspect of social action, so much so that a general form for such linkage processes can be defined. The most useful conventional name for this linkage process across quantitative scales is *aggregation*: the formation of sums, products, vectors, or parametric statistics. The converse is *disaggregation*, the reduction of such sums, products, vectors, or statistics into more variable and specific compartments.

Aggregation and disaggregation involve shifts in the locus of numerical certainty from the small to the large. For example, a statistic such as the average household size in the United States may leave us uncertain about the size of a particular household; knowing the particulars of one household does not tell us much about the whole country. Both aggregation and disaggregation thus involve the problem of inference and have given great impetus to developing the modern mathematical statistics of sampling and estimation.

Aggregation takes a variety of social forms. For example, in the market for consumption products aggregation means the accumulation of consumer utilities or preferences, as expressed by monetary bids, into aggregate demand for all consumer goods and services. In political organizations aggregation is the summation of loyalties, affinities, or political support through determinative processes such as voting or commitment of arms into the operative control of offices. In social control aggregation is the collection of moral and ethical attitudes into "public opinion."

Disaggregation proceeds in the opposite manner down the same paths. In the market buyers and sellers face discrete decisions between allocation of resources to broadly and finely discriminated options; disaggregation is a process of budgeting. In politics the scope of command is divided into particular territories and levels. In moral behavior there are broader and finer degrees of conformity and deviance. In each instance there is a complicated mediation process, which works through monetary prices and contracts linked to properties in the case of markets and through other media appropriate to politics, moral valuation, or other requisites.

Quantitative micro-macro linkage problems can be addressed by a range of social arithmetical and scaling devices (Duncan 1984). A preeminent case is the use of statistics in that original and still common sense suggested by its etymology (Martin 1981): state-istics. The original uses of statistics as essential tools of large-scale governance lay in ancient imperial (later, feudal and royal) levies of taxation and military conscription. The much later advent of representative democracy added new statistical uses and requirements. For example, statistics figure heavily in the development of systems of welfare entitlements, environmental and other regulatory regimes, and revenue distribution schemes. They also permit bureaucratic entities to identify priorities in fields ranging from epidemiology to fiscal policy (Prewitt 1986). Of course, the replication of governmental statistical methods in private household, financial, and corporate management—the more common direction of diffusion than the reverse flow—further extends the realm in which statistical devices are used to bridge micro and macro levels. Polling systems in service to electoral politics or marketing also broaden the uses of statistics.

At the same time, the ability of individuals to grasp macroelements and make private decisions that affect the macro through aggregative or other properties relies extensively on statistics. Overall unemployment and inflation rates, more than individual economic position, have proved to be key factors in voter behavior through their effects on the expressed views of voters, potential candidates, and parties. Organizations such as Amnesty International and (prior to its suppression) Helsinki Watch use counts of human rights violations. Arms negotiators and monitors deal in electronic intelligence, much of which is statistical. No in-depth news story is complete without its statistical sidebar, delineating a count or chronology of bodies, dollars, barrels of oil, or other relevant aggregates.

MEMBERS AND GROUPS

Although considerations of objective quantities in time and space are essential to all processes that extend into the physical world, what is most distinctive in human action, considered qualitatively, is conscious agency: the point of view of the actor as part of a situation. Action is sociological to the degree that it can be described in terms of the exchange of performances and sanctions between two or more actors who share some elements of a symbolic order. Here we move from the scaling of physical dimensions into the realm of groups and their members. These certainly have a major physical component. For example, we often count the members of a group as spatial entities, as though they were coterminous with or inhabitants of physical bodies. This yields the ecological idea of a human population, the number of member-bodies in a fixed spatial frame or territory, and the growth or decline of such populations through vital events, which is the core interest of modern demography.

Physical presence, however, is not a necessary aspect of membership. The essence of membership is identity recognizable by one's near and distant partners in interaction or sharers of information. A member may continue to be treated as belonging to a symbolic order after the relevant body is deceased, as in the "Estate of . . . ," or when the body is elsewhere (for example, the absentee owner or voter who is counted to be the resident of a given place for taxation or electoral purposes). There are also, of course, explicitly fictive members who have only a nonbiological or supernatural existence: the legal being of a corporation or the peculiar status of literary and mythic figures, not to mention religious and ancestral heroes, martyrs, and other recipients of ideological or filial veneration. Of course, collectivities as such can be members, as states in a federal union, families in a clan or club, union locals in a federation, divisions in a conglomerate, and departments in a university.

Temporal considerations are important, such as year of birth to establish relations of membership in the form of a cohort, or years since birth to establish group membership in terms of age. These are, of course, fundamental measures in demography. The dimensions of membership are more complex than assignment in space and time, however. We are most often concerned with memberships that are not primarily spatial or temporal in designation, but roles or statuses within explicitly bounded functional wholes; that is, social systems (members of a pair engaged in a conversation, incumbents of positions in kinship networks, offerers of labor in employment markets, holders of bureaucratic offices of religious confessions or doctrines—one could multiply examples endlessly). Both individuals and collectivities can be bounded or identified using attributes that are basically nonspatial and nontemporal: women voters, stockholders in AT&T, Spanish speakers. (Of course, spatial and temporal boundaries can be used to segment these categories: women who cast presidential ballots in New Hampshire in 1984, AT&T stockholders at the time of the breakup, etc.)

The dimension of groups and their members incorporates a central micro-macro distinction and associated linkage problems, but with an emphasis other than differences in scale. The emphasis is familiar, in fact: It is the perspective of micro- and macroeconomics, the part and the whole. In this case micro and macro are not matters of scale and measurement, or of equilibrium and rational maximization, but of consciousness, belonging, inclusion—and their opposites, amnesia, alienation, exclusion.

A principal aspect of linkage processes which connects social parts with social wholes and members with groups is identification. This is a transaction in which some degree of individuality and individuated interest and control is lost or forgone in the process of combination with other actors. Identification need not be total, of course. In the market for commodities, including commoditized services, identification with products is "brand loyalty." In organizations identification extends to parties, factions, or corporate entities, for which members make sacrifices of personal discretion. Organizations in turn can identify with other organizations. Moral identification is the use of "litmus tests," symbolic tokens, or other moral trials to map individual differences of opinion into distinct classes.

Identification may begin with distinctive biological characteristics that have transparently salient significance for individuals (e.g., visible markers of age, gender, or race). Their bases can also be rendered problematic and manipulated; Garfinkel (1967) documents a classic case. There are, in addition, biological identifiers of more subtle kinds that create membership in groups, such as the so-called high-risk groups identified by a variety of epidemiological investigations on heart disease, congenital disorders, unusual infectious illnesses, and so on.

Identification solves two kinds of behavioral problems. It standardizes expectations in certain domains for large numbers of individuals or social units that may be treated identically insofar as group membership determines treatment. Conversely, it economizes normative standards by supplying a relatively standard package of attitudes and behaviors that some may adopt toward others in terms of their group memberships.

Qualitative linkages that run in the reverse direction, from wholes to parts, are differentiation processes. Consumer markets are segmented according to specific demographic and style-of-life characteristics; organizational roles are functionally divided into spheres of responsibility; there are moral assignments into statuses, presumptive grades of worth and integrity.

CULTURE

These mechanisms of group identification and differentiation especially suggest the importance of cultural communications and information systems. A cultural system considered as a whole is like a membership library, containing stored, partially ordered symbolism that is in discontinuous circulation in a variety of contexts and purposes. In particular, formation of audiences, patronage networks, and participant groups for performances, publications, and ritual enactments is the classical locus of cultural linkage, rendering group boundaries and purposes concrete to members, socializing and enculturating them, embedding meanings into habit and thereby turning them into facts.

The ubiquity of television and arguments for its role in shaping the "global village" are well known. I would like to consider here two less thoroughly known instances in which personal and mass communication technologies subserve the linkage of micro and macro. First is the case of motion pictures. At the commercial level the typical modern movie production process is primarily a sequence of financial and technological deals in which a variety of groups are formed. A piece of intellectual property—a copyrighted script or literary document—becomes the subject of a series of contracts for use or appropriation of highly varied goods and services. Schedules of detailed assembly are invented: Scenarios are assigned to filming units; sets, ancillary properties, and graphic images are constructed; narrative scenes are staged by actors and technical specialists whose services have been contracted. Filmed records of the proceedings are made and edited; further graphical, musical, textual, and linked commercial materials are associated with the film; all are distributed and redistributed under complicated financing arrangements; and the revenues generated are divided in even more complicated schemes.

This complicated assembly of parts into wholes is itself only one part of what goes on. Screening of the picture is the communication of a story to an audience; it stirs certain kinds of emotional responses. Performance creates "catharsis," bringing feelings of identification and membership to consciousness, where they can be further worked and studied in critical writings. People seldom see movies alone; movies become the occasion for social groupings (dates, nights out). As they are discussed, written about, and remembered, as filmmakers, actors, and anthropomorphic inventions become expressive symbols in other cultural and personal enterprises, pictures help to construct the social reality of the times, just as earlier cultural productions such as passion plays, circuses, marches, musical performances, and funereal edifices have done since earlier times. Film connects strongly to regimes of style and expressive symbolism, which work through mass media and merchandisers: This is the realm of iconic communication through which "superstars" of design, fashion, and entertainment help to order the demand for and character of consumer products and styles of interaction.

In short, movies exemplify the power of culture to use technology to create qualitative, symbolic linkages among individuals, to unite groups into more inclusive enterprises, and to shape the consumer "tastes" that economists are generally content to treat as exogenously given.

A second example is the computer, originally a piece of intellectual fancy, which has been adopted from the esoteric cultural level of an obscure mathematical idea to the "mainframe" systems thinking of large-scale social organization and which is now moving on to the more dispersed level of the personal computer. The fundamental idea for a universal logic machine was invented by two mathematicians, Babbage in the 1840s and Turing in the 1930s. The mechanical means to implement these ideas were substantially worked out in secret British cryptological intelligence laboratories whose purpose was to analyze German military communications and thereby piece together the "big picture" of military strategy during World War II. These developments were brought to fruition in the United States after the war, largely under the guidance of another mathematician, von Neumann, and largely as a result of analysis, in wartime operations research, on how to determine algorithmically the most efficient distribution and use of resources in the logistics of worldwide mechanized warfare. Reflecting these origins, the largest users of computers for many years were the Department of Defense and the switching networks of the Bell Telephone System. Subsequently airline companies, educational institutions, and other large-scale enterprises acquired mainframe machines to help record and efficiently organize the scheduling and routing of complex flows of information, goods, services, and financial resources.

The first minicomputers, installed in small business offices and scientific laboratories in the early 1970s, were viewed still as centralized resources for controlling, recording, and analyzing information flows but ones for which physical miniaturization and lowered costs permitted such functions to be dispersed to remote sites. The thinking behind these machines, as expressed in their software environments, was still in terms of rapid batch data-processing capacity.

The 1980s brought radical change to the functions to which computers were applied, particularly a shift from centralized data control and analysis to creating and manipulating text and pictures. Computers began to work more and more in real-time interaction and communication as their primary design mode and to be a common part of daily work life for large segments of the adult work force. They also began entering the intellectual development of younger and younger children through the explosive growth of personal computers in schools and homes, computer graphics in television animation, video games, and so on (Turkle 1984).

In the fifty years since Turing imagined his universal programming machine, this instance of personal mathematical creativity grew first into a collective mechanism with broad systematic practical purposes and then into an expanding set of possibilities for developing individual creativity and expanding the network of interaction. Accompanying this development, the information culture of computing has grown apace, especially the software culture of operating system logics, programming languages, telecommunications, word processing, data bases, spread sheets, and graphic libraries. This still nascent culture, once the exclusive and formidable province of "hackers," is likely to continue growing into a major source of cultural linkages between macro and micro, making possible the formation and integration of groups on the basis of images and information. The effectiveness and durability of such electronically mediated linkages may be a critical question of the age.

POLITICS

A rather different problem in micro-macro linkages is the relation between state and citizen. The literature on this problem, stretching from Thucydides through Machiavelli to Weber and on to the present day, is enormous and remarkably able; my intention here is only to indicate the relevance of qualitative micro-macro concepts to some familiar points in political theory.

The smallest microunit of modern political action systems is authority to make a new decision in a manner that may become binding (at least through its consequences) on another. A political environment becomes most volatile when there are multiple decision makers of roughly equal power and when opportunities exist to form and re-form factions or coalitions. Sophisticated analyses of micro coalitional rationality include "prisoner's dilemma" games (Rapoport and Chammah 1965; Axelrod 1984) and the extensive theoretical developments built on the paradox of voting, demonstrated by Condorcet two centuries ago and in more modern form by Arrow (1963). Attempts to derive general (macro) political equilibria from micro-level relations of this kind must be unstable, indeterminate, or saved only by appeal to residual factors, for reasons elaborated in Parsons's (1937) famous analysis of the utilitarian dilemma. Two-person or small n-person communication game experiments, however, are worthwhile sources of insight into the effects of so-called noncontractual normative and institutional foundations of social order, or their absence. The main line of understanding these elements has been the study of the legitimation of rule through legal, charismatic, and traditional authority.

In contrast to approaching politics as a form of communication—that is, as a field of competitive or cooperative discourse—the control and deployment of instruments of coercion at every level, from fisticuffs to weapons of mass extermination, have been viewed as the essential core of the subject. A good example of macropolitical analysis along these lines is Skocpol's (1979) study of states and revolutions. Her fundamental interest is the equilibrium—or disequilibrium at critical points in time—of national states. The analysis hinges critically on relations between states, particularly in the form of military incursions in the historical cases she studies at length, or transfer of military technology in the more contemporary cases.

Even at highly aggregated levels it is also possible to analyze the sources of collective violence, whether internal or external in purpose (that is, rebellion, revolution, or war), in intentional or micro terms. Thus "just wars" are undertaken for defensive purposes: to punish aggressive states or to give deliverance to those oppressed by them; security concerns of nations and states may yield as equilibria the long-term occupation, subjugation, or incorporation of whole territories beyond the national borders of a state. "Holy wars" are undertaken for sacred purposes, to effect ideological or religious ideals of a more perfect world by violent purge or conversion of elements judged to be profane, evil, or unenlightened. Other wars are undertaken for economic advantage, such as expropriation of wealth (including natural resource wealth) or acquisition of more favorable terms of exchange; these are colonial and imperial wars. Actual cases can combine variable elements of each of these analytical types. Insurrection, rebellion, mass oppression, and intimidation may also set the justice of political order as a standard against which the gain and cost of violence is gauged, or may have religious, ideological, or expropriative motives. A further variant is international terrorism, seeking through violence an external forum of historical or international justice for domestic political losers.

At the individual level microanalyses look for the intentions behind instances of private violence. There is an exchangist or utilitarian rationale: One person goes to the trouble of imposing his or her will on another to acquire a personal economic gain (that is, to get goods or services in exchange for withdrawing the threat of pain). There is also the individual use of violence for the sake of personal justice, the visitation of punishment for prior or anticipated objectionable acts. The capabilities to impose coerced exchange or exact private justice do not require external instruments; sufficient means to bully, assault, or rape can be fashioned from surprise, outnumbering the target, or interpersonal differences in strength, size, experience, agility, and so forth. Coercion can be rational in either the exchange or juridical senses, but it can also spring from cruelty, meanness, or sadism, tastes for the spectacle of damage or suffering by the other; this irrational type shades into violence conducted by the deranged or "temporarily insane." Of course, these are analytic types, which may in varying combination characterize a concrete instance.

Individual violence can also be approached from a macro or systemic perspective, looking beyond the particular reasons for individual acts of violence. The social rate of violence—and more critically in the present context, the social meaning of violence—has the character of an equilibrium, a result of reaching a balance between social forces, as Durkheim long ago argued with respect to suicide and homicide (self-directed and other-directed violence). A comprehensive macroanalysis of private coercion would take into account the economy of weapons and the efficacy of policing, to be sure. The overriding factors, however, would involve socialization—the strength and character of identification with others as members of meaningful systems of interaction—which directs and gives form to strains toward violence.

RETHINKING ECONOMIC ACTION

In line with the foregoing reexamination of qualitative and quantitative attributes and linkages, it is possible to rethink the micro- and macrocategories of economic action. The basic metric of economic action is, of course, money. Money is a fundamental tool for weighing sums and for budgeting. Money is used to measure territory, persons considered as providers of labor and services, property rights and privileges, personal property in the form of commodities and contracts for consumer services, and durable capital goods and contracts. Money is also used in coordination with temporal measures to establish the "current value" of prospective streams of future income or other economic activity. The control of money is closely linked to the apparatus of the state, which protects and enforces rights of property and in turn responds to the ability of large propertied interests to dispose resources to the state through taxes, bribes, loans, or control of military resources.

Behind the economic system lies the general problem of securing factors of economic production from other uses, to turn parts of other systems into parts of the economy. Potentially productive natural resources must be extracted in sufficient quantity. Investors must be stimulated to form investment capital, bringing their resources out of other uses such as destructive consumption and hoarding. Labor must be engaged in productive activities rather than being left to leisure ones. Managerial skills and talents (human capital) must be recruited and developed. These four "must be's" require an interface between the medium of the economy, money, and other media for linking micro and macro, such as power, influence, and commitments, with which social wholes constituted for other than primarily economic purposes engage their memberships.

The components of the modern production system can all be viewed fruitfully in the expanded perspective of qualitative and quantitative micro-macro relations. It is necessary first to expand and recast the classical categories of production—land, labor, and capital—which were basically developed in relation to traditional agricultural production.

In the agricultural case, land factors were fairly simple, for land ranged from prime farmland to nonarable desert and could be gauged in terms of natural beneficence (soil, topography, and climate) and resultant yields. Labor was an unskilled resource: "hands," or muscle power. Capital was agricultural tools, such as horses, oxen, cattle, plows, storage and milling facilities, and earlier products in durable form: seed, oil, wine, cured meats, dried fruits or vegetables.

The early manufacturing version of these factors of production grew up alongside the agricultural and was not all that different from it; indeed, the factors of the agricultural system of dairy and cash-crop farming apply easily to low-technology machine manufacturing. Land factors are the portable products of extractive processes, particularly wood, cotton, wool, coal, and ores. Labor is still basically unskilled, but muscle per se is supplemented by or even forgone in preference for endurance, discipline, or "clever fingers." Capital is still essentially a matter of small-scale facilities or tools (machinery, buildings, vehicles) or small-scale financial resources convertible directly into either tools or resources. Finally, because of the alienability of property under postfeudal factory and freehold systems, a fourth category arises: entrepreneurial activity, which mobilizes the combination of components.

The modern productive system substantially modifies the essential nature of the four productive factors. Land is represented by rights of acquisition or control over specialized materials such as petroleum feedstock or fuel, ammonia, phosphates, rare or precious metals, and measured water. The cost of land factors is now composed to a much larger extent of monopoly price components representing cartel compacts, patent rights, royalties, and market orders. Land-rent differentials are not based, as before, largely on natural beneficence but on access to markets (i.e., urban real estate locations). The micro and macro problem with regard to land factors is essentially acquisition and adaptation: arranging delivery, controlling inventory, and negotiating contracts. Corporate resource management makes full use of the statistical devices of large-scale territorial governance and the intricate diplomatic protocols of trade and military-industrial relations. In all of these matters the trade association, a government-centered distributive organization, is an essential medium through which access is arranged, certain benefits are distributed, and rules are set for its members.

Labor, or human capital, is working skills or talents that need to be induced, motivated, and employed to advantage. Labor cost factors are increasingly affected by the negotiable relative worth of different skills rather than the cost of sustenance and customary standards of living. The labor problem is how to command interdisciplinary teamwork and subordination instead of aggressiveness or disengagement (Burawoy 1983). The fundamental tools of control are the power to hire and fire and the availability of monetary rewards and punishments, but these are inadequate without people-management tools: motivational and ideological communications, personnel testing and evaluation, graded compensation systems, and joint operational and executive committees. The role of unions and professional associations in these areas is substantial, but the role of governmental labor and pension legislation—especially laws pertaining to membership rules and requirements—is even more significant.

Capital is an almost purely financial category, particularly with the rapid obsolescence of real goods and the massive scale by virtue of which transfer of technology is accomplished by world market "turnkey" purchases, financially based mergers and acquisitions, and the like. Earlier notions about capital cost as the cost of persuading investors to forgo direct consumption and to put capital at risk have been vastly revised. Credit now reflects transaction costs plus inflation expectations plus risk estimators plus speculative competition for funds, further subject to tax incentives and subsidies, all modified by the fiscally based credit creation and control policies of central governments and banks. In addition, for large borrowers the terms of credit may include acceptance of the policy dictates of lending institutions. The development of central banking institutions and the affiliation of lenders into deposit insurance combines, check clearinghouse operations, currency control pacts, and the like is one of two major facts of modern credit making. The other fact is that public access to industrial and commercial wealth is channeled through membership in stock exchanges and investment partnerships under the occasionally watchful eye of governmental regulators and courts.

Entrepreneurial ability is divided between the management of internal costs—focusing on competitive price efficiency and requiring attention to "management tools" that are informational in character, such as linear programming, forecasts, cost-benefit analyses, and technical specifications—and marketing skills—that is, advertising, branding, distributive systems, product differentiation, and packaging. Additional important problems such as commercial theft and industrial espionage and externalities such as pollution are related to governing system responses. These problems are controlled through regulation, accounting, inspection, auditing, and dispute resolution through administrative and civil courts. In all of these matters the professions of law, accounting, and economics have made major inroads.

Although money is the basic measure of the modern economy, this review should serve to indicate that its effectiveness in linking large-scale enterprise to particular transactions depends on intermediary arrangements (involving banks, professional associations, trade associations, unions, regulators, arbitrators, outside directors, independent accounting practices, litigators, and other organizational modalities) to link employees, investors, managers, and property owners in networks of group membership far more extensive than the firm and household of classical theory.

CONCLUSION

The attachment of the terms "micro" and "macro" to the levels of individual thought processes on the one hand and capitalism or the state on the other are useful for classifying the current main interests of substantial numbers of social theorists. If we are too insistent on confining our language to these levels, however, the problem of linkage between micro and macro becomes impossibly wide. Freeing them from that particular reification, seeing that micro-macro linkage problems emerge wherever a smaller part deals with a larger whole or vice versa, makes these linkages more tractable. This is probably why they are managed so well so often in practical activities, although this management obviously has not yet been perfected. Large and small, part and whole are cultural instruments of thought which sociology shares as a universal human patrimony.

More particularly, social measurement and social membership give order to the relations between micro and macro and give us the subject matter of our discipline. This is not a call for theories of the middle range, for leaving aside either the state or the individual act. The point is, rather, that states relate to individual actions exclusively through the groups that constitute them, and individuals enter into these relations in their capacity as members of political groups and as manipulators or subjects of political measurement processes. Parallel points apply to the economy, the world system, Christianity, Western rationalism, and so on. The task for theorists is to be perceptive in penetrating these practical relations, rigorous in separating the essential from the ephemeral and (this is not the same) the particular from the universal, disciplined in envisioning plausible alternatives for the future in light of our knowledge of the past, and wise in our judgments about the present.

ACKNOWLEDGMENT

I would particularly like to thank Mark Gould and David Sciulli for planting the seeds of my thinking in certain key parts of this essay; the hundreds of contributors to the NAS/NRC ten-year outlook on research opportunities in the behavioral and social sciences for an unusual interdisciplinary education; and the editors of this volume for many things but especially for their deep reservoir of patience.

REFERENCES

Arrow, Kenneth J. 1963. *Social Choice and Individual Values*. 2d (enlarged) ed. New York: John Wiley.

Astronomy Survey Committee. 1982. *Astronomy and Astrophysics for the 1980s*. Vol. 1. Washington, D.C.: National Academy Press.

Axelrod, Robert. 1984. *The Evolution of Cooperation*. New York: Basic Books.

Baum, Rainer. 1976. Communication and Media, pp. 533–556 in Jan J. Loubser, Rainer Baum, Andrew Effrat, and Victor Meyer Lidz, eds., *Explorations in General Theory in the Social Sciences*. New York: Free Press.

Becker, Gary S. 1981. *A Treatise on the Family*. Cambridge, Mass.: Harvard University Press.

Burawoy, Michael. 1983. Factory Regimes under Advanced Capitalism. *American Sociological Review* 48:587–605.

Collins, Randall. 1981. The Microfoundations of Macrosociology. *American Journal of Sociology* 86:984–1014.

Duncan, Otis Dudley. 1984. *Notes on Social Measurement: Historical and Critical*. New York: Russell Sage Foundation.

Eisenstadt, S. N., and H. J. Helle, eds. 1985. *Perspectives on Sociological Theory*. Vol. 1. *Macrosociological Theory* and Vol. 2. *Microsociological Theory*. Beverly Hills, Calif.: Sage.

Garfinkel, Harold J. 1967. Passing and the Managed Achievement of Sex Status in an "Intersexed" Person. Part 1, pp. 116–185, and Appendix to Chapter 5, pp. 285–288, in *Studies in Ethnomethodology*. Englewood Cliffs, N.J.: Prentice-Hall.

Granovetter, Mark. 1985. Economic Action and Social Structure: The Problem of Embeddedness. *American Journal of Sociology* 91: 481–510.

Hechter, Michael, ed. 1983. *The Microfoundations of Macrosociology*. Philadelphia: Temple University Press.

Kahneman, Daniel, Paul Slovic, and Amos Tversky, eds. 1982. *Judgment under Uncertainty: Heuristics and Biases*. Cambridge: Cambridge University Press.

Klein, Lawrence R. 1986. Macroeconomic Modeling and Forecasting, pp. 95–110 in Neil J. Smelser and Dean R. Gerstein, eds., *Behavioral and Social Science: Fifty Years of Discovery*. Washington, D.C.: National Academy Press.

Knorr-Cetina, Karin D., and Aaron Cicourel. 1981. *Advances in Social Theory and Methodology: Towards an Integration of Micro- and Macro-Sociology*. London: Routledge & Kegan Paul.

Landes, David S. 1983. *Revolution in Time: Clocks and the Making of the Modern World*. Cambridge, Mass.: Harvard University Press.

Liddell, Henry George, and Robert Scott. 1940. *A Greek-English Lexicon*. 9th ed., rev. and augmented by Henry S. Jones and Roderick McKenzie. Oxford: Clarendon.

Luhmann, Niklas. 1976. Generalized Media and the Problem of Contingency, pp. 507–532 in Jan J. Loubser, Rainer Baum, Andrew Effrat, and Victor Meyer Lidz, eds., *Explorations in General Theory in the Social Sciences*. New York: Free Press.

———. 1982. *The Differentiation of Society*. Translated by Stephen Holmes and Charles Larmore. New York: Columbia University Press.

Martin, Margaret S. 1981. Statistical Practice in Bureaucracies. *Journal of the American Statistical Association* 76:1–8.

Mills, C. Wright. 1959. Uses of History, pp. 143–168 in *The Sociological Imagination*. London: Oxford University Press.

Münch, Richard. 1982. *Theorie des Handelns: Zur Rekonstruktion der Beiträge von Talcott Parsons, Emile Durkheim, und Max Weber*. Frankfurt am Main: Suhrkamp.

Nelson, Alan. 1984. Some Issues Surrounding the Reduction of Macroeconomics to Microeconomics. *Philosophy of Science* 51:573–594.

Nelson, Richard R., and Sidney G. Winter. 1982. *An Evolutionary Theory of Economic Change*. Cambridge, Mass.: Harvard University Press.
Olson, Mancur. 1965. *The Logic of Collective Action*. Cambridge, Mass.: Harvard University Press.
———. 1982. *The Rise and Decline of Nations: Economic Growth, Stagflation, and Social Rigidities*. New Haven: Yale University Press.
Parsons, Talcott. 1937. *The Structure of Social Action: A Study in Social Theory with Special Reference to a Group of Recent European Writers*. New York: McGraw-Hill.
Prewitt, Kenneth. 1986. Public Statistics and Democratic Politics, pp. 113–148 in Neil J. Smelser and Dean R. Gerstein, eds., *Behavioral and Social Science: Fifty Years of Discovery*. Washington, D.C.: National Academy Press.
Rapoport, Anatol, and A. Chammah. 1965. *Prisoner's Dilemma*. Ann Arbor: University of Michigan Press.
Schelling, Thomas C. 1978 *Micromotives and Macrobehavior*. New York: Norton.
Schwartz, Barry. 1975. *Queuing and Waiting: Studies in the Social Organization of Access and Delay*. Chicago: University of Chicago Press.
Skocpol, Theda. 1979. *States and Social Revolutions: A Comparative Analysis of France, Russia, and China*. Cambridge: Cambridge University Press.
Turkle, Sherry. 1984. *The Second Self: Computers and the Human Spirit*. New York: Simon & Schuster.
Williamson, Oliver. 1975. *Markets and Hierarchies*. New York: Free Press.
Zerubavel, Eviatar. 1981. *Hidden Rhythms: Schedules and Calendars in Social Life*. Chicago: University of Chicago Press.
———. 1985. *The Seven Day Circle: The History and Meaning of the Week*. New York: Free Press.

CHAPTER FOUR

The Evolutionary Differentiation between Society and Interaction

Niklas Luhmann

I.

Historical sociology has been unable to develop theoretical and empirical research programs. The prevailing opinion among historians is that the requirements of theory and concrete historical facts will never meet. In my view, however, it is a lack of good theory, not something intrinsic about sociology, which has prevented convincing sociological research on the nature of historical development. Sociologists simply are not sufficiently familiar with historical facts. Nor are their theories very well attuned to the historical transformations of societies; their theoretical frameworks are too simple for that. Contemporary sociological theories are not, in this view, sufficiently abstract to allow the kind of complex research design that historical research demands.

The intention in the following essay is to improve on this situation and to demonstrate at least some ways in which sociological and historical research can be connected. Starting from rather conventional methodological prescriptions, it will derive its concepts from a more distinctive theoretical framework. It will then formulate a hypothesis, try to operationalize it, and, finally, make some suggestions about possible verification. Although the theoretical framework that I propose to apply—the theory of self-referential social systems—has, paradoxically, a self-referential relationship with these methodological prescriptions, I shall neglect these doubts and difficulties, proposing simply to impress the public by "manufacturing knowledge" for the task at hand.[1]

II.

Within the general framework of a theory of self-referential systems, we can define autopoietic systems by their ability to reproduce the elements of which they consist by using the elements of which they consist.[2] Autopoietic systems are not only self-organizing systems, able to form and change their own structure; they also produce their own elementary units, which the system treats as undecomposable, as consisting of an ultimate "substance." Hence autopoietic systems are closed systems dependent on themselves for continuing their own operations. They define and specify their own boundaries. The environment, of course, remains a necessary condition for self-organization and for autopoiesis as well,[3] but it does not specify system states. It interpenetrates as "noise," as irritation, as perturbation, and may or may not set off internal efforts of interpretation and readaptation. It does not produce inputs that specify the operation of the system.[4]

Social systems in particular are autopoietic systems that use meaningful communication as their basic operation.[5] Social systems, according to this theory, consist of communications and nothing but communications—not of human beings, not of conscious mental states, not of roles, not even of actions. They produce and reproduce communications by meaningful reference to communications.[6] The reference to other communications (i.e., previous or future communications) is necessary to bring about communication; otherwise no one would recognize an intended communication as communication. Communication, therefore, by necessity occurs within a context of recursive self-reference. It is possible only as the operation of an autopoietic system *sui generis*. It is at the same time communication *about* something, and this "something" can be other communications or topics of a different kind. In this sense social systems differentiate themselves by using communication as autopoietic operations and reintroduce the difference between system and environment into the system.[7] Why? Because being constrained to communicate *about* something, they cannot avoid the distinction between communicating about communication and communicating about something else. The basic operation both differentiates and defines the system, using self-referential connections *to enforce upon itself the distinction between self-reference and external reference as a mode of adding further operations*. We must therefore distinguish implicit and explicit self-reference. With implicit self-reference the system produces communication and thereby *differentiates* itself. With explicit self-reference the system communicates about its own communication and thereby *identifies* itself. The crucial point is that implicit and explicit self-reference cannot be disassociated from each other. They can be distinguished by an observer, but they cannot be separated because communication can be produced only as communication about something.

We must now distinguish two different types of social systems according to whether or not they monopolize communication. I call these types societies and interactions.

Social systems are *societies* if they include all operations that, for them, have the quality of communication.[8] Societies are encompassing systems. Their environment contains many things, events, living systems, and even human beings but no meaningful communications. As soon as something is recognized as communication it is included in the system. Societies expand and shrink according to changing communication potentials, and their structures vary according to the task of communication management. Historically, societies may be said to expand because of increasing communication potential;[9] currently, in fact, only one society exists, the world society that includes all meaningful communication and excludes everything else.[10]

Social systems are *interactions* if they must recognize that their environment contains communications that cannot be controlled by the system. Interactions therefore need social boundaries. They conceive of themselves as face-to-face interactions and use the presence of persons as a boundary-defining device. If new persons arrive, their communications have to be included into the system by some ceremonial recognition and introduction. Even the persons at hand, however, present an ever-present potential for communication outside the system. They can leave the system and talk elsewhere about it or its participants. Interactions therefore adapt to external social conditions by taking into account the other roles of their participants.

In both cases the system itself (and never the environment) defines the boundary. Boundary definition and boundary maintenance are parts of autopoietic reproduction. The ways of handling boundaries and of managing the coupling between system and environment differ, however. Societies are *evolving*, not *adapting* systems. They evolve by changing the structures that provide linkages between communications, and they evolve without too much environmental restraint. Talking about an environment does not necessarily mean adapting to an environment. The religious ecology of older societies may have been particularly conducive to evolution because it is particularly easy to talk about sacred matters—

so easy that a counterdose of secrecy is required to restore the seriousness of the matter.[11] At any rate, the evolution of the societal system generated a highly complex, ecologically maladapted societal system.[12]

Interactional systems, on the other hand, are not *evolving* systems but *adaptive* systems. They operate within a social environment. They realize society by using communication, and they find themselves exposed to societal conditions in their environment. Their boundaries are highly permeable, and their own structures are always preselected by considerations of social fitness. They are not only disturbed by social environments or milieus; they internalize a set of requirements for appropriate behavior. They may, of course, evade social rules and outwit controls, but even this requires highly adaptive social behavior. It cannot be simply a matter of indifference. To do this, special self-protective devices are necessary.

These differences will, in the long run, generate an increasing differentiation between society and interaction. Differentiation can never be separation. Interaction remains communication—remains, as it were, consummation of society. It cannot leave the society and head off into its environment. Exploring new possibilities will simply enlarge the society. Nor can the society reproduce itself without providing possibilities for interaction; it cannot exist only in print. Hence differentiation between society and interaction happens within the societal system, possibly with secondary impact on the ways in which the societal system itself draws its boundaries. It has, then, a double effect on both types of systems. The society will become more of a society and the interaction will become more of an interaction. The society will be increasingly able to realize the prospects of a large, complex, encompassing system, one no longer tied to the limited possibilities of face-to-face interaction. It will loosen its dependence on interaction. The interaction, on the other hand, will be able increasingly to realize possibilities of social reflexivity and intimacy, no longer being overburdened with the function of reproducing the society and taking care of multifunctional responsibilities. It will loosen its dependence on society. Each type of system will be better equipped to realize its inherent potential. In this process both systems, the society and the interaction, will become more complex, each in its own way.

III.

In approaching historical facts, albeit in highly speculative and inferential ways, we will first have to identify evolutionary thresholds that may (and this remains to be proven) increase the difference between society and interaction. Evolution is not a continuous matter. It proceeds in jumps, adapting to strategic innovations that reverse the ways in which autopoietic reproduction of the society can be handled.[13] Literature offers two main candidates: the techniques of preserving and spreading communication and the forms of system differentiation.

The invention of writing, alphabetic literacy, and printing develop possibilities of social communication without interaction. Given these techniques, the society can expand beyond the spatial and temporal limitations of interaction. This "literate revolution" changes the total system, including the uses of oral communication. Oral communication in everyday settings becomes transformed by new possibilities and new constraints because it can now be chosen by preference and refer to a written and printed body of knowledge.[14] The classical arts of dialectics and rhetoric are postalphabetic inventions using techniques that specialize in persuasive oral communication under the constraints of knowledge stored in written texts.[15]

Whereas we can find little sociological research exploring the historical consequences of writing and printing, the differentiation of society under various labels—especially the division of labor and the origins of social class—has been a topic since the inception of sociology.[16] In seeing social differentiation as system differentiation—that is, as the emergence of system/environment distinctions within a system—we can roughly distinguish segmentation, stratification, and functional differentiation according to whether the differentiation is based on equality of the subsystems, on distinctions of rank, or on societal functions.[17] The transition from one type of differentiation to another will increase the potential for social complexity and thereby will change the conditions to which the differentiation of society and interaction responds. Seen from the point of view of evolution, types of system differentiation are forms of organizing complexity that stabilize themselves as "punctuated equilibria." Within a relatively short span of a few centuries only they will realize their level of complexity. Then the transformation into another type will become highly improbable, because in the present system it would be seen as a "catastrophe" in René Thom's use of the expression (that is, a sudden switch to another state of stability). The change from segmentation to stratification, the change from symmetry to asymmetry, that occurred by narrowing the access to prominent positions, is a case in point. The transformation of traditional societies, based on social strata, into modern society, based on the primacy of one-function systems, can be seen in the same way. Highly improbable, destabilizing, "catastrophic" development is possible. It happens from time to time and not always with destructive results. If it can happen through evolution, the theory of evolution is, as it were, called upon to explain the probability of the improbable.

Given this theoretical framework, the increasing differentiation of society and interaction can be investigated at several points. The Greek city around 600 B.C. offers good opportunities to observe the change from segmentary to stratificatory differentiation that coincided with the diffusion of alphabetic reading and writing and a strong new emphasis on the (equally asymmetric) difference between center and periphery. The results were a sharp distinction between economic (household) and political (public) interaction[18] and the well-known generalization of moral expectations concerning the sphere of political virtue.[19] Within the context of this traditional ethical-political semantics, however, society remains identified as interaction. It is the transition to a regime of functional differentiation which makes it impossible to maintain this identity, an identity that presupposed that politics was an upper-strata affair. Not before the second half of the eighteenth century will the traditional semantics collapse, and even in current times political theory is not free of reminiscences and revivals.[20]

IV.

I shall now concentrate on the period before the political and economic transformations of the late eighteenth and nineteenth centuries. These so-called revolutions made it obvious that the societal system could no longer be conceived as a network of interactions, as the "*doux commerce*" of the eighteenth century to which Karl Marx liked to refer ironically. My question is, how was this sudden change prepared by slow structural developments and by semantic adaptations to new conditions? If the hypothesis of increasing differentiation between interactional systems and the total society is true, we have to expect two different kinds of changes. On one hand, the society and its primary functional subsystems will become less dependent upon rules of interaction and will require an understanding of their own structural conditions. On the other hand, interactions will also become more dependent on their own autopoietic self-realization, particularly on something that can be summarized as "taking the role of the other" (Mead) or as adapting to "double contingency" (Parsons).

The first genuine semantic reaction to the increasing complexities of functional differentiation, especially to commercial and political developments, remains conservative. It looks for involution,[21] not evolution, for reinforcement and elaboration of traditional means of describing the world and the situation of human practice. We observe an explosion of sin and anxieties[22] and an increasing awareness of secret and occult features of the world. The world appears to be decaying because its possibilities are increasing and the interactional means are no longer appropriate to deal with them. During the seventeenth century, however, after long debates between "ancients and moderns," this outlook changes toward a more optimistic one.[23] Progress becomes visible, especially in the arts and sciences, and it becomes conceivable that its rules and conditions will be discovered.

Within this semantic and intellectual context, disappointments with the results of well-intentioned practice can be attributed to misunderstandings and misapplications of "natural laws." This mode of thinking leads to a new economic theory that explains problems of international trade by theories of "balance of trade" and by assumptions about the price mechanism, the circulation of money, and the effects of competition.[24] It is no longer the quality of the product or the hard labor that counts, or the honesty of the merchant who would have to fix a "just price" with a sidelong glance toward his eternal life. Competition, in particular, is a noninteractional way of relating to others. The market decides, nothing else. The concept of "economy" changes its meaning and comes increasingly to focus on "political economy"—an antique term that refers to an economic system as seen from the point of view of a total society rather than from the perspective of private households or business.[25] Seen from an evolutionary point of view, these debates and semantic developments were triggered by rather accidental conditions or random events—for example, by the decline of English exports, the spectacular economic and political success of the Dutch, or the problems of the belated and overdue monetary reform in England. Apparently, however, the pull toward functional differentiation was strong enough to derandomize such events and to interweave them to form a general pattern of new structural meanings.

The same holds true for the political sphere. In the course of the seventeenth and eighteenth centuries the term "state" changed its meaning from the old notion of "status" (state "of" something or somebody) to a term denoting an object in its own right. By the end of the sixteenth century it was possible to talk about "governing the state,"[26] but it was not until the seventeenth century that the old discussion about the rights and duties of a prince and the dangerous and responsible interaction of the prince and his counselors was replaced with broader discussions about political representation of interests, political opposition, and international equilibrium. The "absolute state," of course, retards semantic developments, but by the middle of the eighteenth century the concept of the state was ready to receive "constitutions" and "revolution."[27]

The scientific subsystem, conversely, seems to steer a different course. It undoubtedly intensified interaction during the seventeenth century. It certainly promoted contact among scientists, exchange of ideas, exchange of letters, visits, meetings, and academies as institutionalized places for the development and distribution of new knowledge. A second look, however, reveals an important trait of these interactions: They are no longer self-serving. They depend on common access to published books. They no longer aim at the successful management of the present situation. Comparing old wisdom and modern science, Thomas Sprat rejects sacred mysteries and occult essences of nature. For the ancients "this was a sure way to beget a Reverence in the People's Heart toward *themselves*: but not to advance the true Philosophy of *Nature*."[28] The same point is made as an argument against Greek rhetoric: Greeks "lov'd rather to make *sudden* conclusions, and to convince their hearers by argument; than to *delay* long, before they fixed their judgement; or to attend with sufficient patience the labour of experiments."[29] Both points reject interactional impression management in the interest of long-range goals. They plead not for autopoietic but for allopoietic interaction in order to serve the "advancement of learning," that is, the function of science. Whenever interaction is brought inside a functional subsystem, it has to fit into societal lines of differentiation and to adapt to rather improbable rules of behavior[30]—it cannot, as it were, merely amuse itself. The involutional tendencies of the sixteenth century, the exaggerated insistence on the twin techniques of mystification and rhetoric, are here turned into evolutional tendencies, and this requires an increasing differentiation between societal functions and the internal logistics of interaction systems. At this time, of course, society still was never described as a functionally differentiated system. The old "civil society," that is, the society of political interactions, remained the center of the discussions.[31] As in the case of medieval works of art, however, to see the stylistic and semantical innovations meant looking not at the main figures but at the marginal ones. The new conceptualization of the societal system begins with functional area studies of a sort. The results of these studies no longer fit into the interaction paradigm of the society but will require a new theory of society.

V.

At the second level, that of interaction systems, we find corresponding phenomena. The description of human interaction becomes sophisticated—both as description and as suggested orientations and behaviors. In general the rules of interaction shift from requiring attention to other social roles of the participants to the mediation of the contributions within the interaction system itself. Thus society becomes less directly relevant to interaction. As social environment it does not intrude directly into the social bargainings of the interaction system. Of course, during the seventeenth and eighteenth centuries and even beyond, considerations of social rank remained predominant. As things developed, however, and certainly from the beginning of the eighteenth century, it became less and less appropriate to insist on rank differences and formal recognition. Social status has its effect by being presupposed, by being mentioned ("name dropping"), by being underplayed and overestimated—all of which offers the opportunity to achieve equality in spite of status differences. Placed on its own in this way, interaction tends to level off social status,[32] albeit by using it for interactional purposes. Pride became a sin not only for theologians, and the snob was invented to make sure that in spite of all decline of religion and morality there remained at least one sin that could not be forgiven. At the end of the eighteenth century it became possible even to boast of low birth to prove one's capacity to overcome obstacles.[33]

In this case as well, theorizing about these imminent developments is often formulated for special cases only, the structural conditions for which eventually will disappear. In this way new insights into interactional complexities are gained: Behavioral possibilities can be tested on isolated islands of social rationality that have no connection with the functional subsystems of the societal system. The main fields of experiment and study are these:

1. social conversation—the retreat for members of the highest strata of society who have lost their social functions;
2. love-making—outside of marriage and family politics;
3. the intrigues of court life—outside of the bureaucratic administration of real problems such as state financial revenues, war, international politics, and legal affairs.[34]

It was, of course, received tradition to describe human beings as social animals that depend on social conditions for their existence. Within the context of interaction, this general condition becomes a matter of how to evoke positive *or* negative reactions by moves that please *or* displease others.[35] So begins the teaching of "double contingency."[36] The awareness of double contingencies autocatalyzes the development of social systems.[37] Once interactional systems are sufficiently differentiated, one can expect structural developments and semantics that cope with these contingencies; in fact, some of the consequences are easy to observe.

First of all, *motives* become increasingly important and therefore suspect. Traditional societies ascribe motives and do not require much exploration of "real" motives—either in economic (household) or in political (public) affairs. Suspicion as to motives first develops as a problem in interactional settings in the confessional.[38] This movement ends in admitting that one cannot know the real motives of others. One has to make a consensual rule that it is appropriate behavior to ignore them,[39] or one must, as in the case of love, create motives by reciprocal illusions. Given these insights, the religious system must find its own way of solving the problem of false devotion—either by appealing to the Lord[40] or by relaxing standards,[41] but no longer by using the forms and ways of interaction itself.

As a result of all this, a new intensity of *social reflexivity* can be observed, of "taking the role of the other." One must carefully observe the other and calculate one's own behavior from the other's point of view. In conversation one must avoid the presentation of one's own superiority and special knowledge; one should choose topics that give the other a chance to contribute his or her own point of view. A whole battery of rules is reformulated in terms of social reflexivity. For instance, one who talks too much uses time others could use to talk.[42] One has to avoid sharp contradictions and the expression of opinions that may hurt others.[43] Even praise must be handled carefully, lest it be mistaken for flattery by observers or by the addressee.[44] In general, the recommendation is to use "finesses" only when necessary and only under the appearance of not using finesses.

Under these conditions—(1) altruistic and selfish attitudes of oneself and the other, (2) possibilities for dissimulation and sincere behavior by oneself and the other, and (3) social reflexivity—the interaction system develops a combinatorial space of immense complexity.[45] Hence no participant can know the state of a "simple" two-person interaction system. This explains the interest in rules and recipes in the seventeenth century and the rather desperate reliance on sentiment, taste, and natural morality in the early eighteenth century. At any rate, interaction systems become differentiated by their own self-generated complexity, which has to be reduced on the spot and can in no way be used to serve the functions of the societal system.

In addition, a new phenomenon surfaces: *paradoxical, self-defeating communication*. In many cases, devotion being the prime example, communication has to be unintentional.[46] Once invented, this paradigm spreads. As a lady, you cannot deny your interest in being seduced without reinforcing the hopes of the lover.[47] You cannot say that you know that your lover does not really love you anymore without giving the impression that you yourself would like to bring the affair to an end.[48] You cannot maintain that you are an individual different from everyone else without comparing yourself to others.[49] You cannot communicate sincerity without producing counterintuitive effects and evoking suspicion. In other words, you now have to proceed in an intentionally unintentional manner (or in a carefully careless one, as the English are supposed to do) and thus rely on the politeness of others who will not bluntly say that they have found you out. The social system of interaction has to deal with paradoxical communication; that is, to ignore its existence.

In light of these complications there must be an adaptation of the mechanisms of social control and social sanction. "Ridicule" is supposed to play its part here.[50] This mechanism has, moreover, the advantage of being self-referential: To use it wrongly is itself ridicule.[51] It can be applied only in interactional settings, however, and not in public affairs. It presupposes "the liberty of the Club."[52] It differentiates between interaction and society. Last but not least, this new way of conceiving interaction requires new guarantees that interrelationships will be smooth, harmonious, and, above all, moral. How, then, will sufficient trust be generated?

The writers of the seventeenth and eighteenth centuries are not prepared to trust social accommodations alone. The more the internal adjustment of social interaction becomes visible, the more external guarantees appear to be necessary. The guarantees for adequate *social* behavior become *personalized*. It is no longer the social status of a person but his or her internal dispositions that count. A new test of morality is invented: how the person behaves without observers and without considerations of social esteem and reputation. Public virtues lose their authenticity.[53] Even honesty, the old public virtue of *honestas*, finds itself transferred into the darkness of unseen private sentiments. "Why shou'd a Man be honest in the Dark?" is still a rhetorical question.[54] But the answer reads that this only proves "natural" morality.

Through differentiation interaction systems gain new possibilities of achieving their own mode of social communication. They also retain possibilities that are of no use or are even dysfunctional for the complex subsystems that specialize in functions such as science, law, economy, or politics. By differentiation, interaction systems tend to become symmetric and personalized. This means that they cannot tolerate contradiction because for them contradiction means conflict, quarrel, and strife.[55] If they loose the corset of social stratification, they must repress contradiction all the more by strictly interactional means. The literature abounds with exhortations to avoid direct contradictions and sharp confrontations.[56] It is too easy to put an end to interaction if no larger social context makes it obligatory. Hence interaction has to be smooth, pleasing, and self-reproductive.

Functional subsystems require the inverse pattern. They use asymmetric relations, corroborated by professional and/or organizational structures, and they must encourage contradiction as a means of control, advancement, and improvement. This leads to highly artificial rules for interactions, which then become "dried up" and functionally specialized—and unpleasant. Again, the interaction rules established within the Royal Society for the Improving of Natural Knowledge are an interesting case in point.[57] In spite of the formal equality of all fellows, the society must recognize the asymmetry of the relation between the researcher and his or her critical audience. In spite of its interactional mode of communication, it must encourage polite distrust, delay in acceptance and critical contradiction.[58]

With almost desperate idealism, Friedrich Schiller's letters ("On the Aesthetic Education of Man")[59] continue to recommend the unity of interaction and society. Fichte, too, continues to see the rules of harmonious interaction as an ideal model for society—even if it takes millions of years.[60] They did not inaugurate the nineteenth century. The new motto became not "unity" but "difference."

VI.

It was the French Revolution that, in a spectacular way, made it unavoidable that society and interaction should be recognized as different affairs. The best intentions for restructuring the societal system were badly handled in interaction. The rhetoric of humanity leads to the guillotine as the most humane and fastest way of killing people without spilling too much of their blood. The revolutionary theater, a large body (about a thousand) of newly written pieces, presented human ideals on the stage—but in a manner quite different from real-life developments. The famous festivals of the revolution, planned to symbolize society by interaction, came off as artificial, irritating, and, worst of all, ridiculous.[61]

It would be erroneous, however, to see this differentiation between interaction and society as a sufficient description of the state of affairs in the nineteenth and twentieth centuries. Real society is more complicated than that. It uses the loose coupling of interaction and society for many different purposes. First, loose coupling makes it possible to deregulate interaction but also to regulate it in terms of special conditions and special functions. Informality and organization come from the same root. Both presuppose the interruption of cross-cutting references to all other roles of the participants. This is the main evolutionary achievement. Given this basis, interaction systems can either develop by self-regulation constrained by their own history or they can submit to highly specialized conditions of professional or organizational discipline. Only great and reliable indifference on the part of the system toward general social conditions allows for functional specialization and specified input/output relations. Neither professional work on the basis of asymmetric and unreciprocated relations between professionals and clients nor the complex organizations of modern bureaucracies would be possible without this combination of decoupling and recoupling, of loose coupling and tight coupling between interaction systems and their social environment.

With all these possibilities of differentiation, modern society is not necessarily less integrated than traditional societies. Defining integration as the reduction of degrees of freedom of the components of a system,[62] we see at once that integration presupposes degrees of freedom. Highly complex systems need and can afford more variety. More variety, however, does not equal less integration; it makes it possible and necessary to choose between loose and tight integrations within the same system. This means that we find organizations and informal gatherings, political states and social movements, coupling by closure and coupling by input.[63] It remains true that under such conditions, symbols that represent the unity of the system within the system must be highly general or they remain controversial. These symbols, "civil religions," or ideologies are not effective instruments of integration, however;[64] at best, they symbolize the meaning of integration.

All this is complex but not particularly confusing. In addition, however, the idea of smooth, peaceful, harmonious personal interaction becomes a source of ideologies. When ideologies speak about freedom, equality, or human dignity, the suggestion is that these ideas become tangible in interaction. Here they have to make a difference—where else, indeed, could they do it? Moreover, interaction itself is described as the retreat of humanity. "*Gemeinschaft*," "solidarity," and, nowadays, life-world offer a semantics of warmth and well-being.[65] This, of course, presupposes the suppression of violence as an everyday experience. Happiness is to be gained in retreat from society—for example, in love and marriage,[66] requiring free entry into and exit from this retreat, at least for the man. No one would think of restoring the narrowness of medieval households as the only milieu for one's whole life. One needs an evil society to feel happy elsewhere. Early socialist thinkers claimed that everything would be fine if all did their work without capitalists channeling the profit into their own pockets.[67]

In these various ways the difference between interaction and society reenters the society as ideology in terms of good and bad. It becomes a distorted topic for theories that describe modern society. Of course, such a re-entry of the distinction into the distinguished is possible only after the distinction has been made. The structural differentiation between interaction and society as different ways of realizing the autopoiesis of social systems is the result of evolutionary transformations of the societal system. When sufficiently obvious, it transforms the societal system. When sufficiently obvious, it can be used at the semantic level to equip communications that describe the system within the system. Such self-descriptions of the society respond in peculiar ways to structural conditions. They simplify. They evaluate. In our case it seems that the semantics of happy, personal, harmonious interaction as opposed to cool, reckless, impersonal, capitalistic, bureaucratic society was and is particularly likely to give expression to the reality shock modern society receives by its own realization. What was intended as progress and immaculate growth, as wealthy and enlightened humanity, emerged as a functionally differentiated system with all its risks, instabilities, insecurities, and contradictions. This makes it highly suggestive to hope for healthy, human, satisfying interaction, for reasonable consensus and practical understandings. Even if we can live to some extent in such interactions, however, they can never be the society whose evolution will be our destiny.

VII.

The distinction between interaction and society has been formulated as a distinction of (self-referential) *systems*. The distinction of micro and macro is formulated as a distinction of *levels*. The concept of system has *empirical* references; the concept of level has *logical* references. The concept of system can be used to *include* self-references as empirical phenomena.[68] The concept of level has been invented to *exclude* self-references insofar as they amount to tautologies or paradoxes.[69] The micro/macro distinction reduces the complexity of the description of an object, disregarding reciprocal interdependencies among the levels. For instance, we can say that disorder at one level may be seen as order at another without confronting the paradox of saying that disorder is order.[70] This expedient may be used whenever unavoidable. Wherever we can replace it with systems theory, however, we should use the more powerful conceptualization.

NOTES

1. In the sense of the term provided by Karin Knorr-Cetina, *The Manufacture of Knowledge: An Essay on the Construction and Contextual Nature of Science* (Oxford: Pergamon Press, 1981).

2. For general orientation see Humberto R. Maturana and Francisco J. Varela, *Autopoiesis and Cognition: The Realization of the Living* (Dordrecht: Reidel, 1975); Francisco J. Varela, *Principles of Biological Autonomy* (New York: North-Holland, 1979); Heinz von Foerster, *Observing Systems* (Seaside, Calif.: Intersystems Publications, 1981); Milan Zeleny, ed., *Autopoiesis: A Theory of Living Organization* (New York: North-Holland, 1981); Paul Dumouchel and Jean Pierre Dupuy, eds., *L'auto-organisation: De la physique au politique* (Paris: Seuil, 1983).

3. See Heinz von Foerster, "On Self-Organizing Systems and Their Environment," in Marshall C. Yovits and Scott Cameron, eds., *Self-Organizing Systems* (Oxford: Pergamon Press, 1960), pp. 31–50.

4. This does not preclude the possibility of an *observing* system *describing* relations between inputs and system states. In this sense, Varela proposes the distinction between "input-type description" and "closure-type description." See his "Two Principles for Self-Organization," in Hans Ulrich and Gilbert J. B. Probst, eds., *Self-Organization and Management of Social Systems: Insights, Promises, Doubts, and Questions* (Berlin: Springer, 1984), pp. 26–32.

5. Extensively treated in Niklas Luhmann, *Soziale Systeme: Grundriß einer allgemeinen Theorie* (Frankfurt: Suhrkamp, 1984). See also Niklas Luhmann, "Society, Meaning, Religion—Based on Self-Reference," *Sociological Analysis* 46 (1985): 5–20.

6. The same point could be made, of course, for actions. See D. Rubinstein, "The Concept of Action in the Social Sciences," *Journal for the Theory of Social Behaviour* 7 (1977): 209–239. Or for decisions cf. Robert M. Emerson, "Holistic Effects in Social Control Decision-Making," *Law and Society Review* 17 (1983): 425–455. Then, however, the interconnection of actions and decisions implies communication as the more basic operation. Hence, any social system will treat as action or as decision only what can be communicated as action or as decision.

7. See the concept of "reentry" in George Spencer Brown, *Laws of Form*, 2d ed. (London: Allen & Unwin, 1971).

8. For them. There may be, of course, operations that qualify as communication for an observer but that are invisible or inaccessible to the system itself.

9. See Niklas Luhmann, "The Improbability of Communication," *International Social Science Journal* 23 (1981): 122–132.

10. See Niklas Luhmann, "The World Society as a Social System," *International Journal of General Systems* 8 (1982): 131–138; also in R. Felix Geyer and Johannes van der

Zouwen, eds., *Dependence and Inequality: A Systems Approach to the Problems of Mexico and Other Developing Countries* (Oxford: Pergamon Press, 1982), pp. 295–306.

11. For an account of very loose and pragmatic dealings with sacred matters, counterbalanced by secrecy, see Fredrik Barth, *Ritual and Knowledge Among the Baktaman of New Guinea* (Oslo: Universitetsforlaget and New Haven: Yale University Press, 1975).

12. Obviously, then, sociology cannot use a strictly Darwinistic theory of evolution that insists on adaptive selection. Biologists also express increasing doubts. See, for example, Gerhard Roth, "Conditions of Evolution and Adaptation in Organisms as Autopoietic Systems," in D. Mossakowski and G. Roth, eds., *Environmental Adaptation and Evolution* (Stuttgart-New York: Fischer, 1982), pp. 37–48.

13. See Niklas Luhmann, "Das Problem der Epochenbildung und die Evolutionstheorie," in Hans-Ulrich Gumbrecht and Ursula Link-Heer, eds., *Epochenschwellen und Epochenstrukturen im Diskurs der Literatur- und Sprachhistorie* (Frankfurt: Suhrkamp, 1985), pp. 11–33.

14. For examples drawn from an already extensive field of research, see Eric A. Havelock, *Preface to Plato* (Cambridge, Mass.: Belknap, 1963); idem, *The Literate Revolution in Greece and Its Cultural Consequences* (Princeton: Princeton University Press, 1982); Walter J. Ong, *The Presence of the Word: Some Prolegomena for Cultural and Religious History* (New Haven: Yale University Press, 1967); idem, *Interfaces of the Word: Studies in the Evolution of Consciousness and Culture* (Ithaca, N.Y.: Cornell University Press, 1977); Jack Goody, ed., *Literacy in Traditional Society* (Cambridge: Cambridge University Press, 1968); Elisabeth L. Eisenstein, *The Printing Press as an Agent of Social Change: Communications and Cultural Transformations in Early-Modern Europe*, 2 vols. (Cambridge: Cambridge University Press, 1979).

15. This, it seems to me, is the reason why the topic of and theories concerning artificial memory had become important within the context of dialectics and rhetoric. It was more than a question of improving one's own memory and capacity to "find" arguments (*inventio*). One had to compete with others who also had free access to a written body of knowledge and therefore divergent memories. After the introduction of printing, these theories exploded and vanished because personal memories and references to texts diverged too much and their convergence had to be organized in other ways. Compare Frances Yates, *The Art of Memory* (Chicago: Chicago University Press, 1966).

16. And, of course, before. See Niklas Luhmann, ed., *Soziale Differenzierung: Zur Geschichte einer Idee* (Opladen: Westdeutscher Verlag, 1985).

17. See Niklas Luhmann, *The Differentiation of Society* (New York: Columbia University Press, 1982), pp. 229 ff.

18. For the onset of this process, see Peter Spahn, "Oikos und Polis: Beobachtungen zum Prozeß der Polisbildung bei Hesiod, Solon und Aischylos," *Historische Zeitschrift* 231 (1980): 529–564.

19. See Joachim Ritter, *Metaphysik und Politik: Studien zu Aristoteles und Hegel* (Frankfurt: Suhrkamp, 1969); Christian Meier, *Die Entstehung des Politischen bei den Griechen* (Frankfurt: Suhrkamp, 1980). For the corresponding underevaluation of economic (household and commercial) interactions see also Peter Spahn, "Die Anfänge der antiken Ökonomik," *Chiron* 14 (1984): 301–323.

20. See Stephen Holmes, "Aristipus In and Out of Athens," *American Political Science Review* 73 (1979): 113–128.

21. For "Involution" as "progressive complication, variety within uniformity, virtuosity within monotony," see Alexander Goldenweiser, "Loose Ends of a Theory on the Individual, Pattern, and Involution in Primitive Society," in Robert H. Lowie, ed., *Essays in Anthropology, Presented to A. L. Kroeber* (Freeport, N.Y., 1936), pp. 99–104.

22. See Jean Delumeau, *La peur en occident XIVe-XVIIIe siècles* (Paris: Fayard, 1978); idem, *Le péché et la peur: La culpabilisation en Occident XIIIe-XVIIIe siècles* (Paris: Fayard, 1983).

23. By the way, it is interesting to see that the topic of *antiqui/moderni* itself changes its meaning. Since ancient times it had been a rhetorical device for distributing praise and blame. Only in the late sixteenth century did it become a systematic device for describing and evaluating one's own society. See Elisabeth Gössmann, *Antiqui und Moderni im Mit-*

talalter: Eine geschichtliche Standortbestimmung (München: Schöningh, 1974); Robert Black, "Ancients and Moderns in the Renaissance: Rhetoric and History in Accolti's *Dialogue* on the Preeminence of Man of His Own Time," *Journal of the History of Ideas* 43 (1982): 3–32; Richard F. Jones, *Ancients and Moderns: A Study of the Rise of the Scientific Movement in Seventeenth-Century England*, 2d ed. (St. Louis, 1961).

24. See Joyce O. Appleby, *Economic Thought and Ideology in Seventeenth-Century England* (Princeton: Princeton University Press, 1978).

25. For the development of the continental terminology, reacting to increasing complexity and differentiation, see Wolf-Hagen Krauth, *Wirtschaftsstruktur und Semantik: Wissenssoziologische Studien zum wirtschaftlichen Denken in Deutschland zwischen dem 13. und 17. Jahrhundert* (Berlin: Duncker und Humblot, 1984).

26. See Ciro Spontone, *Dodici libri del Governo di Stato* (Verona: Pigozzo & de Rossi, 1599).

27. There is, of course, an immense literature about the history of political ideas but astonishingly little knowledge focusing on the concept of the state, which was nevertheless the carrier-concept of all political innovations. See, however, Paul-Ludwig Weihnacht, *Staat: Studien zur Bedeutungsgeschichte* (Berlin: Duncker & Humblot, 1968); Wolfgang Mager, *Zur Entstehung des modernen Staatenbegriffs* (Wiesbaden: Steiner, 1970). For the most part literature either projects the term unhistorically into the past, reading terms such as *societas civilis*, *res publica*, or commonwealth as "state" or discusses "theories of the state" since the eighteenth century, comparing, for instance, continental with English or American traditions. See Kenneth H. F. Dyson, *The State Tradition in Western Europe: A Study of an Idea and Institution* (Oxford: Robertson, 1980).

28. *The History of the Royal Society of London* (London: J. Martyn, 1667), reprint edited by Jackson I. Cope and Harold W. Jones (St. Louis, London, 1959), p. 5.

29. *The History of the Royal Society*, p. 7.

30. See Thomas Sprat, praising the members of the Royal Society: "They have escap'd the prejudices that use to arise from Authority, from unequality of Persons, from insinuations, from friendships; But above all, they have guarded themselves against themselves, lest the strength of their own thoughts should lead them into error . . ."; and as a result: "they have perpetually preserv'd a singular sobriety of debating, slowness of consenting, and moderation of dissenting" (The History of the Royal Society, pp. 92, 91).

31. See Manfred Riedel, "Gesellschaft, bürgerliche," in *Geschichtliche Grundbegriffe: Historisches Lexikon zur politisch-sozialen Sprache in Deutschland*, Bd 2 (Stuttgart: Klett, 1975), pp. 719–800.

32. "Dès qu'un grand Seigneur m'admet à sa conversation, je ne luy dois ce qu'il me doit, je m'acquitte quand je fait ce qu'il fait. Il me parle, j'écoute, je parle" (Pierre de Villiers, *Nouvelles Réflexions sur les défauts d'autrui*. Paris: Collombat, 1697, Vol. 1, pp. 213 f.).

33. See Sénac de Meilhan, *Considérations sur l'esprit et les moeurs* (London, 1787), p. 133.

34. For all three fields there exists a large body of contemporaneous literature—mostly copying preexisting literature—which is partly provocative, partly moralistic. Without literature (i.e., without print) the innovation hardly would have become a self-reinforcing "fashion." For recent retrospective research, see Christoph Strosetzki, *Konversation: Ein Kapitel gesellschaftlicher und literarischer Pragmatik im Frankreich des 18. Jahrhunderts* (Frankfurt: Lang, 1978); Ulrich Schulz-Buschhaus, "Über die Verstellung und die ersten 'primores' des Héroe von Gracián," *Romanische Forschungen* 91 (1979): 411–430; Claudia Henn-Schmölders, *Die Kunst des Gesprächs* (München: DTV, 1979); Niklas Luhmann, "Interaktion in Oberschichten: Zur Transformation ihrer Semantik im 17. und 18. Jahrhundert," in idem, *Gesellschaftsstruktur und Semantik* (Frankfurt: Suhrkamp, 1980), I: 72–161; idem, *Liebe als Passion: Zur Codierung von Intimität* (Frankfurt: Suhrkamp, 1982) (English translation forthcoming).

35. "Since men by nature are addicted to conversation, and one dependeth upon another [note the presupposed congruence of interaction and society], therefore it importeth much, to know how to second or crosse other men's affections, how we may please or displease them, make them our friends or foes," says Thomas Wright, *The Passions of the*

Minde in Generell (1604), rev. ed. (London: Dawlman, 1630), reprinted with an introduction by Thomas O. Sloan (Urbana, Ill.: University of Illinois Press, 1971), p. 96.

36. As discussed by Talcott Parsons and others, "Some Fundamental Categories of the Theory of Action: A General Statement," in Talcott Parsons and Edward A. Shils, eds., *Toward a General Theory of Action* (Cambridge, Mass.: Harvard University Press, 1951), p. 16.

37. See Luhmann, *Soziale Systeme*, pp. 148 ff.

38. See Alois Hahn, "Zur Soziologie der Beichte und anderer Formen institutionalisierter Bekenntnisse: Selbstthematisierung und Zivilisationsprozeß," *Kölner Zeitschrift für Soziologie und Sozialpsychologie* 34 (1982): 408–434.

39. "Were we to dive too deeply into the sources and motives of the most laudable actions, we may, by tarnishing their lustre, deprive ourselves of a pleasure," teaches the Countess Dowager of Carlisle. *Thoughts in the Form of Maxims Addressed to Young Ladies on Their First Establishment in the World* (London: Cornell, 1789), p. 81.

40. "If we are moved to seem religious only to vent wit, Lord deliver us" (John Donne, "A Litany," XXI, *The Complete English Poems*. Harmondsworth, Middlesex: Penguin, 1971, p. 323).

41. As in the case of the much-criticized Jesuit practice. See, for example, Pierre de Villiers, *Pensées et réflexions sur les égaremens des hommes dans la voye du salut*, 3d ed., 3 vols. (Paris: Collombat, 1700–02), 2: 93, 125. See also Alois Hahn, "La sévérité raisonnable—La doctrine de la Confession chez Bourdaloue," in Manfred Tietz and Volker Kapp, eds., *La pensée religieuse dans la littérature et la civilisation aux XVIIe siècle en France* (Paris, Seattle, Tübingen, 1984), pp. 19–40.

42. See, for example, Jacques du Bosq, *L'honneste femme* (Rouen, 1639), pp. 56 ff., esp. p. 59. For rules against "grands parleurs" and for recommendations on attentive listening and silence, see also Nicolas Faret, *L'honneste homme, ou l'art de plaire à la Cour* (1630), new ed. (Paris: Presses Universitaires de France, 1925), pp. 73 ff.; Madeleine de Scuderi, "De parler trop ou trop peu, et comment il faut parler," in idem, *Conversation sur divers sujets* (Lyon: Amaulry, 1680), 1: 159–204; Claude Buffier, *Traité de la société civile, et du moyen de se rendre heureux, en contribuant au bonheur des personnes avec qui l'on vit* (Paris, 1726), pp. 119 ff. The topic as such is old; it can be traced back to Plutarch.

43. Originally a question of peace and a precaution against provoking violence; now a question of pleasure and "*doux commerce*." See the "Regle generale pour conserver la paix: Ne blesser personne, et ne se blesser de rien" in Pierre Nicole, *Essais de Morale*, 6th ed. (Paris: Desprez, 1682), I: 229; and a few decades later Buffier, *Traité de la société civile*, 4: 78, "douceur de la Société civile"!

44. See Ch. G. Bessel, *Schmiede deß Politischen Glüks* (Frankfurt, 1673), pp. 55 ff.

45. Alfred Kuhn, *The Logic of Social Systems: A Unified, Deductive, System-Based Approach to Social Sciences* (San Francisco: Jossey-Bass, 1974), pp. 273 f., calculates 9^7 possible states of the system!

46. "Qui voudra être devot pour en faire profession, ne le sera pas; qui le sera veritablement, en fera profession sans penser de le faire," remarks de Villiers, *Pensées et réflexions* (1700), 2: 98.

47. Claude Crébillon fils, *Lettres de la Marquise de M. au Comte de R. (1732)*, new ed. (Paris, 1970).

48. Benjamin Constant, *Adolphe* (1816), *Œuvres* (Paris: éd. de la Pléiade, 1957).

49. Charles Duclos, *Considérations sur les Moeurs de ce siècle* (1751), new ed. (Lausanne: Rencontre, 1970), pp. 291 f. And even stronger: People who want to say something about themselves "jouent leur propre charactère" (p. 293).

50. See Jean Baptiste Morvan de Bellegarde, *Réflexions sur le ridicule, et sur les moyens de j'éviter*, 2d ed. (Amsterdam, 1701); Duclos, *Considérations*, pp. 287 ff.; Anthony, Earl of Shaftesbury, *An Essay on the Freedom of Wit and Humour* (1709), *Characteristicks of Men, Manners, Opinion, Times*, 2d ed. (1714, reprint, Farnborough, UK: Gregg, 1968).

51. "Rien n'est si ridicule que de vouloir attacher du ridicule aux talens, et de paraître dédaigner de qu'on n'est pas en état de faire," to give the formulation of a current topic by d'Alembert, *Dialogue entre la Poésie et la Philosophie*, in *Œuvres complètes* (reprint. Geneva: Slatkine, 1967), 4: 373–381, esp. p. 381.

52. Shaftesbury, *Characteristicks of Men*, pp. 75 f.

53. See Richard Blackmore, *An Essay upon False Vertue*, in idem, *Essays upon Several Subjects* (London: Curll, 1716), 1: 237–290.

54. See Shaftesbury, *Characteristicks of Men*, p. 25.

55. It stirs up passions, according to the teaching of rhetorics. Cf. Thomas Wright, *The Passions of the Minde in Generall*, rev. ed. (London: Dawlman, 1630, reprint Urbana, Ill.: University of Illinois Press, 1971), pp. 68 ff.

56. For example, see Pierre Charron, *De la sagesse* (no date, no place), II ch. IX, § 16; Nicole, *Essais*, p. 230; Buffier, *Traité de la Société civile*, pp. 91 ff.

57. See Sprat, *The History of the Royal Society*.

58. It is interesting to see to what extent the seventeenth century was inclined to recommend normal interaction rules (to keep in due temper, to avoid superfluous talk, etc.) as fit for scientific research. See the section on "Their manner of Discourse" in Sprat, *The History of the Royal Society*, pp. 111 ff.

59. Ed. by W. Henckmann (München, 1967). See also Klaus Disselbeck, *Integrierender Geschmack und ausdifferenzierte Kunst: Eine systemtheoretische Untersuchung zu Schillers Briefen 'Über die ästhetische Erziehung des Menschen'* (Diss., Tübingen, 1983).

60. "Und dau're es Millionen und Billionen Jahre," in Johann Gottlieb Fichte, *Einige Vorlesungen über die Bestimmung des Gelehrten* (1794), *Ausgewählte Werke* (Darmstadt: Wissenschaftliche Buchgesellschaft, 1962), 1: 217–274, esp. p. 239.

61. See Mona Ozouf, *La fête révolutionnaire 1789–1799* (Paris, 1976); Hans Ulrich Gumbrecht, "ce sentiment de douloureux plaisir, qu'on recherche, quoiqu'on se plaigne": "Skizze einer Funktionsgeschichte des Theaters in Paris zwischen Thermidor 1794 und Brumaire 1799," *Romanistische Zeitschrift für Literaturgeschichte* 3 (1979): 335–373; idem, "Skizze einer Literaturgeschichte der Französischen Revolution," in Jürgen von Stackelberg, ed., *Europäische Aufklärung*, III, *Neues Handbuch der Literaturwissenschaft* (Wiesbaden, 1980) 13: 269–328.

62. Following a suggestion by Robert Anderson, "Reduction of Variants as a Measure of Cultural Integration," in Gertrude E. Dole and Robert L. Carneiro, eds., *Essays in the Science of Culture in Honor of Leslie A. White* (New York: Crowell, 1960), pp. 50–62. It may be unnecessary to mention that this measure of integration, be it of cultural objects or of social systems, has nothing to do with the mental state of empirical persons, hence nothing to do with "consensus."

63. See Varela, *Two Principles*.

64. For such an opinion see Rudolf Smend, *Verfassung und Verfassungsrecht* (1928), reprinted in idem, *Staatsrechtliche Abhandlung und andere Aufsätze* (Berlin: Duncker & Humblot, 1955), pp. 119–276.

65. For "Gemeinschaft" see Manfred Riedel, "Gesellschaft, Gemeinschaft," in *Geschichtliche Grundbegriffe: Historisches Lexikon zur politisch-sozialen Sprache in Deutschland* (Stuttgart: Klett, 1975), 2: 801–862; and, of course, Ferdinand Tönnies, *Gemeinschaft und Gesellschaft* (Leipzig, 1887). For "solidarity" see J. E. S. Hayward, "Solidarity: The Social History of an Idea in 19th Century France," *International Review of Social History* 4 (1959): 261–284. The neoromantic term "life-world" is not yet ready for historical analysis, but see Ulf Matthiesen, *Das Dickicht der Lebenswelt und die Theorie des kommunikativen Handelns* (München: Fink, n.d. [1983]).

66. See Josef Droz, *Essai sur l'art d'être heureux*, nouv. éd. (Amsterdam: Diederichs, 1827); Jules Michelet, *L'amour* (Paris: Hachette, 1858).

67. See Thomas Hodgskin, *Labour Defended Against the Claims of Capital, or the Unproductiveness of Capital Proved with Reference in the Present Combinations Amongst Journeymen* (1825), reprint of the 1922 ed. (New York: Kelley, 1969), esp. pp. 51 f.

68. See the literature in note 2.

69. But see Paul Watzlawick, Janet H. Beavin, and Don D. Jackson, *Pragmatics of Human Communication: A Study of Interactional Patterns, Pathologies, and Paradoxes* (New York: Norton, 1967); Anthony Wilden, *System and Structure: Essays in Communication and Exchange* (London: Tavistock, 1972); Douglas R. Hofstadter, *Gödel, Escher, Bach: An Eternal Golden Braid* (Hassocks, Sussex: Harvester Press, 1979). These authors

use the concept of level to describe the collapse of the difference of levels and to approach, in this way, the problems of self-reference, circularity, "tangled hierarchy," and paradoxes.

70. In a very similar sense and as a functional equivalent, the distinction of manifest or visible (e.g., disorder) and latent or invisible (e.g., order) has been used, at least since the eighteenth century. As far as I know, it has never been formulated as a distinction of "levels." But why not?

PART TWO

Rational Action and Macrostructure

CHAPTER FIVE

Collective Phenomena and Rational Choice

Reinhard Wippler and Siegwart Lindenberg*

1. INTRODUCTION

Behind the many controversies that rage in sociology, general agreement on a minimal program seems to exist: The central task of sociology consists of showing how social behavior and collective phenomena (such as belief systems, institutional arrangements, and structural patterns) are socially determined. Physical or psychic characteristics and other "non-social" factors are thus ruled out as relevant causes. How, then, can collective phenomena be explained? This question is often phrased in terms relevant to the conference on which this book is based: How can macrosocial phenomena be explained? This is the master question behind many interpretations of the so-called micro-macro problem. Unfortunately, within the minimal program there is no agreement on the micro/macro distinction, except that "micro" always refers to smaller units than those implied by "macro." We will argue that the various meanings attached to this distinction have generated micro/macro problems that stand in the way of an adequate solution of the master problem.

One can find at least four different specific senses in which this distinction is used. First, the micro/macro distinction refers to the *scope* of the phenomena studied. Although there are no clear cut-off points, interacting individuals are clearly micro whereas the value system of a society, for example, is clearly macro. In accordance with the minimal sociological program, the micro level in this view is constituted by interaction

*The sequence in which the authors are listed was decided by flipping a coin.

and not by individuals, because individuals are said to belong to the domain of psychology (Mayhew 1980) or because paying attention to individuals on the micro level is believed to lead to psychological reductionism (Knorr-Cetina 1981). The micro/macro problem, then, consists of combining theoretical and empirical statements about micro-level and macro-level phenomena. The current proposals describing how to realize such a combination, however, are not satisfactory. Neither the decomposition of statements about macro-level phenomena into statements about micro-level phenomena nor the aggregation of micro-level phenomena for the purpose of arriving at macro-level statements has yet resulted in even approximately satisfactory explanatory theories. Similarly, the attempt to conceptualize regularities at the macro level as being actively construed within microsocial action (Cicourel 1981) has only led to reformulations of the phenomena at different levels without adding to the explanatory power of macrosocial theories.

The second meaning refers to the place of micro- and macro-level phenomena in empirical analyses. Often the *indicators* for constructed variables refer to observable units that are smaller than the constructed units. For example, the indicators for a value system (macro) are statements made by individuals (micro). In this case the micro/macro problem is seen as a technical one of appropriate measurement models. Solutions to this technical problem, however useful they may be for empirical studies, leave unsolved the theoretical problem of explaining macrosocial phenomena.

A third meaning of the micro-macro-level distinction is related to a theoretical strategy advocated by Homans. It is controversial among sociologists precisely because it is considered by some to fall outside the minimal sociological program (e.g., Mayhew 1980). Homans argues as follows: Statements about lawlike regularities are indispensable in scientific explanations. There are virtually no lawlike propositions about collective phenomena (macro) in sociology, however, and thus sociologists should borrow their most general propositions from psychology if they are not willing to restrict themselves to purely descriptive work. The micro level of sociological analyses is hence reserved for *psychological propositions* furnishing the mechanisms that make social processes work. Homans's theoretical strategy is an important step toward a theoretically anchored sociology, but this is a result more of his concern with scientific explanation than of his treatment of the master problem. The use of this strategy worked best when applied to spontaneous groups (i.e., to phenomena considered micro by many authors) and when it did not result in the explanation of macrophenomena in historical settings or in nontrivial predictions about macroprocesses.

A fourth meaning of the micro-macro-level distinction can be derived from distinctions common in *economics*. This version somewhat resembles the third because the core of microeconomics is composed of rational choice theory. The two differ in at least one respect, however: Whereas the behavioral units of Homans's micro level are exclusively individual actors, the decision-making units in microeconomic analyses may be not only individuals but also social systems such as households and firms. Have economists arrived at a theoretically satisfactory solution to the master problem? As far as we know this problem has not yet been solved (see, for instance, Weintraub 1979).

None of these micro/macro distinctions has generated a theoretically convincing answer to the question of how macrophenomena can be explained. Could it be that the problem was not adequately conceived? Does the couching of the micro/macro distinction in terms of levels prevent solutions that could lead to a theoretically meaningful macrosociology? It is to this question that we will now turn.

2. ANALYTICAL AND THEORETICAL PRIMACIES

Let us rephrase the minimal sociological program in the following way: Social conditions are always influenced by social conditions, and as a consequence society (in the wide sense in which Simmel uses the term) should always have analytical primacy for a sociologist. Thus a sociologist should be interested in how society works, and an analysis (be it an explanation, description, or interpretation) should be considered sociological only if it points to the influence of social conditions (be it on human cognitions, human actions, or social conditions themselves).

As long as one applies the minimal program to situational descriptions (e.g., Cicourel), conceptual analysis (e.g., Parsons), orienting statements (e.g., Marx), and empirical generalizations (e.g., Rogers and Shoemaker 1971), there is no need to make it theoretically more elaborate. If the program is applied to the establishment of sociological propositions, however (e.g., Zetterberg 1965), a serious complication arises. When sociological propositions are tested, assumptions about uncontrolled variables (boundary conditions) have to be made (e.g., Blalock 1974). This problem is as severe as the instability and variability of the boundary conditions. If boundary conditions are stable and uniform, then the hypothesized regularity will not be disturbed. If, conversely, these conditions vary with different time-space coordinates, they will render the proposition true at one time or locality and wrong at another. For sociology the latter is typically the case. Sociological boundary conditions are institutions and social structural conditions. They differ widely and change considerably over time, which is exactly why there is a task for sociologists and why sociological propositions are bounded by historical periods and places. Thus boundary conditions are very significant in sociology. If they could be specified, they could be added to the propositions themselves and, if technically possible, controlled for in tests of the proposition. How could we begin to get a systematic handle on these conditions? There is nothing in the minimal program that would help us in this task. The program must be expanded, but how?

In the philosophy of science there exists a formal way of dealing with this problem of boundary conditions: the inclusions of a theoretical level for which boundary conditions are more stable and more uniform. Popper (1972) calls it the search for *depth*. What could this level be in sociology? In the preclassical period (especially in the time of Hume and Adam Smith), the answer was *human nature*. There is an invariant core to human nature, so that propositions about human nature are less subject to the disturbing influence of changing boundary conditions than are propositions about social conditions. Given that human beings are involved in everything social, this seemed to be a straightforward suggestion.

In our time Homans was the first to drive this point home. He argued that only psychological propositions are general—that is, not bounded by historical periods. Therefore, we should always link social conditions to variables in general psychological propositions. What varies historically or by locality is this link. Take, for example, one of Homans's general propositions about human nature: "Men are more likely to perform an activity, the more valuable they perceive the reward of that activity to be." A sociological proposition would truly hold generally if the reward values of particular social conditions remain constant and are the same everywhere. As this is not the case, we must systematically control changing boundary conditions, and the psychological proposition tells us where to look in order to do this: For any given time and place, investigate the reward values of social conditions.

Homans thus changed the minimal program for sociology to include investigation of the link of social conditions to variables in psychological propositions. In other words, *he added to the analytical primacy of society the theoretical (or explanatory) primacy of the individual* (i.e., of human nature).

Few, if any, sociologists had made this distinction between analytical primacy and theoretical primacy. Homans himself was not very explicit on this point. To many it seemed as if Homans had actually suggested giving analytical primacy to the individual, attempting to "reduce" sociology to psychology. Small wonder that many sociologists rejected this standpoint as a complete contradiction of the minimal program of sociology. They were reinforced in this belief by the fact that Homans had concentrated his own work on small groups, leaving to others the task of showing how more complex social conditions could be linked to psychological propositions. The micro/macro problem as one of connecting levels of theory was thus explicitly introduced into sociology. Some actually tried to solve it linguistically (e.g., Hummell and Opp 1971); others, through creating macro analogues for micro problems (e.g., Blau 1964); still others, through deductive hierarchies (e.g., Hummell 1972). A controversy followed (e.g., Spinner 1973), and somehow the whole thing remained in limbo—never resolved, never truly vital for what most sociologists actually did, and yet nagging. Quite a number of sociologists who had at first followed Homans's program enthusiastically turned away and embraced the so-called unadulterated minimal program all the more longingly (foremost among them being Peter Blau).

Why did Homans's attempt to enlarge the minimal program meet such a fate? Was it wrong to assume that the individual level of human nature was more stable than the social level? Or was it wrong to assume that boundary conditions could be explored by inclusion of the individual level even if it was more stable? There are sociologists who maintain that the social level is indeed more stable than the individual level and that therefore one is ill-advised to expect an improved grasp of boundary conditions from inclusion of the individual level. As evidence for this belief, they point to the fact that social regularities often show only in aggregated data (i.e., when one abstracts from the chaotic pattern of individual accidents). Some patterns do not even emerge by aggregation but only by looking at longer historical developments, in which the individuals involved are merely pawns of sweeping historical forces. Thus even if the individual level was more stable (which it seemingly is not), it would not help us to come to grips with social boundary conditions. In this functionalists and Marxists could find common ground against the so-called reductionists. Unintended consequences of human action had already been used by Marx and Engels to combat the view that human intentions had an explanatory standing in the social sciences (see Marx [1873] 1981).

In other words, if there is any need to elaborate the minimal program of sociology (so the argument goes), it consists of adding explicitly that for sociology not only the analytical primacy but also the *theoretical (or explanatory) primacy lies with society.*

2.1. THE FAILURE TO DISTINGUISH BETWEEN INDIVIDUAL$_1$ AND INDIVIDUAL$_2$

Much confusion has surrounded the stability arguments on both sides. Although it is true that we often gain stability by aggregation, this says nothing against the assumed stability of human nature. Given that social conditions are not identical for individuals but are distributed in a certain way in a population, it is obvious that we may find considerable differences when looking only at some concrete individuals but a pattern when looking at a large sample.

The idea that individuals are pawns of sweeping historical forces is similarly confusing. If this means that at every point in time individuals are constrained by the status quo and that therefore history is unlikely to take certain random turns, it merely states that we do not expect individuals to react randomly to given social conditions. This does not speak against a constant human nature, nor does it indicate that knowledge of human nature is superfluous for the explanation of why history shows certain long-term developments. Similarly, unintended consequences point to the fact that it would be unwise to assume that individuals are not interdependent. They say nothing about the explanatory status of intentions. There are many convincing examples in the literature (for example, Merton 1957:421–434; Schelling 1971; Boudon 1977) that show intentions to be relevant to the explanation of unintended consequences.

The confusion is on both sides, however. Homans was right, in our view, in tackling the problem of incomplete sociological propositions by insisting that the sociological program must be expanded. He was also right in maintaining that the individual should have theoretical (or explanatory) primacy for sociologists. He was wrong, however, in equating the kinds of propositions needed with psychological propositions, thereby inviting the view that somehow there was a micro (psychological) level that had to be linked to a macro (sociological) level. For psychologists (and especially behavioristic psychologists) both the analytic and the theoretical primacy lie with the individual. Focus and language of psychological theories are not meant to deal with the influence of social conditions; rather, they are meant to show uniformities irrespective of social conditions. This renders them cumbersome or even useless for the job Homans had intended. This is the kind of individual level many sociologists have in mind when they reject "individualistic" explanations. In order to distinguish it from other meanings of the term, let us give it an index. "Individual_1" refers to concepts and theories about the individual within a framework for which both the analytic and the theoretical primacies lie with the individual.

By contrast, in the social sciences and certainly within sociology, we need "individual" in a different sense. "Individual_2" refers to concepts and theories about the individual within a framework within which the analytic primacy lies with society and the theoretical primacy with the individual. This is the meaning of *methodological* individualism (as opposed to, say, psychologism). What is the difference? In order to qualify for the label "individual_2" a theory must satisfy at least the following conditions (see Lindenberg 1983):

1. It must not require much information about each individual to which it is applied.
2. It must allow us to model institutional and social structural conditions as defining intermediate goals and constraints of action (i.e., it must allow the analytical primacy of society).
3. It must allow psychological (including physiological) theories to influence its assumptions. For example, the information-processing capacities of individuals must not be fixed by axiom.
4. It must allow us to express our degree of ignorance explicitly. Thus it must allow us to introduce simplifying assumptions in such a way that they can be replaced with more complex assumptions as our knowledge increases (method of decreasing abstraction).
5. It must be well corroborated as a theory that explains behavior of human beings in the aggregate, inclusive of resourceful behavior.

Let us briefly elaborate each point. First, good psychological theories of behavior may exist that require so much information about each individual that they are useless for a science that is interested in the behavior of aggregates. Take, for example, theories of clinical psychology. They were meant to deal with concrete individuals and require much information about each case. The same is true for many learning theories that ideally require the entire learning history of each concrete individual. For the social sciences the *direct* application (see point 4) of such theories is a misuse of such theories.

Second, a theory of social action for the social sciences must allow us to integrate the social and the individual *on the same level.* It must thus allow direct integration of our concerns: the analytic primacy of society and the theoretical primacy of the individual. For example, profit maximization must not be seen as a motive (i.e., $individual_1$) but as an intermediate goal created by certain institutions given resourcefulness of human beings ($individual_2$). Given that psychological theories serve a different purpose, they make it impossible to model the interrelation of the social and the individual on the same level, except in very simple cases. The fact that Homans restricted his own work to small groups with initially no institutional context simply reflects the difficulty of using an $individual_1$ theory for $individual_2$ purposes.

Third, given that $individual_2$ theories are still theories about human nature, advances in $individual_1$ theories must be capable of having an impact on $individual_2$ theories. This is possible only if the $individual_2$ theories meet requirement 4; namely, the explicit possibility to replace certain simplifying assumptions by more realistic ones. Requirement 4 is also essential for dealing with requirements 1 and 2. Its importance can hardly be overrated. Social conditions can be very complex and can affect social action in complex ways. Without the ability to simplify we would be trapped in a vicious circle: We would have to know what we are trying to find out. Conversely, without the ability to make our assumptions more realistic as we understand social conditions and human nature better, we could not improve our theories. Requirement 4 thus stipulates a process of theorizing in which we successively approximate reality. Although sociologists traditionally have been attuned to the task of simplification through ideal types, they have not been accustomed to this method of decreasing abstraction because ideal types do not allow the successive replacement of simplifying assumptions by more realistic ones.

The fifth requirement stipulates that the action theory capture human nature to such a degree that it actually works for predictions and explanations on the aggregate level. For this task it is essential that the theory accommodate not only the influence of social conditions (requirement 2) but also the possibility of creative or resourceful behavior. Many institutions exist only because human beings are also resourceful agents. For example, institutions dealing with problems of control are resourceful solutions to problems created by resourceful behavior (see North 1981). Because people do not always behave the way they are told, institutions are developed or adopted in order to induce people to follow the expectations or to neutralize the effect of their "deviance."

2.2. RATIONAL CHOICE THEORY VERSUS INDIVIDUAL$_3$

The only theory to date that can be made to meet all five requirements is the theory of rational choice in various forms of elaboration. The *homo oeconomicus* most sociologists associate with the term "rational choice" is a construction of a phase in economics in which requirements 1 and 4 seemed more important than the rest. This led to violations (or partial violations) of requirements 2, 3, and 5. Durkheim and Weber reacted against this version of *homo oeconomicus* rather than against a theory that could meet all five requirements. They also reacted against psychological theories that, even if much improved since then, violate requirements 1, 2, and 4.

Eventually sociologists created their own *homo sociologicus* (in two versions; see Lindenberg 1983), which was supposed to remedy the shortcomings of *homo oeconomicus* and of psychological theories. They thus came up with yet another meaning of "individual": the individual as a thoroughly social product. This "individual$_3$" was meant to accommodate the analytic and theoretical primacy of society. It achieved integration of the individual and the social (as opposed to Homans, who worked with individual$_1$) but at the price of abandoning a theory of action and without being able to demonstrate that a theory of action is unnecessary. With individual$_3$, requirements 4 and 5 are totally violated, whereas requirements 2 and 3 are partially violated. Only a very limited selection of institutional and social structural constraints is recognized (namely, those that make for conformity), and only a limited set of psychological assumptions are admitted (namely, those that explain socialization).

The irony of individual$_3$ is that it also prohibits the proper analysis of institutions, although it was devised to facilitate just that. As mentioned earlier, many institutions are the resourceful response to resourceful behavior; individual$_3$ cannot possibly accommodate this kind of behavior. Another irony is this: "Individual$_3$" creates a problem of scope (micro/macro)—namely, the question of how the analysis of interaction, situations, and small groups should be linked to the analysis of large social and cultural systems. At the same time, "individual$_3$" makes it impossible to erect an explanatory structure in which these different kinds of analyses could be integrated, as it neglects the explanatory importance of theories of action.

To summarize, it is useful to distinguish three different meanings of the term "individual" in three different contexts. Individual$_1$ is used in a context in which the analytical and theoretical primacy lies with the

	individual$_1$	*individual*$_2$	*individual*$_3$
analytical primacy	individual	society	society
theoretical primacy	individual	individual	society

FIG. 5.1

individual; individual$_2$ is used in a context in which the analytical primacy lies with society and the theoretical primacy with the individual; and individual$_3$ is used in contexts in which both analytical and theoretical primacy are given to society (see fig. 5.1).

If individual$_1$ is used for sociological purposes, the problem of *theoretical levels* (micro/macro) arises because individual$_1$ theories are unable to integrate the individual and the social. In this sense the level problem is the result of the misuse of a theory, and from that we cannot expect much regarding the solution to this problem.

If individual$_3$ is used for sociological purposes, the problem of *scope* arises as a micro/macro problem. This problem cannot be solved, however, because there is no explanatory structure to integrate micro- and macroanalyses. In other words, without laws we are unable to explain anything, and if we are unable to explain, the problem of scope (micro/macro) can at best be a linguistic problem.

Only individual$_2$ allows both: the integration of the social and the individual on one level *and* explanation. Progress in this context is the shift from problems that lead to a dead end to problems the solution of which contributes cumulatively to our knowledge. Shifting from individual$_1$ and individual$_3$ to individual$_2$ constitutes such a progressive problem shift, in our view. What kinds of theoretical and methodological issues *do* arise through this shift?

3. ISSUES INTRODUCED BY THE USE OF INDIVIDUAL$_2$ FOR SOCIOLOGICAL PURPOSES

Given the analytical primacy of society and the theoretical primacy of the individual, two problems must be dealt with in order to move in the direction of a solution to the master question (i.e., how to explain macrosocial phenomena). The first is called the "bridge problem" (Lindenberg 1981) and the second, the "problem of transformation" (Lindenberg 1977). We will explicate both problems and sketch some solutions. In addition, from a methodological point of view the structure of deductive arguments for the explanation of collective phenomena will be briefly analyzed.

3.1. THE BRIDGE PROBLEM

The central point about $individual_2$ is that the social and the individual are linked at the same level. For this purpose some bridges must be built, and we have just argued that rational choice theory allows this to happen in such a way that we do not lose sight of either the influence of social conditions or the fact that individuals can be the focus of initiative.

Rational choice theory has basically three elements: wants, subjective probabilities, and alternatives. The bridge problem consists of formulating propositions about the influence of social conditions on these three elements and of formulating propositions under which conditions they are subject to individual initiative. For example, it can be argued that individuals have basic *wants* but that institutions and the social structure provide the "production function" (see Becker 1976; Lindenberg 1984) for these wants. In other words, social conditions determine what individuals are materially striving for. In this vein Adam Smith distinguished three classes: landowners, entrepreneurs, and laborers. Although the basic wants for individuals in all three classes are the same, they strive for different (and possibly conflicting) goals because of the institutions existing in Britain at the time: landowners maximize rents, entrepreneurs profit, and laborers wage. Similarly, Downs (1957) argued that politicians in democracies, no matter what their convictions, must maximize votes. An example of social influence on *subjective probabilities* is given by Olson (1965); rising group size diminishes the subjective probability that the individual contribution to the production of a collective good has a noticeable effect. The question here is not whether these propositions are true as stated but that they exemplify what is meant by bridge propositions. *Alternative courses of action* are obviously influenced by social conditions. For example, certain alternatives are approved and others disapproved, which affects their price. Laws, norms, income, networks, technology—these social conditions affect the set of feasible alternatives, and propositions about this influence are needed to explain social behavior.

One can easily see that the so-called structuralism (although often thought to be an alternative to rational choice theory) consists of the formulation of certain bridge propositions for a (mostly unstated) theory of action. Any rational choice theory applied in sociology would require such structural assumptions, but these assumptions are not enough. Individuals are also clever in discovering opportunities created by the structural constraints; that is, they are endowed with the ability to enlarge the set of structurally given feasible alternatives. For example, certain entrepreneurs perceive the potential of a technological invention for increasing their profit. Others are ingenious in finding tax loopholes; still others create religious organizations that draw large followings.

Bridge propositions, together with rational choice theory, thus explain individual behavior as *social* behavior in two senses: (*a*) socially constrained behavior and (*b*) resourceful behavior that is made possible by certain social conditions. Given the analytical primacy of society, the formulation of bridge propositions is the main task in explaining social behavior. Rational choice theory only provides the vehicle by which this is made possible.

3.2. THE PROBLEM OF TRANSFORMATION

The explanation of individual behavior as social behavior does not yet solve the master problem. Specifically it does not tell us how a particular collective phenomenon, such as an institution, arises from social action. For example, knowing how individuals vote in an election does not tell us the distribution of seats in parliament for the various parties. For that we need to know how the votes are "transformed" into parliament seats. We must know the relevant institutions governing the electoral process. Even voters are often ignorant of these rules, although the rules determine the final outcome in an important way. Obviously this is not merely a technical problem of aggregation; it is a *theoretical* problem (of which the technical problem of aggregation may at best be one aspect; see also Knorr-Cetina 1981). This theoretical problem is not identical to linking levels of analysis, for two reasons. First, the individual and the social levels have already been integrated into the explanation of social behavior (bridge problem); and, second, the transformation of social behavior into certain collective phenomena in nontrivial cases is itself a social process rather than a logical connection of different levels.

In order to take all relevant conditions of transformation into account, very detailed analyses must be carried out (see, for instance, Raub 1984:chap. 4). Given that rational choice theory does not govern the process of transformation, the question arises regarding how to detect the conditions relevant for solving the transformation problem in a particular problem area.

In our opinion, *background knowledge* plays an important role. Many descriptive sociological studies, especially those in the "qualitative" and ethnographic tradition, form a rich source for attacking the problem of transformation because they focus on rules, procedures, and other relevant conditions. The same holds true for historical and legal studies. That personal experience can also represent an invaluable source of background knowledge is vividly reflected in the history of Lipset's research on union democracy. Lipset's familiarity with the union (Lipset 1964) enabled him to detect several conditions that are crucial for the transformation of democratic activities of members into a democratically functioning union. Background knowledge is similarly useful for solving the bridge problem. In light of this analysis it seems fruitless to search for a *formal* integration of results from, say, ethnographic studies (micro) with so-called macrotheory about societies.

To specify constellations of social conditions under which certain actions do or do not result in a particular collective effect is required for the completeness of deductive arguments in sociological analyses. Specification of such constellations also facilitates the search for changes that must be brought about in order to prevent certain seemingly unavoidable unwanted effects. For instance, one of the examples Merton uses in his analysis of self-fulfilling prophecies refers to the transformation of the actions of depositors intent on preserving their savings into the insolvency of the bank that keeps their saving accounts. Merton suggests that this disastrous transformation of individual actions into a collective phenomenon that results from the working of a self-fulfilling prophecy can be put to a halt by creating "appropriate institutional and administrative conditions" (1957:435–436). Unfortunately, he does not specify which conditions are required; that is, which changes in banking regulations would prevent the insolvency of a bank, even if rumors influence the behavior of its depositors (see Wippler 1978).

Other examples of seemingly unavoidable negative effects that can be clarified by specifying constellations of conditions relevant for the transformation problem are the tendency toward oligarchy in constitutionally democratic organizations (see Wippler 1981, 1982) and the high level of frustration that can be found among groups in exactly those situations that offer individuals many opportunities for the improvement of their situation (see Boudon 1977:especially chap. 5).

3.3. THE DUAL STRUCTURE OF SOCIOLOGICAL EXPLANATIONS

What are the methodological consequences when attention is given to the bridge problem and to the problem of transformation? A two-step argument is required for taking into account both that individual choices are made under institutional and structural constraints and that the transformation of individual actions into collective phenomena is mediated by (often complex) constellations of institutional and structural conditions. This dual structure of explanation has been described in more detail elsewhere (see Lindenberg 1977; Lindenberg and Wippler 1978; Raub and Voss 1981). Here we restrict ourselves to a sketch of this logical structure.

The first step consists of the explanation of "individual effects" (i.e., the behavior of the actors involved). These effects are derived from general assumptions about human nature (i.e., the principles of rational choice theory) in conjunction with initial conditions (i.e., the results of bridge propositions). The connection of these individual effects with the collective phenomenon to be explained (the collective effect) in the second step requires sentences that yield such a connection. As this deductive step represents the methodological part of the problem of transformation, these sentences are called "transformation rules." In the most simple case a transformation rule consists of a partial definition connecting individual effects with the collective effect. In most interesting cases, however, more assumptions are needed in order to complete the second step. For instance, transformation rules may take the form of mathematical models or statements about institutional rules. They are logically equivalent to the general assumptions about human nature in the first step. Thus in the second step of sociological explanations, collective effects are derived from the transformation rules and a constellation of conditions (boundary conditions) that contain, among others, the individual effects contained in the first step.

Although the dual structure of explanation refers only to a simple building block, theories of sociologically interesting collective phenomena may be quite complex and constructed as a combination of several such building blocks. Social circumstances that are introduced as given in the context of a particular explanation—either as initial condition in the first or as boundary condition in the second step—may in turn form the explananda and vice versa. Collective phenomena can thus be linked in an explanatory way. The explained collective phenomena become, in turn, the conditions that help to explain other collective phenomena. In short, we need both requirements: full acknowledgment of the analytical primacy of the society *and* explanation.

4. CONCLUSION

Usually the question of how to relate microphenomena and macrophenomena in sociological theory is treated as a problem of levels. Depending on the meaning that is given to the micro/macro distinction, the proposed solutions reduce this theoretical problem factually to one of language use, to a technical problem of indicators, or to the logical problem of reduction or aggregation. None of these solutions has led to a theoretically meaningful macrosociology. We therefore maintain that the problem has not been stated adequately. We propose to conceive the problem differently, starting with the distinction between the analytical primacy of the social (in accordance with the minimal sociological program) and the theoretical primacy of the individual (in accordance with the requirements for explanations).

Reference to individuals in the context of sociology may take different forms; which form it takes depends on the context in which individuals are placed. In a context in which both the analytical and the theoretical primacy are given to the individual ($individual_1$), theories are unable to integrate the individual and the social. In a context in which both primacies are given to the social ($individual_3$), theories are unable to explain anything. Only when analytical primacy is given to the social and theoretical primacy is given to the individual ($individual_2$) is it possible to integrate the social and the individual on one level *and* to explain.

Using $individual_2$ makes it clear that the explanation of collective phenomena should be a two-step explanation in which the first consists of the *social* explanation of human behavior (the bridge problem) and the second consists of showing how social behavior is transformed into collective phenomena (the problem of transformation). Although much remains to be learned about both steps, it is sufficiently apparent that they jointly constitute an answer to the master problem of how macrosocial phenomena can be explained without getting sidetracked into a seemingly barren concern with the integration of micro and macro levels of analysis.

The problem shift we propose also implies two other shifts. First, the search for general *sociological* laws that are meant to hold independent of institutional and under structural changes is fruitless (a similar point is made by Boudon 1984). It only leads to the ill-conceived problem of levels. Second, background knowledge (whatever its source) is of crucial importance for solving the bridge problem and the problem of transformation in nontrivial cases. Generally, descriptive studies are thus much more relevant for sociology as an explanatory enterprise than current journals and university curricula would have us believe.

REFERENCES

Becker, Gary S. 1976. *The Economic Approach to Human Behavior*. Chicago: University of Chicago Press.

Blalock, Hubert H., Jr. 1974. Beyond Ordinal Measurement: Weak Tests of Stronger Theories, pp. 424–456 in *Measurement in the Social Sciences*. London: Macmillan.

Blau, Peter M. 1964. *Exchange and Power in Social Life*. New York: John Wiley.

Boudon, Raymond. 1977. *Effets pervers et ordre social*. Paris: Presses Universitaires de France.

———1984. *La place du désordre, critique des théories de changement social*. Paris: Presses Universitaires de France.

Cicourel, Aaron V. 1981. Notes on the Integration of Micro- and Macro-Levels of Analysis, pp. 51–80 in Karin Knorr-Cetina and Aaron V. Cicourel, eds., *Advances in Social Theory and Methodology*. London: Routledge & Kegan Paul.

Collins, Randall. 1981. On the Microfoundations of Macrosociology. *American Sociological Review* 86:984–1014.

Downs, Anthony. 1957. *An Economic Theory of Democracy*. New York: Harper & Row.

Gadenne, Volker. 1979. Die Unvollständigkeit sozialwissenschaftlicher Hypothesen. Eine Analyse des Problems der Exhaustion, pp. 95–116 in Hans Albert and Kurt H. Stapf, eds., *Theorie und Erfahrung*. Stuttgart: Klett-Cotta.

Hechter, Michael, ed. 1983. *The Microfoundations of Macrosociology*. Philadelphia: Temple University Press.

Homans, George C. 1974. *Social Behavior: Its Elementary Forms* (1961). New York: Harcourt.

Hummell, Hans J. 1972. Zur Problematik der Ableitung in sozialwissenschaftlichen Aussagensystemen. Ein Plädoyer für Formalisierung. *Zeitschrift für Soziologie* 1:118–138.

Hummell, Hans J. and Karl-Dieter Opp. 1971. *Die Reduzierbarkeit von Soziologie auf Psychologie, eine These, ihr Test und ihre theoretische Bedeutung*. Braunschweig: Friedrich-Vieweg & Sohn.

Knorr-Cetina, Karin D. 1981. The Micro-Sociological Challenge of Macro-Sociology: Towards a Reconstruction of Social Theory and Methodology, pp. 1–47 in Karin Knorr-Cetina and Aaron V. Cicourel, eds., *Advances in Social Theory and Methodology*. London: Routledge & Kegan Paul.

Lindenberg, Siegwart. 1977. Individuelle Effekte, kollektive Phänomene und das Problem der Transformation, pp. 46–84 in Klaus Eichner and Werner Habermehl, eds., *Probleme der Erklärung sozialen Verhaltens*. Meisenheim: Hain.

———. 1981. Erklärung als Modellbau. Zur soziologischen Nutzung von Nutzentheorien, pp. 20–35 in W. Schulte, ed., *Soziologie in der Gesellschaft*. Bremen: Zentraldruckerei der Universität Bremen.

———. 1983. The New Political Economy: Its Potential and Limitations for the Social Sciences in General and for Sociology in Particular, pp. 7–66 in Wolfgang Sodeur, ed., *Ökonomische Erklärungen sozialen Verhaltens*. Duisburg: Verlag der Sozialwissenschaftlichen Kooperative.

———. 1984. Normen und die Allokation sozialer Wertschätzung, pp. 169–191 in Horst Todt, ed., *Normengeleitetes Verhalten in den Sozialwissenschaften*. Berlin: Dunker & Humblot.

Lindenberg, Siegwart, and Reinhard Wippler. 1978. Theorienvergleich: Elemente der Rekonstruktion, pp. 219–231 in Karl O. Hondrich and J. Matthes, eds., *Theorienvergleich in den Sozialwissenschaften*. Neuwied: Luchterhand.

Lipset, Seymour M. 1964. The Biography of a Research Project. Union Democracy, pp. 96–120 in P.E. Hammond, ed., *Sociologists at Work*. New York: Basic Books.

Marx, Karl. 1981. Nachwort zur zweiten Auflage des ersten Bandes des "Kapital," pp. 424–427 in Karl Marx and Frederick Engels, eds., *Ausgewählte Schriften in zwei Bänden*. Band I (1873). Berlin: Dietz.

Mayhew, Bruce H. 1980. Structuralism versus Individualism. Part 1. Shadowboxing in the Dark. *Social Forces* 59:335–375.

Merton, Robert K. 1957. *Social Theory and Social Structure*. rev. and enlarged ed. Glencoe, Ill.: Free Press.

North, Douglas C. 1981. *Structure and Change in Economic History*. New York: Norton.

Olson, Mancur. 1965. *The Logic of Collective Action*. New York: Schocken.

Opp, Karl-Dieter. 1979. *Individualistische Sozialwissenschaft, Arbeitsweise und Probleme individualistisch und kollektivistisch orientierter Sozialwissenschaften*. Stuttgart: Ferdinand Enke.

Popper, Karl R. 1972. *Objective Knowledge. An Evolutionary Approach*. Oxford: Clarendon.

Raub, Werner. 1984. *Rationale Akteure, institutionelle Regelungen und Interdependenzen*. Frankfurt: Verlag Peter Lang.

Raub, Werner, and T. Voss. 1981. *Individuelles Handeln und gesellschaftliche Folgen, Das individualistische Programm in den Sozialwissenschaften*. Neuwied: Luchterhand.

Rogers, Everett M. and F. F. Shoemaker. 1971. *Communication of Innovations. A Cross-Cultural Approach*. New York: Free Press.

Schelling, Thomas C. 1971. Dynamic Models of Segregation. *Journal of Mathematical Sociology* 1:143–186.

Spinner, Helmut J. 1973. Science without Reduction: A Criticism of Reductionism with Special Reference to Hummell and Opp's "Sociology without Sociology." *Inquiry* 16:16–94.

Weintraub, E. Roy. 1979. *Microfoundations: The Compatibility of Microeconomics and Macroeconomics*. Cambridge: Cambridge University Press.

Wippler, Reinhard. 1978. Nicht-intendierte soziale Folgen individueller Handlungen. *Soziale Welt* 29:155–179.

———. 1981. Erklärung unbeabsichtigter Handlungsfolgen. Ziel oder Meilenstein soziologischer Theorienbildung? pp. 246–261 in Joachim Matthes, ed., *Lebenswelt und soziale Probleme*. Frankfurt: Campus.

———. 1982. The Generation of Oligarchic Structures in Constitutionally Democratic Organizations, pp. 43–62 in Werner Raub, ed., *Theoretical Models and Empirical Analyses*. Utrecht: E. S. Publications.

Zetterberg, Hans L. 1965. *On Theory and Verification in Sociology*. 3d enlarged ed. Totowa, N.J.: Bedminster Press.

CHAPTER SIX

Microfoundations and Macrosocial Behavior

James S. Coleman

Much of social theory involves accounting for the functioning of some kind of social system. In most sociological research, however, observations focus not on the system as a whole but on some part of it. In fact, the most natural unit of observation is the individual; and in the development of quantitative methods of research dependence on individual-level data, most often in the form of interviews, sometimes in the form of administrative records of behavior, and sometimes in still other forms, has increased greatly. This has led to a widening gap within the discipline between theory and research: Social theory continues to be concerned with the functioning of social systems of behavior, whereas empirical research—particularly quantitative research—is largely concerned with explaining individual behavior.

This focus on individual behavior as the phenomenon to be explained is not completely misplaced in sociology, nor is it new. For example, in one of the sociological classics, *Suicide*, first published in 1897 (1951), Durkheim attempted to explain suicide rates in different societies and among different population groups within a society. Although he described the suicide rate as a *social* fact and was engaged in a polemic against social psychology, Durkheim was engaged in explanation of individual behavior. The only aspect of this work that made it social was that the explanatory variables Durkheim used were explicitly social: the absence of strong social norms, which he termed the degree of anomie in society, or the degree of social isolation among individuals.

However, given that much of social theory is concerned not with individual behavior but with the functioning of social systems of behavior, and given that the most common and most natural observations are of individuals, a central intellectual problem in the discipline is the movement from the individual level, where observations are made, to the systemic level, where the problem of interest lies. This has been called the "micro-to-macro problem," and it is a problem that is pervasive in the social sciences generally. In economics there is microeconomic theory and macroeconomic theory; and one of the central deficiencies in economic theory is the weakness of the linkage between them, a weakness papered over with the idea of "aggregation" and with a ubiquitous concept in macroeconomic theory, the "representative agent."

What I propose to do in this essay is to show some of the problems involved in making a proper micro-to-macro transition, to point to some instances in which the transition has been made, and to indicate steps toward doing so in some areas where it has not been done successfully. In the process I will discuss Protestantism and the rise of capitalism, theories of revolution, economic markets, marriage markets, labor force problems and job markets, panics, and collective decisions.

To explore what is involved in making a proper transition from micro to macro, I will turn first to an instance in which it was not done properly. The example is another classic in sociology, Max Weber's *The Protestant Ethic and the Spirit of Capitalism* (1958). At one level of detail Weber is simply expressing a macrosocial proposition: The religious ethic that characterized those societies that became Protestant during the Reformation (and particularly those that were Calvinistic) contained values that facilitated the growth of capitalist economic organization.

At a finer level of detail Weber's single proposition breaks into three: one having an independent variable characterizing the society, with the dependent variable characterizing the individual; a second with both independent and dependent variables characterizing the individual; and a third with the independent variable characterizing the individual and the dependent variable characterizing the society. Thus the proposition system begins and ends at macro levels, but in between it dips down to the level of individual. The propositions may be put, somewhat crudely, as follows:

1. Protestant religious doctrine generates certain values in its adherents.
2. Individuals with certain values (referred to in item 1) adopt certain kinds of orientations toward economic behavior.

3. Certain orientations toward economic behavior (referred to in item 2) on the part of individuals help bring about capitalist economic organization in a society. (The central orientation to economic behavior is characterized by Weber as "antitraditionalism.")

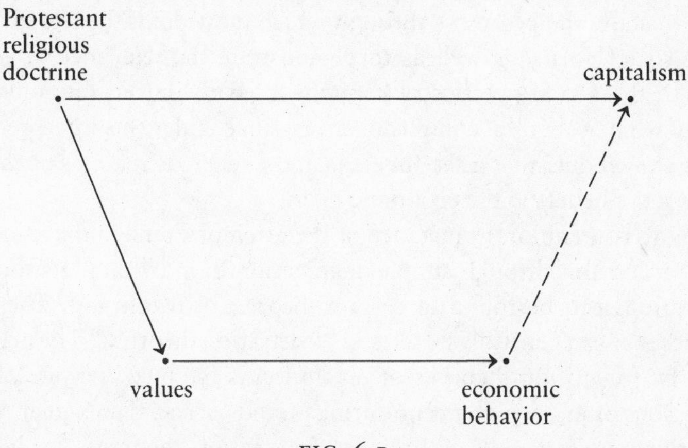

FIG. 6.1

Figure 6.1 shows a way of diagramming such multilevel systems of propositions. The upper horizontal arrow represents the macro-level proposition. The three connected arrows beginning at the same point going down to a lower level and back up to the final point represent the three linked propositions labeled 1, 2, and 3.

In this set of propositions the third is of most interest, for it is the third which moves back up from the individual level to the societal level. Thus in contrast to Durkheim's work on suicide, in which the phenomenon of ultimate interest could be described as individual behavior, here the phenomenon of ultimate interest is clearly macrosocial, characterizing the society as a whole. It is in the third proposition that Weber's theory is weakest, however, for it is here that some combination of individual actions is necessary to generate a macrosocial outcome. The orientations toward action of a worker in a capitalist enterprise are not the same as those of an entrepreneur, yet both are necessary to the enterprise. The orientations necessary to begin such enterprise are not the same as those necessary to continue it. In short, capitalist economic organization is a system of action, and to show how that system comes into being, or even how it functions once in being, the aggregate value orientation of the population is not sufficient.

Some would defend Weber on the grounds that he was not attempting to account for the rise of capitalism but only the "spirit" of capitalism. This, I believe, is a rather weak defense, for if Weber were attempting merely to account for the spirit of capitalism, then is that to be regarded as a property of the society (that is, a shared norm) or as a constellation of beliefs on the part of the individual Protestant? If the former, Weber failed to show the processes through which individuals' beliefs give rise to the social norm (as well as to demonstrate the relevance of such a norm to the actual practice of capitalism). If the latter, one must ask exactly what Weber's accomplishment is, since under this interpretation he has shown only that a set of beliefs in the religious realm is consistent with a set of beliefs in the economic realm.

A more contemporary instance of the attempt to make the micro-to-macro transition through simple aggregation of individual attitudes or orientations can be found in certain theories of revolution. These are theories that can generally be termed "frustration theories." The problem taken by frustration theorists of revolution is the puzzling one of why revolutions often seem to occur during periods of social change in which conditions are generally improving. Frustration theorists resolve this problem by arguing that the improving conditions in the society create frustration on the part of individual members of the society, leading to revolution. Like Weber's propositions in the Protestant ethic, there are three linked relations. The first is from the system level to the individual level; the second is wholly at the individual level; and the third is from the individual level to the system level. Figure 6.2 shows these propositions diagrammatically.

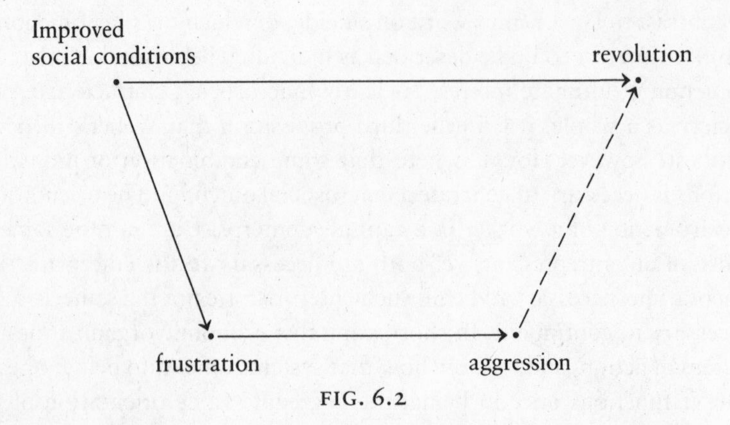

FIG. 6.2

The first relation takes several forms, depending on the source of frustration as viewed by the theorist: "short-term setback" in the theory of

James Davies (1962); "relative deprivation" in the work of Ted Gurr (1970); rising expectations induced by rapid change in the work of others. The second relation is merely a frustration-aggression proposition from psychology. The third relation is implicit: a simple aggregation of individual aggression somehow to magically produce a social product (that is, revolution). Yet this bypasses important social processes: A revolution involves organization and the interplay of actions on the part of a number of actors.

In both instances the micro-to-macro transition is made simply by aggregation of individual orientations, attitudes, or beliefs. If the theoretical problem is, however, a problem involving the functioning of a social *system*, as it is in the case of explaining the rise of a capitalist economy, or in explaining the occurrence of a revolution, then it should be obvious that the appropriate transition cannot involve the simple aggregation of individual behavior.

WHAT IS AN APPROPRIATE TRANSITION FROM MICRO TO MACRO?

If the two foregoing examples illustrate failures to make the transition from micro level to macro level, then what can be said about successful transitions? A first observation is that good social history makes the transition successfully. Good social history, attempting to establish a causal connection between, for example, the advent of Calvinist religious doctrine and the rise of a capitalist economy in the West, shows not only how the doctrine affects the behavior of individuals but how that behavior then comes to be combined, how the social organization takes place which constitutes capitalist enterprise. After reading such history the reader would be left in no doubt about the character of the argument—about whether a change in workers' behavior, an increase in entrepreneurial behavior, more diligent behavior on the part of managers, or all of these were claimed to be the result of Protestantism and to lead to the growth of capitalism.

It is one thing, however, to be able to trace the development of social organization in a particular instance and quite another to develop generalizations about such processes. It is still another to construct models of the micro-to-macro process. Clearly some form of interdependence must be modeled in cases such as those just described, for the phenomenon to be explained involves social organization, not merely aggregated individual behavior.

The most successful example of modeling this transition is the model of a perfect market in neoclassical economic theory. The starting point is a set of individuals, each possessing a particular utility function, a particular set of goods, and a behavior principle that states that a person will act so as to maximize utility subject to the initial resources with which he or she begins. The ending point is a general equilibrium: a set of prices for goods and an equilibrium distribution of goods among the actors. This achievement was, I believe, an extraordinary intellectual feat. The feat was accomplished for an idealized social system, one in which actors were independent, goods being exchanged were private, and tastes were fixed. Close inspection of this theory can give some indication of the extent of the social assumptions. There are, it is assumed, no social barriers to inhibit information flow and exchange agreements; there is complete intermixing among a large set of independent actors; there are no consumption externalities (that is, no social interdependencies in consumption); the goods exchanged are alienable and not inherently attached to the person, as is true for labor services.

There is another difficulty to this accomplishment as well: It has somewhat the character of an existence proof in mathematics. It specifies that with appropriate properties for the utility functions there will be equilibrium; but it cannot be directly applied to particular situations to make the micro-to-macro transition. Nevertheless, it provides a general intellectual framework for making the transition, a model to shape the way we conceive of this transition.

The question then arises as to whether some modification can allow the transition to be made in areas of social science other than economics. The answer, I believe, is yes. I have been working on the development of such models for some time, using the perfect market model with modifications. In this I have employed the strategy of assuming a specific form of the utility function, which allows empirical use of the model with quantitative data. Various applications of this model have been made: to community decision making, resource exchange among interest groups, so-called influence processes in a social network, and others. One arena to which application can be made, and in which some work has been done, is the so-called marriage market. There is a demographic phenomenon known as the "marriage squeeze," which occurs in this way: When there is a sharp increase in the marriage rate, as there was after World War II, a problem exists for the cohorts of females born about the time of the increase or shortly thereafter. There are not enough men for them to marry. Men marry women who are, on average, two years younger than themselves. This means that the normal mates for females born in

1946 would be males born in or around 1944. The 1946 cohort was large, however, and the 1944 cohort was small. Thus there is a marriage squeeze for women; a larger number never marry, and a larger number marry younger men or much older men who are divorced or widowed. Something like the reverse is true if there is a sudden drop in the birth rate: a marriage squeeze for men.

The problem lies in the fact that given this squeeze produced by a sudden birth rate change, it is not at all clear what will "give"—how the scarce men will be distributed among the surplus of women. The absence of a model for assortative mating by age when there are cohort size fluctuations means that demographers have been stymied in their goal of developing what is called a two-sex population model for moving a population forward through generations.

It is clear that marriage can be seen as taking place in a kind of market but one that is quite special, with each actor having only one commodity—himself or herself—to barter and with exchange rates governed by the constraint of one-to-one rather than by exchange at equal value. Models for such matching marriage markets have been developed—for example, by Gale and Shapley (1962), Becker (1974), Sanderson (1980), and Schoen (1983). Theorems have been proved about the stability of particular matching algorithms (Roth 1983). Thus solutions for the marriage squeeze problem of demographers have been attempted that would facilitate a two-sex population model, but this is only a beginning. It is necessary to formulate a model that when supplied with age-by-age marriage rates over a sufficient number of years with varying cohort sizes will give estimates of the utilities of men and women of particular ages for women and men of particular ages, and the structure of the process through which marriages take place.[1] This in turn would lead to predictions about marriage rates when birth rates are known.

This is a case in which the model of the market process provides the appropriate device for moving from the micro to the macro level. It does so in effect by solving simultaneously a set of individual maximizations, which results in a macro-level outcome that is internally consistent. Put in the same diagrammatic form as figures 6.1 and 6.2, this is shown crudely in figure 6.3.

An illustration that shows the feasibility of micro-to-macro models in the area of matching markets is the procedure by which graduates of medical school are matched with hospitals for residency training. Hospitals submit lists of first choices, second choices, and so on, for their residency positions, and applicants submit their choices of hospitals,

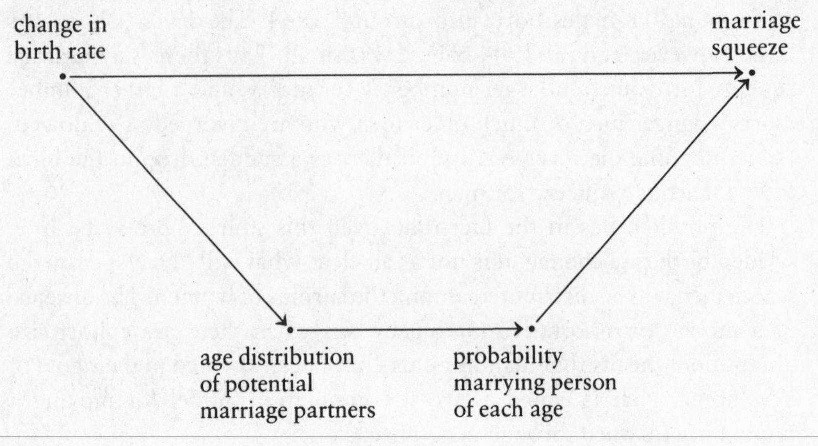

FIG. 6.3

rank-ordered. A computer algorithm, in use since 1957, matches hospitals and applicants. The algorithm constitutes a matching process, and a stability theorem for this process has been proved showing that assuming no changes in preference orders, no resident and hospital that are not matched would both prefer each other to the hospital and resident, respectively, with which they are matched (see Roth 1983).

This example illustrates another point as well. Before the matching algorithm was introduced, matches occurred through bilateral agreements in a market that was in continual turmoil. The algorithm introduced an *institution* that imposed a particular structure on the system. A model of the market before this institution would necessarily be somewhat different from the model of the market after the institution came into being. Thus the micro-to-macro model not only begins with numbers of applicants and places and with preference orders for each actor; it also contains, implicitly or explicitly, a model of the institution, process, or structure through which the matches take place.[2]

COLLECTIVE BEHAVIOR

The preceding example may suggest that any model for the micro-to-macro transition that begins with rational actors at the micro level must take the form of an exchange market. This is not the case, as the following example illustrates.

Some attempts have been made to explain the occurrence of a panic, often leading to injury and death, when a fire alarm is sounded in a

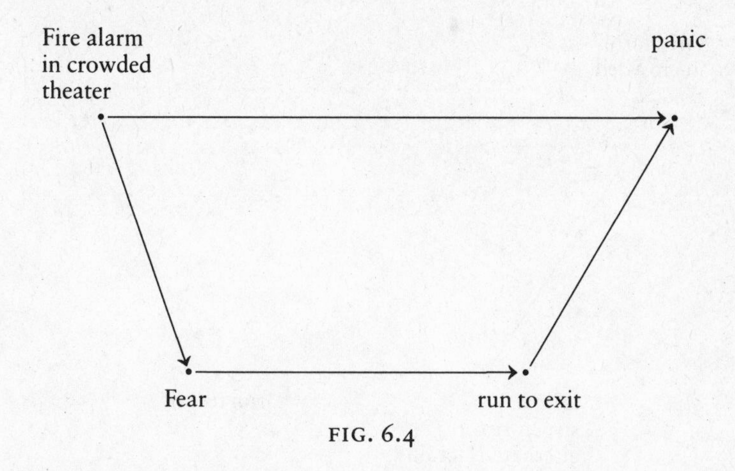

FIG. 6.4

crowded public place. The macro-level relation is the effect of sounding a fire alarm in a crowded building in producing the crowd behavior known as panic. Earlier attempts at explaining this dipped down to the micro level in the following way: The fire alarm created in each person a sense of panic or fear of being trapped. This leads to running toward an exit, which, simultaneous with others' running, leads to jamming and blocking of the exits. The propositions are shown in figure 6.4.

A different explanation was subsequently posed by Mintz (1941) and Brown (1965). Brown showed that the fire alarm created for each person a prisoner's dilemma situation in which purely rational behavior would lead to running: If others were orderly, one was better off dashing toward an exit, whereas if others were not orderly but dashed toward an exit, one was also better off dashing toward an exit than staying behind. Figure 6.5 shows the set of propositions involved.

This explanation has the virtue of accounting for the phenomenon without assuming any form of irrationality, as was necessary in the first explanation, although the micro-to-macro transition is properly carried out in both models. It is deficient, however, in explaining too much. It accounts for the existence of panics and jams but fails to predict the many cases in which no panic occurs and in which persons exit in an orderly fashion. A modification of the explanation is this: In contrast to the prisoner's dilemma situation, there is communication in the crowded theater among those inside. Thus each person has an additional option besides running madly or walking in an orderly fashion: This is to transfer partial control over this action to others, running if they run but walking if they walk. Under what conditions will an individual do so

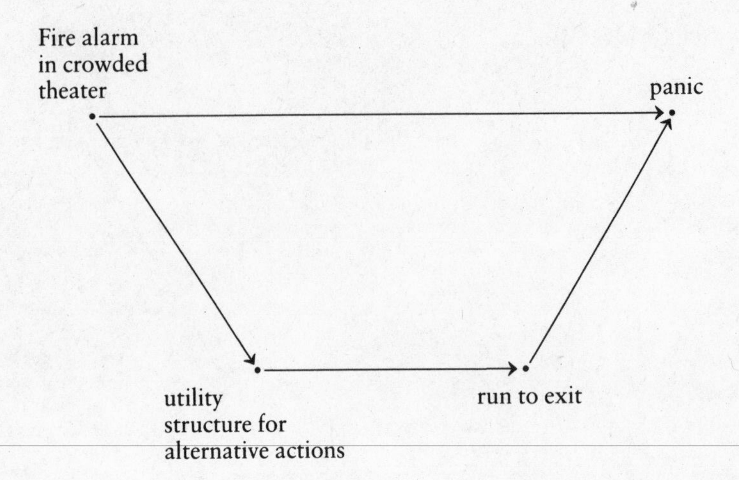

FIG. 6.5

rather than to run unilaterally, as the prisoner's dilemma would dictate? It can be shown (Coleman 1981) that it is rational for one to do so if and only if others have transferred to oneself partial control over their actions. Figure 6.6 shows this modified set of propositions.

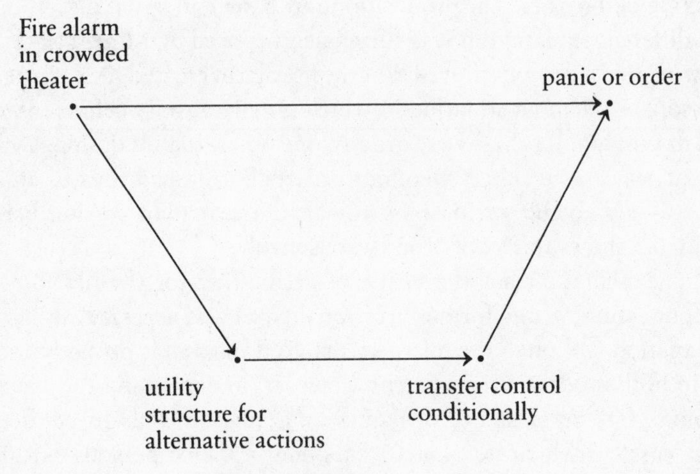

FIG. 6.6

This modification allows a considerably richer set of predictions. First, it does not predict that panic will always occur. Second, it predicts that certain persons, particularly those who are at the center of attention (such as actors on the stage when the alarm is sounded), will be less likely to run than others, and most likely to run will be those who are likely to be unobserved by others.

As this example illustrates, macro-level phenomena—a panic in this case—can be generated by rational actions that involve no exchange whatsoever. In the model based on the prisoner's dilemma, the individual will take an action unilaterally; that is, dashing toward an exit. In the elaboration of this, under certain conditions, the individual may take another action unilaterally instead: to unilaterally transfer to others in the theater control over the decision to run or to walk.

Such unilateral transfer of control over one's actions, a transfer made rationally, may occur in a wide range of situations quite different from panic. It is the operational description of what we do when we place trust in another person or persons. The widespread role of trust in society, and even systems of trust, indicate that this kind of rational action (which may, as in the panic model, be taken conditionally on certain actions of others) may be important in a number of micro-to-macro transitions, just as exchange in a market context is important in a number of others.

STRATIFICATION RESEARCH IN SOCIOLOGY

It is useful to turn to a body of research that is central to sociology in order to ask how the micro-to-macro transition might be made properly. The body of research is in "social stratification" or "status attainment," and it almost completely fails to make the micro-to-macro transition. Ordinarily research in social stratification treats a change of job as if it were an individual decision: The determinants are background characteristics of the individual, aspects of life history that affect occupational mobility. The destination occupation is regarded as unlimited in number of open jobs; taking a new job of a particular type is analyzed in exactly the same manner as the change of an attitude. Jobs are scarce commodities, however, and a new job is obtained only in competition with others. Or, to put it differently, taking a new job involves *two* mutually contingent decisions: a decision of the job seeker and a decision of the organization in which the job is located. Both decisions are made in the presence of other competing jobs or job seekers.

In short, as in marriage it is a matching process, carried out in a market structure. As in any such matching process, the final action depends not merely on the job seeker's interest in this job but also on the job-seeker's interest in other available jobs; and not merely upon the organization's interest in this job seeker but also on its interest in other available job seekers. In addition, these actions depend on the interest of other organizations in this and other job seekers, and in other job seekers' interests in this and other organizations. That is, the action depends intrinsically and directly on the distribution of other job seekers and of other jobs and of the distribution of interest at each point in these distributions. Thus only if the research problem remains at an individual level (What should one do to improve occupational position, assuming everyone else remained as at present?) can this interdependent structure of the labor market be ignored.

In general, the use of sample surveys to study social stratification makes it necessary to ignore the interdependence. There has been, however, an evolution in the use of sample surveys which brings them closer to macrosocial problems. One stage of this evolution is the use of a well-defined social unit, such as the American adult population. By this single change the work becomes potentially relevant to macrosocial outcomes, for the sample now characterizes a social unit about which statements might be made. A milestone marking this evolutionary stage is Blau and Duncan's *The American Occupational Structure* (1967).

The uncompleted nature of the evolution, however, is evidenced by the fact that the relations studied by Blau and Duncan—and by others working in this tradition—remain wholly at the individual level. The nationally representative sample allows descriptive characterization of the occupational distributions and movements but cannot provide parameters for a model of the labor market process, because individuals' movements are treated as wholly independent. Figure 6.7 shows the individual-level character of the proposition.

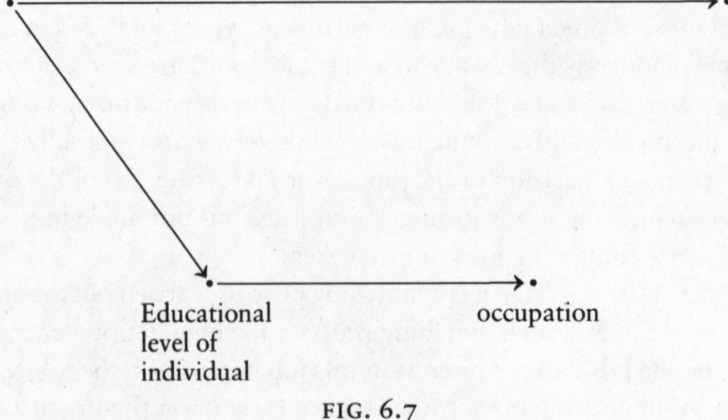

FIG. 6.7

When changes occur in the occupational structure, every effort is made in research of this kind to separate out any influence of the change in occupational distribution, so that "pure" occupational mobility of the individual, uninfluenced by structural changes, can be isolated. It may be that this attention to individual life chances derives in part from the ideological background of the discipline, focusing it on questions such as the amount of status or occupational inheritance that exists over generations, a question that can be answered by remaining at the individual level. Or it may be that this attention is focused by the fact that the research is based on a sample of individuals drawn randomly.

The next evolutionary stage is marked by the book *Inequality*, by Jencks and his colleagues (1972). In that book the authors focused on an explicitly macrosocial question: Does the level of education in society affect the inequality of income? This, in contrast to Blau and Duncan and others following that tradition, asked a macrosocial question and by doing so attracted far wider attention, beyond the committed members of the discipline. What is curious about this work, however, is that the empirical analysis carried out focused completely on an individual-level question. Based on data from a national sample, Jencks and associates asked, Does schooling lead to higher achievement? Based on other surveys, they asked, Does more education lead to higher income? The answers to these questions, whatever they may be, do not provide an answer to the macrosocial question. This can be seen in figure 6.8; it is the lower horizontal proposition to which nearly all the research in this book was directed.

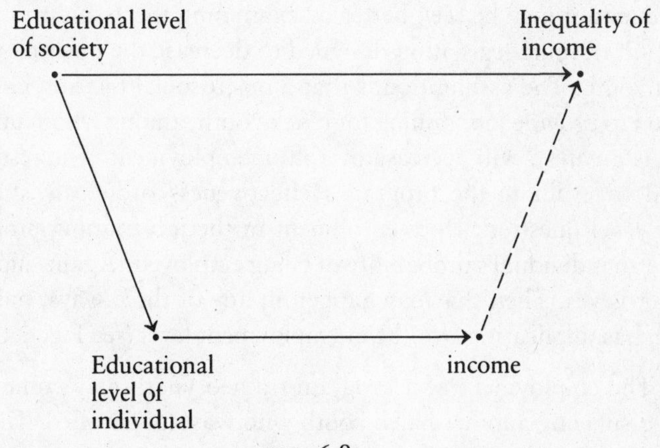

FIG. 6.8

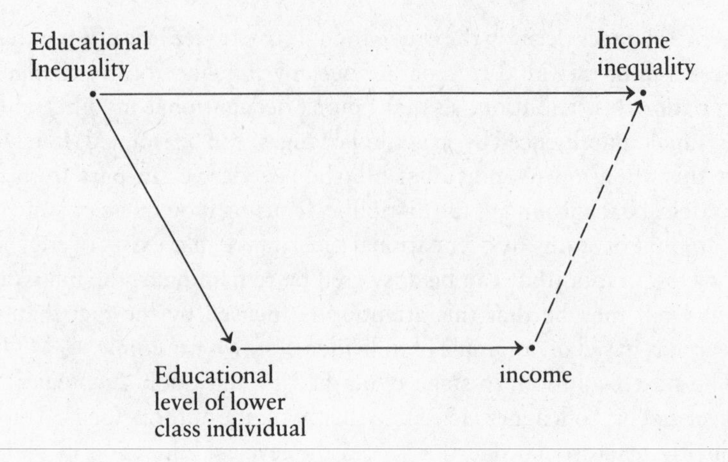

FIG. 6.9

Now suppose the independent variable in the macrosocial question were put in somewhat greater correspondence to the dependent variable. Suppose Jencks and colleagues really meant to ask, Does the *inequality* of education affect equality of income, as shown in figure 6.9? Suppose Jencks had found from the individual-level analysis that an individual's level of education strongly affects that individual's income. Would this have provided an answer to the macro-level question? Again, it would not, because of the absence of an appropriate micro-to-macro transition, which would show how a change in the *distribution* of persons with different levels of education leads to a change in the distribution of income and the quantity of income.

The matter may be seen better by examining the assumptions underlying job training legislation designed to decrease the unemployment of black youth. The assumption is that a macrosocial relation holds: Legislation to provide job training for black youth, among whom unemployment is greatest, will decrease overall unemployment. The research designed to evaluate the program's effectiveness ordinarily studies the micro-level question: Does enrollment in the job training program increase an individual's probability of being employed? Again, suppose the answer is yes. Then this may happen in any of three ways, only one of which has implications for the unemployment level (see Fig. 6.10):

1. The employment of a program-trained youth may come through displacing another black youth who was not enrolled. This would leave the black youth employment rate unchanged.

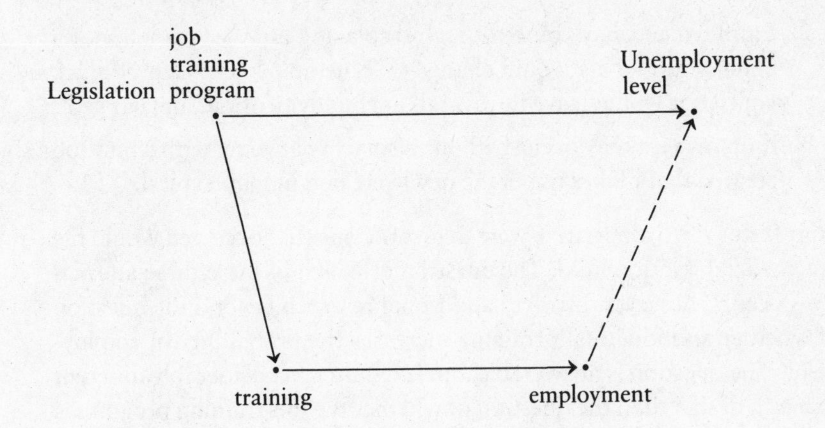
Legislation
job training program
Unemployment level
training
employment

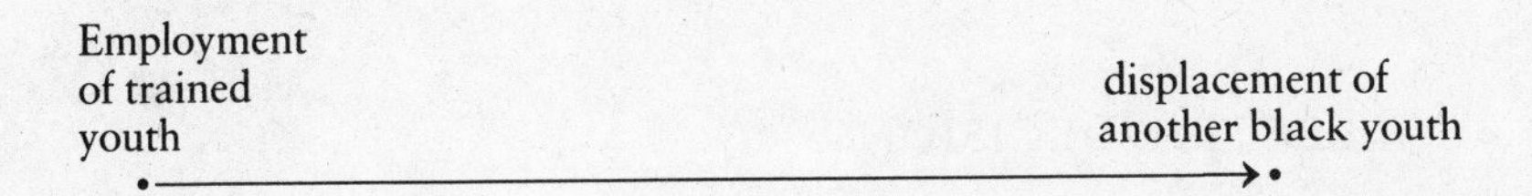
Employment of trained youth
displacement of another black youth

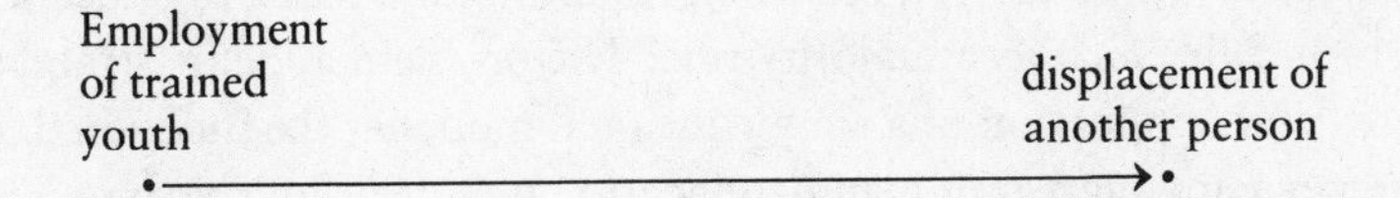
Employment of trained youth
displacement of another person

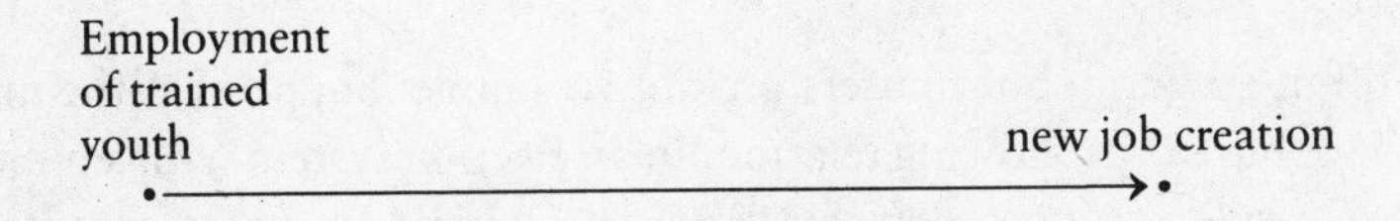
Employment of trained youth
new job creation

FIG. 6.10

2. Employment may come through displacing another person, not a black youth. This would change the unemployment rate of black youth but would leave the overall unemployment rate unchanged.
3. Employment may occur without displacing anyone, with a new job created that makes use of the newly created human capital.

Only if this third alternative were in fact the one that occurred would the macrosocial relation hold. The question of which of these three alternatives occurs, however, involves additional research beyond the question of whether an individual's training increases the probability of employment. The question is answerable, but it requires a considerably different research design than the question of whether the job-training program is effective. If that research were undertaken, it would be a beginning toward constructing a micro-to-macro model necessary for questions such as that posed by Jencks and associates or that which legislators assume in legislating job-training programs.[3]

COLLECTIVE DECISIONS

Now I will turn to a very different form of micro-to-macro transition, one that appears to be directly handled through simple aggregation. This is the process of arriving at a collective decision through voting. The micro-level action is casting a vote, and the macro-level outcome is a collective decision arrived at through counting the votes, together with a decision rule, such as a majority rule. The problem appears straightforward, and application of a simple rational model at the individual level, together with aggregation and application of a decision rule, models the process. At the micro-level each individual has a preference order, and this preference order leads to a vote. The micro-to-macro transition occurs through counting of votes and application of a decision rule to produce a macro-level election outcome. Figure 6.11 shows these relations.

So far, so good, but matters are not so simple. Suppose at the macro level we have the following relation: In an election system with a plurality decision rule, a contest between candidates H and J leads to an outcome in which J wins, as shown in figure 6.12. This could be studied at the micro level, as polls do, by eliciting preferences of a sample of prospective voters, aggregating them, and predicting the election outcome. Now suppose we add another candidate, say R, to give an H, J, R contest. One would suppose that the macro-level relation would now be either (a) the

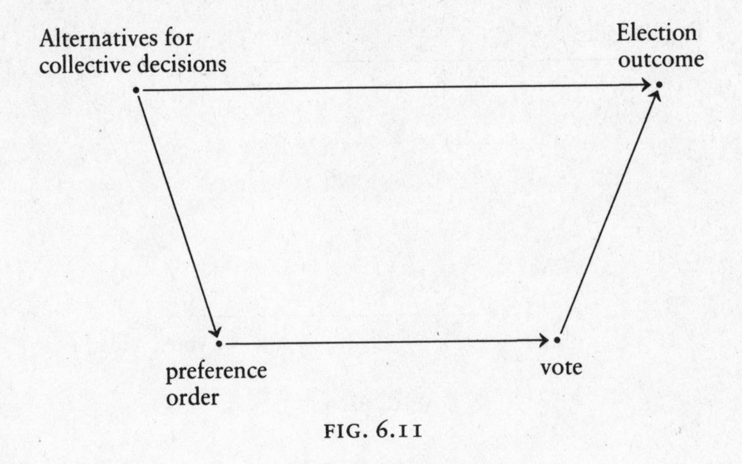

FIG. 6.11

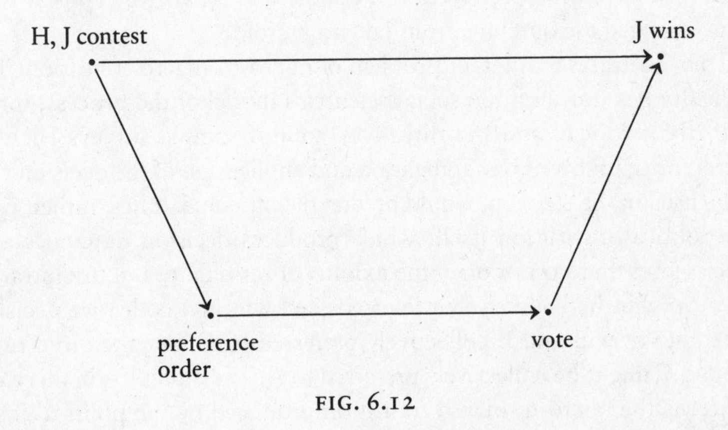

FIG. 6.12

H, J, R contest leads to election of J, as before, or, (b) if R were higher than J in a sufficient number of the preference orders, election of R. However, as Arrow proved in a dissertation written at the University of Chicago, which later became famous as the Arrow impossibility theorem, it is quite possible that H would win, as indicated in figure 6.13—and that there is *no* method of aggregating votes, no decision rule, that can prevent such a possibility (Arrow 1952).

As the letters I have used indicate, with H for Harold, J for Jane, and R for Richie, the 1983 mayoralty election in Chicago is probably an example of this. In a contest between Harold, Jane, and Richie, Harold was the winner, whereas a contest between Harold and Jane alone would

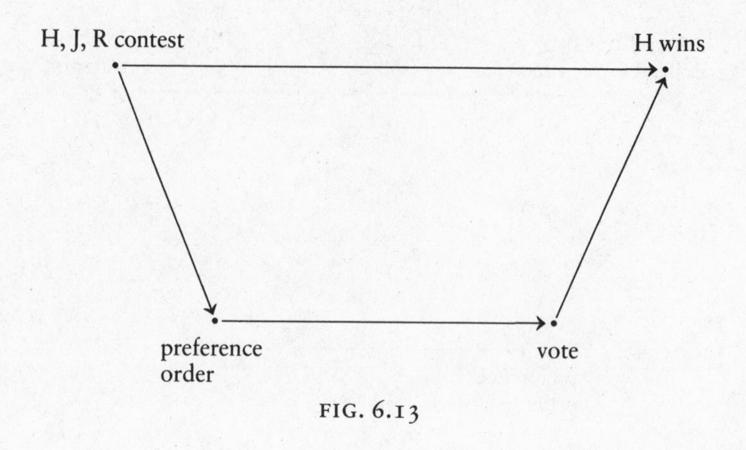

FIG. 6.13

likely have resulted in Jane as winner. The addition of Richie, an "irrelevant alternative" who did not win in the three-way contest and would likely not have been preferred by a majority in a two-way contest with Jane, changed the outcome from Jane to Harold.

This illustrates a different problem of micro-to-macro transition. The difficulty lies not with the social scientist's model of the process, for in both the two-way and the three-way contest sample surveys eliciting preferences, followed by aggregation and application of the decision rule to be used in the election, would predict the outcome. It lies, rather, with the political institution itself, which produces decision outcomes at a macro level that do not obey the axioms of rationality but are intransitive. A might be collectively preferred (i.e., win in a collective decision outcome) over B and B collectively preferred to C, but then in a turnaround C might be collectively preferred to A. The difficulty, in this case, concerns the micro-to-macro transition produced by the political institution, the decision rule. Different decision rules produce different kinds of collective "irrationalities." For example, in a Hare system, such as that used for election of the Council of the University Senate at the University of Chicago, Brams showed that the following relation can hold: In a contest between A, B, and C, an increase in attractiveness of A can lead to a change in the outcome from A winning to B winning—indeed a perverse result (Brams 1982). Figure 6.14 shows this diagrammatically.

It can be shown that the fault with the political institutions that produce the macro-level outcome from micro-level actions lies in the kind of individual action generated, usually a vote. A vote, as an all-or-nothing action, extracts too little information from the individual about *order* of preference and *intensity* of preference—and until now, no institution has

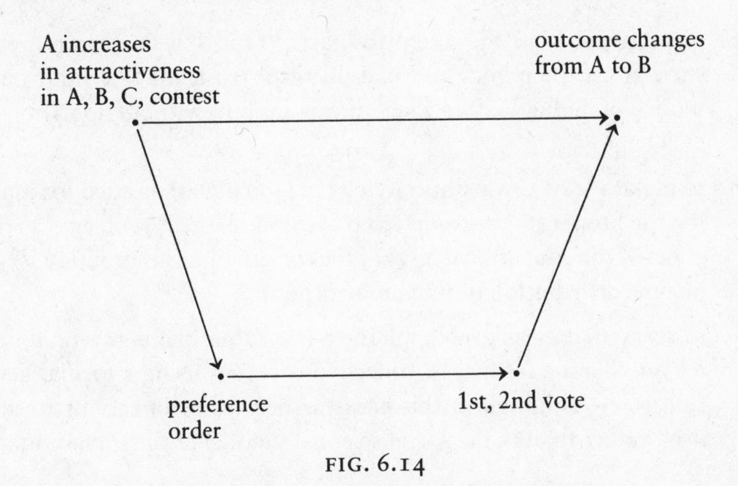

FIG. 6.14

been found which extracts sufficient information about order and intensity of preference that the micro-to-macro transition is freed from the faults I have described—although some institutions have been devised which contain fewer of the faults than do those most commonly in use.

CONCLUSION

I have tried to do several things in this essay:

1. to suggest the central importance of a proper model of micro-to-macro transition for using micro-level data to study the macro-level or system-level relations that constitute a major portion of social theory;
2. to show extensive and widespread failure to develop appropriate models for the micro-to-macro transition in a wide range of phenomena, from assortative marriage by age to occupational mobility;
3. to argue that the neoclassical economic theory of perfect market exchange systems constitutes a model for the micro-to-macro transition, although the model is appropriate only for an idealized social system with complete communication;
4. to show that using the conceptual framework of a market but with certain modifications other micro-to-macro transitions may be successfully made—as, for example, in marriage markets, labor markets, and other matching markets;

5. to point out that the micro-to-macro transition in certain areas, such as escape panics and placement of trust, may be built on a model of individual rational behavior but without markets or exchange;
6. to make a start toward specifying the kind of data needed for making the proper micro-to-macro transition for such problems as the effect of the educational level of the society (or a subgroup in it) on income distribution or unemployment; and
7. to show that comparable micro-to-macro problems can be found for another area—that is, collective decisions using a formal decision rule—although in this case the defect lies in the institution itself rather than in the social scientist's model of the transition.

The question remains, where does that leave us? Are there any general directions we can pursue in developing appropriate models of the micro-to-macro transition and in designing research that will aid in making that transition? I believe the answer is yes, pursuing a path that I alluded to earlier, a path suggested in the discussion of marriage markets, panic, placement of trust, and occupational mobility. To embark on that, however, would require another chapter. I will end simply by asserting that these examples taken together suggest a general direction toward solving this problem.

NOTES

1. This last point may be somewhat obscure. A model in which men propose, choosing from among the total set of women available, whereas women choose from among the subset of men who propose, will give different predictions than one in which women propose. Thus with appropriate data the two models with different structures of the process can be compared for their predictive power.

2. There is another point as well. This institution was established by the hospitals principally to reduce the extra transaction costs they incurred through bilateral negotiations. The algorithm used gives that outcome, among all possible stable outcomes, that is most favorable to the hospitals and least favorable to the applicants. It is not clear that applicants are better off through introduction of this institution than they were before its introduction. This exemplifies the fact that social institutions do not emerge in a power-irrelevant way but depend upon the distribution of power prior to their introduction.

3. It is sometimes argued that only macro-level research (i.e., to see whether unemployment is actually reduced by a job-training program) can answer the questions. Such research, however, constitutes a very crude instrument. It seems possible that appropriately designed surveys, which traced not merely the job-training enrollee into a job but also traced the former occupancy of that job, first determining if another occupant was displaced, then, if so, continuing to determine the prior occupancy of the job taken (if any) by the displaced person, and so on.

REFERENCES

Arrow, Kenneth. 1952. *Social Choice and Individual Values*. New York: John Wiley.

Becker, Gary. 1974. A Theory of Marriage. Part II. *Journal of Political Economy* 82.

Blau, Peter, and Otis D. Duncan. 1967. *The American Occupational Structure*. New York: John Wiley.

Brams, Steven J. 1982. The AMS Nomination Procedure is Vulnerable to "Truncation of Preferences." *Notices of the American Mathematical Society* 29, 2:136–138.

Brown, Roger. 1965. *Social Psychology*. New York: Free Press.

Coleman, James. 1981. Rational Behavior in Panic Situations, pp. 91–106 in Gordon Tullock, ed., *Toward a Science of Politics*. Papers in Honor of Duncan Black. Blacksburgh: Public Choice Center, Virginia Polytechnic Institute and State University.

Davies, James. 1962. Toward a Theory of Revolution. *American Sociological Review* 27:5–19.

Durkheim, E. 1951. *Suicide* (1897). New York: Free Press.

Gale, David, and Lloyd Shapley. 1962. College Admissions and the Stability of Marriage. *American Mathematical Monthly* 69:9–15.

Gurr, Ted. 1970. *Why Men Rebel*. Princeton: Princeton University Press.

Jencks, Christopher et al. 1972. *Inequality*. New York: Basic Books.

Mintz, Alexander. 1941. Non-Adaptive Group Behavior. *Journal of Abnormal Social Psychology* 36:506–524.

Roth, Alvin E. 1983. "The Evaluation of the Labor Market for Medical Interns and Residents: A Case Study in Game Theory." Mimeographed, University of Pittsburgh.

Sanderson, Warren. 1980. Economic-Demographic Simulation Models: A Review of Their Usefulness for Policy Analysis, pp. 433–542 in *Laxenburg, Austria; IIASA Reports Volume 1, No.* 2. Laxenburg: Austria.

Schoen, Robert. 1983. Measuring the Tightness of a Marriage Squeeze. *Demography* 20, 1:61–78.

Weber, Max. 1958. *The Protestant Ethic and the Spirit of Capitalism*. New York: Scribner.

PART THREE

Interpretive Action and Macrostructure

CHAPTER SEVEN

Complexity and Behavior Structure, Planned Associations and Creation of Structure

Hans Haferkamp

My approach in handling micro- and macroareas in sociology differs from those of others, such as Gurvitch (1942), who propose two separate sociologies—a micro and a macro—which have different subjects and methods and therefore preclude the formation of general theories. I also contrast my approach with "imperialistic theories"—that is, theories that are devoted primarily to one level of explanation but that claim to be more general. Such theories do not differentiate between micro- and macro areas. For example, social systems theorists claim to generate explanations at both levels. Other approaches, following Piaget, propose that there is no macrostructure apart from intentional construction.

I am sympathetic with those theoretical approaches that acknowledge differences between the micro and macro levels, but I would go further and emphasize the existence of many concepts that are common to both areas as well as others that are specific to each area. I also emphasize processes and structures connecting these levels.

To begin with, I make a basic distinction: The micro level involves a *small number of actors* who are able to observe one another. The maximum number of actors is that of a small group, comprising about thirty persons who are in the same place at the same time. The concept "face-to-face interaction" characterizes this micro level. At the micro level persons, actions, patterns of behavior, and particular aspects of the situation are observable in their totality. By their own admission, researchers are likely to select and reduce what is observed, but this is a question of where the researcher's attention is directed.

In contrast, the macro level has *many actors* who are not in direct interaction with one another. At this level the researcher is able to observe only indicators of actions and patterns of behavior. Examples of units at the macro level are social movements, masses, and societies, about which it is possible to observe only uniformities based on statistical indicators and representations of utterances (speeches, addresses), which must be translated into statements about underlying actions.

There are many other ways to distinguish between micro and macro levels, but these cannot be consistently upheld. For example, it is not helpful to put an immense number of "small" meaningful, coordinated social actions into one category and a small number of large, ultrastable, unintentional, and incomprehensible "structures" into another. This distinction has been discussed in terms of "action and structure" (see J. Berger 1978). My position contrasts with the generalizing structure-theoretical approach, such as that of Habermas (1982:57), who argues that "not even in borderline cases can material reproduction be explained as the intended result of a collective cooperation" (my translation). There are not only intentionally constructed microsocial associations but also *intentionally constructed far-reaching associations* in which single actors foresee the shape and consequences of very far-reaching interwoven actions, which are realized step by step. We must also recognize, however, that there are ego and alter ego processes in the life-world which are not equipped with meaning, actual or related to the situation, and which show structures, or *regularities*, that are unknown to participating actors.

It is thus my thesis that theories for analyzing the micro and macro levels must (1) analyze "meaningful action," (2) grasp behavior ranging from elementary behavior to the structure of social behavior, (3) analyze the intentional construction of large and inclusive social associations, and (4) analyze the processes of creating social structures that are not consciously understood by the acting subjects in the moment of genesis. These ingredients can be represented systematically as shown in figure 7.1. In sociology theories on field 1 (complex meaningful action) are widely available, as are theories on field 4 (creation of social structure), if they are not constructed as theories of action. Theories on fields 2 (behavior structures) and 3 (planned associations of actions), however, are seldom developed.

COMPLEX MEANINGFUL ACTION

The two main aspects of action are meaningful ascription and unintentional behavior. From this *duality of action* I will discuss briefly the area

Meaning \ *Range*	*Intended by actors*	*Not intended by actors*
Microarea: ≤30 actors	(1) Complex meaningful action	(2) Behavior structures
Macroarea: >30 actors	(3) Planned associations of actions	(4) Creation of social structure

FIG. 7.1

of ascription of meaning. This is an area of sociology that has provided many useful concepts; for example, interactionists' formulations of the "knowing, active subject as the source of human conduct" (Knorr-Cetina 1981:4). In theories of interaction, however, it is not often recognized that many definitions of situations and meanings are neither created by the actors nor specifically related to the situation. As Weber (1913) argued, actors' definitions are always related to parts of a general stock of knowledge, institutions, and culture. I wish to retain this reference to differing definitions of situations and, in so doing, to underline Cicourel's critical observation that microsociologists often put forth unconvincing conceptions of "social interaction as local, self-contained productions" (1981:53). So-called individual definitions are social in a very important sense because they are socially transmitted. Social action is marked by *intentionality* and relation to culture: Actors give their action a meaning, but this meaning is not self-created; conversely, actors operate within the framework of the general representations of their society's culture.

STRUCTURE OF SOCIAL BEHAVIOR

The second aspect of the micro level is different. According to Habermas (1981), the analysis of unintentional action is not really a subject for sociology. This position is understandable insofar as most sociological studies regard meaningful behavior as involving an exact connection between a specific behavior and a specific ascription of meaning. In such cases an understanding of the physical aspects of behavior is indeed irrelevant for the sociologist. This assumption seems to underlie the main streams of sociological action theory and may explain the tendency for sociology to stress the definition of situations and the sociology of knowledge. It also may explain why, until recently, the findings of analytical action theory have not been accepted and why their relevance for sociology has been ignored. Habermas (1982:2) reflects this dominant assumption in his remark that sociological action theory is not interested in the distinctions made by analytical action theory. According to Habermas (1981, 1:370), such distinctions are anachronistic.

The distinction between behavior and ascription of meaning has also disappeared from the tradition of symbolic interactionism since Blumer, as well as from action theory based on the sociology of knowledge ranging from Schütz to P. L. Berger, Luckmann, and Matthes.

In contrast to these positions, I maintain that action theory must deal with (*a*) the physical expressions of actors, (*b*) the material and physical elements of the situation, and (*c*) antecedent causes and effects of behavior. Mead's distinction between behavior and interpretation can be reconstructed in a partial theory of behavior—namely, that the actors *generate behavior*. When newly created, this behavior is *only* behavior and acquires meaning for the actor only after it is registered, given a meaning, and interpreted by another actor (Mead 1934:47). If Mead's observation is correct (and I contend that it is), then we must develop concepts that are consistent with individuals' experiences in the life-world. In daily life we see how often people surprise or disappoint themselves or others. To explain this kind of phenomenon we must resort to the fact that physical states and unintentional behavior frequently determine behavior that is later interpreted as meaningful. When an actor has an accident caused by fatigue, the course of events leading to the accident must be analyzed as carefully as the interpretation of the events following the accident.

Support for the importance of material and physical elements is found in Weber's (1913) statement that in the process of the construction of reality, peculiarities of all aspects of the situation, including *uncomprehended social facts*, play a role. Weber clearly included external processes and subjective factors in the field of explanation. These open up possibilities, set limits, and generate certain processes. In this connection I support Callon and Latour (1981:284), who argue that we must consider "a whole gamut of tools, regulations, walls and objects. . . . We must now gather up . . . and examine with the same method the strategies which enlist bodies, materials, discourses, techniques, feelings, laws, organizations."

Explicit recognition of the antecedent causes and effects of behavior eliminates a deficiency in interactionists' approaches, noted by Alexander (1982). This author points out that "arrangements established prior to the individual activity in that particular moment are not considered as significant foci of study. Theorists either will not acknowledge such a priori elements or else will regard them only as parameters in relation to which actors have an ultimate discretion" (p. 94). We must therefore take into consideration *causes at work behind the actors and effects not intended by the actors*. Among these antecedent *causes* are fatigue, or lack of vigilance (*Wachheit*). Also included would be hunger, thirst, sexual needs, passions—in short, the whole range of determinants of unconscious behavior. It is clear that the origin of these factors cannot be explained in sociological terms, but because they affect social behavior and social acts a sociological analysis must be invoked to assess their effects. Other antecedent causes of behavior include the characteristics of planned institutions or structural creations that determine that behavior, although such determination is often not recognized by the actors. The existence of power, for example, may promote uncomprehended patterns of submission, unrecognized by both those who exercise power and those who submit to it.

If these observations are correct, then it is necessary for us to identify those theoretical traditions that have generated social action theory. We must work on philosophical action theory and examine how concepts and distinctions such as reasons and causes, consequences and effects, and intentional and unintentional behavior can be integrated into sociological action theory (compare Haferkamp 1981). Philosophical action theorists, of course, work predominantly with "atomistic models of behavior"; what is crucial, however, is how sociologists make use of these models in analyzing their own domains of interest.

This argument is related to another criticism of action theories—namely, that they are restricted to the actual experience of the actors involved. If action theories consider both conscious reasons and perceived consequences as well as unconscious causes and unperceived effects, they move beyond the limitations imposed upon them by critics among the system theorists and materialists. The analytical concern of action theory is both with planned and manifest behavior and with emergent behavior and the effects of behavior that are interpreted only later by actors.

My proposal is in agreement with Parsons's (Parsons et al. 1951) and Graumann's (1980) attempts to include the behavior in action theory. Other theoretical positions (for example, that of Goffman) might also be integrated with this approach. Twenty years ago Goffman (1963) distinguished between talking, writing, gesturing, and other intentional signs and unintentional spontaneous, expressive utterances that are not premeditated but involuntary. At the present time, when intonation, stress, phonological aspects of speech, gaze, and body movement, conversational turn-taking rules, and code switching have become the subject of microsociological research, we must acknowledge that social action is composed of both nonverbal and verbal elements, neither of which is reducible to the other. Still other elements are relevant, such as the psychology of the unconscious (Giddens 1979: 58–59) and some aspects of sociobiology (Claessens 1980:29–92). When we examine effects of behavior, we enter an area of research in which much work has been done from the perspective of the older functionalist theory—in particular by Merton (1957) in his elaboration of the concept of latent function. Situations are complexly stratified and finely structured; if we attend only to the verbal definition of a situation, as Blumer does, then our approach is too simple. I agree with Knorr-Cetina that sociologists tend to consider "topics and concepts *below* or *above* the level of purposive, meaningful action" (1981:18); I argue that we must integrate these topics into the study of action.

When studying meaningful action, the investigator commonly identifies the actor as the unit of analysis. This is also the case when we consider social definitions of situations. This focus on persons can be abandoned when we analyze the relation between behavior in situations and its antecedent causes. At this point we concentrate on the *interaction* in situations; this interaction is the unit of analysis. At this level we can also locate the dynamics and organization of behavior that may be above and beyond actors' awareness. For example, we find that initiators in small groups are always in positions of advantage in determining group processes, although they themselves may be unaware of their position. Bales shows that in such groups two types of leadership are usually present: instrumental and expressive. Working with Parsons, Bales found that the emergence of leadership in groups goes by a specific phase movement of which the actors are not aware (Parsons and Bales 1953:71–73). Even if aware of certain processes at work, such as the creation of leadership, actors subsequently regard such processes as a characteristic of specific participants or a characteristic of the specific situation.

This distinction between meaningful action and unintentional social behavior is analytical, given that at the microarea there is often a mixture of meaningful action and unintentional behavior. Any phenomenon might be a consequence of action as well as a cause of behavior, an effect of behavior as well as a reason for action. In addition, unintended behavior may be transformed into controlled action. It is obvious, for example, that at the micro as well as the macro level there are differences in influence and power. Actors are able to determine the course of their actions and to profit from ongoing processes of action to different degrees. These processes are marked by a mixture of comprehended and uncomprehended social facts.

ASSOCIATIONS OF ACTIONS

At the macro level I make a comparable distinction. I consider a duality comprising associations of actions on one hand and processes of creating structure on the other. Associations of actions are constructed intentionally; plans and systems are outlined and the actors live accordingly. Examples are found in the precise execution of programs of technology (space flights) and in planning for war. From this perspective we must also include intentionally produced life conditions and their consequences, such as specific family and kinship systems, economic organizations as well as political associations, and cultural complexes as well as political motivations and achievements.

At this level we observe *processes of negotiation between equals and power-based transactions.* My theoretical position in this regard rests on the observation that transactional patterns are created by one or more persons and that small groups are carriers of such creations. These creations are transmitted to other groups in the society. The creation of a religion is such a process; lawmaking also frequently occurs this way. I also place theories of influence that explain how specific systems of knowledge are transmitted at the macro level. New knowledge may be the basis of influence. Influence and power are very important mechanisms connecting the micro and the macro levels. On the basis of influence and power, associations of actions are classified together. On one hand they are responsible for uniformity of action; on the other they are the basis for the distribution and coordination of different action patterns in different associations (see Haferkamp 1975). Callon and Latour name these processes "translations": "all the negotiations, intrigues, calculations, acts of persuasion and violence, thanks to which an actor or force takes, or causes to be conferred on itself, authority to speak or act on behalf of another actor or force. . . . Whenever an actor speaks of 'us', s/he is translating other actors into a single will, of which s/he becomes spirit and spokesman" (1981:279). Whoever succeeds in this process of translation is a macroactor.

A major precondition for succeeding with a new association of actions is to work within inclusive systems of meaning—"symbolic universes"

(Berger and Luckmann) or "black boxes" (Callon and Latour). Inside these systems many actors are ordered to positions and definite patterns of action: "They can enter alliances with iron, with grains of sand, neurons, words, opinions and affects. . . . Strength thus resides in the power to break off and to bind together" (Callon and Latour 1981:292). Such plans bring actors who are spatially and temporally separate into a relationship. The condition for accomplishing plans, therefore, is that actors must have an image of the world, of society, or of a plan of organization, as well as influence or power.

Positive suggestions along these lines are found in the theory of problematization, which deals with the definition of social problems, the transmission of these definitions, and the ways of solving the problems. Here I cite Eder (1982), who argues that very early in human history the world was seen as deriving from intentional thought and associations of human actions. Implicit in this formulation is the notion that it is possible to intervene in these processes, to change them, and to direct them toward desired goals. If we agree with Eder, then this is exactly the characteristic of societal development. Eder further states that the processes of construction, selection, and transmission are often understood by actors; that they have cognitive maps of interrelationships; and that these interrelationships are marked by the interchangeability of members and the dominance of the whole arrangement in relation to its parts, as is the case in team games. In this instance Weber's theory of the state is also supported. We recall his statement, that a state exists only when the actors' orientation of action is directed to a conception of the existence of a state. This approach does not mean that society, state, and structures of behavior in state and society and between different states and societies are subsumed under a single conception. Differing conceptions, maps, and images of society are held by different actors. The consequences are conflict, a struggle for power, and/or negotiations among actors or groups of actors (Strauss 1978). The cognitive maps derive from the partly successful attempts of actors with disparate power to structure society, to convince other actors, and to transmit conceptions of social interrelationships. For example, established churches and sects with traditions as well as new religious movements try, with a small number of actors, to enlarge their memberships. Similar patterns develop in other contexts—parties of the state and fanatics, multinational enterprises and unsuccessful inventors, members of the educational system and alternative pedagogic movements—*each has plans and maps for all.* In pursuit of such plans actors initiate relevant acts (work, study, beat, shoot, etc.). A few illustrative examples are in order.

Members of a political party wish to press their particular political goals. They succeed in winning positions on the executive board of the party and are successful at the polls. Members of the party then become members of the government and carry out their plans. Armies occupy a country on the basis of plans formulated by very few officers. A revolutionary cadre murders an entrepreneur. An isolated member of a resistance plans an assault. A small number of actors, in conflict with multinational corporations, educate the people on means of self-support or create gift shops for the needy.[1] Ten or twenty years later the results are referred to as fundamental "opaque" social changes, and sociologists and political scientists approach funding agencies for large sums of money to research such processes of change in order to discover latent functions, hidden regularities, and so on—a redundant exercise if sociologists and political scientists would look at events as they occur.

It is possible to explain large associations of actions, such as the market or class relations, in a similar way. The disintegration of a "self-regulating" market economy, separated from the life-world and from political and legal institutions, from moral commandments and definite duties—in short, from an ethic of duties—was an actor-planned, intentional process of objectification (*Verselbständigung*). This was later followed by a process of reification, as discovered by Marx and further analyzed by Berger and Pullberg (1965) and Berger and Luckmann (1966). These genetic processes of objectification and reification must be analyzed in terms of actions. Empirical evidence for this thesis is shown by the results of the historical "protest research" conducted since the 1960s (Hobsbawm 1967; Thompson 1966; Tilly, Tilly, and Tilly 1975).[2]

The rise of the market economy throughout Europe in the eighteenth and nineteenth centuries met the tradition-based resistance of lower strata, who tried to stop the liberalization of material care from the norms of tradition (*altes Herkommen* in the German Peasant's War) and of the "good and just price" (in the English hunger revolts). They referred to a "moral economy" (Thompson 1966) in their actions, which suggests an allocation of goods not on the basis of a price mechanism but on norms of just distribution. In punishment actions (against profiteering and the hoarding of corn), blockades (against the exporting of food), and price riots the continuous and enduring resistance of the mob is expressed against the objectification (*Verselbständigung*) of a purely market-regulated economy in contrast to the traditionally funded demands for obligatory welfare (*pflichtgemässe Fürsorge*). At the other pole we find the actions of entrepreneurs leading to a moral neutralization of the market economy. The objectification of the market therefore is grounded on conflicts between large groups of actors as well as differences in their power and symbolic universes. On one hand we find the *wertrational* actions and conceptions of protests by people in the lower strata; on the other we find the *zweckrational* actions of entrepreneurs, furthered sovereigns, and princes of different states.

Similar processes occur in the formation of classes. When J. Berger states that Ricardo's exploration of an inverse relation of wages and profit is a theoretical achievement of the first order which has no foundation in the knowledge of the actors of Ricardo's time (1979:202), then we must reply that the actors in the life-world of that time were conscious of the wage-profit relationship. How else can we explain the embittered fight of workers against entrepreneurs for higher wages at the cost of profit and vice versa?

We can explain not only the genesis of these structures but also their reproduction through intentionality. (For the importance of the difference of genesis and reproduction and the claim that action theory can explain the reproduction of the market or of classes, see J. Berger 1978:155–156.) How else can we understand the more than 100-year struggle between workers' movements and the associations of entrepreneurs and the accompanying demands, conceptions, and visions of both sides? How else can we understand the present conflicts between trade unions and entrepreneurs and the public discussion of their positions?

We see organization at the macro level as "ongoing systems of negotiation" (Joas 1981:8), and the contrasting concept to structure on this level seems to be the ordering of the associations of actions.

Enduring success in these activities that direct social change is assured on the basis of the contribution that is made to the existing needs of society members. Actors who contribute can demand that their conceptions be followed. The one who "pays the piper calls the tune." The ability of actors to supply important services to other actors is decisive in influencing associations of actions. Without this ability no association of actions can be influenced. This is the central hypothesis in explaining the ordering of large associations. Certainly there are changes in the ability to supply services and thus to keep in power; and it is self-evident that these actors construct conceptions and plans for their own benefit.

THE CREATION OF SOCIAL STRUCTURE

We must go beyond the construction of the macro level as an intentional result, however. For instance, economic considerations partly determine interactions in the life-world, and politics partly shape interactions in everyday life, both in ways not intended by actors. Surely there are variations in the power to shape such interactions, but the fact is that power is always there.

We can neither reduce the macro level to an aggregate of micro levels nor maintain that the only adequate concept of a society is the image held by the people of that society. The macro level takes shape partly through the creation of social structure. It does not consist of "procedures of counting," or of "interpretations," or of the "building of conceptions of society" (Cicourel 1981). For Cicourel the macro level is composed of a great number of microprocesses such as the development of reports, statistics, and plans, as well as through the collecting, adding, and collating of data. All that is called structure or seen as indicators of structure is produced in interactions. Cicourel stresses that there is no structure without the interaction of group members (1981:66). In constructing documents we find many strategies of interaction in which specific details are enhanced or neglected in order to produce a coherent totality.

Careful examination of Cicourel's work reveals that he only describes the outer shape of structures; to put it bluntly, he describes the distortions and ornaments of connections among the outcomes of actions that develop at the macro level. Beneath these ornaments and distortions we find the hard core of the macro level. I suggest that a comparable distinction such as that between meaningful action and structures of behavior at the micro level might be applied at the macro level.

An action-theoretical analysis of macrostructures is not problematic when the structures are *decoded* or *deciphered* by the actors and when the actors profit from their knowledge. Sociological and historical studies have shown that it is predominantly sovereigns and politicians who profit most from the knowledge of decoded systems; yet Bendix (1978), in *Kings or People*, points to a sufficient number of cases that show that ordinary people can initiate changes once they understand certain processes. Learning about medical or biological problems changes people's habits in daily life. Bales's (1953) discovery of phases in interaction process has influenced many currently widespread books on group dynamics. Going further, we can say that the fact that a structure is opaque does not mean it is inaccessible to knowledge, merely that it is not recognized, although it affects actors. I find the claim of analyzing structures in terms of action theory unconvincing when based only upon the ability of actors subsequently to recognize a structure. A part of the analytic task is to analyze the creation, existence, and reproduction of structure *before* the actors become aware of these processes.

This is a very difficult task within a traditional action-theoretical frame of reference, because in that tradition the concept of action is bound to the intentionality of the actors. In contrast, we point to the case in which the content of structure creation is not comprehended, not meaningful for the actors, and not even observable from the perspective of a researcher. Researchers can only recognize *indicators* of these large structural creations. That it is unrecognized by actors does not mean a lack of ability on the part of actors to create, reproduce, and act upon social structures; indeed, actors' struggles, their uncoordinated interactions in making their status and relative privileges secure, have unintended consequences that create and reproduce social structure. The basic principle in the creation of unintended social structure is that it is *appropriate, advantageous, and selective* of the effects of its actions. Appropriate actions contribute, often unnoticed, to the achievement of a specific quality in living conditions. Fine (1979) writes that an element of behavior that is repeated and becomes part of structure is one that does not undermine the structure and position of the actors who act out this structure. It is one that stabilizes the status quo. The appropriateness of this behavior is the basis for its transmission to other actors or groups of actors. Thus social structures survive independent of the will of the actors. In time actors recognize the value of the new structures and relate to them.

As Weber has shown, there can be a paradox of intentions (*Wollen*) and effects (*Wirkung*) of social action. The actions that have an *effect* that is appropriate and advantageous are selected and reproduced. For example, the central effect of life compatible with the Protestant ethic was that life was better for an important group of social actors. Their lives were better adapted to the necessities of the rising rational market economy. For entrepreneurs it was of greater advantage to live not in the Catholic but in the Calvinistic manner. This Calvinistic life-style enabled them to adapt to the conditions of an emerging mercantile economy.

Through action, moreover, former intentions are often destroyed by effects. In Weber's example the better the life of the actors, the more the relevant parts of the Protestant ethic decreased. The simple association of a rational market economy with better living conditions—as foreseen by other actors without the roundabout reasoning of the Protestant ethic—becomes recognized by the actors, who profit from this development and therefore further this structure. Unintentionally, the reformers encourage the rise of an economy that has effects far beyond or even in contrast to all they had in mind before. When the heads of ascetic movements fully recognize these paradoxical relations, they do not reject their Protestant ethic, which is at this time a "prison of thoughts." Instead they further the association very consciously: "We must admonish all Christians to win whatever they can, and to save whatever they can, which means in the end to become rich" (Weber 1920:197, my translation).

These processes cannot be analyzed within an action-theoretical frame of reference so long as action theory is bound to the conception of intentionality of actors. When this link is broken, then it will be possible to analyze the core of social structure within the framework of action theory.

The concepts of *appropriateness, advantage, and selection* are action-theoretical concepts and remain in that context. There are also traditions of action and interaction theory which discuss uncomprehended structures. Beside Weber's empirical works on the paradox of will and effect it is possible to note Mead's (1934) analysis of the role of life-process in the construction of interaction, and the works of Ferguson (1969) and Gehlen (1962) on the advantage of institutions.

Situations promoting changes in recognized social structures—changes that may not be recognized by the actors—occur because the surrounding conditions are no longer the same and the original structures are thus no longer appropriate and advantageous. When the reproduction of associations of actions is transformed, structure becomes problematic. Institutions based upon a previous process of creating a social structure persist beyond their usefulness and contribute to the deterioration of living conditions unnoticed by the actors; actors react too late, and either the destruction of or a regressive movement in societies results. The Roman Empire, the French monarchy, and the present-day economies of some countries constitute relevant examples.

CONCLUDING REMARKS

In the theory espoused we include a complicated relationship among uncomprehended structures, planned institutions of creative intentional action, and unplanned behavior. In addition we often find processes of transformation. Behavior becomes meaningful action and structure becomes clear to actors, who then structure such effects intentionally. Intentional shaping at the macro level is facilitated when those actors who are great achievers and in positions of power and domination become aware of the appropriateness and advantageousness of social relations. Because of this position, they are able to use their knowledge to prevail over others and to realize their intentions.

ACKNOWLEDGMENT

I am grateful to Hyacinthe M. Ellis for her assistance in writing the first version of this essay in English and for her fruitful critical comments.

NOTES

1. A system operates, in some cities in Germany, in which shops are organized to receive old or discarded personal effects from donors who, in return, acquire the right to articles they need which have been left in the shops by other donors. There is no limit to the amount of such articles a donor-member may take.

2. For the following information on social historical research I have to thank Stephan Fuchs, who also gave me some further suggestions. I also thank Susanne Bartsch for critical comments on this topic.

REFERENCES

Alexander, Jeffrey C. 1982. *Theoretical Logic in Sociology. Vol. 1. Positivism, Presuppositions, and Current Controversies*. London: Routledge & Kegan Paul.

Bales, Robert F. 1953. The Equilibrium Problem in Small Groups, pp. 111–161 in Talcott Parsons, Robert F. Bales, and Edward A. Shils, eds., *Working Papers in the Theory of Action*. New York: Free Press.

Bendix, Reinhard. 1978. *Kings or People*. Berkeley, Los Angeles, London: University of California Press.

Berger, Johannes. 1978. Soziologische Handlungstheorie und politische Ökonomie, pp. 146–157 in K. O. Hondrich and J. Matthes, eds., *Theorienvergleich in den Sozialwissenschaften*. Neuwied: Luchterhand.

———. 1979. Wie viele Soziologien? Antwort auf Hans Joas. *Zeitschrift für Soziologie* 8:201–203.

Berger, Peter L., and Stanley Pullberg. 1965. Reification and the Sociological Critique of Consciousness, History and Theory. *Studies in the Philosophy of History* 4:196–211.

Berger, Peter L., and Thomas Luckmann. 1966. *The Social Construction of Reality*. New York: Doubleday.

Callon, Michel, and Bruno Latour. 1981. Unscrewing the Big Leviathan: How

Actors Macro-Structure Reality and How Sociologists Help Them to Do So, pp. 277–303 in Karin Knorr-Cetina and Aaron V. Cicourel, eds., *Advances in Social Theory and Methodology: Toward an Integration of Micro- and Macro-Sociologies*. London: Routledge & Kegan Paul.

Cicourel, Aaron V. 1981. Notes on the Integration of Micro- and Macro-Levels of Analysis, pp. 51–80 in Karin Knorr-Cetina and Aaron V. Cicourel, eds., *Advances in Social Theory and Methodology: Toward an Integration of Micro- and Macro-Sociologies*. London: Routledge & Kegan Paul.

Claessens, Dieter. 1980. *Das Konkrete und das Abstrakte. Soziologische Skizzen zur Anthropologie*. Frankfurt: Suhrkamp.

Eder, Klaus. 1982. *Genese und Struktur einer gesellschaftlichen Pathologie. Untersuchungen zur Entwicklungsgeschichte der politischen Freihheitsrechte in Deutschland zwischen 1770 und 1880*. München: Habilitationsschrift.

Ferguson, Adam. 1969. *An Essay on the History of Civil Society*. Farnborough: Gregg International.

Fine, Gary A. 1979. Small Groups and Culture Creation. *American Sociological Review* 44:733–745.

Gehlen, Arnold. 1962. *Der Mensch*. Frankfurt: Athenäum.

Giddens, Anthony. 1979. *Central Problems in Social Theory. Action, Structure and Contradiction in Social Analysis*. London: Macmillan.

Goffman, Erving. 1963. *Behavior in Public Places: Notes on the Social Organization of Gatherings*. New York: Free Press.

Graumann, Carl F. 1980. Verhalten und Handeln. Probleme einer Unterscheidung, pp. 16–31 in Wolfgang Schluchter, ed., *Verhalten, Handeln und System. Talcott Parsons' Beitrag zur Entwicklung der Sozialwissenschaften*. Frankfurt: Suhrkamp.

Gurvitch, Georges. 1942. *Sociology of Law*. New York: Philosophical Library Alliance Book Corporation.

Habermas, Jürgen. 1981. *Theorie des kommunikativen Handelns*. Vols. 1 and 2. Frankfurt: Suhrkamp. English translation 1984: *The Theory of Communicative Action*. Vol. 1: *Reason and the Rationalization of Society*. Boston: Beacon.

———. 1982. *Erläuterungen zum Begriff des kommunikativen Handelns*. München. English translation 1985 in G. Seebass and R. Tuomela, eds. *Social Action*. Dordrecht: D. Reidel.

Haferkamp, Hans. 1975. *Soziologie als Handlungstheorie*. Opladen: Westdeutscher Verlag.

———. 1981. Handlungsintentionen und -folgen. pp. 262–274 in J. Matthes, ed., *Lebenswelt und soziale Probleme. Verhandlungen des 20. Deutschen Soziologentags zu Bremen 1980*. Frankfurt: Campus.

———. 1985. Critique of Habermas's Theory of Communicative Action, pp. 197–205 in G. Seebass and R. Tuomela, eds., *Social Action*. Dordrecht: D. Reidel.

Hobsbawm, Eric J. 1967. *Labouring Men*. New York: Anchor Books.

Joas, Hans. 1981. Handlung und Struktur, pp. 3–12 in W. Schulte, ed., *Soziologie in der Gesellschaft*. Bremen: Universität Bremen.

Knorr-Cetina, Karin. 1981. The Micro-Sociological Challenge of Macro-Sociology: Towards a Reconstruction of Social Theory and Methodology, pp. 1–47 in Karin Knorr-Cetina and Aaron V. Cicourel, eds., *Advances in Social Theory and Methodology. Toward an Integration of Micro- and Macro-Sociologies*. London: Routledge & Kegan Paul.

Matthes, Joachim, and Fritz Schütze. 1973. Zur Einführung. Alltagswissen, Interaktion und gesellschaftliche Wirklichkeit, pp. 11–53 in Arbeitsgruppe Bielefelder Soziologen, eds., *Alltagswissen, Interaktion und gesellschaftliche Wirklichkeit I*. Reinbek/Hamburg: Rowohlt.

Mead, George H. 1934. *Mind, Self, and Society: From the Standpoint of a Social Behaviorist*. Chicago: University of Chicago Press.

Merton, Robert K. 1957. *Social Theory and Social Structure*. New York: Free Press.

Parsons, Talcott, and Robert F. Bales. 1953. The Dimensions of Action-Space, pp. 63–109 in Talcott Parsons, Robert F. Bales, and Edward A. Shils, eds., *Working Papers in the Theory of Action*. New York: Free Press.

Parsons, Talcott, et al. 1951. Some Fundamental Categories of the Theory of Action: A General Statement, pp. 3–29 in Talcott Parsons and Edward A. Shils, eds., *Toward a General Theory of Action*. New York: Harper Torchbooks.

Schütz, Alfred. 1932. *Der sinnhafte Aufbau der sozialen Welt*. Wien: Springer.

Strauss, Anselm. 1978. *Negotiations*. San Francisco: Jossey-Bass.

Thompson, Edward P. 1966. *The Making of the English Working Class*. New York: Vintage Books.

Tilly, Charles, Louise Tilly, and Richard Tilly. 1975. *The Rebellious Century 1830-1930*. Cambridge, Mass.: Harvard University Press.

Weber, Max. 1913. Über einige Kategorien der verstehenden Soziologie. *Logos. Internationale Zeitschrift für Philosophie der Kultur* 4:253–294.

———. 1920. *Gesammelte Aufsätze zur Religionssoziologie*. Tübingen: J. C. B. Mohr (Paul Siebeck).

CHAPTER EIGHT

Interaction Ritual Chains, Power and Property: The Micro-Macro Connection as an Empirically Based Theoretical Problem

Randall Collins

Micro and macro approaches to sociological theory have existed for many years, but the issue of how to relate them has become acute only within the last ten or twenty. This has happened largely because of empirical claims made by proponents of the micro approach. The early symbolic interactionism of Mead or Thomas lived at peace with the macrosociology of the time; but this microsociology was largely philosophical rather than empirical, and the conception of macrostructure to which it was attached would strike most sociologists today as idealized and naive. Militant symbolic interactionism dates from Blumer in the 1950s. Blumer stressed a processual interaction as seen in actual empirical encounters and used this to critique macrosociology in general, and especially what he saw as the reifications of functionalist theory. The same opponent called forth Homans's behaviorist microreductionism; again, Homans was coming from an empirical base—small group research—and he charged his macro opponents with being empirically unrealistic as well as unfruitful in explanatory theory. Homans's followers then spawned exchange theory, as a way of relinking with the macro level. The linkage, one might say, was reasserted all too easily, and Homans's criticisms of traditional macrotheory were too quickly forgotten.[1]

The most militant micro attacks on macrotheory were still to come. This happened because microsociological research became a good deal more precise and a good deal more micro. The so-called participant observation of loosely bounded situations gave way to much closer studies of carefully defined aspects of face-to-face interaction. Erving Goffman was a prime mover in this area, not merely for pioneering the topic of everyday life as a subject for empirical research but for giving it a theoretical basis—especially his Durkheimian conception of rituals in ordinary social encounters. The micro front was joined by ethnomethodology, conversational analysis, cognitive sociology, and related approaches. All of these, it should be stressed, differ from older philosophical subjectivisms precisely because they are forms of empirical research, albeit a theoretically informed empiricism. In fact, the microrevolution of the 1960s and 1970s was in large part a movement of new research techniques—especially tape recordings, although more recently other devices—for collecting the truly fine-grained data of naturally occurring interaction, hence the new militancy of microsociology against macrosociology. For from the point of view of the observation of situational behavior, all other sociological concepts—organizations, cultures or "cultural traditions," norms, states, societies or "social formations," classes—are merely derivative, summaries, glosses, perhaps even reifications and outright myths. The alleged empiricism of "hard data" and survey research is turned on its head, viewed merely as constructs from the micro situations that make up the research process itself.

So much for historical background. I do not wish to review the metatheoretical debates on the primacy of micro or macro, or the reduction or irrelevance of one as opposed to the other, or even some abstract conceptual scheme in which both live in harmony. I prefer to approach the issue as one of building generalized explanations of the empirical world. Seen from this angle, we have two polar types of research: very fine-grained empirical analyses of conversational and nonverbal interaction on one hand, and the range of more traditional research on macrostructures, on up to the level of the economics and geopolitics of the world system, on the other. The question then becomes, Do micro and macro forms of research have anything to do with each other? Or was the furor of the 1960s and 1970s simply the adding of one more research specialization, now carried out with very fine-grained empirical methods but of interest only within another specialized niche in the overpopulated academic world?

My answer is no. Modern microsociology is more than a trivial addition to the academic scene. That is not to say that heuristically, as a matter of practice, macrosociologists cannot go on studying the world system, the structure of the state, or any other macrotopic without using micro research methods or invoking microtheory. Macrostructures are a distinct level of analysis on just this pragmatic level: One can make generalizations about the workings of the world system, formal organizations, or the class structure by making the appropriate comparisons and analyses of its own data. What I will argue, nevertheless, is that the effort to connect micro- and macrotheories is worth making. It is not absolutely necessary to do so; each level can proceed well enough without the other. I believe, however, that the power of explanatory theory on either level will be enhanced if we can show their mutual penetration in a fairly precise way.

THE MICROTRANSLATION OF MACROSTRUCTURES

How can macrostructure be composed out of micro events? Clearly it is so composed: What is "empirical" meets us only in the form of micro encounters, and any macrostructure, no matter how large, consists only of the repeated experiences of large numbers of persons in time and space. Our macroconcepts are only words we apply to these aggregations of microencounters. The fact that these words—"nation," "society," "corporation," and so forth—are part of the discourse of everyday life merely presents us with another item of data and does nothing to ensure that the terms correspond accurately to the aggregation of microencounters that actually takes place.

Nevertheless, this gives us the clue to the real dimensions of macrostructures: precisely the lines along which aggregation of microencounters takes place. Macrostructure consists of nothing more than large numbers of microencounters, repeated (or sometimes changing) over time and across space. This gives us exactly the dimensions of macrostructures: the sheer *numbers* of persons and encounters involved; the amount of *time* taken up by encounters of various kinds and their repetitions; and the configuration they make in physical *space*. Time, space, and number: These are the only macrovariables, and every other macroterminology is metaphorical and ultimately should be translated into these.[2] Everything else in a theory is microprocesses. Moreover, it is at the micro level that the dynamics of any theory must be located. The structures never *do* anything; it is only persons in real situations who act. It is on the micro level that we must show the energizing processes, both those that cause structural change and those that are responsible for maintaining and reproducing the structures from one occasion to another (that is to say, the "glue" that holds structures together).

This may sound as if I am giving a great deal of prominence to the micro. That is true, but we should bear in mind that the theoretical issue is not merely one of showing how macrostructures are composed of aggregations of microencounters, and formulating all laws determining macrostructures in terms of aggregations of microevents in time, space, and number. My own previous writing (1975, 1981*a*, 1981*b*) has tended to stress that goal, but I would now add that this exercise in the "microtranslation of the macrostructure" also has a use in the opposite direction, perhaps even a more immediate use: It shows how microevents, the behavior of individuals in situations, are themselves determined by where they are located in the larger network of microencounters around them in time and space. Macrosociology, seen in a fine-grained way, becomes the key to understanding much of what goes on in the realm of microsociology.

More on this below, when I will discuss the theory of interaction ritual (IR) chains. For the moment I would like to illustrate my point that macrostructures are to be explained by principles that aggregate microprocesses in time, space, and number. Here is an example: One principle, which is congruent with a fair amount of data, I have labeled the *principle of social density*, after Durkheim's discussions of this subject (Collins 1975:75–76). This proposes that the more individuals are exposed to networks of social encounters that are diverse and cosmopolitan, the more their ideas will be abstract, relativistic, and concerned with long-term consequences. Conversely, individuals in localistic and enclosed networks think and speak concretely and particularistically, with a short-term outlook and a "magical" attitude toward forces in the larger world. The distribution of such experiences is one dimension of an explanation of class cultures, if one looks at it from the point of view of a macropattern. The dynamics of this principle result from the ritual nature of interaction, a microprocess (explained in greater detail elsewhere; see Collins 1975:92–103, 153–154). The principle itself, however, is somewhat more macro than that, for it speaks of the number of encounters of various kinds that one has over a period of time, which is at least a local extension of experience beyond one immediate situation. It does not deal with the entire macrostructure in the largest sense, but it does locate the individual in what might be called the "mesostructure," the network of repeated encounters around him or her.

It should be apparent that the distinction between micro and macro levels is a continuum, not a dichotomy. Microevents are situational; but these can be prolonged, repeated, or aggregated, in time, and the number of encounters spreads out in space, as far as one wishes to look. There is an element of macrostructure in almost any microprocess, in that it is affected by (1) the spatial configuration in which it takes place, such as the sheer physical density of the interactive situation itself, and (2) the number of times such situations (or other types of situations) have been repeated in the past by these individuals. Thus individuals will come into any microsituation with a past history of encounters in other microsituations, and these make up the ingredients of what will happen in that particular situation. This encroaches again on the theory of interaction ritual chains, to be discussed later.

Notice that we can pick out any part of the continuum of time and space upon which to focus theoretically. Thus we have very localistic parts of macrostructure, in the aforementioned "principle of social density" affecting individual outlooks. At the opposite extreme we can deal with the large-scale world arena of states, a large-scale focus in historical time and geographical space. Here again we would expect that explanatory principles would be built around sheer temporal, spatial, and numerical relationships: in this example, among the armed groups and material (spatial) conditions of their supply and communication that make up the state. In fact, I have argued elsewhere (Collins 1981*c*, 1985) that the essence of explaining the power of states is contained in the principles of their *geopolitical* relationships. The growth, contraction, and other structural changes in the military and materially extractive networks that make up states are determined, I have proposed, by certain principles of their long-term spatial relationships and the sheer numerical relationships of their populations and material (in other words, space-occupying) possessions. The social dynamics of the struggle for legitimacy, which makes up the microexperiential reality of the struggle for power, are crucially affected by the rises and falls in military threat based on these geopolitical factors. Thus again at the ultra-macro level, explanatory theory can be resolved into time, space, and number conditions affecting microexperiential events. I could also add as an illustration, in a longer discussion of this topic, an intermediate-sized macrostructure, such as formal organizations, and show how organizational structure is determined by the sheer physical and numerical layout of work, as this sets the stage for struggles for control between organizational authorities and their subordinates (Collins 1975:chap. 6).

I will glide past a fairly complex body of theory at this point and state that the *microtranslation* (as opposed to *microreduction*) of macrostructures is theoretically fruitful; that it is more than a program for the future; that it leads to what I hope are more powerful explanatory generalizations on levels of many sizes of the macrocontinuum.

INTERACTION RITUAL (IR) CHAINS: THE EFFECT OF MACRO UPON MICRO

Let us now consider the opposite issue: the location of individual microexperience within the aggregates of microencounters that make up the macrostructure. This is the model of interaction ritual (IR) chains. The terminology is from Goffman (1967); what it implies is that interactions are not merely instrumental but are procedures that both generate and consume symbols representing group membership. There is nothing particularly mysterious about these symbols; for the most part they are embedded in the cultural codes with which people speak. An interaction typically is the negotiation of a momentarily shared conversational reality. The extent to which some type of conversational reality is created depends upon the motivations and resources of the individuals who come to the encounter. That is, what conversation is produced depends on how much individuals wish to speak to one another in a certain fashion and what stored memories, vocal styles, and the like they bring that will enable them to do so. These motivations and resources come from previous encounters; hence the notion of a *chain* of interaction rituals.

To summarize quickly, every conversation gives some increment to the cultural capital of the individuals who take part in it. This cultural capital can, in turn, be invested in future conversations. Furthermore, there are various kinds of conversations one may participate in: some more formal, Goffmanian "front-stage"; others more "backstage"; some quite intimate. Some conversational topics are "cheap" and common; they cost little but produce little in the way of distinctive ties among the individuals who take part in them. Other kinds of conversations enact one's membership in a network of power, or create ties in relatively exclusive social circles. Thus underlying the manifest content of conversations is a continual negotiation about one's social memberships. There is a marketlike aspect to the series of conversations that takes place over time as individuals attempt to move toward those symbolic exchanges that bring them the best return on the conversational capital they have accumulated so far. Hence the outcome of any conversation is an "emergent situation," in the sense that it cannot be predicted in advance merely from knowing the past history of only one participant. If we know the past history of all the participants, however, we should be able to judge theoretically who will want to talk with whom about what, and whether the other will reciprocate, and hence what further social ties will be enacted.

One might ask a fundamental question in all such market or market-like models: What is the common denominator among all the different types of conversational exchanges, so that individuals can weigh which type of "good" they would like to attain? How does one decide whether he or she should aim for a conversation that will be entertaining as opposed to one that implies membership in a high-prestige group, or again one that brings intimate ties but in a very small localized connection? There is no conversational equivalent of monetary currency which reduces all these to a common value. Nor, for that matter, do various conversational choices present themselves to individuals with clear and full information of what is available, even from the persons standing immediately in front of them. In general, there are considerable limits simply to translating conventional economic theory into these kinds of social exchanges. Individuals do choose, however, and there seems to be a pattern in how they do so. I argue that the common denominator of conversational choice is emotional rather than cognitive. (This is in keeping with models, both rationalistic and ethnomethodological, that converge on the principle of "bounded rationality," the inability of individuals to weigh complex decisions consciously.)

Let us look at this again from the point of view of a chain of interactions. Each conversation in that chain is a negotiation, which results in the inclusion or exclusion of the individual in some kind of local group membership. One result that the person stores from this, as I have said, is cultural capital: things to talk about in future conversations; another is an increment or decrement in emotional energy. Persons who dominate their conversations acquire more energy, more self-confidence, and a greater tendency to take the initiative in subsequent conversations and to put their cultural capital to use. Similarly, one need not dominate the conversation—as it need not be an authority situation, but possibly an egalitarian, sociable, or even an intimate encounter—in order to gain an energy increment; one need only be fully accepted into group membership. So we have on one hand occasions in which persons gain more emotional energy, which in turn gives them an emotional resource to bring to subsequent conversations. On the other hand, persons who are dominated in conversational situations (which may be as a result of enacting an authority situation as the recipient of orders from another) or who are excluded from informal membership situations lose emotional energy.

In any given encounter, then, all the participants who enter it have both some *cultural capital* and a given degree of *emotional energy* set by their past conversations. There is also a third "resource" that circulates:

one's *social reputation* and identity, as circulated not so much in one's own talk as in the network of other people's conversations in which one might figure as a topic. When we come to each new encounter, then, whether that encounter will prove to be attractive to both participants or to one side more than the other, and also who will be able to dominate the interaction, depends on the match among the participants of cultural and emotional resources that are brought to it. Individuals do not have to reflect consciously on these matters[3]; the conversation will run off by a force of its own, will be a success or a perfunctory failure, will be one-sided or two-sided, and so forth, depending on the balance of resources brought into the situation. The emotional energy, in my view, is pivotal in this. It determines what each person will *feel* about the conversation he or she is getting into: how much one wants to talk to the other person, whether it is a high or low priority in comparison to what else each might do, and how successful each will be in bringing off the kind of conversation he or she would like to enact. This is true in various kinds of conversational situations, ranging from a boss trying to control a worker, a boy trying to strike up an acquaintance with a girl, the amount of humor shared by casual acquaintances in the hallway, or a wife feeling whether or not she is in the mood to confide in her husband. (It is particularly noticeable, I might add, in determining the kinds of conversations intellectuals have with one another.)

As I have indicated, these chains of interaction rituals can be viewed from several perspectives. We can take a micro-oriented view: In this case we wish to predict what will happen in the microsituation. This becomes a theory of individual motivation and a theory of micronegotiations. If we focus on the individual, viewed as a continuous entity across a string of interactions, we then have an explanatory theory of individual personality. We might notice, incidentally, that the individual person is not the ultimate microunit. A "personality," in fact, is a macroconstruct of an intermediate size: the true microunit is the encounter, and we abstract out an individual when we trace him or her across a number of encounters. What we call a "personality" is simply a reification, or perhaps one might say a repository, of ways of thinking, feeling, and acting that are the results of a string of interaction rituals. If we want a practical intervention dealing with this level—that is, a therapy—I suggest that this would take the form not of psychoanalysis but of "socioanalysis": the understanding of individuals' moods, emotional energy levels, and abilities or inabilities to deal with various kinds of social situations as caused by their past history of encounters in the kinds of conversational networks that constitute their "markets."

From another angle, however, the aggregate of individuals' thoughts and conversational behaviors makes up a macropattern. This is most usefully seen, I would suggest, as the set of class cultures that segregate people across the stratified social landscape. To put it another way, the associational aspect of stratification, which Weber called status groups, consists empirically of people who are habitual conversational partners in nonhierarchical situations, that is, conversations that are "sociable" rather than order-giving and practical. The term "community" is a rough metaphor; in fine-grained reality it actually consists of various types of networks of repeated conversations among certain persons. A status group has its consciousness, of whatever form it may take, precisely because of the membership-identifying content of the interaction rituals that are carried out in conversations; to put it in a way that combines the perspectives of diverse theorists, it is these conversational rituals that produce the moral solidarity of the group, which might also be called its ideological construction (or distortion) of reality. Let me add, in contrast to theories that assume that normative phenomena are somehow the results of societywide rules, that microempirically, moral solidarity is an episodic and local phenomenon, that the groups it ties together are friends, factions, perhaps at most larger status groups or social classes, not the whole society, and that moral solidarity is more a weapon of group conflict than an agency of pansocietal integration.

Let me add that as an empirical matter, if one wishes to describe accurately the condition of class consciousness, ideology, or culture across a society, the proper way to do so would be to sample the typical conversations across the landscape. Questionnaire methods, on the contrary, sample artificial situations and arrive at officially constructed "attitudes" brought out for precisely those situations. Attitudes in this sense I think are somewhat mythical. A truer picture could be obtained by sampling the range of situations in which people are actually talking and thus creating their mental realities of the moment.

THE PRIMACY OF THE MACROSTRUCTURE: POWER AND PROPERTY

I would like now to raise an objection to this focus on conversations. One might say, "Doesn't this focus elevate conversation to a higher position than it really has?" As my colleague Jonathan Turner points out, the world is not a perpetual cocktail party, and most possibilities for conversations are much more structured to begin with. Workers must reply to their bosses; housewives are stuck with talking to their husbands, children, and neighbors. Even at cocktail parties is it not the case that the prestige that makes someone the object of many attentions has less to do with the conversational capital he or she can present than with his or her preestablished social position, so that powerful and important persons get conversational offers that persons in lower positions do not? Again, even the content of what people say may be determined less by this bargaining among cultural capitals and accumulated energies than by the sheer roles they occupy: the boss giving orders, the colleagues passing information, and so on.

There is some validity in this objection. The valid part is that, generally speaking, the larger macrostructure seems to be primary in shaping microencounters. This is already explicit in the model of interaction ritual chains: What happens at any point in the chain (i.e., where the personal chains of different individuals intersect) is determined by what has been accumulated in the previous chains themselves—which is to say, by where they are located in the macronetwork. We should not simply leave it at this, however, and declare that social roles, previously acquired, determine most of subsequent behavior. The "role" of being a boss, a worker, an expert, and so on is neither merely given nor encoded as a script to which everyone passively adheres. It is something enacted, and not without struggle. Real resources uphold these structural identities or "positions": above all, property and power. The question is, What makes these real? In other words, how do they translate microempirically?

Property, I think, is an overwhelmingly central (and badly neglected) feature of structured microsituations. In fact, what makes microsituations relatively more "formal" or "structured" is usually the presence of property. How does property present itself in microsituations? It is above all the material setting in which the interaction takes place and the display of a habitual connection of some individual to that setting. I am defining "property" without reference to the legal niceties as to who can make what claim and what is recorded on documents. That is not to say that these latter, macroaspects of property cannot sometimes be activated in the interactional chain. In most immediate microsituations, however, "possession is nine-tenths of the law," as American lawyers say. In fact this makes sociological sense. To hold an "office" is actually not so much a structural abstraction as, more than likely, a particular physical place that one habitually possesses. The way people know who has what structural "position" in a formal organization tends to be, first, by the physical places in which one usually finds them. This may indeed be backed up by legal claims, but it is equally possible for nonlegal owners to obtain local possession rights by sheer habitual appropriation of desks, telephones, keys, and the like. A large part of enacting a role is making use of the physical setting and giving signs that one belongs there and that others do not. Thus I am disputing a cognitive definition of what organizational structure is; it is *not* primarily dependent upon individuals having to carry around in their heads a set of rules and definitions of who is what, or indeed on having very much consciousness of what the organization officially looks like at all.[4]

Moreover, what kind of physical setting one appropriates is crucial for the interactions that take place within it. The Goffmanian presentation of self is sometimes referred to as "impression management"; this can also be called control of the "means of emotional production," an extension and empirical specification of what Marx and Engels called the "means of mental production." When we add to this the material means of communication, we have a material property that gives some persons better access to larger social networks than others. Thus we have a way in which property translates into power: not as a macro-level metaphor but as a microempirical process by which some persons have better access to mobilizing allies and hence to mounting a coercive threat, whereas others are isolated and thus less capable of mobilizing power and hence of appropriating further property in the subsequent interactional chain. The micro-macro continuum is thus not merely an analytical device for sociological observers; it is part of the system of stratification itself, in that access to the macrostructure is itself stratified and is indeed the fundamental dimension of social class.

Property, in the long run and in the legal sense, is backed by external agencies of enforcement. Most property gets into people's hands initially because it is passed along to them through a chain of authoritative owners and their agents, and threats to property are ultimately fended off by calling on persons elsewhere in the macrostructure to bring legal and ultimately coercive actions to bear. In macro terms, property is backed by the state; in an analytical sense power is more fundamental than property. In the microrealities of everyday life, however, power tends to be enacted above all in the form of property.

It is easiest to see this if we think empirically about formal organizations. There is a long research tradition about organizations which has found power to be peculiarly elusive. The formal orders given by the authorities are undermined by the informal structure; in effect, what is said on paper, as the macrostructure, does not easily translate into what is observed in the conversational interactions that make up the microreality of the organization. (See, for example, Clegg [1975], who went seeking power relationships in a business firm in ultra-empiricist fashion with a tape recorder.) Organization theory has gone too far, however, in dispensing with authoritative power, as if the formal hierarchy does not exist in empirical reality at all. It most certainly exists because there is one aspect of it that is constantly enacted: It is enacted as sheer physical possession of certain offices, machines, places to be, as well as paychecks and other concrete emoluments. A boss may not easily control what his or her subordinates are doing, but the boss does control who stands where, who is in the building in the first place, and who gets paid. It is this fairly concrete chain of dispersion of physical property that constitutes the central structure of power in almost every organization.

I am well aware that there are other theories about organizational power. Exchange theory, for example (Blau 1964), attempts to derive it from the greater expertise that leaders contribute to the common good of the organization, in return for which they receive subservience from less skilled subordinates. It is not difficult to recognize this as ideology; its empirical reality might be found in some kinds of informal exchanges, but it is far from a realistic picture of the formal chain of command itself. To establish an organization one does not need expertise and respect; the sine qua non is property, whether in the form of investment capital or a budget, which can be used to hire subordinates. As is quite clear from actual struggles over organizational control, a takeover bid succeeds or fails based upon the financial resources of a particular faction—that is, its connection in the financial network. As a limiting case, of course, there may be an actual political revolution, in which the coercive power of the state is reappropriated by a mobilized group, which in turn can be used to take over organizational properties and the command structures built upon them. Even in this, however, there is the loop between property and power: For it takes material means of intercommunication and mobilization, which makes it possible for a revolution to take place at all. Conversely, as Weber emphasized, any organization formed by voluntary mobilization of a group acquires its permanence as a social entity only by becoming routinized in the form of property.

If one were to ask what upholds the macroworld as a social structure, I believe the proper reply is *property*. This is a theoretical reply from the point of a microtranslated macrotheory, not a reified macrotheory. If society consists of nothing more than a long series of microinteractions spread out in time and space, the question "What is structure?" reduces to "What causes the typical, if intermittent, repetition of encounters?"

The most fundamental, implicit, and taken-for-granted aspect of microbehavior is the enactment of property. In microreality this need consist of nothing more than the appropriation of a particular part of physical space. There is little or no higher-level cognitive processing necessary for this; people do not do it because they have internalized the norms of property, or because it is a semantic rule that people are constantly monitoring. On the contrary, there is an implicit struggle over exactly this appropriation and over the process of giving and taking orders, of showing oneself as impressive or unimpressive, that results from the use of these material resources. Property nevertheless is reenacted quite regularly on the micro level because it is the taken-for-granted background upon which the interaction rituals of everyday life are staged.[5]

NOTES

1. Thus Homans's own analysis (as well as Blau's) of the emergence of stratification is vitiated by the easy functionalist assumption that exchanges are generally balanced, and hence that powerful persons *must* be presumed to give back something especially valuable to their subordinates.

2. A truly scientific sociology would consist of relational propositions among these variables, rather than among our commonsensical (and ideological) labels for macrostructures. Schegloff (see his chapter in this volume) goes even further, arguing that our commonsensical observations even on the *micro* level must ultimately give way to the truly fundamental microphenomena that conversational analysis and other ultra-detailed empirical research are uncovering.

3. Indeed, individuals cannot reflect on them to any great extent. This would constitute a cognitive overload, unrealistic from the point of view of what we know of human beings' real-life cognitive capacities. This implies that theories (such as Habermas 1981) that place self-reflectiveness at the center of language are wrong: Self-reflection is a special and limited case, usually possible only in some specifically protected intellectual situation rather than in ordinary social life.

4. This points to one of the inadequacies of another recent effort to solve the micro/macro problem, Giddens's (1984) "structurationism," with its heavy reliance on micro-situated rules and other phenomena of cognition.

5. Property is generally "indexical," in the ethnomethodological sense. It mostly takes the form of the "here and now," inexpressible in general except by pointing to it in a concrete situation. One "points" implicitly with one's body when one occupies, with a sense of appropriating it, one's own home, one's place of work, and so forth. This is usually all that it takes, not a lot of high-level cognitive processing, to keep the macrostructure intact.

REFERENCES

Blau, Peter M. 1964. *Exchange and Power in Social Life*. New York: John Wiley.

Clegg, Stewart. 1975. *Power, Rule, and Domination*. London: Routledge & Kegan Paul.

Collins, Randall. 1975. *Conflict Sociology. Toward an Explanatory Science*. New York: Academic Press.

———. 1981*a*. On the Micro-Foundations of Macro-Sociology. *American Journal of Sociology* 86 (March):984–1014.

———. 1981*b*. Micro-Translation as a Theory-Building Strategy, in Karin Knorr-Cetina and Aaron V. Cicourel, eds., *Advances in Social Theory and Methodology: Toward an Integration of Micro- and Macro-Sociology*. London: Routledge & Kegan Paul.

———. 1981*c*. Long-Term Social Change and the Territorial Power of States, in *Sociology Since Midcentury. Essays in Theory Cumulation*. New York: Academic Press.

———. 1983. Micro-Methods as a Basis for Macro-Sociology. *Urban Life* 12:184–202.

———. 1985. *Weberian Sociological Theory*. London and New York: Cambridge University Press.

Giddens, Anthony. 1984. *The Constitution of Society*. Berkeley, Los Angeles, London: University of California Press.

Goffman, Erving. 1967. *Interaction Ritual*. New York: Doubleday.

Habermas, Jürgen. 1981. *Theorie des kommunikativen Handelns*. Frankfurt: Suhrkamp.

CHAPTER NINE

Between Micro and Macro: Contexts and Other Connections

Emanuel A. Schegloff

I.

When persons talk to each other in interaction, they ordinarily talk one at a time and one after the other. When their talk is not produced serially in this manner, they generally act quickly to restore "order"; someone quickly steps in to fill the silence; someone stops talking (or several someones do) to resolve the simultaneous talk; or if two or more of the participants continue talking, their talk takes on a special character of "competitiveness" (it is louder or higher pitched, for example). These special states of silence or competitiveness, however, are quickly resolved in favor of "normality," one at a time, no more, no less.

I want to call whatever mechanism, device, or set of practices that produces these effects a form of social organization. What is organized by this organization is both a set of social actions (looked at in one way) and a set of actors (looked at in another way). Whatever else the participants may be doing—announcing, requesting, complaining, on one hand, and listening, displaying understanding, agreeing, on the other—they are constitutively realizing a course of action in their talking and listening. Although a turn at talk, or some smaller utterance unit within it, may have enacted through it a number of acts of the kind we conventionally call (after Austin and Searle) "speech acts," the conduct of conversation (or, more generally, "talk-in-interaction") itself represents a course of action. The participants who "bring it off," whether by talking or by withholding talk at the "right" places and supplying it at others, do so in their capacities as "prior speaker," "current speaker," "recipient," and the like. The units (such as sentences) out of which such a course of action as "talking in a turn" is constructed are structures with describable, interactionally relevant properties. For example, their structure allows anticipation of their possible completion, the imminence of which can be detected by hearers, and used as grounds of contingent action. Accordingly, a possible next speaker can begin to gear up to talk as such projected possible completion comes "into view"; a current speaker can anticipate such a possibility and modify the manner of his or her talk so as to circumvent, ward off, or fight off such a start by another (e.g., by suddenly speeding up the talk, not pausing for a breath at the point of possible completion, but rushing ahead into a next sentence and pausing at a point of maximum grammatical control, such as after a preposition but before its object).[1] Coordination between actors is thus present, as are anticipation and modification of coordination. Although a single person seems to have talked, obviously the participants together have produced the bit of discourse, action, and interaction that has resulted.

What I have just described is a bit of the turn-taking organization for conversation[2]—that is, one aspect of a "speech exchange system." Although it is not what sociologists ordinarily think of as "social organization," in many ways it is the apotheosis of social organization. It operates in, and partly organizes, what would appear to be the primordial site of sociality: direct interaction between persons. It coordinates the behavior of the participants—*all* participants—by allocating differentially at any moment differing opportunities for differing types of participation. The types of participation are partly defined by different types of social acts—single or multiple instances of the empirical version of a basic social unit: the unit act. This bit of social organization is part of the medium, or the "enabling" institution, for a substantial proportion of the conduct of which all the other major social institutions are composed. Finally, as a coherent set of practices or rules, it is, or constitutes, a structure of action and thereby escapes the polarity of individual and aggregate.

The relationship we depict between micro- and macroanalysis (recognizing without further comment the utter relativity and likely hopelessness of these terms) may well reflect whether we start from the micro or macro end of the continuum, and it is likely to reflect as well the kind of microanalysis or macroanalysis on which we base our approach. I approach the theme from what is ordinarily considered the micro end of the spectrum. Of the several kinds of microsociology now active—symbolic interactionist analysis, role theory of various types, exchange theory of various types, small group theory, status expectations theory, phenomenological analysis, and the like—I come to the topic from the active practice of "conversation(al) analysis" (CA for short).

It is not clear how the kind of microanalysis CA does (if it *is* microanalysis) is to be related to macro-level theorizing or whether it should be. This kind of work is concerned with understanding how courses of interaction come to have the detailed trajectory and character they do. This is accomplished in part by coming to understand how the recognizable social actions that participants enact are done and done recognizably.[3] This form of analysis takes seriously the relevance of the fact that the interactions we are examining were produced by the parties for one another and were designed, at least in part, by reference to a set of features of the interlocutors, the setting, and so on, that are relevant for the participants. The fact that these interactions are structured and progressively restructured by the participants' orientations does not serve (from this point of view) to make "objective" analysis irrelevant or impossible; it is precisely the *parties*' relevancies, orientations, and thereby-informed action which it is our interest to describe, and to describe under the control of the details of the interaction in which they are realized. It is what the action, interaction, field of action are to the *parties* that poses our task of analysis. One of our most insistent and recurrent findings is the so-called local character of the organization of interaction (that is, its turn-by-turn, sequence-by-sequence, episode-sensitive character), and this is one basis for the problems that arise in attempting to relate its analysis to so-called macro.

In what follows I shall take up three types of linkages between the micro and the macro proposed or embodied in recent literature. I shall consider them in the context of conversation and interaction analysis as a genre of microanalysis, in some cases focusing on the outcome of a macro-micro linkage and in other cases on the difficulties involved. I will then consider a kind of inversion of the way the issue is frequently posed, and sketch a different kind of treatment of the problem.

II.

In this section I will examine one proposed form of the linkage between micro and macro: variation in microphenomena between cultures or societies. I will begin by describing a domain of phenomena referred to in conversation analysis as the organization of "repair."[4] Only a brief account will be given here.

By "repair" we refer to efforts to deal with trouble in speaking, hearing, or understanding talk in interaction. "Trouble" includes such occurrences as misarticulations, malapropisms, use of a "wrong" word, unavailability of a word when needed, failure to hear or to be heard, trouble on the part of the recipient in understanding, incorrect understandings by recipients, and various others. Because anything in talk can be a source of trouble, everything in conversation is, in principle, "repairable." The actual behavior by which repair is effected, or at least undertaken, is socially and sequentially organized. The social organization of repair casts the parties to the conversation into one of two categories with respect to the possibility of repair: the speaker of the trouble-source (or "self," as we refer to him or her) and all others ("other"). Opportunities to repair, and activations of them, are distributed differentially between self and other. For example, the speaker of a turn in which trouble occurs has the initial opportunity to deal with that trouble in the same turn in which the trouble occurs; the initial opportunity is thus for "self-repair." The import of this is that others, who may well be able to effect the repair (e.g., they know the missing word, they know the speaker meant "buy" rather than "sell," etc.), withhold doing so while the current speaker (self) is still talking. Only after self has finished the turn at talk and has not repaired the repairable does some other address it.

Further, if one distinguishes between undertaking to repair something (i.e., *initiating* repair) on one hand and *solving or completing* it on the other, then another bit of social and sequential organization may be noted: Just as self has the first opportunity to initiate repair, so overwhelmingly does self (the producer of the trouble source) have the first opportunity to complete or solve it, even if an other initiated the repair. That is, when self has not initiated repair and an other has then done so, generally other merely initiates the process and, in the first instance, leaves it to the speaker to do the actual repair. There is, then, a kind of division of labor and prerogatives.

The distinction between self and other discriminates as well between the forms of talk used by the several parties in doing the work of repair and the characteristic trajectories the talk follows until successful resolution of the trouble (or, very rarely, failure) has occurred. Thus "same-turn self-repair" is characteristically initiated by an abrupt self-interruption, a disjunction marked by cutting off a word in progress followed by an effort to deal with the trouble. Repair initiated by some other ordinarily takes the form of a whole turn in which one of a limited set of question constructs ("huh?"; "who?"; partial repetitions of prior turn, etc.) is used to give some indication of what the trouble was in the preceding turn. There are additional positions from which repair can be initiated, additional resources for doing so, and considerable interactional import attached to the whole matter. For example, repair is a major resource in maintaining and restoring intersubjectivity or mutual understanding in interaction, and it supplies a major vehicle for both the expression and the circumvention of disagreement and, with it, conflict. These are not central to my purpose here, however.

What is striking is the apparent constancy of this organized domain of behavior to a fine level of detail across variations in the most macro contexts with which social scientists ordinarily deal. I will cite three instances to depict both this constancy and the striking way in which such variations as are found are neatly adapted to special features of the macrocontext.

First, there is the report by Moerman[5] on materials gathered by recording in peasant villages in Thailand. The macrounit in this case is a society with a history and a national social structure quite different from those of the United States; a more local (though still macro?) social structure of a peasant village that is no less strikingly different from the variety of "local contexts" in the United States from which the data were collected on which the original accounts of repair were based (which range from urban ghettos to middle-class suburbs to rural exurbs); a culture and value system drawn from sharply different origins; and a language genetically and structurally unrelated to English. Moerman reports (and shows) that where his corpus contains adequate materials, repair in Thai conversation is well described, and in detail, by the account developed on American materials.

A second report is by Besnier,[6] who studied conversational interaction in Tuvaluan, a language spoken by a society of some 400 persons on an island in the South Pacific. Besnier describes and documents a remarkable similarity between the organization of repair in that locale and what has been described for the United States. One minor divergence from the U.S. materials is of interest, however, and relates in an interesting way to a claim about the ethnopsychology and ethnoepistemology of the South Pacific, as described by Ochs.[7] Ochs and others[8] claim (in the first instance about Samoa but also about other South Pacific cultures) that the

Western notion of "intention" plays a substantially weaker role there. Further, members of Samoan and other cultures who hold this view do not believe one can (or ought to) guess explicitly another's intentions. This view is derived from ethnographic inquiry.

Consider the relationship of this claim to the following observation about conversational behavior. In Besnier's display of the range of types of initiation and completion of repair in Tuvaluan conversation, he depicts the following type of occurrence. A speaker produces a turn to a point just before completion—for example, to just before a projected last word. She then pauses. In the cases Besnier reproduces, and others he describes, the recipient of that (uncompleted) turn then uses a form commonly used elsewhere when recipients of talk with trouble in it initiate repair: a partial repeat (in this case, of the last word or two before the silence set in) plus a question ("who?" "what?" "where?" etc.) of the type appropriate for the type of word that has been "withheld." The prior speaker then supplies the missing word as a solution to the repair initiator. In American (and other) materials, such talk, in which a speaker hesitates just before what is potentially the last word, is sometimes met by the recipient supplying a candidate last word for the incomplete turn (sometimes with "question" intonation), which the prior speaker may accept or reject.[9] When asked if this type of response occurs in Tuvaluan as an alternative to the partial repeat plus question word, Besnier reports (personal communication) that it does not.

Note that this divergence between American and Tuvaluan practice fits nicely with the claim that these South Pacific peoples do not believe in guessing the intentions of others; the practice used by other societies or cultures, but not by them, involves explicitly just such guessing.[10] In respects other than this, however, the organization of repair among the 400 inhabitants of this South Pacific island is just like that in societies of wholly different character.

A third case comes from fieldwork by Irene Daden among the Quiche-speaking Indian peasants of the Guatemalan highlands.[11] As was noted earlier, in the general discussion of repair, the initial opportunity to deal with trouble is afforded the speaker of the trouble-source, in the same turn at talk as the one in which the trouble occurred. This may then be referred to as "same-turn, self-initiated repair." Speakers begin such repair with a "repair initiator." A repair initiator alerts the recipient to the possibility that what will follow in turn may not be a continuation of the preceding talk but, rather, may be disjunctive with it; it may restart the turn, or replace a word just used, or make some other such change in the prior talk rather than continuing it.

The most common same-turn repair initiator in English and in other European languages is what we call a "cutoff," what linguists call a "stop" (most commonly, a glottal stop). This involves a sudden stop of the speech stream, or self-interruption. It should be noted that this stop has no semantic sense in Continental European languages and English; nor does it affect meaning. It is, as the linguists say, not "phonemic" in English. It *is*, however, phonemic in Quiche. Therefore it is not surprising that Daden reports that Quiche speakers do not use the cutoff or stop as a same-turn repair initiator. When English speakers do not use a stop, they often use a sound stretch; they prolong some sound in a word they are producing and then proceed to the repair. Like cutoffs, sound stretches are not phonemic in English. However, *brief* sound stretches *are* phonemic in Quiche. They are not used as same-turn repair initiators in Quiche. Quiche speakers do primarily use overlong sound stretches (which are not phonemic for them) to initiate same-turn repair.

Several points should be noted. First, "same-turn repair initiation" is a kind of occurrence and a locus of action only by reference to this theoretical account of an organization of repair in conversation. When this account is used to examine conversational behavior in radically different social, cultural, and linguistic contexts, it proves in each of them to be a locus of systematic action. Second, there is some variation in how the action is achieved, but the variation is extraordinarily minor relative to the constancies that make it observable in the first instance. Third, the differences between Quiche and other cultures with respect to repair seem to be designed precisely for the host language and its phonological structure.

To summarize this part of the discussion, I have described a type of social organization of behavior, the organization of repair. This is *social* in many respects: It allocates rights among classes of persons; it accords the status of action types to determinate bits of behavior; and it is an important ingredient in other fundamental types of organization in interaction—most notably the organization of agreement and disagreement and thus of the embryo of conflict. We have in hand a detailed description of the resources deployed in this bit of organization and the placement and nature of these deployments. This "microdomain" shows extraordinary invariance across massive variations in social structural, cultural, and linguistic context and relatively minor variations fitted to those variations in context.

The finding that the phenomena of repair may not vary substantially by society, culture, or language does not make them not social or their study nonsociological. There is a tendency under such circumstances to think of invariants as universal categories or properties or capacities of mind. It should be clear, however, that we are dealing with matters of *conduct* and of *conduct in interaction*. There is temporal and sequential organization between actors and types of actors, actions and types of actions. Options, practices, and rules for ordering them are involved. They are addressed to plausibly generic organizational exigencies of interaction. Should we not expect in the first instance not variation but invariance in this domain and other such domains?

III.

In the previous section I considered one mode of relating micro and macro levels: possible variation in the former by reference to the latter. Next I will examine a second mode of relating the two: examining the operation of microprocesses (in interaction, for example) when participants are involved who display variation on attributes considered to be relevant at the macro level—most commonly class, ethnicity, and gender. From a substantial literature I have selected one line of research in particular because of its intersection with some work of my own which allows me technical access to its details. The problems I seek to address are quite general, however, and by no means are specific to these inquiries or these investigators. The work I will discuss is concerned with some aspects of the organization of turn-taking in conversation with respect to gender relations, and in particular the much-cited work of West and Zimmerman on the study of interruption—a phenomenon transparently a by-product of turn-taking organization (though not exclusively so, as there are units other than turns at talk which can be interrupted).[12]

A particularly well-known finding has been the reported asymmetry of interruption between the sexes—men interrupting women far more frequently than the opposite. When furnished with an appropriate definition or account of interruption (such as "talk by another when a prior speaker is still talking and is not 'in the vicinity' of possible turn completion"), this finding aims to link an asymmetrical outcome in the talk to differential attributes of the participants of a macrorelevant type. What is commonly seen as differential between men and women in a finding such as this (as in findings of this kind concerning other mixed conversational pairings, such as professional/client) is differential status or power, of which the interruptions are presumed to be a symbol and for which they are a vehicle.

Such findings, and the research strategy of which they are a product, however attractive for their policy implications, present certain problems. One concerns the need in this type of analytic enterprise to show that characterizations the investigator makes of the participants are grounded in the participants' own orientations in the interaction.[13] This is not at all clear (except, perhaps, statistically) for the characterization of the participants in gender terms in this research tradition (or in class, ethnic, or other such terms in cognate research traditions). Second, the differential attributes are not conversation-specific in any straightforward way. That is, these identifications of the participants are not analytically linked to specific conversational mechanisms by which the outcomes might be produced; however relevant to the macroconcerns that motivate their use, they risk being arbitrary in their relation to the interactional events they are invoked to account for. Indeed, the most serious problem is that early introduction of such linkages to macro-level variables (and, with them, to a compelling political/vernacular relevance) tends to preempt full technical exploration of the aspects of interaction being accounted for and the micro-level mechanisms that are involved in their production. There is a potential for analytic losses at both the micro and macro levels. Let me illustrate with the case of gender differences in interruption.

Technically, occurrences in which a woman is speaking and a man (in the middle of her talk) says "But-" or "Bu-" or "B-" (where "-" is a mark of self-interruption or cutoff) are all interruptions. They are not, however, the kind of event central to the finding that men disproportionately interrupt women. The prototype occurrence for that finding is one in which a woman is talking, a man starts in the middle of her talk and continues talking until the woman withdraws before finishing what she was saying. If this is so, then we must recognize that there is a stretch of time in which both parties are talking at the same time, and we can ask whether there is some order or organization to the several speakers' conduct when there is simultaneous talk and, if so, whether or not that order might be relevant to the outcome. There *is* a systematic organization to the talk produced by more than one speaker talking at the same time.

Without entering into a technical elaboration and without specifying those occasions of simultaneous talk which are exempt from this organization, I can briefly mention some of these mechanisms. There are several forms of talk by which speakers show that they will not withdraw from the "overlap," such as increased volume or pitch or repeating parts of the turn. Each party to the overlap can activate these forms, and each can react to the other's use of these forms—ordinarily in the next beat or syllable after the other's introduction of one of them. One type of response to the other's continuation at talking or deployment of these forms of "competitive" speaking is to drop out of the overlap and yield the turn to the other—at least for the moment. Another response type is to continue in the face of the competition, and perhaps even to become competitive (or more competitive) oneself.

There is much more to the organization of overlapping talk than this, but the foregoing should provide sufficient background to note that the resolution of an overlap is, in the first instance, not determined or effectuated by the attributes of the parties; otherwise the outcome of an interruption would be entirely determined at its beginning. The resolution is arrived at by the conduct of the parties during a stretch of talk in which both speak simultaneously, during which each does or does not deploy resources of competitive talk such as raising the voice, and during which each has responded to the deployment of such resources by dropping out, by holding firm, or by upping the competitive "ante" in return. It may well be that women are interrupted more than they interrupt, but the introduction of such an "external" attribute early in the research process or the account can deflect attention from how the outcome of the conversational course of action is determined *in its course*, *in real time*. Once this process has been explicated, much of the interest it had may well have been "secularized" and appear anonymous rather than gender-specific.

Once again, what is needed is the capacity to specify technically the parameters of the relevant organization of action or interaction through which macroattributes have whatever different effects they have, if any. In the case of interruption, one may well be able to describe differential courses of action (e.g., in invoking competitive resources or in responding to them) that systematically make it likely that this one or that one will "lose." Whether gender per se will turn out to be a macro-relevant attribute relating to these is not clear.[14] Perhaps it is one "proxy" for high/low power or status. Indeed, such differences may come to embody for some investigators what high/low status amounts to interactionally, although establishing the relationship to external status (as measured by noninteractional measures) may be quite problematic. For understanding interaction it is the former (the "intrainteractional"), not the latter, that is consequential, and it is not necessarily tied directly to macro-level phenomena. (For example, it appears from published stenographic transcripts that former President Richard Nixon regularly yielded to aides John Ehrlichman and Robert Haldemann when they found themselves talking simultaneously, although their "external" status would have predicted the opposite outcome.)

It should be obvious that some cases of competitive simultaneous talk involve matters other than status or power tests altogether. There are, for example, some types of utterance that require a particular turn position to get done; wisecracks, for example, must be done in the turn following the one that touched them off and with which they play. Other turn types, most notably efforts to address troubles in hearing or understanding the preceding talk, also appear to take priority over competing talk. The developing turn of a speaker who persists in competitive overlap can thus reveal the activity being prosecuted through the turn as the basis for its speaker's persistence, and this, rather than power-related matters, can be the basis for another party's withdrawal.

More consequentially, aside from the several alternatives to status/power as accounts for persistence to survival, there are at least three other criteria of success in competitive talk besides the survival (or outlasting the other) criterion implicit in the preceding discussion. The most important of these is that one's own turn be the one to which ensuing talk is addressed. Success by this criterion can be of greater consequence to the further course of the talk, is by no means guaranteed by survival in overlap, and may be enhanced by quite different modes of conduct in overlap than are relevant to survival.[15] These important aspects of the study of the organization of simultaneous talk as part of the study of turn-taking have a way of being preempted when the research focus turns early to relating aspects of this organization of talk to macro-relevant variables.

The issue is, of course, a general one and by no means limited to the particular research enterprise through which I have tried to explore it. All kinds of conversational, linguistic, so-called nonverbal, and other interactional behavior have been related to such classical dimensions of social organization as class, race, ethnicity, and gender. Although one may choose to proceed along the lines of such a strategy in order to focus on important aspects of social structure in a traditional sociological sense, the risks of underspecification of the interactional phenomena should be made explicit, and with them the risks of missing the opportunity to transform our traditional understanding of what is important in social structure. Although the trade-off may be made in order to benefit important sociological or sociopolitical concerns, even these concerns may suffer if the interactional phenomena are not completely explored on a technical basis.

IV.

A third type of proposal for relating micro to macro levels is that they be mediated by one of a class of bridging notions collected under the rubric "context." "Context" is sometimes taken to refer to the matters examined in the previous sections of this essay: cultural/societal context and the context of interactional participants of a certain type or types. (Much of the following discussion may therefore be relevant to that of the prior sections as well.) Additionally, however, some have proposed contexts of a scope intermediate between the largest structures of a society and the details of interaction—"contexts of the middle range," one might call them. Prototypical here are institutional and/or organizational contexts[16] such as "bureaucratic," "medical," "legal," "classroom," "formal," and the like, or by characterizations of the activity to be done (e.g., "getting-acquainted conversation," "task-oriented group," etc.) or the relationship of the participants (e.g., "conversation between strangers").

My concern about this tack is that it raises the familiar problem of multiple description. The set of ways of describing any setting is indefinitely expandable. Consequently the correctness of any particular characterization is by itself not adequate warrant for its use; some kind of "relevance rule" or "relevancing procedure" must be given to warrant a particular characterization. Here I must vastly oversimplify by suggesting that there are two main types of solution. One is the positivistic one (in one of the many contemporary uses of that term): Any description the investigator chooses is warranted if it yields "results," statistically significant or otherwise attested, with the further possible proviso that these results be theoretically interpretable. The second type of solution requires for the relevance of some characterization *by the investigator* some evidence of its *relevance to the participants* in the setting characterized; that is, reference is made to the intrinsic or internal ordering and relevance assertedly involved with sentient, intentional actors. We are operating with the second of these positions, and it is therefore required that we be able to warrant any characterization of the parties or setting by showing that it is relevant to the parties, and relevant to them at the time of the occurrence of what we are claiming is related to them or contingent on them.

For example, Sacks[17] showed a number of years ago that there is no general unique solution to the problem of how relevantly to characterize a member of society, and I tried to show[18] that formulating place is also a matter contingent on various interactional features. Those papers were concerned to show how the terms used by *conversational participants* reflected the facets of the situation and action that the parties were treating as relevant. Those "internal to the setting" relevancies then serve as constraints on an *investigator's* characterization of the setting.

So the fact that a conversation takes place in a hospital does not ipso facto make technically relevant a characterization of the setting, for a conversation there, as "in a hospital" (or "in the hospital"); it is the talk of the parties that reveals, in the first instance *for them*, whether or when the "setting in a/the hospital" is relevant (as compared to "at work," "on the east side," "out of town," etc.). Nor does the fact that the topic of the talk is medical ipso facto render the "hospital setting" relevant to the talk at any given moment. Much the same point bears on the characterization of the participants: For example, the fact that they are "in fact" respectively a doctor and a patient does not make those characterizations ipso facto relevant (as is especially clear when the patient is also a doctor); their respective ages, sex, religions, and so on, or altogether idiosyncratic and ephemeral attributes (for example, "the one who just tipped over the glass of water on the table") may be what is relevant at any point in the talk. On the other hand, pointed use of a technical or vernacular idiom (e.g., of "hematoma" as compared to "bruise") may display the relevance to the parties of precisely that aspect of their interaction together. It is not, then, that some context independently selected as relevant affects the interaction in some way. Rather, in an interaction's moment-to-moment development, the parties, singly and together, select and display in their conduct which of the indefinitely many aspects of context they are making relevant, or are invoking, for the immediate moment.[19]

One additional constraint needs to be mentioned: that relevant contexts should be procedurally related to the talk said to be contingently related to them. That is, there should be some tie between the context-as-characterized and its bearing on "the doing of the talk" or "doing the interaction." Curiously, then, although it may be problematic to warrant "in a hospital" as a formulation of context, or "doctor/patient" as an identification of the participants, it may be relatively straightforward to warrant "two-party conversation," or "on the telephone" as contexts and "caller/called" as identifications of the participants. Because they are procedurally related to the doing of the talk, evidence of orientation to them ordinarily is readily available.

To suggest, however, that warranting the invocation of vernacular characterizations of context is problematic is not to say it is impossible. Rather, I mean to direct attention to the need for examining the details of the talk and other behavior of the participants to discern whether and how it displays (in the first instance to coparticipants but also to professional analysts) an orientation to context formulated in some particular fashion. The literature includes a number of efforts along these lines.[20] An indication of one line worth trying might be the following.

Take the observation that "physicians routinely . . . ask questions, and patients routinely provide responses."[21] Rather than treating this as the observation that persons independently formulated as physicians disproportionately engage in a particular form of conduct, one might ask whether these persons can be "doing being doctor" by conducting themselves in a particular way. One is then directed to close examination of the conduct in order to specify in what respects it might constitute "doing, and displaying doing, doctor." One might note that constructing turns as questions is one part of "doing being doctor," and one might be drawn into further specifying aspects of the talk (e.g., the type of question, the manner of the asking, the manner of doing recipiency of the response, etc.) as parts of this process—*if*, that is, there are such specifiable aspects. If there are, then attacking the problem in this fashion allows a claim of the participants' orientation to the "doctor/patient"-ness of the interaction, rather than the more positivistic correlation of a type of activity with an independently given (but not demonstrably party-relevant) characterization of the parties.

The point, then, is not merely to impose a formal (or formalistic) constraint on the use of certain forms of description, but to be led by such a constraint to a new direction of analysis, with the promise of additional, and possibly distinctive, findings. I have sketched one such possible direction for the characterization of the participants in interaction, but this does not have a readily apparent application to the characterization of "context."

Let me suggest an alternative. Rather than treating the detailed course of conversation and interaction as micro-level phenomena, which invite connection to macro levels of analysis through intervening contexts vernacularly characterized as earlier described, *modes of interactional organization might themselves be treated as contexts*. Indeed, it is ironic to find some critics insistently taking conversation analysis to task for not setting its findings into context or for not incorporating context into its inquiries.[22] For much of this work can be viewed as an extended effort to elaborate just what a context is and what its explication or description might entail. In the great surge of studies in a number of the social sciences (but particularly in anthropology,[23] linguistics,[24] and sociology[25]) beginning in the early 1960s which was concerned to (re-)assert and elaborate the importance of variation, social setting, and context, one frequently saw references to "the different meaning some sentence or action would have 'in the context of an academic lecture' as compared to 'the context of ordinary conversation.'" These "contexts" were treated as transparent; everyone would know what those different contexts were and how they would affect the meaning of something said or done in their course. Of course, that transparency is merely apparent. What constitutes ordinary conversation as a context, and how it lends the character or "accent" it does to actions and utterances produced in its course, for some of us has been a matter for empirical inquiry and sustained analysis.

Given limitations of space, I cannot give a full characterization of "ordinary conversation" as a speech exchange system, and thereby as a type of context for social action.[26] A speech exchange system is specified by the form of organized solutions it has to such generic problems as managing the allocation and size of turns among the parties, providing for the organized production of stretches of talk into coherent sequences and courses of action (sometimes organizing successive utterances, sometimes dispersed ones, for example), furnishing orderly means for dealing with troubles of speaking, hearing, and understanding the talk so as to allow the action to proceed there and then, providing orderly procedures for the starting and ending of episodes of concerted interactional activity, and the like. Speech exchange systems vary in these terms; differing organization in some respects often implicates other differences. (For example, the different turn-taking systems underlying "conversation" and "formal meetings," respectively, can implicate differences in the organization of sequences; differences between "conversation" and "ceremonies" appear to implicate differences in the organization of repair; etc.) In this essay I can give only a brief illustration of how speech exchange systems can be seen to furnish relevant and procedurally consequential contexts for a range of different activity types. I will do so by elaborating a bit on comparative speech exchange systems.

As noted earlier, one basic aspect of speech exchange system variation is in turn-taking systems. So, for example, in ordinary conversation determination of both who shall speak next and when that one should speak (i.e., when current turn should end) is accomplished in a local, turn-by-turn manner and not by some predetermined pattern. In contrast, many meetings preallocate every other turn to the chairperson and give to the chairperson the power to allocate, in those turns, who shall have rights to speak in the others. Many ceremonies, rituals, and formal debates, on the other hand, may fully specify the order and length of all turns, being thereby at the opposite end of the "local allocation" versus "preallocation" spectrum. In general it appears that other speech exchange systems, and their turn-taking organizations, are the product of transformations or modifications of the one for conversation, which is the primordial organization for talk-in-interaction. Below I sketch some aspects of a turn-taking system that organizes a substantial range of activities in very different vernacularly conceived contexts as an exploration of an alternative, more technically specified version of this notion. Note that this brief description is not based on the same amount of data and analysis as that on which our understanding of conversation is based; therefore it is rough and to be used only for illustrative purposes.

Consider, then, such diverse occasions as classrooms[27] of a "traditional" kind (at least in the United States) and presidential press conferences.[28] In cases of both types of event, quite a few persons are present, most of them as official participants; 20 to 30 in the classroom situation, as many as 200 or more in the case of the press conference. For turn-taking purposes, however, it is important to note that they are organized as two-party speech exchange systems. In each case one of the parties has one incumbent or member (the teacher, the president) and the other party (the students, the press corps) has many. In both cases turns are distributed as they generally are in two-party turn-taking systems: They alternate between the parties. It is this alternation, and the consequent exclusion of another reporter as next speaker after a current speaker-reporter, which makes clear that those are *two-party* interactions, even though *multiperson*.

In both cases the speech exchange system is designed to organize particular types of utterance or actions—questioning and answering. In the case of the classroom it is the one-person party (the teacher) who does the questioning and the multiperson party who does the answering. In the press conference the multiperson party (the press corps) does the questioning and the one-person party (the president) does the answering.

Similar "devices" are used to select which of the persons who compose the multiperson party shall speak for that party when it is that party's turn. In the classroom situation the teacher produces a question and allows a set of candidate-next-speakers to be assembled. Some students signify self-nomination into the candidacy pool by raising their hands. The teacher may wait and encourage more students to enter the pool (for example, by seeking them out by eye contact); the students may try to avoid this prodding by averting their eyes, by suggesting that they are "working on the problem," by assuming preoccupied, studious, puzzled faces, and the like. At some point the teacher selects someone from among the students to speak, usually (but not always) from the candidacy pool. The duration of the turn thereby assigned is primarily determined *by the teacher*, who can continue looking expectantly at the student after the apparent possible completion of the "answer" turn, or can begin talking at a possible completion point even if it appears that the student is prepared to go on. The teacher may then solicit additional answering talk from other students, and the selection process may repeat. After each answer or answer part the teacher may offer an assessment of that answer before soliciting more, or before beginning another cycle by taking a next turn to do either another question or "telling" talk. Various other behaviors occur simultaneous with all of this, of course, but a great deal of it is structured by reference to this organization. (An example is other students monitoring the "answer" a called-upon student is giving and shooting their hands into the air as early as possible after a possible error or after possible closure that has not exhausted the possible answer; but such behavior is obviously attuned to, and attempting to preempt, the turn-taking system as otherwise described.)

In the case of the press conference, when the president is ready to take questions (after an initial statement or round of greetings), it is so announced. Members of the press corps then self-nominate into a candidacy pool by hand-raising and by other behavior (to be discussed later). The president selects one of them to ask a question, then addresses himself (ostensibly) to the question. Unlike the classroom case, here the answerer *does* determine (for the purposes of organizing the occasion of the talk) when the answer is complete. Under one form of organization (variations to be discussed later), as soon as the reporters hear the president coming to a possible completion of the response, they prepare to raise their hands to enter the candidacy pool at the earliest possible nonoverlapping point (e.g., on the last syllable). Once again the president selects which of the reporters will get that party's next turn. Because the answerer, rather than the questioner, has determined what will be treated as an adequate answer, and because of the way this turn-taking system operates to produce a flurry of candidacies for next speaker, the prior questioner does not get the opportunity to pursue the answer with a "follow-up" question. It is then up to the next reporter selected, who undoubtedly has a prepared question to ask, to decide (without consultation with others, for there is no time) whether to use the turn to follow up on the preceding question-answer exchange, or to ask the prepared question. The issue, then, is one of achieving a concerted course of action by a party whose incumbents cannot coordinate their activities in any explicit way. When a next question has been asked the cycle continues.

Consider the following additional points. When Ronald Reagan took office, he and his staff experimented with several changes in the organization of press conferences. The first changes were introduced, so it was said, in the interests of decorum. It was thought unseemly for reporters to be leaping from their seats, waving their hands in the air, and calling out "Mr. President," often while the president was finishing a response. Therefore the practice was changed; the press corps were requested to raise their hands quietly; no calling out, no standing up, no waving of arms. These changes are obviously cosmetic: they are not structural or organizational but affect only the signs by which bids for speakership are displayed.

For the next press conference different changes were introduced. This time, all members of the press corps were assigned numbers, and well in advance of the actual press conference numbers were drawn at random, thereby fixing both the identities of the question askers and the order in which they would ask their questions. That is, the system was changed from one in which half the turns were preallocated to a one-person party, who in turn chose turn by turn who would speak for the other party, to a system with full preallocation of next-speaker identities (though not of turn size and not fully of turn allocation because, as we shall see, under this system follow-up questions became possible—that is, additional turns for the same speaker from the press corps).

This change *was* organizational and it did yield different outcomes. For example, under the old system, as the president would be finishing a turn a clamor would start up, bidding for his attention, and his eyes would sweep the room scanning through the waving arms. He would not, as speakers otherwise often do, return his eyes at the end of the utterance to the one whose question had prompted the response. This was the physical vehicle for the blockage of follow-up questions. At the first press conference with the new organizing format, President Reagan at first forgot the change; as he ended his response to the first question, he began sweeping the room with his eyes, looking momentarily puzzled at the absence of waving arms bidding for his attention. Then he remembered, remarked at having forgotten the change, and consulted a note on the podium on which were listed the names of the questioners in order. He called the next questioner. As he finished his answer to the second question, his eyes returned to the questioner who was still standing, "receiving the answer." This momentary mutual gaze opened the possibility for a further question, and the reporter grasped the opportunity, asked a follow-up question, and got another answer. Later in the same press conference another reporter asked a pointed question, which the President answered in a guarded and hesitant manner. What was striking was that as he brought his answer to a close, he visibly withheld his glance from returning to the still standing reporter, looked instead at the list on the podium, and with hardly a breath after his answer's completion called out the name of the next questioner. The avoidance of follow-up was no longer ensured by the turn-taking organization of the talk; instead, it was revealed as a forcibly achieved, and nakedly apparent, evasion. Future press conferences returned to the former format. Note that the turn-taking system in effect can have, in these and many other and deeper respects, important consequences not only for the sequential organization of the talk and other aspects of interactional form (which are, of course, of central importance to the formal sociology here); it can also (and thereby) affect the substance of what gets talked about and how.

I have meant in the preceding discussion to illustrate the notion of speech exchange system as context by describing several seemingly different activities in speech-exchange-system context terms and to suggest some of their similarities and, in the framework, some of their differences. I then explored some organizational variations within one of these formats—the press conference—emerging with a suggestion of some ways in which the substance of the talk can be affected. Among this system's practices are the following: the organization of a multiperson setting by a two-party format; a one-person party and a multiperson party; single-person party selects speaker for multiperson party from self-assembled candidate pool; the set of practices organizes limited action-type interaction, ordinarily a colloquy of move (such as question) and response (such as answer), though not restricting assignment of the action types between the party types. A substantial part of the conduct of vernacularly different occasions, such as the press conference and the classroom, is organized by some such device. Two points are central. First, these ways of formulating context are procedurally relevant; they directly implicate sequential conduct of the interaction. Second, in the very ways in which the parties organize distribution of their participation, they exhibit their orientation to, and constitute the reality of, their contexts so understood.

The effects of different turn-taking practices on the character of interaction, and on the substance of what gets talked about in interaction, may be appreciated by considering the discussion periods following the papers at the conference on which this book is based (and many others). For the first several papers, the chair of the session called on persons who requested the floor, and after each had asked a question or offered a comment, the floor reverted to the presenter of the paper for a response. This format encouraged the development of a "colloquy," an extended exchange of remarks between the presenter and one other person, after which such a colloquy might develop with another member of the audience. Because each person invited to participate sustained an extended exchange with the deliverer of the paper, however, relatively few persons from the audience were able to participate.

After the first several papers, the chairs of the sessions adopted another practice (whether at the suggestion of the conference organizers or spontaneously I do not know). Rather than allowing the speaker to respond to each question or comment after it was put forward from the audience, a number of questions or comments were collected and the speaker was then asked to respond to them in turn. The effect of this practice was to limit the interaction with each audience member to a single exchange—for example, to a single question and its answer. For unlike the earlier format, the response by the speaker was not followed by a search for another intervention from the floor—a search that could find the prior questioner for a follow-up. A response by the speaker was followed by the speaker consulting his notes to find the next intervention to which a response was in order. Only in a few cases did the participant whose intervention had just been addressed forcibly seek to retake the floor to follow up the response. In some cases this effort succeeded, but only after having produced an atmosphere of contentiousness (not always warranted by the substance of the exchange); in other cases it failed, sometimes being suppressed by the chair, enforcing the procedures that had been adopted.

What differs between these two forms of turn-taking practices is not only the mechanism by which opportunities to participate were distributed, and the relative concentration or dispersion of these opportunities among more or fewer participants. The character of the talk, the topics likely touched on, the depth of pursuit of particular topics (that is, the substance of the matters under discussion) are also involved.

Consider the different contingencies each of these arrangements makes more or less likely, the substantive stances it makes sense for a participant to make explicit or to inhibit—that is, the direction the discussion may substantively take. Especially for nonpresenters, certain stances vis-à-vis some presentation will not be interactionally feasible (or will entail substantial reputational costs) because of the access to the floor and the length of speaking turn they require, and the impossibility or unsuitability of accomplishing those floor requirements in these interactional circumstances. Indeed, such considerations inform the expectations of those who attend such affairs about what can be realistically expected from them and what cannot; or, rather than "what cannot," what can occur only between formal sessions (or in the discussion participants may arrange for the future to follow up contacts made here) in which a different speech exchange system can operate. Just as interactional context can demonstrably control what participants in conversation think to say, stories they are reminded of, and the like, so it is likely that the points participants make in the conference sessions are the survivors of an interactional process that cuts more deeply than seeing that some critique that has come to mind cannot be pursued under these circumstances. It is likely to constrain what comes to mind in the first place. Thinking afterward of what one might have said is not simply a matter of lacking social wit.

Finally, this bears in another way on the micro/macro issue. About ten years ago, in offering some comments on the import of the model of turn-taking we were then presenting, we wrote:

> Turns are valued, sought, or avoided. The social organization of turn-taking distributes turns among parties. It must, at least partially, be shaped as an economy. As such, it is expectable that, like other economies, its organization will affect the relative distribution of that which it organizes. Until we unravel its organization, we shall not know what those effects consist of, and where they will turn up. But since all sorts of scientific and applied research use

conversation now, they all employ an instrument whose effects are not known. This is perhaps unnecessary.[29]

If such conferences as this, conversations among colleagues and work sessions and seminars with students, as well as survey and demographic interviews and talk in the course of fieldwork are important shapers of the content of a body of knowledge, and if they are in turn shaped and constrained by the turn-taking systems in effect in those activities, then the body of knowledge is being "effected" by conversational practices. How, then, shall we think of such a body of knowledge? As a product or element of macrostructure? Of microstructure? How does it matter?

V.

The predominant thrust of the social sciences in the direction of variation and comparative analysis leads those committed to that stance to be unsatisfied by any "unitarian" analysis. From their point of view, until some "depth" is achieved by determining how some described phenomenon differs in different social classes and cultural settings, or under different work conditions, until the historical circumstances under which some practice arose are made explicit, yielding a comparative understanding for its basis, unless the social structural circumstances are described under which some phenomenon waxes or wanes, there is no satisfaction; there is no stable, even if temporary, intellectual resting place. This stance drives every apparently unitary analysis to find some variation. On the other side is the stance that finds in every discovered variation the challenge to find and articulate some yet more general account that allows the variants to find an appropriate place under its umbrella. These contradictory and potentially complementary impulses do not necessarily coincide with the boundaries of macro and micro or their possible relationship. Still, at present there does appear to be an elective affinity between macro-micro integrationists and variationism on one hand and those who rest comfortably without such integration and unitarianism on the other. It is the latter which is the minority position, and it would be salutary if its message were better received.

When conversation analysis points to various features of talk-in-interaction and proposes that together they evidence the operation of a systematic solution to certain general organizational problems of interaction, one response is to propose that these are not the interesting facts about conversation; they are so common as to be obvious and, being common and obvious, are not relevant. It is what differs by class, ethnicity, culture, gender, institutional setting, organizational context, and so on that is interesting. The impression is thereby fostered that it is only by its linkage to macro themes that microanalysis becomes "respectable" and finds its *raison d'être*.

One can argue to the contrary, however, that any discipline that takes the understanding of human action as its goal must be answerable to such microanalysis as seems to offer a rigorous account of the details of social action *in its own terms*. Ideally such microanalysis will involve a capacity to yield effective and informative analysis of the details of actual, singular episodes or courses of action and interaction. Such a "single-case-competent" analytic apparatus should provide a proximate, or first-order, account of determinate episodes of interaction on one hand and, on the other hand, should provide a "hook" or "receptacle" for linkage with other theories at other levels. The nature of the linkage of other levels of analysis to that account will be shaped and constrained to an important extent by its characteristics, as may be the very terms in which other levels of analysis may themselves be couched. Compatibility with the terms of a microanalysis adequate to the details of singular bits of interaction is a (perhaps *the*) major constraint on articulation with other orders of theorizing.

The upshot of these considerations is that at least some of the favored contemporary ways of relating macro to micro levels of analysis are problematic. Efforts to link to the level of culture and society in the search for variation are unassured of success and uncertain in motive. Efforts to relate levels of analysis via macro-relevant attributes of the participants in micro-level processes threaten underdevelopment of a full technical exploration of the micro-level processes. Efforts to bridge the levels by the use of vernacular conceptions of context are vulnerable to challenges to the adequacy of their warrant and to the directness of their linkage to details of the actual conduct of interaction. I have tried to suggest one direction in which a solution might be found, at least with respect to the last of these tacks; it challenges us to replace vernacular formulations of context with technical ones—where, however, the "technical" may do better at capturing the real relevancies for participants than do the vernacular. How far this will take us, and whether now is the time to be taking this path, is not entirely clear. The issue in the end is not what the traditions and current tendencies of our disciplines ask of us but the integrity of our materials—what is necessary to come to terms effectively with the details of the lives in interaction of which the ordinary society is so largely fashioned.

ACKNOWLEDGMENT

Many thanks to Renee Anspach and Elinor Ochs for discussion of several of the themes touched on here at various stages of the essay's development, and to Charles Goodwin, Douglas Maynard, Michael Moerman, Melvin Pollner, Anita Pomerantz, Melvin Seeman, and Don Zimmerman (as well as several of the participants at the German/American Conference, "Relating Micro and Macro Levels in Sociological Theory," for which it was first prepared) for useful critical response to earlier versions. Jennifer Mandelbaum provided not only these but indispensable assistance and encouragement throughout.

NOTES

1. Emanuel A. Schegloff, "Discourse as an Interactional Achievement: Some Uses of 'Uh Huh' and Other Things That Come Between Sentences," in Georgetown University Roundtable on Languages and Linguistics, Deborah Tannen, ed., *Analyzing Discourse: Text and Talk* (Washington, DC: Georgetown University Press, 1981).

2. Harvey Sacks, Emanuel A. Schegloff, and Gail Jefferson, "A Simplest Systematics for the Organization of Turntaking for Conversation," *Language* 50 (1974): 696–735.

3. Harvey Sacks, "On the Analyzability of Stories by Children," in John J. Gumperz and Dell Hymes, eds., *Directions in Sociolinguistics* (New York: Holt, Rinehart & Winston, 1972), p. 332.

4. Emanuel A. Schegloff, Gail Jefferson, and Harvey Sacks, "The Preference for Self-Correction in the Organization of Repair in Conversation," *Language* 53 (1977): 361–383.

5. Michael Moerman, "The Preference for Self-Correction in a Tai Conversational Corpus," *Language* 53, 4 (1977): 872–882.

6. Niko Besnier, "Repairs and Error in Tuvaluan Conversation" (unpublished paper, December 1982).

7. Elinor Ochs, "Talking to Children in Western Samoa," *Language in Society* 11 (1982): 77–104; and "Clarification and Culture," in Georgetown University Roundtable on Languages and Linguistics, Deborah Schiffrin, ed., *Meaning, Form, and Use: Linguistic Applications* (Washington, DC: Georgetown University Press, 1984).

8. Alessandro Duranti, "Intentions, Self, and Local Theories of Meaning: Words and Social Action in a Samoan Context" (manuscript prepared for the Laboratory of Comparative Human Cognition, University of California, San Diego, 1984); also Elinor Ochs and B. B. Schieffelin, "Language Acquisition and Socialization: Three Developmental Stories and Their Implications," in R. Shweder and R. LeVine, eds., *Culture Theory: Essays on Mind, Self, and Society* (New York: Cambridge University Press, 1984).

9. This is not merely a psycholinguistic adaptation to a missing word; it is not invariably a word search. It can have strategic interactional use, as when the speaker is engaged in something interactionally "delicate," such as offering an assessment of a third party without being sure that the interlocutor shares the judgment. Then the speaker may speak until just before the point of the assessment term, hesitate, and leave it for the recipient to supply a candidate term, thereby showing that they hold the same assessment. The two can thus produce the assessment together. "Assessments" are, of course, one interactional specification of norms and values.

10. There is some indication, therefore, that some variations in repair practices may serve to implement distinctive cultural values or ethnotheories. Showing this, however, will require overcoming some difficult analytical problems.

11. What follows is based on preliminary fieldwork by Irene Daden, reported in Irene M. Daden and Marlys McClaren, "Same-Turn Repair in Quiche (Maya) Conversation: An Initial Report" (unpublished manuscript, University of California, 1978). The report should be treated with caution because subsequent extended fieldwork did not focus on these matters.

12. See Don H. Zimmerman and Candace West, "Sex Roles, Interruptions and Silences in Conversation," in B. Thorne and N. Henley, eds., *Language and Sex: Difference and Dominance* (Rowley, MA: Newbury House, 1975); Candace West and Don H. Zimmerman, "Women's Place in Everyday Talk: Reflections on Parent-Child Interaction," *Social Problems* 24 (1977): 521–529; and Candace West, "Against Our Will: Male Interruptions of Females in Cross-Sex Conversation," *Annals of the New York Academy of Sciences* 327 (1979): 81–97.

13. See section 4.

14. Subsequent work by West ("Why Can't a Woman Be More Like a Man?" *Work and Occupations* 9 (1982):5–29), in which some of these overlap resolution devices are examined in terms of pejorative relations between the genders/statuses, leaves the question unresolved.

15. Furthermore, even with respect to the *onset* of simultaneous talk to which this tradition of work is addressed in the first instance, as early as 1973 Jefferson suggested various interactional issues that could be implicated in precisely placed onsets of talk while another was still talking. Although much of that work may not be directly in point for "interruption," it is unlikely that no such range of interactional uses is involved in interruption onsets, as alternatives to, or in combination with, the gender/status/power considerations that have hitherto been the focus of attention. See Gail Jefferson, "A Case of Precision Timing in Ordinary Conversation: Overlapped Tag-Positioned Address Terms in Closing Sequences," *Semiotica* 9 (1973): 47–96.

16. Aaron Cicourel, "Notes on the Integration of Micro- and Macro-Levels of Analysis," in K. Knorr-Cetina and A. Cicourel, eds., *Advances in Social Theory and Methodology: Toward an Integration of Micro- and Macro-Sociologies* (Boston: Routledge & Kegan Paul, 1981), 51–80.

17. Harvey Sacks, "An Initial Investigation of the Usability of Conversational Data for Doing Sociology," in David N. Sudnow, ed., *Studies in Social Interaction* (New York: Free Press, 1972), 31–74.

18. Emanuel A. Schegloff, "Notes on a Conversational Practice," in ibid., pp. 76–118. That paper offered as one conclusion of its analysis the following, which is directly relevant to the theme of this essay: "This is pertinent to some ways in which 'contextual variation' affects interaction. It is being proposed that the much invoked 'dependence on context' must be investigated by showing that, and how, *participants* analyze context and use the product of their analysis in producing their interaction. To say that *interaction* is context-sensitive is to say that *interactants* are context-sensitive, and for what and how that is so is an empirical matter that can be researched in detail. One dimension has to do with the ways in which interactants particularize their contributions so as to exhibit attention to the 'this-one-here-and-now-for-us-at-this-point-in-it' character of the interaction" (p. 115).

19. That investigators may share with the participants the common cultural knowledge that is thereby employed, and use it in conducting analysis (see Cicourel, "Notes on Integration"), is beyond question. Not every aspect of the talk, however, invokes all the same aspects of context. One may not need to know about hospitals, or that a fragment of conversation is drawn from a conversation that occurred in a hospital, to understand and appreciate a perfectly coordinated turn transfer displayed in it. For any next candidate conversational phenomenon it may not be knowable in advance what, if any, contextual sensitivities it bears. When data fragments are displayed in conversation-analytic research reports with no discursive description of "context," a claim may be read that none is specially relevant to the phenomenon being explicated.

20. For example, J. M. Atkinson, "Understanding Formality: Notes on the Categorization and Production of 'Formal' Interaction," *British Journal of Sociology* 33 (1982): 86–117; John Heritage, *Garfinkel and Ethnomethodology* (Cambridge: Polity Press, 1984), 280–290; Douglas W. Maynard, *Inside Plea Bargaining* (New York: Plenum Press,

1984), chap. 3; and, along somewhat different lines, Jurgen Streeck, "Embodied Contexts, Transcontextuals, and the Timing of Speech Acts," *Journal of Pragmatics* 8 (1984): 113–137.

21. Paula A. Treichler, Richard M. Frankel, Cheris Kramarae, Kathleen Zoppi, and Howard B. Beckman, "Problems and *Prob*lems: Power Relationships in a Medical Encounter," in Cheris Kramarae, Muriel Schulz, and William O'Barr, eds., *Language and Power* (Beverly Hills, CA: Sage, 1984), 68, citing Richard M. Frankel, "Talking in Interviews: A Dispreference for Patient-Initiated Questions in Physician-Patient Encounters," in G. Psathas, ed., *Interactional Competence* (Norwood, NJ: Ablex Publishers, in press); and Candace West, "'Ask Me No Questions . . .': An Analysis of Queries and Replies in Physician-Patient Dialogues," in S. Fisher and A. D. Todd, eds., *The Social Organization of Doctor-Patient Communication* (Washington, DC: Center for Applied Linguistics, 1983), 75–106.

22. For example, see Cicourel, "Notes on Integration," and other recent papers of his.

23. E.g., John J. Gumperz and Dell Hymes, *Directions in Sociolinguistics*.

24. E.g., William Labov, *Sociolinguistic Patterns* (Philadelphia: University of Pennsylvania Press, 1972).

25. E.g., Erving Goffman, "The Neglected Situation," in John J. Gumperz and Dell Hymes, eds., "The Ethnography of Communication," *American Anthropologist* 66, II (1964): 133–137.

26. Treating conversation, speech exchange systems, and forms of interaction more generally as a bridge between macro and micro makes some sense in view of some developments in the social sciences over the last two decades or so. As many have noted, one trend has paired in dialectical development the emergence of a set of powerful themes drawing on linguistics and psychology into the so-called cognitive sciences, with a related though opposed flourishing of the thematics of human variation in anthropology. The former has focused on what goes on "in the head," has strained in the direction of universalism, has treated as the enduring reality the embodied, minded self or cognizer, and has treated action as the externalization of plans and intentions hatched by the cognizer in the mind. One anthropological stance has stressed, in contrast, cultural particularism, public culture, and the social situatedness of all conduct and practice. Interaction as an autonomous and structured field of action may be seen to mediate between them.

27. For other treatments, see H. Mehan, *Learning Lessons* (Cambridge, MA: Harvard University Press, 1979); and A. McHoul, "The Organization of Turns at Formal Talk in the Classroom," *Language in Society* 7 (1978): 183–213.

28. These formulations of context are the type to which I have just objected. I use them here as vernacular terms to enlist the reader's recognition in commonsense terms (and outside the scope of a technical analysis of detailed data) of the familiar scenes to which I mean to be referring. The ensuing discussion begins to develop a technical characterization for some set of activities that goes on in the vernacularly named context. The goal is to arrive at technical characterizations of the one or more speech exchange systems organizing the several kinds of activity that occur there. For other efforts to develop descriptions of turn-taking organizations for speech exchange systems other than conversation, see J. Maxwell Atkinson and Paul Drew, *Order in Court* (London: Macmillan, 1979), chap. 2 ("Examination: A Comparison of the Turn-Taking Organizations for Conversation and Examination"); and David Greatbatch, "A Turn-Taking System for British News Interviews" (unpublished paper, Department of Sociology, University of Warwick, 1984).

29. Sacks, et al., "A Simplest Systematics," 701–702.

REFERENCES

Atkinson, J. M. 1982. Understanding Formality: Notes on the Categorization and Production of "Formal" Interaction. *British Journal of Sociology* 33:86–117.

Atkinson, J. M. and Paul Drew. 1979. *Order in Court*. London: Macmillan.

Besnier, Niko. 1982. "Repairs and Errors in Tuvaluan Conversation." Unpublished paper, Linguistics Department, University of Southern California.

Cicourel, Aaron V. 1981. Notes on the Integration of Micro- and Macro-Levels of Analysis, pp. 51–80 in Karin Knorr-Cetina and Aaron V. Cicourel, eds., *Advances in Social Theory and Methodology: Toward an Integration of Micro-and Macro-Sociologies*. Boston: Routledge & Kegan Paul.

Daden, Irene, and Marlys McClaren. 1978. "Same Turn Repair in Quiche (Maya) Conversation: An Initial Report." Unpublished paper, University of California, Los Angeles.

Duranti, Alessandro. 1984. "Intentions, Self, and Local Theories of Meaning: Words and Social Action in a Samoan Context." Unpublished paper, Laboratory of Comparative Cognition, University of California, San Diego.

Frankel, Richard M. forthcoming. Talking in Interviews: A Dispreference for Patient-Initiated Questions in Physician-Patient Encounters, in George Psathas, ed., *Interactional Competence*. Norwood, NJ: Ablex.

Goffman, Erving. 1964. The Neglected Situation. *American Anthropologist* 66, 6: 133–137.

Greatbatch, David. 1984. "A Turn-Taking System for British News Interviews." Unpublished paper, University of Warwick.

Gumperz, John, and Dell Hymes, eds. 1964. The Ethnography of Communication. *American Anthropologist* 66, 6 (whole issue).

Heritage, John. 1984. *Garfinkel and Ethnomethodology*. Cambridge, Mass.: Polity Press.

Jefferson, Gail. 1973. A Case of Precision Timing in Ordinary Conversation. Overlapped Tag-Positioned Address Terms in Closing Sequences. *Semiotica* 9:47–96.

Labov, William. 1972. *Sociolinguistic Patterns*. Philadelphia: University of Pennsylvania Press.

Maynard, Douglas. 1984. *Inside Plea Bargaining*. New York: Plenum Press.

McHoul, A. 1978. The Organization of Turns at Formal Talk in the Classroom. *Language in Society* 7:183–213.

Mehan, H. 1979. *Learning Lessons*. Cambridge, Mass.: Harvard University Press.

Moerman, Michael. 1977. The Preference for Self-Correction in a Tai Conversational Corpus. *Language* 53, 4: 872–82.

Ochs, Elinor. 1982. Talking to Children in Western Samoa. *Language in Society* 11:77–104.

———. 1984. Clarification and Culture, in Georgetown University Roundtable on Languages and Linguistics, 1984, Deborah Schiffrin, ed., *Meaning, Form, and Use: Linguistic Applications*. Washington D.C.: Georgetown University Press.

Ochs, Elinor, and B. B. Schieffelin. 1984. Language Acquisition and Socialization: Three Developmental Stories and Their Implications, in R. Shweder and R. LeVine, eds., *Cultural Theory: Essays on Mind, Self, and Society*. New York: Cambridge University Press.

Sacks, Harvey. 1972a. An Initial Investigation of the Usability of Conversational

Data for Doing Sociology, pp. 31–74 in David Sudnow, ed., *Studies in Social Interaction*. New York: Free Press.
———. 1972b. On the Analyzability of Stories by Children, pp. 325–345 in John Gumperz and Dell Hymes, eds., *Directions in Sociolinguistics*. New York: Holt, Rinehart & Winston.
Sacks, Harvey, Emanuel A. Schegloff, and Gail Jefferson. 1974. A Simplest Systematics for the Organization of Turn-Taking for Conversation. *Language* 50, 4:696–735.
Schegloff, Emanuel A. 1972. Notes on a Conversational Practice: Formulating Place, pp. 75–118 in David Sudnow, ed., *Studies in Social Interaction*. New York: Free Press.
———. 1981. Discourse as an Interactional Achievement: Some Uses of "Uh Huh" and Other Things that Come Between Sentences, in Georgetown University Roundtable on Languages and Linguistics, 1981, D. Tannen, ed., *Analyzing Discourse: Text and Talk*. Washington, D.C.: Georgetown University Press.
Schegloff, Emanuel A., Gail Jefferson, and Harvey Sacks. 1977. The Preference for Self-Correction in the Organization of Repair in Conversation. *Language* 53, 2:361–383.
Streeck, Jürgen. 1984. Embodied Contexts, Transcontextuals, and the Timing of Speech Acts. *Journal of Pragmatics* 8:113–137.
Treichler, Paula A., Richard M. Frankel, Cheris Kramarae, Kathleen Zoppi, and Howard B. Beckman. 1984. Problems and *Prob*lems: Power Relationships in a Medical Encounter, pp. 62–88 in Cheris Kramarae, Muriel Schulz, and William O'Barr, eds., *Language and Power*. Beverly Hills, Calif.: Sage.
West, Candace. 1979. Against Our Will: Male Interruptions of Females in Cross-Sex Conversation. *Annals of the New York Academy of Sciences* 327:81–97.
———. 1982. Why Can't a Woman Be More Like a Man? *Work and Occupations* 9, 1: 5–29.
———. 1983. "Ask Me No Questions . . . ". An Analysis of Queries and Replies in Physician-Patient Dialogues, pp. 75–106 in S. Fisher and A. D. Todd, eds., *The Social Organization of Doctor-Patient Communication*. Washington, D.C.: Center for Applied Linguistics.
West, Candace, and Don H. Zimmerman. 1977. Women's Place in Everyday Talk. Reflections on Parent-Child Interaction. *Social Problems* 24:521–529.
Zimmerman, Don H., and Candace West. 1975. Sex Roles, Interruptions, and Silences in Conversation, pp. 105–129 in B. Thorne and N. Henley, eds., *Language and Sex: Difference and Dominance*. Rowley, Mass.: Newbury House.

PART FOUR

Affective Action and Macrostructure

CHAPTER TEN

Psychoanalysis as the Macro-Micro Link

Edith Kurzweil

Most sociologists will agree that macroanalyses deal with collectivities, and microanalyses with social processes between two or more individuals—that is, with small groups. Few of them, however, can agree on a satisfactory way to move from micro to macro levels of analysis. This was simpler so long as microsociology was content to remain philosophical rather than empirical, when it was not necessary to demonstrate *exactly* how intimate social processes intrinsic to aggregates of face-to-face relations—of reciprocity, symbolization, exchange, or dependency—causally, and step by step, "translate" into analyses of institutions, communities, changes in demographic variables, and other properties of populations.

As we know, Talcott Parsons was the first sociologist to attempt such a synthesis. When, for instance, Jürgen Habermas talks (in relation to questions of social action and social order) of the conditions linking the actions of alter and ego, and then to their life-world, he takes the Parsonian synthesis for granted. So do most systems theorists, although some of them, such as Siegwart Lindenberg and Reinhard Wippler, indicate clearly that much remains to be learned about how social behavior translates into social phenomena (see later discussion in this chapter). In other words, when constructing our paradigms, we do not always keep in mind that Parsons did not successfully demonstrate the mechanisms of interpenetration, and of evolving changes, within and between personality and social systems.

In this essay I will begin by showing how Parsons proposed, in "Superego and the Theory of Social Systems," to bring together the Freudian theory of personality (it had failed to conceptualize personalities as parts of systems) and the Durkheimian social system (it neglected personal motivation). We recall that Parsons wanted to account adequately for microphenomena in a macrotheory that would be able to subsume intentional as well as unintentional action. He did so with the help of the Freudian concept of the superego and in line with his specific understanding of culture. Other applications of Freudian theory—in Germany and France--derived from other social and intellectual premises. Therefore, I shall maintain that Parsons was influenced by his own location in American society and by his theoretical expectations of convergence. This is not to detract from his vast knowledge of other cultures, but only to argue that his generalizations, though applicable to other societies, relied on his own American intellectual perspective, on a specifically American perspective on Freud's ideas. For Parsons addressed the type of Freudian theory that was being pursued by American (and emigré) psychoanalysts in the 1940s and 1950s and that had appealed to many anthropologists, without considering the fact that in other countries Freud's works would be interpreted differently.

In Parson's theoretical scheme, both personality and social systems were postulated as interactive systems; and they were being mediated and stabilized by a *common culture*, by a commonly shared system of symbols.[1] In order to provide an inclusive step-by-step scheme, Parsons then proceeded to relate the elements of the common culture that individuals inevitably share to his three modes of action orientation: cognitive, affective, and evaluative. We are all familiar with his definitions and functions of norms within each of his systems and with how any orientation of action will properly be symbolized. By focusing on the *inter*active system between ego and alter, on conventions of language, and on moral standards that are at the core of the stabilizing mechanisms of social interaction, we recall, Parsons illustrated how "*all the components of the common culture* are internalized as part of the personality structure."[2]

We remember also that when Parsons proposed to achieve the macro-micro link by adapting the Freudian concept of the superego in 1951, psychoanalysis was at the height of its success in America. We did not know, however, that by then such psychoanalysts as J. Lampl de-Groot and Jacques Lacan were beginning to indicate that this particular thrust of psychoanalysis was better suited to the American intellectual climate than to postwar European conditions.[3] The emphasis on the division of the personality into id, ego, and superego at the expense of Freud's earlier focus on drives, said a number of Europeans, was well suited to American notions of scientific analysis; and the stress on ego components seemed more suitable to the general optimistic and adaptive nature of the American personality than had Freud's so-called topographical theories.

This is part of the post facto argument by a number of prominent French and German psychoanalysts and sociologists. Before addressing these questions, however, and before showing what led Parsons to criticize Freud for neglecting the components of interaction that are regulated by moral norms, I must briefly reconstruct the context and some of the problems that led to the psychoanalytic discussions Parsons encountered when he offered his own means of theoretically linking individual and social phenomena.

I.

From the time Freud established that the symptoms of hysterical patients had originated in response to social interactions, both he and his disciples had felt justified in reconstructing individuals' defense mechanisms as responses to events (or their perception), and in moving easily from micro- to macrophenomena. In the wake of their discoveries, they all had great hopes of curing neuroses and other mental disturbances in line with the advances of psychoanalytic science. So they continued to assume, for some time, that the uncovering of individuals' unconscious trauma would result in cure, as soon as unconscious connections and clues would be interpreted. We recall that psychoanalysis then was thought to be in a position to help "neutralize" the destructive impulses of individuals, and some went so far as to believe that these impulses would be eradicable. Therefore, in its "micro-scope," psychoanalysis was to cure individuals' aggression, which, in turn, would reduce neurosis in general. In its "macro-scope" it was to militate against aggressiveness and war, mostly through newly gained insights by political figures. (Freud's famous letter to Einstein, the "inevitability" of the death instinct, or *Totem and Taboo*, are some examples of the Freudian linkage.)

Freud's early formulations did not lend themselves to the stringent analysis Parsons's system required. The heuristic divisions within the personality structure, however, as postulated in the contributions of 1914 and 1915 and more so in "The Ego and the Id" (1923), were amenable to stressing any one component over the other two. Until then psychoanalysts had not talked of egos or selves in very specific ways. To Carl Jung, the self would become an important archetype (next to the soul, which was central to the collective unconscious represented by the *anima* or *animus*). His formulations were unsystematic, vaguely connected to individuation and symbolization, and they originated in active imagination and in the amplification of dreams. Such unscientific constructions would have been unacceptable to Freud, even if he had not already been suspicious of Jung before their final break in 1913. In addition, Jung was referring to already formed personalities, or to individuals as social beings, so that Freud, who increasingly rooted his psychoanalysis in early family experience (Oedipus complex), had to reject these views. (The centrality of the family romance, of course, would be compatible with the importance Parsons accorded the family in his social system.) Freud required more complex structures than the Jungian self could accommodate. Expanding on what already had become a self—that is, what in subsequent formulations roughly would correspond to the ego component of personality structure—required an open theoretical system that would allow for both the evolution of human drives and their continuous integration into the personality, in response to the environment. Because Jung increasingly denied the centrality of sexuality, he was able to settle for a more undifferentiated notion of self than Freud, who expected to account for the ongoing changes within psyche, biology, and culture and for their continuous impact on one another.

During this time Freud also defended psychoanalysis against all simplistic application to political ends, and in particular against Adler's impatience with theoretical preoccupations. For Adler was willing to compromise in order to introduce psychoanalysis into the school system through teachers and social workers; he expected to further political consciousness. The arguments between Freud and Adler revolved around how the psychoanalytic vision was to be realized—that is, on whether or not the jump to macrophenomena would be made at the expense of microanalysis. (Adler too was an excellent therapist, but he helped his patients to confront problems rather than to deal with unconscious materials.) That is why Adler's formulation—inferiority complex, masculine protest, or positive tendencies—would have been useless for Parsons, even if he had not been hostile to Adler's Marxism.

II.

Adlerian and Jungian psychoanalysis, then, proved inapplicable to Parsons's social system. So were the derivations by the "culturalists," such as Erich Fromm, Karen Horney, Harry Stack Sullivan, and Wilhelm Reich. The latter, for the most part, had been elaborated within American culture and to some extent did appeal to its populist streak. In spite of their different foci, these analysts expected psychoanalysis to contribute to some kind of human liberation: Fromm insisted on the freedom from domination; Horney argued that self-fulfillment would lead to self-realization by removing neurotic conflict; Sullivan promised to get there through interpersonal relations; and Reich attempted to liberate genitality. The so-called classical psychoanalysts as well expected to implement Freud's larger promises, but they did not address them in such an immediate context. Parsons inevitably found their methods most in tune with his own: Their societal visions, though primarily derived from working with the unconscious of patients, focused on unconscious defense mechanisms and on their reactivation in therapy. By abstracting from their cases, and through a backward tracing of the gradually unfolding memories, American psychoanalysts refined their scientific knowledge. In this process they increasingly came to focus on the ego components of personality.

Because classical psychoanalysts were more and more concerned with formulations of microphenomena—that is, with intrapsychic mechanisms and structures—they often generalized too loosely to macrostructures. Parsons criticized them for it and proposed to supply the bridge between psychoanalysis and sociology. In this context he chided psychoanalysts for subsuming the object world under "external reality" and for postulating "ego-functions" as adaptive processes.[4] His criticism, I believe, was valid. The strict (heuristic) separation between the functions and structures of the personality (that is, the confinement of learned responses to internalization by the superego), Parsons pointed out, does not adequately account for the fact that both ego and superego derive from the same cultural patterns. Furthermore, Parsons criticized "the absence of biological contact" and psychoanalysts' nearly exclusive concern with the psychic unconscious at the expense of physical influences on these psyches.[5] In this instance he anticipated objections to "American ego-psychology" by some of the European Freudians. (Lionel Trilling also suggested a need to refer to biology, but he did so in order to render psychoanalysts' discussions less self-referential and to arrive at the literary critic's distanced and "privileged place.")

Parsons himself entered Freudian discussions by noting that the concept of the superego had become dissociated from the sources of affect. He argued that Freud had underplayed the significance of the common culture of expressive-affective symbolism individuals were sharing. Accepting the American Freudians' view of the works on culture (i.e., *Totem and Taboo*, *Civilization and Its Discontents*, or *The Future of an Illusion* were devalued as too speculative for scientific investigation), he, too, concentrated on the theoretical and metapsychological works. The Freudian analysts for whom the superego (mostly) is located in the unconscious were less concerned with the cognitive elements of internalization per se than Parsons, who began by proposing to use the superego as the link between the micro and macro levels in sociological analysis. (Parsons's scientific interest also would exclude the Freudians' so-called sociological discussions of literary works, delinquency, or authoritarian personalities—which, in fact, were decidedly unscientific and speculative.)

Outside the United States, psychoanalysts' cultural concerns were different: Micro-to-macro linkages were more likely to include references to Freud's cultural contributions, and scientificity was secondary. In both France and Germany there was less of a separation between psychoanalysis and sociology, at least in the aftermath of World War II. A number of German Freudians proposed to use psychoanalysis to reeducate all Germans and to make them aware of their collective guilt. Followers of Lacan expected to "reread" Freud because they wanted to politicize their society by mobilizing the "political unconscious."

By then American Freudians had divided over these issues: those who gave precedence to cultural rather than individual phenomena (Fromm, Horney, and Abram Kardiner) had left the fold to form their own intellectual networks. Although they maintained that they were indeed applying psychoanalytic insights to social issues, they did not try to prove the immediate connections between micro and macro levels. In fact, Parsons (and others) did not consider their theoretical formulations rigid enough: He proposed to rely on the ideas of the classical Freudians, precisely because those of the culturalists increasingly were addressing utopian conditions and thereby had lost touch with empirically provable phenomena. Because the Freudians' cultural contributions as well were increasingly separate from the clinical data, some of them welcomed the Parsonian project as a possible tool for their own research.

III.

In America Freudians had considered the concept of the ego as the most useful construct in connecting micro and macro levels of analysis: It was in direct touch with reality, whereas the superego and the id were located largely in the unconscious. (Regarding this point Freudians had their own disagreements, particularly about the start of superego formation: The earlier its origins, the more unconscious it would be.) Essentially American Freudians followed Anna Freud, who had stressed both the ego's need for synthesis because of its link to perceptive reality and the anxiety evoked by gratification of instincts, and Heinz Hartmann, who had found that adaptation to social structure and cooperation are essential to humanity.[6] Given the enormous proliferation and acceptance of these ideas in America (that is, far beyond psychoanalytic and intellectual circles), Parsons did not question their basic assumptions. (German psychoanalysts, some of whom were close to the Frankfurt School, preferred pursuing the dynamic aspects of drive, or id theory; and the French, in line with their pervasive interest in linguistics, talked of *le moi* as arising from individuals' speech.)

I have argued elsewhere that Hartmann's timing, though accidental and partly triggered by his emigration from Vienna via Paris to New York, coincided with a theme that appeared custom-made for America: The structural study of adaptation presented a scientific means of examining a society built upon the successful adaptation of immigrants, at a time when in Europe whole populations were adapting to fascism.[7] Hartmann's paper, in fact, was the forerunner of his seminal contribution (with Kris and Loewenstein), "Comments on the Formation of Psychic Structure," which was to shape American psychoanalysis for many years.[8] Essentially, they interpreted Freud in the following way: (1) They decided to avoid his biological terminology and use only psychological terminology; (2) they planned to avoid metaphoric language and to replace the word "self" with "ego"; (3) rather than talking, like Freud, of superego approval and disapproval, they focused on degrees of tension between psychic organizations; (4) they postulated the origins of object relations (and of defense mechanisms) by the end of the first year of life and linked them to the learning process that replaces the pleasure principle with the reality principle; (5) they summarized Freud's basic ideas on superego functions but made greater allowances than he had for modification during development and for a gradual adjustment during latency; and (6) they declared that cultural conditions were important for superego functions. (On this sixth point they joined other psychotherapists and psychologists who were trying to explain mass behavior.) When social values change rapidly without substituting new ones, or when new ideas of conduct do not supplement the older structure of the superego, American psychoanalysts maintained, individuals become compliant.[9]

Whereas Hartmann et al. urged Freudian analysts to study infant and child behavior in order to verify these hypotheses, Parsons correctly recognized that the psychoanalysts lacked a systematic means of getting at the cultural elements infants and children internalize. His own family system, however, was to serve as the connection between the two realms. In fact, Parsons argued that in the United States, interpretations of Freud focused too much on the power of individuals' instinctual needs and the deleterious effects of their frustrations.[10] Because Freudians were ever more concerned with intrapersonal issues, he found their psychology too biologically oriented, at the expense of societal and cultural influences. Their emphasis, he went on, paid too little attention to Freud's structural differentiation of the personality and its organization as a system, and to the relation of the individual to his or her social milieu during development. Soon the Europeans as well would decry this biological direction, but they would do so by arguing that it ignored class or ethnic differences, lacked Freud's critical stance, and had adopted American values.

Parsons proposed to reassociate the ego with the superego and to emphasize the common cultural aspect of symbolism. He thought that Freud had not sufficiently extended his fundamental analysis from the internalization of moral standards to "the cognitive frame of reference for interpersonal relations."[11] Indeed, Freud had not done so. This had become more of an issue, I believe, in Parsons's intellectual milieu than it had been in *fin-de-siècle* Vienna. The ever greater concern with ego functions, with their ramifications, and with interpersonal relations, had taken root in American intellectual culture. Because the psychoanalysts Parsons spoke to had become part of it, they agreed with him that "the internalization of a common culture of expressive symbolism . . . makes it possible for the child to express *and communicate* his feelings."[12] Thus Parsons postulated internalization by means of reference systems of cognition, expressive symbolism, and moral standards and then linked these to the process of identification. Now he suggested that the Oedipal situation was cultural as well as precultural (in the early attachment to the mother) and that therefore Freud's conception of the ego needed to be modified as deriving from *two* sources: the external environment and the common culture acquired from objects of identification.[13] By postulating culture as a separate source of internalization, Parsons moved somewhat closer to the Jungian paradigm. By defining the borderline between the ego and the id less clearly than did the American analysts, he relinquished some of the theoretical precision he originally had valued. Still, he concluded that his ideas were "broadly in line with the recent increasing emphasis in psychoanalytic theory itself on the psychology of the ego" and thought that his own formulations would provide the bridge between theories of personality and culture.[14] He then proposed to furnish the missing links in his unified theory of the social sciences.

In "Social Structure and the Development of Personality" (1958), Parsons further elaborated on the organization of the personality as a system and on the relation of individuals to their social milieu, especially during personality development.[15] Now he relied more strongly on the convergence between the thinking of Charles H. Cooley, Emile Durkheim, and George Herbert Mead and on role and interaction theories; and he showed how ego development takes place through the learning of social roles in collectivity structures.[16] Arguing once again that the separations between the ego and the id and between the ego and the superego were less distinct than had been assumed, Parsons expanded the principles of object relations through identification of object-cathexis and internalization to all of psychoanalytic theory and personality. His familiarity with all theories was admirable, and his attempt to link macroanalyses and microanalyses was exemplary. Nevertheless, by blurring the heuristic boundaries between the structures of personality, Parsons abandoned the theoretical precision he originally had sought. "Pure" psychoanalytic theory, as we know, ultimately neglects sociological facts. Parsons's sociological analysis, however systematic, no longer could account for the unconscious elements of personality as fully as he had expected.

IV.

When German and French psychoanalysts in the late 1940s addressed the American discussions, they selected the elements useful to their own ends. Some criticized the pragmatic American bent; others objected to the built-in adaptivity that militated against Marxist assumptions; yet others decried the neglect of the death instinct. They all were preoccupied with their own professional rehabilitation after the Nazi debacle, however, so that none of them addressed Parsonian (or any other) grand theory. As Alexander Mitscherlich, German psychoanalyst and investigator at the Nuremberg trials recalled, he had been surprised that "Freudian psychoanalysis in exile had become a broad scientific movement with a very careful system of training . . . and with a psychoanalytic ego-psychology."[17]

Mitscherlich was an ex-communist, had been imprisoned by the Nazis for nine months, and during the war had studied psychosomatic medicine and psychiatry in Heidelberg with Viktor von Weizsaecker. He became the foremost advocate of psychoanalysis after the war, arguing that only with the help of a restructured unconscious could Germans rid themselves of their Nazi past. Both the cultural and individual unconscious needed to be explored, he stated in innumerable public forums and books, in order to understand why Germans had united behind Hitler and to ensure that they would never again follow such a leader. He maintained that by investigating how the Germans' collective identification with their *Fuehrer* had occurred—through the ego ideal and by bypassing true object relations—they might come to terms with this past. He expected them to face it and to relinquish identification with the victors as well (the Russians in the East and the Americans in the West), by coming to understand what unconscious psychological mechanisms had engendered blind compliance.

Clearly, Mitscherlich's agenda required an intimate examination of the links between macro and micro levels of analysis. The "adaptive" qualities of both psychoanalytic ego psychology and Parsonian convergence theory, however, were counterproductive in explaining and accomplishing the necessary break with the immediate past. A Freud/Marx conflict approach would be more useful, he thought, although none of the available ones would do: Wilhelm Reich had perceived fascism as a manifestation of suppressed genitality, but its liberation could not possibly penetrate to individuals' reasons for enslavement to it. Fromm's fascist character traits—authoritarianism, destructiveness, and automaton-like conformity—were descriptive rather than applicable to therapeutic ends. Adler never believed in penetrating the deepest reaches of the unconscious.

Like Parsons, Mitscherlich expected to explain the intricate mechanisms connecting individual and social behavior with the help of psychoanalysis. He aimed primarily to use this knowledge in the field. Given his research with psychosomatic illness, he thought that pinpointing the exact moment when an individual's psychic reaction turned into a somatic symptom (as defense) might provide the clue for generalizations to all individuals and, ultimately, to the entire society. In other words, his macro-micro link, unlike that of Parsons between personality and culture, was postulated to lie at the nexus between individual biology and psyche. To move from there to cultural experience, he stated, required exacting research into the connections between them all. When he established the Sigmund-Freud-Institut in Frankfurt in 1956 (with the help of the Rockefeller Foundation), Mitscherlich set up interdisciplinary teams of psychoanalysts, psychologists, therapists, and sociologists in order to open new avenues of empirical research. Finally, they all expected to uncover the mechanisms that would explain why Germans had "lost their humanity." That was the only means, said Mitscherlich, by which to gain them readmission.

Essentially, German psychoanalysts were learning from their patients' immediate Nazi pasts and from their own didactic analyses. By closely cooperating with social scientists, they tried to explain personal development within familial and social contexts. Through learning all about ego psychology (American and English Freudians were their teachers and models), they would focus on how intrapsychic mechanisms linked to cultural mechanisms. But when they did address how id, ego, and superego related to one another, this was subordinated to the larger, cultural questions. Their basic assumptions as well as their respective research projects covered a broad range; and results were reported in *Psyche*, the widely circulated journal Mitscherlich began to edit in 1946. None of its contributors could be accused of advocating or advancing adaptivity, or of furnishing a grand theory removed from empirical questions.

Mario Erdheim, an anthropologist and psychoanalyst, for example, suggested that an innovative ethnoanalysis could "extricate the dialectic between transference and countertransference" by utilizing the tension every investigator experiences when immersed in a foreign culture. Just as Freud's self-analysis, he reminded us, had been possible at a moment when he had experienced a sort of "social death" resulting from his disappointments over a university career (he had discovered the role of the unconscious), so the "ethnoanalyst" could learn to "note things there which are to become things here."[18] Unlike American Freudians, he relied on *Totem and Taboo* to compare personality formation in primitive and mass society and to examine social conditions that might induce psychic change. He found that in the former personalities were both products of a leader and the basis for ideas of domination from the perspective of the dominated, whereas in the latter "institutions functioned like individuals who had been deprived of personal characteristics."[19] Erdheim further supported this theory by applying it to anthropological findings by others and to empirical situations and by comparing individuals' dreams in a variety of cultures. He found similar themes of domination in family and society, ranging from the Aztecs to nineteenth-century Europeans, and to current Western culture. This argument was as Freudian as it was Marxist.

Erdheim argued, however, that feelings of guilt and social obligation in modern society cannot be accounted for adequately by the American type of ego psychology, and thus a return to Freud's drive theory would be required. The tools provided by *Totem and Taboo*, however, also would not suffice because they are connected (in modern society) to pregenital and phallic/narcissistic drives that soon obstruct id drives. That was why, stated Erdheim, Freud had proposed the heuristic division into id, ego, and superego in the first place, although he had not postulated that ego psychology should dominate. Instead, he went on, all of Freud's work should be considered so that it would be possible to analyze how dominators may utilize crippled egos by using narcissism as their most effective tool. (This concept as well is formulated in the works around 1915. It became central in American psychoanalytic discussions with Kohut's focus on the self after 1971 and in more popular adaptations with Christopher Lasch's and Richard Sennett's use of the concept.[20])

Among the German theorists who argued for the refocusing on inner drives was Thomas Leithaeuser. He maintained that Freud wanted to keep humanity from being delivered through "enlightenment" by excessive entanglements in inner and outer authority relations, as well as from resignation and despair.[21] Helmut Dahmer found that the luxuriating needs of consumer society originate in the same drives that formerly incited people to rebellion and encouraged innovation.[22] In addition, according to Alfred Lorenzer, such spontaneity may occur with the help of a critical-hermeneutic process that genuinely aims to loosen and revivify bodily symptoms, fixed ideas, reified imagination, and obsessive fantasies.[23] Whether we read Klaus Horn's examination of evolving aggressive drives[24] or Karola Brede's view of the roots of psychosomatic symptoms,[25] we realize that they all argue for a return to drive theory—with a concomitant retention of the advances of ego psychology and its analysis of defenses—as the means to reradicalize and revitalize human potential.

Undoubtedly the unpredictability of the Freudian id may provide a more suitable theory for explaining radical social change than a reality-oriented ego psychology. Such a means of effecting the micro-macro linkage, it was thought, might be more likely to penetrate to the postwar Germans' fascist past than would a purely explanatory and functionalist theory. This is not the time to argue to what extent any theory may be able to predetermine practice. These discussions themselves, insofar as they aired the intense fears of another possible totalitarian disaster, put psychoanalysis at the center of German intellectual life and generated a more "democratic" discussion. In one way or another these inquiries, in their idealist thrust, harked back to German romanticism and idealism, to Hegel and Marx, as well as to Freud's own speculations and to his visions for psychoanalysis.

V.

French intellectuals also revived a Hegelian and Marxian tradition. Except for the surrealists, however, only a few paid attention to Freud before the war. Thus the reconstitution of psychoanalysis in 1946 seemed no more than a private meeting. This soon changed after the much-publicized break between classical analysts and Jacques Lacan in 1953 and even more so in the 1960s. As we know, the earlier rift occurred ostensibly over the length of the fifty-minute hour and the training of psychoanalytic candidates. In fact, Lacan vehemently rejected the advances of "American" ego psychology and its acceptance by French psychoanalysts, calling them "pseudo-scientism," "fake professionalism," and an activity that was too isolated from the larger culture. He thought that a psychoanalysis centering on the division of the personality into id, ego, and superego was based on miscognitions. At the same time he purposely separated himself from Sartre's then popular "superficial" view of consciousness, insofar as existentialism did not leave much room for explanations of unconscious mechanisms. Arguing that the ego is not the locus of truth but of *méconnaissances* (that is, of false perceptions), Lacan declared that he would liberate psychoanalysis from all wrong interpretations in order to free the *authentic self*, which he variously called the *I* or the *je* to distinguish it from *ego*.

Lacan frequently credited Hegel as the source of his inspiration. Certainly the latter's contention that consciousness is always subjective, that the scientific object is constructed by subjective mind, and that "self-consciousness is faced by another self-consciousness," was transposed to Lacan's central concept of the mirror image.[26] In this first and usually jubilant reaction to itself in a mirror, as a biological organism, as an entity belonging to the human species, stated Lacan, the infant becomes conscious of itself. At this instant a libidinal dynamism allegedly is revealed—a dynamism potentially present in Freud's studies on narcissism and in the *Ichspaltung* (splitting) of the *imago*. (This discussion of narcissism, however, differs from Kohut's examination of "the relationship between the self and archaic narcissistic self-objects," because unlike

Kohut, who related the ego's anxiety to the vulnerability and awareness of the mature self, Lacan moved into discourses on the infantile psyche.[27]) Because this is postulated as the earliest instance of identification, Lacan located the individual's anticipation of "it-self" (here he also makes an allusion to "id-self" and to the mistranslations of Freud into English) in this moment, and invested it with all the complex emotions and intellectualizations that go into all subsequent relations between the *Innenwelt* and the *Umwelt*.[28] Whereas Parsons, who also located the internalization of culture at this point, did so through the agency of the superego, Lacan introduced yet another complexity: Given that the mirrored body always is perceived in reverse, the ego constructed from this image, itself a product of alienation, *must* be misperceived. Consequently it will continue to remain a source of miscognitions and illusions. In order to reach these layers of problems, maintained Lacan, psychoanalysts had to analyze the discourse of their practices, rather than their patients' psyches alone. They could do so only with the help of language. Therefore Lacan imposed the categories of Saussurean structural linguistics onto the Freudian categories. He postulated binary relationships between *signifiers* (sound image) and *signified* (concept), language system and individual speech, between *metaphor* and *metonym*, in order to help unravel the ambivalences Freud had addressed in the "language of the unconscious." Given that the ego, or the self, is created through language, particularly through the mediations between signifiers and signifieds, language was postulated as the locus of internalizations of both society and the self. In addition, Lacan found a permanent barrier of repression between the language of the Other (the unconscious as "pure" subject of the signifier) and the other (counterparts of the ego), such as objects and persons treated as objects, and connected to the subject in real, symbolic, or imaginary fashion. The relationship between psychoanalyst and analysand, said Lacan, consists in removing this barrier through their discourse—a discourse that also connects the individual to society.

This rereading of Freud through metaphoric language, of course, was diametrically opposed to the American ego psychology that explicitly had ruled out reliance on metaphor. French classical analysts opposed it. Eventually, however, it was Lacanian psychoanalysis that was accepted by an intellectual milieu attuned to linguistic analyses. This led most Freudians to discuss Lacan's ideas, and even refutations helped spread them. Sociologists as well (e.g., Alain Touraine, Michel Crozier, and Jean

Baudrillard), some of whom for a while had addressed Parsonian categories of macro and micro levels of analysis, began to include discourse as components of their theoretical frameworks. Increasingly mediations between spoken and unspoken language, between thought and unthought wishes, dominated French theories. All at times addressed notions of *desire* because it too was found to have its nexus in the emergence of the infant's original mirror image, whose "irreducible demand and need [was] the very source which prevent[ed] it from being reduced to need."[29] This transposition of the Oedipus complex into formulations paralleling linguistic transpositions, in their broader implications, led Lacan to conclude that desire is situated between the natural and the signifying (biology and culture) and therefore affects them both. Furthermore, stated Lacan, desire arises out of the discrepancy between demand and need and is part of neither the symbolic nor the natural order. Such a metaphysical location, of course, not only was anathema to Parsons's project but cannot even be discussed in the same terms.[30]

VI.

At the risk of simplifying, we may observe that Parsons's linking of micro- and macrostructures by means of the Freudian concept of the superego was based on a specific understanding of culture. His integration of Freudian theory into sociology occurred at a time when psychoanalysis had become accepted by a certain sector of the American middle class. Although the Freudian projects in Germany and France were different, there too psychoanalysis was to respond to particular cultural conditions, and psychoanalytic explanations were admissible only after a critical mass of intellectuals had begun to accept some of Freud's notions of the unconscious. In both countries psychoanalysts addressed the sociological questions with the help of interdisciplinary cooperation, although the Germans cooperated with social scientists and the French with philosophers. This in itself indicates a different sense of priorities by leading European analysts.

In America the pursuit of ego psychology, with its focus on empirical research and provable hypotheses, became central, and investigations into neurology, physiology, and experimental psychology tended to remain separate. That American psychoanalysts were mandated (with few exceptions) to have a medical degree conferred legitimation. They were humanists among doctors, however, and their medical peers considered them nonscientific and "soft." Their elaborations of the "science" of ego psychology, however, with its systematizing language, was to further the "scientificization" of their discipline.

This scientific stance put off the Europeans after 1945 not only because 65 percent of the members of the International Psychoanalytic Association then were American and therefore could pass any resolution they pleased, but because the Americans assumed that ego psychology was the only viable psychoanalytic theory. Consequently, attempts to impose ego psychology were countered by criticisms of its adaptive components. European analysts did succeed in reducing the length of sessions and years of analysis required by Americans, not by convincing the Americans on theoretical grounds but by proving that there were only a handful of European analysts and that these had to train many new candidates in order to reestablish the discipline. Still, it is inconceivable that the German critical tradition or the French philosophical one sooner or later would not have penetrated psychoanalytic circles.

In fact, facing the German fascist past with the help of Freudo-Marxism provided the endogenous method that alone could have been effective. Investigations by Mitscherlich's group, and by Jürgen Habermas and his students, continue to rely on these ideas. Some of them use the psychoanalytic components of critical theory to question their own reliance on these two (and a few other) father figures, insofar as dependence on intellectual leadership has become as suspect as that on other leaders. This type of inquiry itself is thought to militate against authoritarianism. The range of these mediations, however, entails reaching back into history, to the generation of the grandfathers. Because young German intellectuals want to understand their "fathers'" errors in order to avoid them in future and to reestablish their former liberal traditions, some psychoanalysts now link their current research to the psychosomaticists Viktor von Weizsaecker and Jakob von Uexkuell, as well as to Hegel, Marx, Kleist, and Schiller. Ego psychology does not lend itself to these efforts, not only because it would be exogenous, less flexible, and opposed to such inquiries but because the process of making Freud's visions their own became the basis for postwar German consciousness.

The French psychiatric tradition—Charcot, Bernheim, and Janet—for a long time had militated against the acceptance of psychoanalysis, as had Cartesianism and the philosophy of Henri Bergson. Content with these theories, the French resisted Freud's ideas, so that before World War II Lacan had been one of only twenty-four Freudians in all of France. In addition, it is doubtful that psychoanalysis would have become so popular had Lacan not led as strong an attack against ego psychology as he did. He initiated the "French Freud"—helped by the advent of "structuralism" and by the events of 1968. This psychoanalysis was as French as it was Freudian. Just as American psychoanalysts after World War I had wanted to rid themselves of "the Pope in Vienna," so French psychoanalysts after World War II expected to reject "the church of ego psychology."

All three theorists—Parsons, Mitscherlich, and Lacan—addressed the links between micro- and macrostructures; they all applied Freudian concepts; and each of them would vehemently have objected to being confined to a national context. Neither Freud's nor Marx's visions accepted national boundaries; and the Parsonian system as well expected to integrate all phenomena. Yet ultimately a certain amount of parochialism infused all these theoretical premises. If this contradicts the Freudian mission (its professional organizations continue to transcend national boundaries), his followers nevertheless continue to remain true to Freud in their own fashion: Using specific parts of psychoanalysis to explain the micro-macro links between individuals and the cultures they help construct only proves the power of Freud's ideas.

NOTES

1. Talcott Parsons, "Superego and the Theory of Social Systems," *Social Structure and Personality* (New York: Free Press, 1970), p. 21.
2. Ibid., p. 23.
3. Jeanne Lampl de-Groot, "On the Development of the Ego and Superego," *International Journal of Psychoanalysis* XXVIII (1947): 7–11; Jacques Lacan, "The Mirror Stage as Formative of the Function of the I as Revealed in Psychoanalytic Experience," in *Ecrits: A Selection* (New York: Norton, 1977), pp. 1–7, and reported in "Bulletin of the International Psychoanalytic Association," *International Journal of Psychoanalysis* 30 (1949): 178–208.
4. Parsons, "Superego," p. 23.
5. Ibid., p. 24.
6. Heinz Hartmann, "Ego Psychology and the Problem of Adaptation," in *Ich-Psychologie und Anpassungsproblem* (Stuttgart: Klett Verlag, 1960); Anna Freud, "The Ego and Mechanisms of Defenses," *The Writings of Anna Freud: Vol. II* (1936; reprint, New York: International Universities Press, 1966), p. 188.
7. Edith Kurzweil, *Four Faces of Freud* (manuscripts, in progress).
8. Heinz Hartmann, Ernst Kris, and Rudolph M. Loewenstein, "Comments on the Formation of Psychic Structure," *The Psychoanalytic Study of the Child* 2 (1946): 11–38.
9. Ibid.
10. Parsons, "Superego," p. 24.
11. Ibid., p. 25.
12. Ibid., p. 27.
13. Ibid., p. 30.
14. Ibid., p. 31.
15. Talcott Parsons, "Social Structure and the Development of Personality," in *Social Structure and Personality*, p. 79.

16. Ibid., pp. 91–92.

17. Alexander Mitscherlich, "25 Jahre Psyche," *Psyche* 25 (1971): 7.

18. Mario Erdheim, *Die gesellschaftliche Produktion von Unbewusstheit* (Frankfurt: Suhrkamp, 1982), p. 34.

19. Ibid., p. 193.

20. See especially Heinz Kohut, *The Analysis of the Self* (New York: International Universities Press, 1971); idem, *The Restoration of the Self* (New York: International Universities Press, 1977); Christopher Lasch, *The Culture of Narcissism* (New York: Norton, 1978); Richard Sennett, *The Fall of Public Man* (New York: Knopf, 1977).

21. Thomas Leithaeuser, "Psychoanalyse in der Sozialforschung," in *Die Psychoanalyse auf der Couch* (Frankfurt: Qumran, 1984), p. 88.

22. Helmut Dahmer, "Wozu brauchen wir eine kritische Theorie der Individuen?" in *Psychoanalyse auf der Couch*, p. 80.

23. Alfred Lorenzer, "Die Kontroverse Bloch-Freud," in *Psychoanalyse auf der Couch*, p. 90.

24. Klaus Horn, "Psychologische Vorstellungen ueber Aggression und erzieherische Konsequenzen," in *Psychoanalyse-Kritische Theorie des Subjekts* (Frankfurt: Roter Druckstock, 1972).

25. Karola Brede, *Einfuehrung in die psychosomatische Medizin* (Frankfurt: Syndikat, 1980).

26. G. W. F. Hegel, *The Phenomenology of Mind*, trans. A. V. Miller (1807; reprint, Oxford: Oxford University Press, 1977).

27. Kohut, *Restoration of the Self*, p. xiii.

28. Edith Kurzweil, *The Age of Structuralism: Lévi-Strauss to Foucault* (New York: Columbia University Press, 1980).

29. Jacques Lacan, *Ecrits: A Selection* (New York: Norton, 1977), p. 302.

30. Yiannis Gabriel, in *Freud and Society* (Boston: Routledge & Kegan Paul, 1983), p. 314, finds a resemblance between Parsons's formation of the ego out of original identification with the mother to Lacan's mirror phase. Lacan, however, "views the ego as the product of a fundamental alienation; it is nothing but an imaginary imago invested with those desirable qualities which the ego would dearly love to possess but does not."

CHAPTER ELEVEN

Micropathology and Macronormality

Karl Otto Hondrich

I.

In this essay I will argue against one tradition of sociological analysis: the idea that a healthy society produces healthy individuals and that pathologies that appear in social systems can be explained by a pathology of the whole system. I argue against the conception that there is an overall correspondence between the whole and its parts. The *correspondence theorem* is deeply rooted in our thinking about social facts: Authoritarian social structure makes for the authoritarian character; families with double bind structures tend to produce schizoid individuals; capitalist social structures force egoistic motivational structures upon individuals, and so on. Basic social theories, be they functionalist, neo-Marxist, psychoanalytic, symbolic interactionist, or critical, all seem to rely heavily on the correspondence theorem, although the founding fathers—especially Marx and Freud—had a flavor for its opponent, which I will call the *contradiction theorem*.[1]

I begin with the *contradiction theorem* not by critically elaborating the sociological tradition but by making eclectic use of it in a spirit of naive discovery. What I seek are cases in which macroprocesses of social association (*Vergesellschaftung*) that are very elementary and by no means pathological nevertheless produce microphenomena that are usually labeled pathological. I will not insist on the labels "normal" and "pathological"; they are more or less a metaphoric or dramatic way of talking.

The theoretically interesting hidden phenomena are contradictory movements on the macro and micro levels of social association.

In the first section of this essay I reflect on the meanings of "pathology" and "normality," trying to relate these terms to everyday language. In the second part I study the following kinds of contradictions between the macro and micro levels: first, as contradictions, within individuals, between collective and individual interests; second, as contradictions between values that claim validity for the total societal system but that can be realized only partially in subsystems; and third, as contradictions between majorities and marginal individuals or groups. In the last part of the essay I will raise a few theoretical questions linked to the contradiction theorem: What is its *raison d'être*? Is it possible that macronormality produces micropathology? What are practical (moral) consequences of the contradiction theorem?

Other important questions are not dealt with in this chapter. They include the problem of limitations of the contradiction theorem and the question *to which degree* micro- and macrostructures are in a relationship of contradiction, correspondence, or independence. (Schegloff's chapter makes an interesting point for the independence of micro- and macrostructures.) The following ideas are, I stress, not more than a first step and demand further elaboration.

II.

The contrasting labels "pathological" and "normal," applied to living systems, may have at least three different meanings: a sociological, a statistical, and a value meaning. First, the state of a personal or social system is considered pathological if it is incapable of performing the expected tasks. As a consequence the person or the social system experiences a loss in self-reliance and independence. A person is defined as being ill; a society becomes dependent on others. This is Parsons's (1958) sociological definition of illness. In a second meaning, derived from Durkheim (1895), normality and pathology are diagnosed comparatively: Those systems deviating most from the average of comparable systems are pathological. This statistical notion of normality and pathology is often criticized by social philosophers for its value neutrality: Normality is always with the average people or systems, which means with the majority, and eccentrics and marginal groups appear as deviant or pathological, whether they are saints or criminals. Therefore, a third notion of normality and pathology is introduced: normality as the realization, pathology as the failure to realize a value or a group of values such as social justice, freedom, or communication among equals.

Critics of this value-oriented notion of pathology usually object that it is arbitrary because the choice of values itself is arbitrary. Therefore, social philosophers have invested much energy in formulating highest value principles upon which all people concerned could be agreed. Nevertheless, all those attempts are in conflict with a trivial sociological fact: In social differentiation there necessarily evolve contradictory values. As a consequence health or normality in the sense of realizing *one* value at best inevitably implies deficiencies in fulfilling other values. In everyday life, the utmost fulfillment of one value or value group is considered not an indicator of health but of pathology: Sophocles' (and Anouilh's) Antigone in her stubborn fulfillment of obligation toward the killed brother, Heinrich von Kleist's Michael Kohlhaas in his self-destructive striving for justice are pathological heroes in their efforts to "really" realize values.

Therefore, in a sociological perspective health and normality lie not in the realization but in the nonrealization of values. That is the point at which the three different notions of normality or pathology come together. The modified version of the value-oriented notion of pathology means that both overfulfillment and underfulfillment of values are pathological.

Durkheim's comparative method gives us a firsthand impression of what over- and underfulfillment mean statistically. Only Parsons's perspective leads us to its sociological meaning, however: Over- and underfulfillment of roles and tasks is performance that weakens and finally destroys the system's capacity to adapt to its environmental conditions. "Normal," conversely, refers to all states and processes that strengthen adaptive capabilities. *Macronormality* means that society's adaptive capabilities increase, particularly by two processes of *Vergesellschaftung*: by embracing ever more people in social association and by having people participate in more social functions. I will not pretend that *Vergesellschaftung* always and under all conditions increases society's adaptive capability, but I assume that ongoing *Vergesellschaftung* is considered a normal and almost inevitable process—fateful (*schicksalhaft*) in its logic, as Max Weber would have put it.

This process produces pathology at the micro level in the sense that it overstresses and destroys adaptive capacities of some individuals and small social systems. They are considered ill, deviant, eccentric, dangerous. In everyday life we are all engaged in a continuous and subtle process of judging people, including ourselves, in this respect. I call this *spontaneous micropathologization*. Nevertheless, what is perceived as pathological from average standards might be judged normal from the point of view of individuals who try to adapt by their own particular means. If we rethink the process from this perspective, eccentrics often win our sympathy. We reverse our judgment: What has been spontaneous micropathologization becomes *reflective micronormalization*, all the more so as we can make society responsible. This results in *reflective macropathologization*, which corresponds to *reflective micronormalization*. I will cease to relate the reflective possibilities here. My point of departure is the level of social reality that I have called spontaneous micropathologization. I will deal with three results of this process—egoism, nonrealization of values, and marginality—and I will show that all three are products of macronormality.

III.

One complaint about individual pathology in modern society concerns the high degree of individuals' egoism or selfishness and the lack of collectivity orientation. Almost all people are egoistic, and many are very egoistic. Selfishness is often regarded as not only a pathology weakening adaptive capacities of macrosystems (Hirsch 1976) but also as pathological with reference to individuals' own interests as far as these are promoted by collective action. Labor unionism is a case in point. The great majority of workers believe that trade unions are important to further workers' interests, as indicated in surveys. Only two of five workers in Western Germany and one of five workers in the United States are members of trade unions, however.

How does one explain this contradiction? Obviously, individual interests are served by nonmembership: not paying the membership fee, not being responsible for unpopular union activities, perhaps gaining some advantages, especially in small firms, where an entrepreneur favors people who do not join unions. Such individual interests are certainly contradictory to collective interests—that is, the special individual interests enforceable only by collective action. Are egoistic interests that go against collective interests indicators of a false consciousness? Not at ali, because the workers concerned are well aware of the conflict among their own interests. Are egoistic interests the result of a competitive social structure? No, because we notice the same conflict of interest in so-called noncompetitive socialist structures.

This issue must have deeper roots, and I will mention three possibilities:

- the differentiation of a collective and an individual perspective in *basic interaction* (in the tradition of Mead);
- the *growing size* of social systems (The explanation follows that of economic theories of collective goods. Economists such as Mancur Olson have continued the tradition of Georg Simmel in this line of analysis.); and
- *crosscutting social circles*, also in the tradition of Simmel.

With respect to the *production of subjectivity by social interaction*, Mead writes, "Apart from his social interactions with other individuals, he (the individual) would not relate the private or 'subjective' contents of his experience to himself and he could not become aware of himself as such, that is, as an individual" (1956:245). I would like to paraphrase Mead's basic idea by adding the notion of interests: Without a common, collective interest individuals would not become aware of their personal, individual interest that is part of the common interest but is at the same time different from and contradictory to it. My wife and I have a collective interest in bringing up our children, but this common interest brings into existence individual and contradictory interests: Who most ably withdraws, almost unnoticed, to his own room and books, letting the other do the collective job? The free rider problem begins in the dyad.

With respect to the issue of size, the larger the number of people with a common interest in producing any collective good—for instance, labor unions' political interests—the smaller the possible share of every individual in that production.

> First, in the large, latent group, each member, by definition, is so small in relation to the total that his actions will not matter much one way or the other. . . . Second, in any large group everyone cannot possibly know everyone else . . . so a person will ordinarily not be affected socially if he fails to make sacrifices on behalf of his group's goals (Olson 1965:62).

It follows that even if individuals are not selfish from the beginning, and even if they are in favor of the collective good, they are inclined to withhold their efforts and let the others perform, given that their own contribution would not be perceptible. The contradiction between egoistic and altruistic behavior or between individualistic and collective rationality is constituted in the collective effort itself. Egoism is the result not of a particular pathological social structure but of *Vergesellschaftung* in its most elementary meaning: the increasing association of people.

Sociologists should be reminded of this point by the economic theory of public goods. One may only imagine that ever-increasing numbers of interaction partners leave less time to the individual for others. In the economists' language, the marginal utility of every individual social contract decreases. This means that individuals—with their own interests—become more important to themselves. The impact of others on individuals' social identity is decreasing. This is a numerical way of explaining the growing impact of individualism and individual interests with respect to collective interests, an analysis in the spirit of Simmel's (1890) and Blau's (1977) structural sociology.

I owe my third argument for the production of individual selfishness by normal macroprocess of *Vergesellschaftung* to Georg Simmel. Simmel described how individual identity—and, I may add, the particularity of individual interests—is developed by belonging to different and cross-cutting social circles. Individuals' participation in many of those circles guarantees that there can be no interest identity between any social circle and its individuals. The conflict of collective and individual interests is inevitable. Perhaps we could imagine a very generalized collective interest of all social subsystems reflected as a totality within the individual. Nevertheless, any decision to act would resurrect the contradiction between the totality and the particularity of interests. Simmel points to *social differentiation* as a source of this contradiction.

IV.

Social differentiation is also the key term for understanding a second macromicro contradiction: the *contradiction between regulative principles*, which, as generalized values, claims to be valid for the totality of society and the fact that it is realized only in parts of the society but so badly realized that we perceive the state of the subsystems as pathological. The amount of lying in politics, of unfaithfulness in sexual love, of inefficiency in scientific research, of violence in family life—are these not obvious examples of pathologies in domains of life that constitute functionally specialized microsystems as part of the social totality?

Even if the answer to this question is positive, it remains as the product of functional differentiation, a normal process of the macrostructuration of society. Functional differentiation means that regulative principles that traditionally permeate social life in a diffuse way become functionally specialized. Those principles or values that are most important in one realm of life cannot be most important in another domain of life. Necessarily they work as contradictory but complementary elements in social life. So the search for truth is the highest principle in science but not in politics. Lying in politics is understandable because it serves the higher value of power; unfaithfulness in sexual love is understandable because of the higher value of passion; inefficiency in science can be explained by the higher value of truth; and power play in families may be tolerated by those suffering because they value emotional bonds more highly than physical health.

Certainly individual decisions may go in other directions. A politician tells the truth knowing that he will lose his power position; a married woman may sacrifice a passionate love to a conventional marital one; or a wife might cut the emotional bond of the family life and file a complaint against a violent husband. We may explain those decisions by Parsons's notion of "interpenetration"[2]: Truth, although not the highest value in politics, nevertheless penetrates from science into politics and cannot be disregarded by politicians; faithfulness, although not basic to passion, nevertheless may come in; judicial trials and files before a court are basically alien to the kind of emotional regulation that is functionally specific to family life, but family members may resort to it.

Values interpenetrate from one functionally specific life domain into another, and this interpenetration is normatively regulated in a subtle way. The point I wish to stress is that interpenetrating values can never take preeminence in functional subsystems other than their own; otherwise all subsystems will lose their identity: A political system in which truth is always preferred to power soon will crumble; preference for faithfulness will be the end of passionate love; the permanent judicial (rather than informal and emotional) regulation of family affairs will mark the end of the family.

If we try to generalize any one of those functionally specific values, intending to make it the highest value for other functional subsystems or for the whole of a society as the macrosystem, this would end in pathology. The problem was analyzed by Max Weber (1964) as one of value tensions between different domains of life (*Lebenssphären*). Functional differentiation, a macrophenomenon, creates values, such as religious brotherhood and scientific truth, that are specific to particular domains of life. Nevertheless, they become generalized as universal values, pushing on the macro level, to penetrate all other domains of life and to determine, on the micro level, the totality of the individual's activity. If one value or a group of values is successful on the micro level, the result is *Gesinnungsethik*. In its purest, heroic appearance, *Gesinnungsethik* is pathological and self-destructive to the individual, as Sophocles' and Kleist's dramas make clear.

Conversely, complete value relativism and opportunism are also pathological. Too much value realization is as pathological as too little. Even an average, socially appropriate degree of value realization is pathological from the point of view of *Gesinnungsethik*. There is no way out of the paradox that a plurality of values on the macro level produces pathologies as to the realization of values on the micro level.

V.

The last microphenomenon to be considered is *marginality*. Rules and standards adopted collectively produce conforming behavior of a majority as a macrophenomenon and nonconformity of marginal groups as contradictory microphenomena. More interesting than this process itself are its dynamics. Any step in the process of *Vergesellschaftung*, embracing more people or giving more people a share in valued things, produces a new kind of marginality and new minorities. Take, for instance, the recent educational boom. In West Germany in the last twenty years this boom decreased the majority of those with elementary education from 80 percent to 50 percent, so that this group has gradually become a minority. The same is true for unskilled labor and for housewives. If we meet a member of those new minorities (which seldom happens among academics), we become involved in a process of pathologization, in which the person herself or himself takes part, complaining, justifying, praising, circumventing, denigrating, or concealing his or her status. This is a historically new phenomenon. It is the consequence of low-status people losing majority status and becoming marginalized.

The reverse process is going on for *growing minorities* such as conscientious objectors (*Wehrdienstverweigerer*), homosexuals, unmarried people, and people without children. Insofar as they switch from hidden to open minorities and from small to large minorities—sometimes even approaching majority status—their members become less pathologized. This normalization process on the micro level is the result of a liberalization of norms, especially judicial norms, on the societal level. Conversely, the growth of such minorities is often discussed as macropathologization. Conservatives in particular look at it as endangering adaptive capacities of the macrosystem, weakening its reproductive force, its motivation for defense, its communal ties that might protect against anomie. Sociologists seem to stay away from potentially fascinating research problems in this respect: Is it a condition for the existence of civil rights that they are not *de facto* realized, except by minorities? And what would be the macroconsequences if all people were to make use of their rights?

There is an additional example in which *Vergesellschaftung* as a normal process of expanding social association leads to contradictions that are resented as individual pathologization. As consumers we profit from the expansion of international markets; we have more choice of cheaper and better products. These advantages of economic *Vergesellschaftung* on the macro level, however, produce disadvantages on the *meso* (middle) level of enterprises. Under the pressure of competition and in order to survive, enterprises must rationalize and dismiss workers. Unemployment and its pathologization on the individual level is the price paid for organizational survival on the *meso* level and for greater satisfaction of consumer needs on the macro level. Critics of consumerism and growth will object that pathologization takes place on the macro level alone, in the collectivity's striving for more and cheaper goods. The implications of this argument have to be examined. Can we and are we to arrest international *Vergesellschaftung* and the dynamics of needs? What does this mean for the adaptive potential of societies? Will stopping the macrodynamics of society decrease the pathologization processes on the micro level, or will it simply "fix" existing pathologies?

VI.

I cannot give ready answers to those questions. Nevertheless, the results of my analysis do contain some suggestions. First, there is no way out of the basic contradiction between normal processes of *Vergesellschaftung* on the macro level and pathologization on the micro level. The contradictions are produced by *Vergesellschaftung* itself. All attempts to gloss over the conflicts and harmonize the inherent contradictions, either by declaring the whole of society as a pathological system or by declaring individual pathologization as a pathology with which we should finish, ignore the basic sociological problem.

What is the *raison d'être* of the contradiction theorem? The explanation inherent in my analysis is a causal-deductive rather than a functional one. I have explained the contradictions between micro and macro levels by basic interaction, functional differentiation, and growth of social systems, norms, and marginalization processes. A variation of these factors also may change the relationship between macronormality and micropathologization. I could add a functional explanation, arguing that the production of contradictions is useful for adaptation and flexibility of social systems on the macro level as well as for the protection of individuals against excessive demands of the collectivity. Nevertheless, a functional explanation cannot explain why contradictions between the macro and the micro level seem to be pronounced in some societies but not in others. Those differences and deviant cases are major challenges to the kind of reasoning I have presented. Is the contradiction theorem not refuted by a society such as Switzerland, which evidently combines a high degree of macronormality with a high degree of micronormality, given that all indicators of crime, suicide, marginalization of foreign workers, and family disorganization are comparatively low?

Two kinds of answers to this question are possible. The first is that Switzerland is a small country with a low degree of functional differentiation; this means that family and community still have more functions (for instance, social security and corresponding social control functions) than they have in comparable countries.[3] This answer remains within the theory of size and functional differentiation as explaining the contradiction theorem. I prefer another answer, which is more intriguing from a functional point of view. Just as deviant individuals fulfill symbolic and adaptive functions within a societal system, so Switzerland fulfills special functions within the international macrosystem. Switzerland is a small country and not only gets a "free ride" as far as military security and international engagement are concerned but also specializes within the international system with respect to internal and monetary security. Having realized values of security and secrecy, it exploits all those countries having average or below-average security. The only internationally prominent Swiss public personality—not a politician but the president of the Swiss National Bank, Fritz Leutwiler—recently declared that Switzerland contributes to making poor countries still poorer by helping their capital "escape" (*Die Zeit*, 23 March 1984).

In this perspective what appears to be Swiss normality on the macro as well as the micro level is no longer normal. For Swiss normality is functionally dependent and partly produced by pathologies of other larger countries in the international system. We can also turn things around and speak of the normality of the international macrosystem in which Switzerland (and its satellite, Lichtenstein, and other small countries such as Hong Kong and Monaco) is a deviant but functionally important microsystem. The whole problem is a case of micro- and macrocontradiction on the level of the international system. Switzerland is as small a model for the world as Albert Schweitzer is for the average citizen.

I will only mention the problem of *macropathology and micronormality*. There are cases in which it is easy to agree about pathology of total societies: war and civil war, extreme rates of violence, external dependency, and indebtedness as consequences of excessive growth efforts, as in South American countries or Poland. What happens in those cases on the micro level? Does macropathology simply produce micronormality—just as macronormality produces micropathology? I suspect that, on the contrary, polarization and extreme contradictory processes will occur on the micro level. There will be, often simultaneously, increasing egoism and altruism, vices and virtues, heroic marginality and opportunistic conformity as well.

VII.

What kinds of morality and practical consequences follow from the contradiction theorem? If normal processes of *Vergesellschaftung* produce individual pathologies, then both macronormality and micropathology are part of an all-embracing normal process. Micropathology, then, in the eyes of a sociologist, is no longer a pathology. Is it possible to declare this sociologist's view as a general wisdom? If everyone were sociologically enlightened and adopted the moral view that "everything goes," everything is normal, and if as a consequence they would no longer take part in individual pathologization, then society could eliminate the tension between macronormality and micropathology and social regulation would no longer function.

This, too, is part of a sociological insight, but it is contradictory to the first one, which allowed moral abstention. The second one obliges me, as a member of the moral community, to take part in a continuing process of individual pathologization. Certainly I can withdraw from this obligation as a moral free rider. But I can do so only so long as I know that others will do the "ugly business" of pathologization for me. Morally, this position is certainly not proper. Nevertheless, society does not work on the basis of moral principles alone but also on the basis of violations against those principles. Perhaps the sociological argument developed as the contradiction theorem can be understood as a counterargument against the generalization principle in ethics. This ethical principle postulates, "If not everyone ought to do A, then no one ought to do

A" (Sobel 1967:390; Bach 1977). Against this the sociologist would adopt a normative version of the contradiction theorem: "If not everyone ought to do A, then at least a few marginal persons or microsystems should do A—but they should not be allowed to do so!" So the sociologist would add: For the contradiction theorem to be realized, it might be better that the generalization principle as contradiction against the contradiction theorem be widely accepted.

NOTES

1. Although Marx was predicting harmony between micro and macro levels for the society to come, for the existing capitalist society he emphasized the contradiction between a competitive macro structure and the destruction of this structure by competing individuals. For Freud the contradiction between cultural development as a macro process and repression of individual needs was inevitable.
2. For a reevaluation of the term in the framework of Parsons's theory see Richard Münch (1982:771 ff.).
3. This is similar to the interpretation of Marshall B. Clinard (1978).

REFERENCES

Bach, Kent. 1977. When to Ask, "What If Everyone Did That?" *Philosophy and Phenomenological Research* 37 (7):464–481.

Blau, Peter M. 1977. *Inequality and Heterogeneity: A Primitive Theory of Social Structure*. New York: Free Press.

Clinard, Marshall B. 1978. *Cities with Little Crime: The Case of Switzerland*. Cambridge: Cambridge University Press.

Durkheim, Emile. 1895. *Les règles de la methode sociologique*. Paris: Presses Universitaires de France.

Hirsch, Fred. 1976. *The Social Limits to Growth*. Cambridge, Mass.: Harvard University Press.

Mead, George Herbert. 1956. *On Social Psychology*. Selected papers, edited and with an introduction by Anselm Strauss. Chicago: University of Chicago Press.

Münch, Richard. 1982. Talcott Parsons and the Theory of Action. II. The Continuity of the Development. *American Journal of Sociology* 87:771–826.

Olson, Mancur. 1965. *The Logic of Collective Action: Public Goods and the Theory of Groups*. Cambridge, Mass.: Harvard University Press.

Parsons, Talcott. 1958. Definition of Health and Illness in the Light of American Values and Social Structure, pp. 165–187 in E. Gartley Jaco, ed., *Patients, Physicians and Illness*. New York: Free Press.

Simmel, Georg. 1890. *Über soziale Differenzierung. Soziologische und psychologische Untersuchungen*. Leipzig: Duncker & Humblot.

Sobel, J. Howard. 1967. Generalization Arguments. *Inquiry* 10:380–404.

Weber, Max. 1964. Richtungen und Stufen religiöser Weltablehnung, pp. 441–483 in *Soziologie-weltgeschichtliche Analysen-Politik*. Stuttgart: Alfred Kröner Verlag.

CHAPTER TWELVE

Depth Psychology and the Social Order

Neil J. Smelser

It has been remarked that any kind of interdisciplinary marriage between the psychoanalytic and the sociological perspectives is difficult, if not impossible, to attain.[1] As one who has explored each extensively, I share this view. In this exploratory essay I will first adduce a number of fundamental obstacles to synthesis between the two sets of perspectives; second, note a number of possible and actual points of contact found in the literature; and third, modestly try my own hand at striking a synthetic chord, taking the theory of the mechanisms of defense as a starting point.

THE PSYCHOANALYTIC TRADITION AND THE SOCIOLOGICAL TRADITION

Actually, it is an error to speak of these two traditions in general terms because both have become differentiated into a number of traditions, characterized by varying assumptions, theoretical emphases, research styles, and methodologies. It is possible, however, to point out several reasons for "noncontact" between one or another facet of the two sets of traditions.

1. In Freud's writings on society, particularly in *Civilization and Its Discontents*,[2] he tended to place stress almost exclusively on the antagonistic relations between civilization and the instinctual side of individuals' lives; he spoke of "hostility to civilization which is

produced by the pressure that civilization exercises, the renunciation of instinct which it demands."[3] Such a dualistic formulation would be unwelcome to many sociologists, including myself. In particular it leaves out the fundamental fact that "civilization" is not a monolithic entity; it should be divided, at the very least, into culture and social structure, with the latter (including institutions such as the family, courts and other legal agencies, and the church) regarded as *mediating* between the strictures of culture and the desires and tendencies of individuals. Or, to put the matter differently, Freud projected the antagonism between id and superego onto society but neglected to note that there is also a functional societal equivalent to ego.

2. Despite his early efforts to develop a scientific physiological model in the *Project for a Scientific Psychology*, Freud's model of science, mainly a psychological adaptation of a medical model, rests on epistemological and methodological bases different from those of the positivistic strands of sociology, associated with the positions of Durkheim and Ogburn.[4] The latter stressed causal association among *aggregated* social facts as the basis for scientific knowledge, whereas Freud stressed clinical inference about uniquely convergent *patterns* of forces in the individual's psyche. In addition, a sociologist such as Durkheim was hostile to what he called "internal facts" (i.e., dispositional psychological forces)—a hostility shared by behaviorists in psychology—and insisted on objectively measurable "external facts." For Freud, the sole field of study was *intrapsychic* representations of instinctual forces and external realities.

3. More generally, the fundamental units and levels of analysis of much of sociology and psychoanalysis differ from one another in apparently unsynthesizable ways. Sociologists are concerned mainly with the objectively determinable opportunities and constraints of the social structure for individuals and groups; psychoanalysts are concerned with various forces, including the external reality of social structure. What is real for sociologists is external reality; what is real for psychoanalysts is the internal representation (including distortion) of that reality. This discontinuity of levels of analysis plagues efforts to synthesize the microscopic and macroscopic generally.

4. The psychoanalytic model of unconscious motivation and conflict, often irrational in character, is difficult to square with two alter-

native models of the mind often employed in sociology and the other social sciences: the rational choice model, in which the actor is in full possession of knowledge about alternative lines of action, calculates costs and gains from each, and acts accordingly; and various phenomenological models, which take the actors' conscious intentions and meanings as the proper representation of psychological reality.

5. For scholars and practitioners in both traditions interested in the potential for change, the psychoanalyst regards the decisive locus for change to be in the pattern of conflicts and defenses in the individual person. Sociologists view the decisive locus of change as existing in the social, political, and economic environments of the individual.

Thus when different parts of the psychoanalytic tradition touch different parts of the sociological tradition, it is difficult to envision any kind of fit or mutual exchange because of discrepancies in fundamental assumptions and formulations. Nevertheless, a number of points of contact can be seen in the literature, among which the following are illustrative:

1. The positivist sociologist, Ogburn, himself underwent psychoanalysis and regarded it as a *means* by which irrational misunderstandings, myths, and fantasies—all antipathetic to the rational, scientific organization of knowledge—could be dispelled.[5]
2. Certain formal *analogies* between psychoanalytic and sociological thought can be noted. The theories of both Marx and Freud concern a system that maintains an equilibrium in tension between conflicting forces. For Marx the tension is expressed in contradictions between the mode of production and the social relations of production, which manifest themselves in antagonism between classes. For Freud the tension is between the instinctual impulses (the id) and various personality establishments (the superego, the individual's sense of reality) engaged in the management and control of these impulses. Both theorists stress, moreover, that the main strategy of control is a form of repression, politicoeconomic in one case and psychological in the other. Furthermore, in each case the repressive forces are buttressed by a number of ancillary devices that lead to distortions of reality and consciousness. For Marx one of the main functions of religion, philosophy, morality, and so on is to disguise the true interests of the workers and to contribute to a false consciousness in them. For Freud various mechanisms of de-

fense, such as projection, isolation, rationalization, and displacement, distort the true nature of impulses and obscure them from the individual. For Marx, moreover, the structure of society results from the efforts of the dominant class to save itself from the destructive impact of societal contradictions; for Freud the structure of the personality (character traits, symptoms, etc.) is geared in large measure toward saving the individual from the destructive impacts of his or her inner conflicts. Finally, for both theorists, freedom from repression is gained by an expansion of awareness (consciousness) of the conflicts besetting the system. For Marx, however, freedom expresses itself in the destruction of the system and the creation of one that is conflict-free, whereas for Freud freedom expresses itself in the dissolution of symptoms and in the increased capacity of the individual to redirect the previously conflict-bound energy into productive activity.

3. One particular tradition in anthropology, known as "culture and personality," interpreted various kinds of social institutions and belief systems as *projections* of intrapsychic conflicts generated by particular kinds of child-training practices.[6] The main theme of *The Authoritarian Personality*[7] and related studies—that one main determinant of prejudice, discrimination, and its attendant inequalities is the projection of ambivalences acquired in dealing with parental authorities—is consistent with this tradition. Also closely related is the work of a number of small group theorists, such as Slater and Cottle, who treat the dynamics of authority and affiliation in small groups in part as reenactments of earlier family dramas and the ambivalences and conflicts created in those dramas.[8]
4. Another tradition, a kind of mirror image of that just noted, treats the structure of personality (conceived in psychoanalytic terms) as partly a product of internalization of objects, role relations, collectivities, and values that constitute the sociocultural environment of the individual. Parsons's treatment of personality development and personality structure[9] is perhaps the most notable example of this line of work. The more recent theoretical work of Chodorow on the perpetuation of the mothering motive through early mother-daughter relations, though differing sharply in emphasis from that of Parsons, is in the same genre of interpretation.[10]
5. A number of sociologists and others have employed different facets of the psychoanalytic tradition in attempting to *diagnose* and *eval-*

uate the contemporary human condition. This characterization applies to many of the works of the early critical theorists, especially Horkheimer, Adorno, Fromm, Marcuse, and Lowenthal,[11] as well as, in a certain degree, to writers such as Norman O. Brown and Christopher Lasch.

6. Finally, some theorists have found use of the psychoanalytic method useful in their formulations. Habermas, for example, likened the psychoanalytic technique to Marxist study, in that both constitute a critical means of cutting through obfuscation and ideological distortion and reaching to the deeper structural dynamics of a situation.[12]

The foregoing are some of the linkages that have appeared, in varying degrees of seriousness and strength, over the decades. It is not within the frame of this essay to evaluate these illustrative efforts, except to say that some of these lines of work, such as the culture and personality approach, appear to have run their course[13] and that, taken together, these linkages do not appear to add up to anything resembling a synthesis of theory or empirical research.

A REFORMULATION AND RECLASSIFICATION OF THE DEFENSE MECHANISM

Over the generations many aspects of psychoanalytic theory as originally formulated by Freud have experienced both discreditation and reformulation: the dualism of Eros and Thanatos as the primary instincts; the psychosexual theory of development (modified, for example, by Erikson);[14] female development, female sexuality, and anatomical determination; the primacy of the Oedipus complex in the development of psychic disorders (in the work of Kohut, for example);[15] to say nothing of the psychoanalytic classification of neurotic and other disorders. The status of all these aspects must be regarded as clouded at best.

Other aspects of psychoanalytic theory, though having experienced many vicissitudes, have continued to remain vital elements in that theory. I have in mind the centrality of the notion of ambivalence toward internal representations and external objects (including persons) as central in the development of character traits, symptoms, and interpersonal relations; the importance of the transference phenomenon, both within and outside of psychoanalytic treatment; and the concept of the mechanisms of defense as characteristic modes of dealing with intrapsychic conflict and anxiety.[16] The idea of the mechanisms of defense prove a particularly valuable guideline in psychoanalytic technique, serving as a basis for recognizing resistances, in the psychoanalytic theory of personality and character, and in various metapsychological frameworks—economic, genetic, and developmental.

Despite this persistence and vitality, however, the theory of defense mechanisms remains problematical on a number of counts. First, the classification of defenses has always had a kind of incomplete, ad hoc quality. The defenses most commonly referred to are those recited by Freud in *Inhibitions, Symptoms and Anxiety*[17] and by Anna Freud in *The Ego and the Mechanisms of Defense*[18]—repression, regression, reaction-formation, displacement, undoing, isolation, projection, introjection, reversal, sublimation, and intellectualization. Since that time other kinds of complex combinations, such as "depersonalization,"[19] have been added, as well as such specific items as "infertility" and "humor" as instances of defense mechanisms.[20] To bring this to its logical extension, Greenson remarked that every kind of psychic phenomenon can be used for defensive purposes.[21] Clearly this kind of classification is not systematic, and clearly the various defenses lie at different levels of conceptual generality.

More important for the purposes of this essay, the concept of defense mechanism has had a primarily intrapsychic reference. Although Freud acknowledged a reference to the external world when he said that "an instinctual demand only becomes an (internal) danger because its satisfaction would bring on an external danger—that is, because the internal danger represents an external one," the reference is still to the instinct and to the *reactive* character of the external agent.[22] Anna Freud more or less repeated the point, indicating that the main source of external (objective) threat is in relation to punishments that may be or imagined to be inflicted if a prohibited instinctual impulse is gratified. In this formulation external reality becomes virtually an extension of the superego. Although Hartmann and others stressed the continuity between defense and adaptation—thereby taking a more positive view of defense and looking in the external direction[23]—as late as 1981 Brenner could define defense in terms of its internal consequence; namely, "the reduction of unpleasure associated with a drive derivative, i.e., with an instinctual wish, or with superego functioning."[24] My view is directly contrary to this and includes the notion that objective threats must receive a definition independent of instinctual drive representation and the superego, though in fact they are always reacted to and perceived in relation to the latter two establishments of the personality.

In working to overcome these two deficiencies in the theory of defense mechanisms I shall proceed by two stages: first, to systematize the classification of defense mechanisms themselves, in reference only to intrapsychic impulses and conflicts (which is the psychoanalyst's point of emphasis); and second, to attempt to generalize this categorization to encompass external (objective) dangers and deprivations as well. In dealing with the latter we come directly into contact with social structure and the social order.

The first basis for classifying defenses is to recognize that defensive operations can be activated at different stages in a model of the process beginning with instinctual arousal and terminating with instinctual gratification. This model, based on Freud's early presentation[25] and formalized later by David Rapaport,[26] constructs a highly generalized sequence, beginning with mounting drive tension, which, when its gratification is delayed, gives rise to the establishment of psychic drive representation, characteristic discharges of affect that are associated with these representations, and characteristic hallucinatory representations of potentially gratifying objects. The tension is reduced when the drive is gratified by some kind of motor activity leading to a change in the state of the organism.

With respect to defense mechanisms, it appears that they can be activated at different stages in this process beginning with instinctual arousal and ending with gratification. Repression, for example, appears to involve a frontal attack on the mental representation of the instinctual drive and to prevent its appearance in the conscious life. Other defenses operate against conscious, though possibly distorted representations of instincts.[27] Freud also spoke of the "suppression of affect," and also suggested that repression can eliminate the "accompanying affective character" of aggressive impulses.[28] At least two of the mechanisms of defense—undoing and isolation—were said by Freud to "take place in the motor sphere."[29] Evidently, then, the defenses can be considered in terms of the different stages between the excitation of some behavioral tendency and its expression in motor activity.

The second dimension by which defense mechanisms can be classified has to do with the basic mode of defense employed by the ego against threatening intrusions.[30] In reviewing the central psychoanalytic writings on the mechanisms of defense, I have found it possible to classify all the major defense mechanisms into four basic modes or directional tendencies:[31]

1. to block the threatening intrusion;
2. to reverse the threatening intrusion into its opposite;
3. to shift the reference of the threatening intrusion; and
4. to insulate the threatening intrusion from its associative connections.

These modes are very general in their formulation. They are formulated without regard to what psychic content is used for defensive purposes; that is, whether the ego uses an interpersonal situation, an affect, a fantasy, or another defense, among others. The modes are formulated without regard to the degree of their effectiveness as maneuvers. Now I shall discuss each basic mode in somewhat more detail, indicating some of the subtypes of each.

1. *Blocking the threatening intrusion.* The most obvious defense is repression, or the turning of the instinctual representation away from the conscious ego.[32] The suppression of affect is another. Denial of the meaning of the instinctual representation is still another. The appropriate form of defense in the behavioral sphere would be the inhibition of motor activity that is threatening to the ego, either directly or because it involves the gratification of a reprehensible impulse.
2. *Reversing the intrusion into its opposite.* In the essay, "Instincts and Their Vicissitudes,"[33] Freud identified two forms of this reversal: first, reversal of the direction of the instinctual aim itself from passive to active (for example, from scopophilia to exhibitionism); and second, reversal of the content, when an instinct is turned around from an object to oneself. Affects also may be reversed (for example, when contempt is transformed into awe or worship). Finally, two of the mechanisms of defense involve new patterns of motor activity which attempt to reverse or nullify the reprehensible quality of other behavioral tendencies; these are reaction formation and undoing.
3. *Shifting the reference of the threatening intrusion.* This category involves the "relocation" of the intrusive element in another place in the ego's environment. Thus it includes various kinds of externalization—for example, the projection of id impulses onto exter-

nal objects, and the projection of the sources of superego anxiety (guilt) onto a remote authority figure. In addition, this mode includes two familiar forms of distortion by the ego: displacement, which shifts the reprehensible impulse from the original object to a substitute object, and rationalization, which, by means of giving new "reasons," proliferating new categories, and so on, shifts the original conflict to a more remote symbolic level. All these shifts are designed by the ego to disguise the threatening intrusion by means of cognitive distortion.

One final manifestation of shifting must be mentioned. With respect to the therapeutic situation, the term "acting out" refers specifically to the externalization of tendencies excited by the transference relation into the behavior sphere, with the same unconscious intent to conceal the relevant internal psychic conflict. I feel it is appropriate to treat acting out in a somewhat more general sense—that is, as a means of defending against any internal psychic conflict by shifting its reference to motor activity. Defined in this more general sense, acting out takes its place among the other types of defense as shifting the reference of the threatening intrusion.

4. *Insulation from associative connections* involves the psychic phenomena that have been referred to variously as isolation of instinctual representations, isolation of affects, depersonalization, "splitting,"[34] and isolation of a behavioral event that "is not forgotten, but, instead . . . deprived of its affect, and its associative connections are suppressed or interrupted so that it remains as though isolated and is not reproduced in the ordinary thought. . . . The motor isolation is meant to ensure an interruption of the connection in thought."[35]

The classification resulting from the two sets of dimensions reviewed is presented in table 12.1. This type of classification involves a logical ordering of the defense mechanisms in relation to one another, rather than presenting them as a simple list of alternative strategies for the ego. It also suggests a principle by which defenses can be regarded as "layered" or organized into hierarchies that constitute more or less fixed establishments of the personality. Let me illustrate this by a simple example. Suppose the ego's main struggle is with a primitive aggressive impulse against a parental figure which has been repressed at an early stage of childhood development. At some subsequent time this repression fails and the impulse breaks through. By way of further defending against the

TABLE 12.1

The Mechanisms of Defense Classified in Terms of Basic Modes and Development Phases of Behavior

<table>
<tr><th></th><th colspan="6">Stages</th></tr>
<tr><th>Stages</th><th>1</th><th>2</th><th colspan="3">3
Psychic Representation (Hallucination) of Gratification Situation</th><th>4
Behavioral Outcome</th></tr>
<tr><th>Modes</th><th></th><th></th><th>3a. Cognitive representation drive</th><th>3b. Relevant affect</th><th>3c. Relevant object</th><th></th></tr>
<tr><td>Blocking</td><td rowspan="4">Libidinal tension</td><td rowspan="4">Delay of gratification</td><td>Repression</td><td>Suppression of affect</td><td>Withdrawal, denial</td><td>Inhibition</td></tr>
<tr><td>Reversal into opposite</td><td>Change of instinctual aim</td><td>Reversal of affect</td><td>Reversal from other to self as object</td><td>Reaction-formation; undoing</td></tr>
<tr><td>Shift in reference of</td><td>Projection of impulse</td><td>Projection of affect</td><td>Displacement; identification; rationalization</td><td>“Acting out”</td></tr>
<tr><td>Insulation from associative connective</td><td>“Splitting” or isolation of impulse</td><td>Isolation of affect</td><td>Depersonalization of experience</td><td>Isolation of behavioral event</td></tr>
</table>

impulse, the ego externalizes it by projecting it onto the father himself, thus altering the source of danger from impulse to the external world. In turn the ego defends against the derived fear of the father by displacing it onto a less immediately threatening object, such as an animal. In turn this phobic result may be further defended against, for example, by forming a counterphobic reaction formation, by acting out in the form of avoidance rituals, or by denying the anxiety accompanying the phobic reaction. Any one of these reactions may be even further defended against by rationalization, or an effort of the ego to make reasonable and consistent what might otherwise appear unreasonable and inconsistent types of beliefs or behavior. Represented graphically, this model reads as follows:

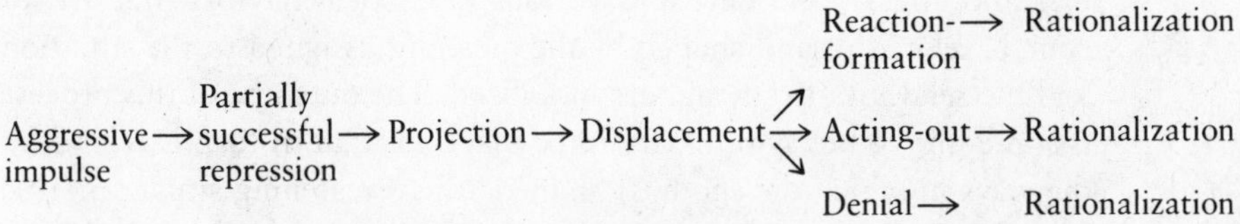

			↗	Reaction-formation →	Rationalization
Aggressive impulse →	Partially successful repression →	Projection →	Displacement →	Acting-out →	Rationalization
			↘	Denial →	Rationalization

By this process of continuously shifting the source toward which the defenses are directed, the ego builds up layer upon layer of defensive positions, some defending against impulses, some against external threats, some against other defenses, and so on. This process of shifting yields a structural result that has been described by Gill as follows: "What is defense in one layer is impulse in relation to another layer. . . . In general, a behavior is a defense in relation to a drive more primitive than itself, and a drive in relation to a defense more advanced than itself."[36] That part of ego structure having to do with defense, then, is best conceived as a hierarchy of defenses, directed toward a multiplicity of different sources and organized in a progression from the deeper, unconscious layers to the more superficial, conscious layers.[37]

GENERALIZATION OF THE SCHEME TO EXTERNAL REALITY

One of the accomplishments of Anna Freud's extension of the theory of defense mechanisms is her formulation of a number of different sources of threat or danger to the ego. She mentioned dread of the strength of the instincts themselves; the anxiety that arises from the objective (external) dangers that may arise if instincts are gratified; and, finally, the anxiety that springs from the "ego's need for synthesis."[38] I will now focus on the topic of objective dangers, but first I would like to expand that to include aspects of objective reality *beyond* those aspects that are threatening in relation to the gratification of impulses. These additional aspects include uncertainties, threats, and deprivations imposed on the ego from outside.

As a starting point, a model of external excitation can be developed, a model that is precisely parallel to the Freud-Rapaport model relating to instincts and their gratification. The model begins with the appearance (or continuation) of a threat or loss of uncertain dimensions. The initial response is anxiety on the part of the ego, and in adapting to this anxiety it develops some kind of cognitive representation of the threatening situation (i.e., gives it meaning), mobilizes appropriate affects (primarily fear and anger), and envisions various kinds of behaviors that are, of course, related to and shaped by the meaning assigned to the situation and the relevant affects that are mobilized. The outcome of this process is some line of behavioral action (or inaction) that in turn is related to the ways in which the ego has "shaped" the threatening situation. This is the kind of general model that has emerged in the psychological literature on stress and coping and the more recent literature on risk.

Furthermore, I posit that the ego, in dealing with external threats and deprivations, uses *precisely the same repertoire of defensive modes* as it does in dealing with instinctual representations and conflicts, and that these can be correspondingly classified with respect to external threats. Denial of objective danger, for example, would be the external counterpart of psychological repression—that is, an effort to block the threatening intrusion.[39] Withdrawal or flight from the scene would be the external counterpart of inhibition. With respect to affective reactions generated by external threats or loss, the same repertoire of suppression, reversal, projection (or, in this case, introjection), and isolation are available.

Empirical studies of coping patterns under stressful or uncertain circumstances seem to give support to such a classification of defensive activities. Defining coping as "the things that people do to avoid being harmed by life-strains," Pearlin and Schooler analyzed reported methods of dealing with strains they encountered as parents, jobholders and breadwinners, husbands and wives. (The strains themselves were also self-reported.) The interviews included a sample of some 2,300 persons in the Chicago area. In categorizing the responses Pearlin and Schooler identified three main clusters: (1) responses that function to control the meaning of the problem, including selective ignoring (denial) and various kinds of rationalizations, such as comparing one's lot favorably with others who are worse off, and devaluation of the importance of that which is deprived (e.g., money); (2) responses that function to control the affects generated by hardships (e.g., having faith, keeping calm, trying not to worry, accepting adversity, etc.); and (3) behavioral responses that attempt to modify the situation (e.g., negotiation of problems or seeking advice in marriage, searching for new jobs, etc.).[40] These three categories, generated inductively, correspond to "cognitive representation," "relevant affect," and "relevant object" in table 12.1, as relevant phases in the excitation of activity.

A recent study of workers in the "dangerous" trades, such as firefighting, working with toxic chemicals, and the like, showed a similar pattern of reactions. The fact that danger is continuously present and must be confronted on a daily basis makes simple denial of the danger a difficult defense to sustain; evidence of this is the high level of continuous anxiety among workers.[41] At the same time, many of the workers apparently try to reduce anxiety by self-assuring phrases such as these: "It's just a normal part of the job"; "What you can't change, you accept"; "It won't happen to me"; and "It's worth the risk."[42] Another belief that is frequently mobilized is that managers are to blame for dangerous workplace design, failing to provide adequate information about dangers, and cutting corners in order to maximize profits, all with the accompanying affect of anger. Managers, for their part, make an effort to define personal safety as a matter of individual workers' responsibility.[43] These beliefs and affects, of course, set the stage for conflict between the two groups. In the "motor sphere," a number of adaptations are also observable, each depending on the belief and affect that has been picked up by the workers: to quit, to resign oneself to living with danger, to complain to government authorities about dangerous situations, to agitate politically for preventive and precautionary measures.

The anxiety generated by—and defenses employed against—situations of threat or loss will vary according to whether the threat or loss is severe, whether it is expected or unexpected, whether it is chronic or acute, and whether it is defined as under or out of one's control. Summarizing some of the research evidence from the literature on risk, Douglas notes,

> Apparently, people underestimate risks which are supposed to be under their control. They reckon they can cope with familiar situations. They also underestimate the low probability risks, those which are rarely expected to happen. They get worried by media reported events that seem dramatic (air crashes with film stars on board) and less worried by undramatic losses (such as death from asthma). The media give "salience" to large-scale disasters from recent

tornadoes and earthquakes, but presumably salience and recency eventually fade into the familiar background.[44]

Pieczenik has argued speculatively that the degree of vulnerability that a population feels in relation to a foreign power will determine the "choice" of types of defense mechanisms. To choose the most extreme case, the tension-fraught cold war relations between the United States and the Soviet Union, in which both parties are vulnerable in the extreme, will involve more projection, distortion, and denial, whereas situations of lesser vulnerability, such as relations between the United States and Canada, will involve less extreme defenses, such as the suppression of ambivalence.[45]

The threat of nuclear war stands as the most extreme example of a threat that is severe, unpredictable, both acute and chronic in its dimensions, and seemingly beyond the control of average citizens. One would expect, therefore, that denial and suppression of affect—what Lifton calls "nuclear numbing"[46]—would predominate as defenses,[47] although these are often buttressed by self-assuring rationalizations ("The balance of nuclear terror secures the peace"; "Limited nuclear wars are possible"). Those who "personalize" the possibility of nuclear war by defining it as mainly in the control of world political and military leaders, moreover, would be those most likely to activate themselves politically on the issue.[48]

There is also evidence that the employment of defenses in situations of danger or loss may have a sequential character. Lindemann's classic study of survivors of those who died in a tragic nightclub fire in Boston in 1943 revealed an initial phase of denial of the death itself, followed by episodes of self-accusation and blame as well as episodes of scapegoating others (introjection and projection), then by a longer period of grief work in which the bereaved's social attachments are realigned.[49] A similar kind of sequencing apparently occurs among survivors of community disasters, with a period of numbness and disbelief followed by a period of assimilation and giving new definition to the event and to one's relations with others.[50]

These are some of the dimensions of the use of defensive strategies in contending with situations or uncertainty, threat, and loss in the ego's environment. This discussion must be complicated, however, by noting the fundamental fact that the ego does not deal with the external world in isolation. The anxiety and other affects, the meaning patterns assigned, and adaptive reactions envisioned with respect to some kind of external threat inevitably set in motion simultaneous *inner* struggles with those kinds of affects, meanings, symbols, and ambivalences that are aroused by association. Adaptive action, then, always involves a kind of ongoing double dialogue, external and internal, and each side of the dialogue affects (and in some cases distorts) the other.

SOCIETAL LINKAGES WITH THE DEFENSIVE PROCESS

In one of its significances, the organization of life into a society is a way of making life more predictable and for that reason less dangerous. Entry into any kind of role (parent-child, employer-employee) simplifies the myriad possible types of interaction with others by selecting out some as appropriate and others as not appropriate. A commonly shared language with a commonly shared grammar, commonly shared norms and understandings, commonly shared values and worldviews are likewise stabilizing, shaping individuals' life-long attachments to persons, objects, and symbols.

At the same time, however, the organization of life into a society brings into being and establishes an almost endless number of possibilities for vulnerability to uncertainty, threat, and loss.

- The organization of social and economic life affects the balance of benefits and threats in the natural environment. The building of reservoirs for purposes of irrigation may reduce the chronic danger of flooding, but it also generates the new danger of massive flooding if reservoirs are destroyed by earthquake. Dozens of additional contemporary examples of environmental poisoning could also be cited.
- The organization of social life also affects the balance of benefits and threats to the health of the organism, as students of sanitation and the epidemiology of diseases will testify.
- The specialization of social life into roles invariably generates inequalities, which in turn involve real and symbolic deprivations.
- The entry into a social role guided by some kind of expectation inevitably creates the possibility that another will not live up to the rules of the game, which is a source of threat or loss.
- Setting up rules of the social game also establishes the possibility that circumstances may cause changes (including disintegration) of those rules, which is also threatening to those who believe in them.

- The same can be said for the value systems and worldviews that are appealed to in order to legitimize the normative; insofar as these are defined in any way as sacred, attacks on them or their erosion constitute a threat.

Above and beyond these possibilities, it should also be pointed out that society—or, more accurately, culture—selects out and defines specific types of action and symbols as threatening, despite the fact that there may be nothing intrinsically threatening about them. For a male to stand less than a foot from another male while conversing is threatening behavior in many Anglo-Saxon cultures; for a male to stand at a distance while conversing in many Mediterranean cultures is regarded as unfriendly and therefore threatening. It is by virtue of cultural selectivity that menstruating women or old people are found disgusting, a style of art found offensive, and communist ideas found menacing. Culture and society, then, contain a reservoir of norms, values, and definitions that determine in large part what is to be defended *against*.

Part of society's social resources are directed toward institutions (medical, law enforcement) that are designed to contend with threatening situations. In addition, society and culture are provenders of preferred psychological defenses against many threats. Language and culture are replete with cautionary and sometimes contradictory adages and proverbs ("Look before you leap"; "He who hesitates is lost"; "A stitch in time saves nine"), which, if believed in and made part of one's code of conduct, will presumably fend off some unidentified range of misfortunes implied in the proverb. Superstitions, rituals, and cliches may serve the same function.[51] As the culture and personality scholars were able to show, the world of myths, fairy tales, and religious belief systems constitutes in part enormously complex systems available for projecting, splitting ambivalent feelings, and sublimation. The same functions can be served by the existing reservoir of stereotypes regarding ethnic groups, foreign countries and their peoples, public leaders, movie stars, and famous athletes.

Until this point, it should be acknowledged, the discussion of the role of society and culture in the defensive process has had a certain unrealistic ring; society and culture have been discussed as though they were unified entities. The truth is that modern, complex societies—despite the existence of some forces that make for uniformity, consensus, and integration on the societal level—are differentiated and diversified into literally thousands of divisions and groups along class, ethnic and racial, cultural, political, age, sex, and life-style lines. These divisions and groups and subunits within them differ from one another, moreover, along the lines we have been discussing; that is, with respect to what in society they define as threatening and as sources of anxiety, how they define these threats and what kinds of affects they mobilize in relation to these threats, and what kinds of purposive action (if any) they envision as a means to contend with them. Indeed many groups—mainly voluntary associations and social movements—are *built* around the anxiety based on the perception of a grave threat (e.g., alcohol, drugs, crime, environmental abuse) and devote their energies to attempting to persuade others to accept their perception, the anxiety they feel about it, and the need to act. Such groups, when formed, also tend to validate and reinforce the selected combination of threat-definition-affect-action for their members and, indeed, make it a normative imperative that their members and prospective recruits believe in that combination of elements and act by that belief.

As indicated earlier, these divisions make for a great deal of group conflict; I mentioned the different reactions of workers and managers to environmental hazards in chemical and other industries. In relation to these kinds of conflict, many societal agencies (courts and regulatory agencies of the state are good examples) frequently mediate the conflicts and, in ruling on them, validate one kind of definition of the situation and its associated defensive complex and invalidate others. Following the example given, if upon receiving a complaint from a group of workers about hazardous waste disposal practices a regulatory agency requires managers to take corrective action, the agency is, among other things, giving validity to the workers' particular complex of beliefs and affects. In this way too, then, society intervenes in and affects the patterning of defensive belief complexes in it.

Considering this matter more generally, it can be argued that the essential feature of much of contemporary politics—perhaps generally, but certainly in societies with democratic political systems—is a struggle over definitions. Political leaders, parties, groups, and social movements all contend in identifying what is wrong (threatening) in society, giving reasons why it is wrong, blaming others for the wrong, saying how we should feel (anxious, indignant) about the wrong, and saying what ought to be done about the wrong. The media, of course, are crucial in these symbolic dialogues and controversies and play an independent role in their outcomes. The importance of these kinds of political struggles over the legitimate definition of the situation is evident, given that those who can effectively resonate with the electorate's own definitions, anxieties, and other affects become the legitimated holders of office and wielders of power.

ACKNOWLEDGMENT

I would like to thank Kim Hayes, my research assistant, for both intellectual and practical aid in the course of preparing this essay.

NOTES

1. Robert S. Wallerstein and Neil J. Smelser, "Psychoanalysis and Sociology: Articulations and Applications," *International Journal of Psychoanalysis* 50 (1969): 698–699; Talcott Parsons, "The Superego and the Theory of Social Systems," in Parsons, Robert F. Bales, and Edward A. Shils, *Working Papers in the Theory of Action* (New York: Free Press, 1953), pp. 13–14; Jerome Rabow, "Psychoanalysis and Sociology," *Annual Review of Sociology* 9 (1983): 555.

2. James Strachey and Anna Freud, eds., *Standard Edition of the Complete Psychological Works of Sigmund Freud* (London: Hogarth Press, 1961), pp. 59–148.

3. "The Future of an Illusion," in ibid., p. 15.

4. Emile Durkheim, *The Rules of Sociological Method*, trans. Sarah A. Solway and John H. Mueller (New York: Free Press, 1958); William F. Ogburn, "Presidential Address: The Folkways of a Scientific Sociology," in *Studies in Quantitative and Cultural Sociology*. Papers presented at the Twenty-fourth Annual Meeting of the American Sociological Society (Chicago: University of Chicago Press, 1930), pp. 1–11.

5. Otis Dudley Duncan, "Introduction," in *On Culture and Social Change: Selected Papers [of William Fielding Ogburn]* (Chicago: University of Chicago Press, 1964).

6. Abram Kardiner, *The Psychological Frontiers of Sociology* (New York: Columbia University Press, 1945); John W. M. Whiting and Irvin Child, *Child-Training and Personality* (New Haven: Yale University Press, 1953).

7. T. W. Adorno et al., *The Authoritarian Personality* (New York: Harper, 1950).

8. Philip E. Slater, *Microcosm: Structural Psychological and Religious Evolution in Groups* (New York: John Wiley, 1966); Thomas J. Cottle, "An Analysis of the Phases of Development of Self-Analytic Groups," in Jan J. Loubser, Rainer C. Baum, Andrew Effrat, and Victor Meyer Lidz, eds., *Explorations in General Theory in Social Sciences Theory* (New York: Free Press, 1976), Vol. I, pp. 328–353.

9. Parsons, "Superego and the Social System"; Talcott Parsons and Robert F. Bales, *Family, Socialization and Interaction Process* (New York: Free Press, 1955).

10. Nancy Chodorow, *The Reproduction of Mothering* (Berkeley, Los Angeles, London: University of California Press, 1978).

11. For a summary and evaluation, see Martin Jay, *The Dialectical Imagination: A History of the Frankfurt School and the Institute of Social Research, 1923–1950* (Boston: Little, Brown, 1973), ch. III.

12. Jürgen Habermas, *Theory and Practice*, trans. M. Viertel (Boston: Beacon Press, 1973).

13. George D. Spindler, ed., *The Making of Psychological Anthropology* (Berkeley, Los Angeles, London: University of California Press, 1978).

14. Erik H. Erikson, *Childhood and Society* (New York: Norton, 1950).

15. Heinz Kohut, *The Analysis of the Self* (New York: International Universities Press, 1971).

16. For a brief account of changes in the concept of defense since the appearance of *The Ego and the Id* in 1923, see Sander M. Abend, "Psychic Conflict and the Concept of Defense," *Psychoanalytic Quarterly* 50 (1981): 67–76.

17. Standard Edition (London: Hogarth Press, 1959), 20:73–174.
18. London: Hogarth Press, 1937.
19. D. Feigenbaum, "Depersonalization as a Defense Mechanism," *The Psychoanalytic Quarterly* 6 (1937):4–11.
20. Therese Benedek, "Infertility as a Defense Mechanism," lecture cited in Samuel J. Sperling, "On Denial and the Essential Nature of Defense," *International Journal of Psychoanalysis* 39 (1958): 37; Masha Mishkinsky, "Humour as a 'Courage Mechanism,'" *Israeli Annals of Psychology and Related Disciplines* 15, 4 (December 1977): 352–363.
21. E. Pumpian-Mindlin, reporter, panel on "Defensive Organization of the Ego and Psychoanalytic Technique," *Journal of the American Psychoanalytic Association* 15 (1967): 150–165.
22. Freud, *Inhibitions, Symptoms, and Anxiety*, p. 164.
23. Hartmann's words were that "defense processes may *simultaneously* serve both the control of instinctual drive and adaptation to the external world." Heinz Hartmann, *Ego Psychology and the Problem of Adaptation* (New York: International Universities Press, 1958), p. 51.
24. Charles Brenner, "Defense and Defense Mechanisms," *Psychoanalytic Quarterly* I (1981): 559.
25. Freud, *The Interpretation of Dreams*, Vol. V (Standard Edition, London: Hogarth Press) Chap. VII.
26. Rapaport, *Organization and Pathology of Thought: Selected Sources* (New York: Columbia University Press, 1951), part seven.
27. Freud, *Inhibitions, Symptoms, and Anxiety*, p. 117.
28. Ibid., pp. 90, 117.
29. Ibid., pp. 119–120.
30. This is the main dimension employed by Patrick Suppes and Hermine Warren in their suggestive article, "On the Generation and Classification of Defense Mechanisms," *International Journal of Psychoanalysis* 56 (1975): 405–414.
31. I omit "sublimation," which is considered here not to be primarily defensive in its significance but rather a form of indirect gratification of instincts. I also omit "regression" as a special form of defense, as it typically involves substituting one of the major forms of defense, employed at an earlier developmental stage, for another.
32. Sigmund Freud, "Repression," (Standard Edition, London: Hogarth Press), XIV: 147.
33. Standard Edition, Vol. XIV, p. 127.
34. Salman Akhtar and Jessica Price Byrne, "The Concept of Splitting and Its Clinical Relevance," *American Journal of Psychiatry* 140, 8 (August 1983): 1013–1016.
35. Freud, *Inhibitions, Symptoms and Anxiety*, pp. 120–121.
36. Merton Gill, "Topography and Systems in Psychoanalytic Theory," *Psychological Issues* 3, 2 (1961): 122–123.
37. Samuel J. Sperling, "On Denial and the Essential Nature of Defense," *International Journal of Psychoanalysis* 39 (1958): 36–37.
38. Anna Freud, *The Ego and Mechanisms of Defense*, pp. 59–64.
39. Edith Jacobson, "Denial and Repression," *Journal of the American Psychoanalytic Association* 5 (1957): 74–77.
40. Leonard I. Pearlin and Carmi Schooler, "The Structure of Coping," *Journal of Health and Social Behavior* 19, 2 (March 1978): 2–21.
41. Dorothy Nelkin and Michael S. Brown, *Workers at Risk: Voices at the Workplace* (Chicago: University of Chicago Press, 1984), pp. 37–49.
42. Ibid., pp. 83–99.
43. Ibid., pp. 50–63.
44. Mary Douglas, "Social Factors in the Perception of Risk," (Report to the Russell Sage Foundation, unpublished manuscript, 30 April 1983).
45. Steve R. Pieczenik, "Foreign Policy, Ego-Defense Mechanisms, and Balance-of-Power Vulnerability," *American Journal of Psychotherapy* 3 (1977): 4–13.
46. Robert Jay Lifton, "Beyond Nuclear Numbing," *Teachers' College Record* 84, 1 (Fall 1982): 15–29.

47. In the early 1970s psychoanalyst Martin Wangh circulated an inquiry to several thousand psychiatric practitioners in the United States, asking about how patients in treatment dealt with their anxieties about nuclear war. The respondents replied almost unanimously that the subject never came up in treatment. This would suggest a high level of denial, and that even in the psychoanalytic situation, people tend to deal with those areas of suffering over which they believe they can exercise some control. Reported in Martin Wangh, "'On Narcissism' in a Changing World," Meeting of the International Psychoanalytic Association (Madrid, July 1983).

48. I should remind the reader that in referring to various kinds of belief about nuclear war—or any other topic mentioned—as "defenses" I am referring to them only as psychic reactions to overcome uncertainty and master anxiety. I am not commenting on the empirical validity or invalidity of various claims to knowledge that these beliefs might entail.

49. Erich Lindemann, "Symptomatology and Management of Acute Grief," *American Journal of Psychiatry* 101 (1944): 141–148.

50. Kai T. Erikson, *Everything in Its Path: Destruction of Community in the Buffalo Creek Flood* (New York: Simon and Schuster, 1976); Leo Rangell, "Discussion of the Buffalo Creek Disaster: The Course of Psychic Trauma," *American Journal of Psychiatry* 133, 3 (March 1976).

51. For an account of the use of "common sense" as a defense against misfortunes, see Clifford Geertz, "Common Sense as a Cultural System," in *Local Knowledge: Further Essays in Interpretive Anthropology* (New York: Basic Books, 1983).

PART FIVE

Synthetic Reconstructions

CHAPTER THIRTEEN

Action and Its Environments

Jeffrey C. Alexander

This essay begins with some reflections on the micro/macro distinction in sociological theory and, on the basis of this critical reflection, suggests that some of the most illuminating and important innovations in this recent discussion need to be reconstructed and brought together. After suggesting a mode of interrelating some individualistic theories, the essay moves from the hermeneutical to the theoretical. A *microempirical model* of individual action is suggested, according to which action is viewed as interpretation and strategization. A microempirical model of order is then developed on this basis in which society, culture, and personality are conceived as action's immediate environments.

1. TERMINOLOGICAL CONCERNS

In the last decade the discipline of sociology resuscitated an old dilemma in a new form—a form, unfortunately, that has done little to resolve the dilemma itself. The perennial conflict between individualistic and collectivistic theories has been reworked as a conflict between microsociology and macrosociology. The distinction, of course, refers to size, and the implication of attaching these adjectives to "sociology" is to suggest that social theory and its empirical correlates involve clear choices between units of different size: small units versus big units. If this were all that has been implied, however, there would be little problem. In truth, much more has been suggested, for "micro" (small size) has usually been linked to a specific empirical focus, the focus on the individual in his or her interactions with other individuals. Although throughout much of this essay I, too, will be examining precisely this empirical issue, I would like to begin by suggesting that this equation of micro with individual is extremely misleading, as, indeed, is the attempt to find any specific size correlation with the micro/macro difference. There can be no empirical referents for micro or macro as such. They are analytical contrasts, suggesting emergent levels within empirical units, not antagonistic empirical units themselves.

The history of the life sciences gives ample illustration of how relative any imputation of macro and micro can be. Physiology, one of the robust life science disciplines, defined its field in terms of determinate interrelations of bodily organs and blood. Biochemistry, a much later development, suggested that interorganic functioning involves significant changes in the chemical properties of the elements from which these bodily organs are composed. More recently, molecular biology has introduced an entirely new level: Fundamental life processes can be understood in terms of molecular and atomic interaction, an understanding that connected biology not only to chemistry but to physics and mathematics as well. This historical declension from large units to small has illuminated new bases of physical organization and further complicated science's understanding of life. It has also enlarged the disciplinary base of the life sciences. It has not, however, except perhaps in the minds of some scientific entrepreneurs, succeeded in privileging one empirical arena over another. The autonomy and integrity of physiological functioning still holds: Basic biological events can be understood in terms of the relations between organs and blood. So can they be understood in terms of chemical shifts, molecular interaction, and, indeed, in terms of the physics of elementary particles.

The issue for contemporary life science is not which level is determinate or which discipline is "right" but, rather, at what level a given life phenomenon should be explained. The properties that are specific to a given level of life process are taken as the variables for a particular discipline; for other disciplines they are considered parameters, not denied as such. If the explanation for an empirical phenomenon at one level leads to the focus on processes that have been taken as parameters (dummy variables), then a different level of analysis is sought. Although this particular search for scientific knowledge may not be able to proceed until these parameters are more fully explored, the significance of the original variables is not eliminated. For example, heart disease is related, in the first instance, to inoperative valves or the breakdown of muscle, but the full causation of this physiological, functional breakdown is incomprehensible without understanding the biology, chemistry, molecular biology, and, ultimately, the physics involved. Still, the latter remain dependent on our knowledge of the heart as an organ and its relationship to blood. Or, to take another example, human reproduction can be "explained" physiologically in terms of mechanical activities of the genital organs. More microscopically, however, it can be explained in terms of the biology of sperm and egg; in terms of the biochemistry of acids, alkalines, and background solutions; in terms of the molecular bonds of genetic material and the mathematical probabilities of recombinant materials; and in terms of the magnetic properties of elementary units and forces.

These layers of life science, of course, are very gross; between them one could introduce a much more fine-grained picture of interdependent levels. This is precisely my point. The terms "micro" and "macro" are completely relativistic. What is macro at one level will be micro at another. Different properties are associated with different levels, and specific problems may demand the conversion of parameters into variables by moving toward larger or smaller units of reference. Each level, however, is homologous with every other, and there is no empirical life process that could subsist on any one level alone. Paradoxically, every empirical phenomenon can be accounted for at every level of analysis; it is simply accounted for in different ways. These different accounts reveal important new properties of the life process itself.

This complex notion of autonomy and interdependence has not been sufficiently understood by the social sciences. The tendency, rather, has been to equate micro with a specific level—the level of individual interaction—and this level has been portrayed as if it were in some kind of competition with all the others. The notion of homology has been lost and, with it, the possibility of integrating the results of this new sociology of individual interaction with more traditional understandings of social life at other levels. Such an integration can proceed only by disregarding the equation of individual interaction with microscopic. There are significant socially related processes that are "smaller" than, or "below," interaction; for example, the complex (largely unconscious) working of the personality and the open program of the individual's biological substrate, which involves not only quasi-instinctual genetic material but the socially related prestructuring of organs such as the hemispherically specialized brain. Equally significant, there are levels of analysis "larger" than that of individual interaction—for example, the level of institutional exchange—which themselves can be viewed as microprocesses relative to structures and processes of still larger scope.

The issue is not whether individual action and interaction are significant but whether theory should focus on this level in a manner that resists the rule of homology and analytic interpenetration. New insights into the structuring of individual action and interaction must be accepted. They must be articulated, however, in a manner that allows them to be interlarded with systematic understandings at every other level. Only in this way can the insights they provide be preserved while a broader, truly general theory of society is maintained.

2. RECONSTRUCTING "MICRO" THEORIES

The challenge is to convert the empirical insights of recent microtheorizing into analytical elements of more general theories. This conversion rests on two tasks. First, the claims of such theorizing to have discovered a completely new subject must be thrown into doubt; second, its claims to a completely empirical method must be skeptically examined.

Although the emphasis of "classical" sociology—of Marx, Weber, Durkheim, and Parsons—has undoubtedly been on larger units of social life, it has been the claims of postclassical, "micro" theorizing, not the proclamations of the classical theorists, which suggested that the objects of this traditional theorizing were anti-individual and anti-interactional as such. This negative claim is merely the other side of a positive one: the assertion, made by all those who have participated in this microrevival, that their emphasis on individual action and interaction represents a new and revolutionary *empirical* discovery. This insight into a completely new phenomenal realm, moreover, usually has been conflated with (i.e., seen as infused by) decisive new formulations at the level of ideology, method, and epistemological presuppositions.

In *Critique of Dialectical Reason*, for example, Sartre (1976) claimed to have discovered, in opposition to all previous Marxism, the realm of individual existence, individual freedom, and contingency. This differentiated empirical realm, he believed, establishes a new form of historical reason, a new theory, which is simultaneously more revolutionary and more tolerant, more sensitive to cultural forms, and more open to historical unpredictability. This new realm also produces a new method (Sartre 1963), one that allows for the past, present, and future to be seen from within every individual act. Touraine (1977) and Bourdieu (1977) have more recently taken up these Sartrean claims, naming (respectively) social movements and social action as new empirical arenas that, by their reference to intention and experience, promise to revolutionize our understanding of the reproduction of society.

Writing in an entirely different tradition, Schutz (1967, [1940] 1978*a*, 1978*b*) took up much the same claims for his own particular microarea. The "life-world," he believed, is an area never previously perceived by social science, let alone illuminated in a systematically theoretical way. Only the perception of this life-world, the subjectively experienced horizon of individual action as defined by the actor, allows for a voluntaristic theory, a theory of motive, a theory of self. It provides, Schutz believed, a perspective drastically at odds with even the most ostensibly interpretive sociology, and it implies not only a new method but an entirely new theory of social life. Berger and Luckmann (1966) and, much more extensively, Garfinkel (1967) later elaborated these claims in a more polemical form, suggesting that phenomenology had discovered an empirical object that justified a new social science itself. Building particularly on Garfinkel's claims, Giddens (1976, 1979) suggested that the discovery of individual reflexivity warrants the formulation of completely "new rules" of sociological method. Habermas (1984), returning to Schutz and linking him with pragmatism, raised the life-world to new empirical and ideological heights (see Alexander 1985*a*). Not only is it a phenomenon sharply separated from such supraindividual structures as norms, institutions, and systems, but it allows for the kind of immediate and satisfying personal experience that can ameliorate the alienation of late capitalist life.

From more distinctly American traditions, similar claims have been established for symbolic interactionist and exchange theory. Purportedly building on Mead, Blumer (1969) claimed that the phenomena of individual interpretation and contingent understanding have been entirely overlooked by every other tradition of sociological work. Once this new empirical realm is recognized, methodological and epistemological perspectives (and perhaps even ideological ones) will end up in a very different place. Although he never implies such theoretical extremism, Goffman (1959) suggests at various times in his work that the dramaturgical element in everyday life—the phenomenon of face-to-face interaction—will revolutionize sociology and overthrow its previous forms. Homans (1961), writing from his later, antinormative perspective on exchange, clearly promises the same thing. Exchange is an empirical phenomenon that has been ignored by almost every earlier form of sociological theorizing; it represents a distinctive realm that is determinate over all others;

it demands a new method, makes new presuppositions, implies a new ideology. Collins's (1981) recent arguments urging the microtranslation of macrosociology have followed in Homans's footsteps, although Collins bolstered his claims for the scientific newness of interaction with the "discovering claims" of Goffman and Garfinkel.

I suggest that the insights of these microtheorists, though much more elaborated and detailed than what has appeared before, are neither as new nor as purely empirical as they would like to contend. For all of his emphasis on the mode of production, Marx ([1867] 1962*a*) still devoted the lengthy tenth chapter of *Capital* to the interactional dimension and strategy of class struggle, and in his political writings (e.g., Marx [1852] 1962*b*) he often described individual strategy and politically contingent decisions. Weber's macrosociology of religion goes even further in this direction, resting upon quite nuanced descriptions of human personality needs (e.g., Weber [1916] 1946). His structural theory of patrimonialism, moreover (Weber 1978:1006–1110), includes detailed disquisitions on the decision-making processes of political actors and their staffs. Durkheim's ([1911] 1965) religious theory refers continually to his understanding of the life-world of the true believer, just as his study of suicidogenic currents (Durkheim [1897] 1951:277–294) depends on the phenomenological reconstruction of individual loneliness and despair. Parsons's functional analysis of the American university (Parsons and Platt 1973:163–222) includes a detailed portrait of student-teacher interaction, and his general theory of polarization and social change depends upon a specific understanding of the psychological deprivation experienced by traditionalist groups (e.g., Parsons 1954).

True, neither Marx, Weber, Durkheim, nor Parsons concentrates for long on such smaller units of analysis, but as these examples indicate, prototheories of more microscopic levels are implied throughout their works. Usually these implicitly theorized microprocesses operate as parameters, allowing larger units to be explicitly variable. At certain times, however, the analysis even of these traditionally macrotheorists takes a decidedly micro shift, taking up directly the behavior of smaller units such as individual personality, individual experiences, and individual interaction. My point here is that every macrotheorist of social systems or institutions makes assumptions about how individuals act and interact; these assumptions are crucial to their large-scale theories even when they are not made explicit—as, indeed, they usually are not. It is no wonder, then, that traditional sociological theorizing has occasionally made the behavior of these smaller units an explicit object of analysis and that the discussions of more recent, self-consciously "micro" sociology are not entirely new.

This leads to my second point: The focus on micro-level processes is not, in fact, entirely an empirical decision to make. Any microsociological analysis refers not merely to an overwhelming empirical fact but to an analytically differentiated, theoretical decision. Sociologists make presuppositions about the nature of social order—about the relative importance of different levels of analysis—and it is often this nonempirical presumption that shifts the burden of empirical discussion toward contingency and interaction and away from social structure. I am suggesting here not only that the individualist emphasis of recent microsociology is not entirely new but also that it may, despite its great empirical insight, be theoretically misplaced. To privilege the arena of microprocess may involve more than an empirical discovery; it may also involve a theoretical mistake. It may rely upon assumptions that deny to the macroparameters of interaction any real determination of this interaction itself.

Before exploring this possibility more fully, I want to suggest that the impact of nonempirical assumptions is actually still more complex. Sociological theories presuppose more than an understanding of the source of structure, or social order. They also proceed from a priori commitments about the nature of human action, particularly assumptions about action's relative rationality. It is this assumption about action which separates microtheories from one another, given that they usually *share* assumptions about order, and which often confounds their predictions about microeffects. No theory is simply a theory of size: Collective (macro) or individual (micro) order can be conceived as operating in radically different ways. In principle individuals can be portrayed as rational and objective or irrational and subjective (and in practice they often are); actors can also be viewed in a more synthetic way (which is rarely the case).

As I have tried to indicate in my earlier work on theoretical logic (Alexander 1982–1983, 1984) each of these decisions about action is ramifying in significant and radically different ways. Rationalist assumptions lead to the underplaying of value components and set the stage, when action is considered at a collective level, for the elimination of the voluntaristic element in social order. Nonrational assumptions rescue subjectivity and voluntarism, but they may idealize action and neutralize the impediments that stand in its way. Because neither of these implications is desirable, the first step toward achieving a truly satisfactory general theory of action is to synthesize rationalistic and nonrationalistic modes of theorizing.

The three great microtheories of the postwar period are symbolic interactionism, phenomenology/ethnomethodology, and exchange/rational choice. Each views itself as a *sui generis* explanation of individual behavior and interaction, as an empirical explanation that covers the entirety of what Parsons called the "unit act." If we examine their presuppositional positions, however, we will see that each theory is no more than a partial description of this primordial microunit. Such a critical examination, moreover, sets the stage for transforming the concrete empirical emphases of each theoretical tradition into analytical dimensions of a more broadly conceived unit act. We can find the theoretical resources for this reconstruction in Parsons's (1937) early description of the unit act, despite the fact that Parsons's own collectivist bias prevented him from ever conceiving of this unit act in a truly microsociological way. Given that the very utilization of Parsons's theory demands the recognition of its anti-interactionist thrust, our synthesis of microtheories within this "action" framework will lead us, finally, to a critical discussion of the presuppositions about order itself.

The action frame of reference that Parsons set out in 1937 includes the following elements: effort, means, ends, norms, and conditions. An action is made with reference to two environments: norms (ideal elements) and conditions (material elements). Means and ends, by contrast, are the products of action. What impels this action is effort. Norms and conditions are macrosociological elements, and by far the greater part of Parsons's systematic theory is related to elaborating their nature and interrelation. Ends and means are situationally specific, given that they are produced by individual action in the world. Every end is a compromise between individuals' effort, their objective possibilities, and their normative standards of evaluation; every means represents some aspect of individuals' conditional world which they have succeeded in putting to use according to their objective possibilities and internalized needs. What carves means and ends from conditions and norms is effort, but it is precisely this ineffable individual effort that for Parsons remains an unexamined black box. Effort is the contingent element of action, the consciousness that Sartre (1956), in *Being and Nothingness*, calls the undetermined "pure event." Effort is the motor, the microprocess, that drives the combination of the other elements. Because Parsons rarely had much to say about action as effort, he can tell us little about this important part of the story of ends and means, the part that sees them as "microtranslations" of norms and conditions. Parsons's analytic differentiation of action still holds, however. It provides the background for a theoretical synthesis of microsociological theories even while it can tell us little about these theories as such.

For it is "effort" that is the real object of exchange theory, ethnomethodology, and symbolic interactionism. Each explains one analytic dimension of effort and in so doing contributes one crucial element to our understanding of ends and means. Each contributes, in turn, to the microexplanation of norms and conditions. Exchange theory explains action as instrumentalizing efficiency and offers an account of how, given ends, norms, and conditions, effort produces usable means through the calculation of immediate costs. Phenomenology and ethnomethodology explain action as an order-seeking activity; they suggest how, given means, norms, and conditions, actors employ cognitive processes in open, contingent situations to establish ends that are consistent with, though not exclusively derived from, overarching rules. Interactionism focuses on neither means nor ends but on the utter contingency of individual interpretation itself. Viewing the latter pragmatically as a response to the intentions and activities of other actors in the situation, it further demonstrates how effort is concerted into means and ends.

Synthesizing microtheories with Parsons's unit act, then, exposes the interactional level of social life as systematically related to more macrostructure. It makes this level variable in a manner that allows the contingent properties of social structure to be discussed in a systematic way. If Parsons's black box of effort is opened up and each microtheory's exclusivist understanding of action is denied, we are directed toward elements that richly complement macroanalysis. Whether parameters or variables, each element can be related to dimensions of collective structure in a way that allows the latter to be seen as products of contingent action without being reducible to it. Exchange theory demonstrates that the material conditions of action are not fixed in some ontological manner "outside" of the acting individual. True, conditions are defined for the purposes of macroanalysis as material elements that cannot be changed; but this "cannot," exchange theory demonstrates (when the shift is made to microanalysis), is only the end result of what is in the first instance a contingent, not determined event. Actors have a finite amount of time, energy, and knowledge that they can apply to changing their external situation. What they decide cannot be changed (in light of these limitations) actors allow a conditional (i.e., purely material and external) status. Environments become "conditional"—they exert a "determinate" force—precisely because they demand so much time and energy if they are to be changed. It is not that a worker *cannot* change his or her class position; the contingent nature of action means that he or she certainly has the freedom to do so. The problem is that the time and energy required to alter the work environment are so demanding that the probabilities of the worker changing it are very small. In this way the worker's economic environment becomes an "objective" condition.

Ethnomethodology and phenomenology indicate, similarly, that the continuity and inertia of cultural patterns—which are emphasized by one stream of macroanalysis—rely on the continued operation of what Husserl ([1931] 1977) called certain "transcendental" features of human consciousness. Culture may be analytically conceived as existing outside of any individual mind, but its supraindividual status depends on individual mental features, particularly on the inclination that consciousness has to make each new mental impression part of the horizon of the impressions that preceded it. If this "horizonal" property of consciousness is placed in a situation where it cannot be successful, where the break between incoming impressions is simply too great, then the orderly consistency of culture (its "determinateness") breaks down, as Garfinkel (1963) demonstrated in his famous experiments on trust. Symbolic interactionism has shown, finally, that the response of others to an actor's activity can sometimes change the interpretation an actor gives even to that activity itself. The power of culture and conditions, then, depends on maintaining pragmatic continuities between actors and situations.

To conclude this hermeneutical reconstruction we must now return explicitly to the problem of order. I have shown that microtheories are not simply empirical discussions; to the contrary, they make a priori assumptions about action's relative rationality. I have suggested that only a synthesis of rational and interpretive microtheory gives action its due, and I have outlined this synthesis by relating each microtheory to a different element of Parsons's unit act. Each theory not only opens up Parsons's black box of effort but relates the now illuminated contingency to normative or conditional elements of a systemic kind. One clear implication of this exercise is that Parsons's macrotheory may be expanded by making variable what it left as parameter—namely, the contingent element of effort. There is another implication of equally great importance. The synthesis of unit act and microtheory demonstrates that the referents of contemporary microtheories are only the "fluid" or open element in larger, more crystallized units. These microtheories, then, cannot be considered theories of social order in themselves. It would be as absurd to deduce norms and conditions from transcendental consciousness and exchange as the other way around.

Each microtheory we have considered has, however, made precisely this claim. In the hands of Homans, Garfinkel, and Blumer, each has been proposed as an empirical theory of society as such. I have argued to the contrary, that the theoretical reconsideration of these claims makes it clear that the processes these theorists posit must be combined with the exposition by the great macrotraditions of collective material and ideal forms. Conflict theory and Marxism describe the allocation of conditional elements that are "declared determinate" by exchange. Cultural studies—hermeneutical, structural, Durkheimian, or Weberian—describe the integrated normative traditions from which "horizonality" and interpretation are constructed and which crystallize it in turn. This, I propose, is precisely what Parsons intended when, in his middle period work, he made allocation and integration the central macroprocesses of his social system theory, whereas means, ends, and effort remained the contingent elements in his conception of the unit act (see Alexander 1986).

This concludes my hermeneutical reconstruction of the micro-macro link. In the remainder of this essay I will suggest that this interpretive reconstruction implies a systematic model of action and order as empirical processes, processes in which contingency plays a different role according to specific historical and institutional conditions.

3. A MICROEMPIRICAL MODEL OF ACTION

In searching for a general term to describe the openness of individual action, such theorists as Giddens (1976) and Gouldner (1970), drawing on Garfinkel, developed the concept "reflexivity." Although it is certainly important to talk in general terms about the quality of action in the free space of contingency, I find this concept not only too general and opaque but also redolent of polemical traditions that imply one-sided commitments. "Reflexivity" is too Sartrean, both in its cognitive emphasis on self-consciousness and in its positive valuation of the individual's separateness—even alienation—from the world. It may also be too idealist, in the sense that it poses a tension between reflexivity and external material conditions, whereas, in my view at least, any general characterization of action must include the sources of conditional behavior within the process of contingency itself.

What might be a more complex way of conceptualizing the basic components of contingent action—the negotiation with the reality that Sartre (1956) calls "consciousness as pure event"—while maintaining a commitment to this generalized mode? I will conceive of action as moving along two basic dimensions: interpretation and strategization. Action is understanding, but it is also simultaneously practical and utilitarian. These two dimensions of action should be conceived as analytic elements within the stream of empirical consciousness. They do not represent different kinds of action, nor do they represent different emphases within a single line of action at different points in time. Every action is both interpretation and strategization; each process ensues at every moment in time.

Interpretation itself consists of two different processes: typification and invention. By the former I invoke the phenomenological insight that all actors take their understanding of the world for granted.[1] They do so because they fully expect that every new impression will be "typical" of the understanding of the world they have already developed. This "typicality" does not operate merely at the gross level of tradition. Even if we encounter something new and exciting we expect this newness and excitement to be understandable: It will be known by us within the terms of reference we already possess. We cannot separate ourselves—except in the fantasy of psychotic experience—from our classification system. The most modern mind therefore is no different from the savage one exalted by Lévi-Strauss (1966), for like the "native" in a premechanical civilization, we are forever—irredeemably, with or without consciousness and intention—turning all that is new into all that is old.

Socialization means learning to typify within the framework provided by one's particular world. Every member of the collectivity must learn to explain, to name, to discover the typical terms of every possible situation. The most basic rule for acquiring sociological citizenship is "no surprises," and typification is the characteristic of consciousness upon which such inclusion depends. Similarly, typification is the hinge upon which later, more particular entries into group life depend, entries that can be seen as secondary socializations. You are a surgeon when you typify the world surgically, a girl when you conceive of every impression girlishly, and so forth. To be socialized into a world is to take your understanding of it for granted, and to live in that world is to document every new object as evidence for this ontological certainty.

Typification, finally, is part of interactional process, not merely a quality within individual consciousness. When we interact with our children we are teaching them what to typify, although we make the assumption that they already know how to do it. Communication between adult persons is not simply aimed at rational consensus, nor is it simply a process of rewarding or sanctioning; it is a deeply hermeneutical process of understanding that proceeds through gestures that typify a tiny selection of ongoing experience, gestures through which we seek to exact from others the same typifications we apply to them in the course of communication.

As this last consideration implies, however, interpretation involves more than the reproduction of an internalized classification scheme. True, even a structuralist like Lévi-Strauss (1966:161–190) has acknowledged that reproduction involves not simply universalization (putting the small into the large—what I have called typification), but also particularization (putting the large into the small). Still, it is reproduction as such that needs amending. The reality our contingency confronts is not quite the same as anything we have encountered before. We are convinced that it is just one more example of the past, but it can never be that alone. Because it is always new and because each successive representation of reality must, indeed, bring past generalization into contact with new objects, there is always something different, something invented, in each successive conceptualization of reality. If we could, by the very act of our consciousness, transform reality so it would be no more than what we have known, then understanding would involve typification alone. Reality is resistant, however. To make it typical is a creative act and not merely a reproductive, typifying act, for we are usually (unconsciously) finding ways of understanding in a slightly new key. Typification actually camouflages shifts in classification. These shifts are what invention is all about. Only because invention is hidden within phenomenological conformity can culture be so plastic and individual action proceed in such an extraordinarily fluid way.

It was, I believe, to just this kind of inventive element that Durkheim ([1898] 1974) referred when he defined representation as composed not only of an "externalization" of prior symbolic expectation but of an "internalization" of the newly encountered objects themselves. It was also what he referred to when he ([1911] 1965:217, 243) insisted on the transforming role "religious imagination" plays within every ritual process. Dilthey ([1910] 1976) implied invention when he stressed the ultimate incomprehensibility of individuals to one another. One tries to make the other's gestures typical, but the irredeemable separateness of human beings ensures that others' gestures retain an element of mystery.

This mystery is created by others' invention and it stimulates ours in turn, for if we can only guess at what "something other" really means we must create some partially new categories of understanding. Interpretation, therefore, is certainly a way of reducing the complexity of the world, as Luhmann (1980) suggests, but the understanding of typification and invention presented here makes them far more active existential interventions than his concept seems to imply.

There is still another major dimension of human consciousness, one that eludes the idealist framework altogether and sets contingent action on a much more "complexifying" course. This is strategization. Action is not merely understanding the world, it is also transforming and acting upon it. Actors seek to carry out their intentions through *praxis* (Marx [1845] 1965), and for this reason they must act with and against other people and things. Such practical action certainly occurs only within the confines of understanding, but within the terms of clearly understood events it introduces the strategic considerations of least cost and most reward. To act against the world requires time, energy, and knowledge. One cannot expend time and energy indefinitely; every expenditure in one direction is a loss in another. We seek the shortest path to our goal, for this will be the least costly in terms of time; but if the shortest path is not really the straightest line, if the objects in our path are piled up or much larger than expected, this time saving may be too costly in terms of energy. Time and energy, then, must be allocated according to least expense.

Every strategic calculation, moreover, involves relevant knowledge. Keynes has shown that knowledge of our environment and the consequences of our action are hardly "perfect" in the classical economists' sense. In his *Treatise on Probability* ([1921] 1973), he demonstrated that every strategic and economizing action depends on calculations about probable consequences, calculations that in turn depend upon our knowledge of the future. This knowledge can only be very sketchy, however; there is simply too much contingency (nothingness in Sartre's sense) to make any safe bets. People cannot know the future, even if they pretend that they are confident about it. Probability, then, cannot be calculated in a mathematical way: It is an empirical proposition dependent on partial and fragmented knowledge. Keynes translated these insights into his book, *The General Theory of Employment, Interest and Money* ([1936] 1965:135–164, 194–209), by suggesting that if calculations about profit (time and energy in my terms) depend on limited future knowledge, then inevitably introduced into investment decisions are subjective elements relating to confidence and trust. The "state of long-term expectations" influences investment. This puts rational calculation into a relationship with "irrational" understanding.

Strategization, then, comes back to interpretation. To the degree that we assume that the future will be like the past, we may calculate a given cost-benefit ratio as profitable, but if we sense that the future may be disjunctive, then the same profit will seem too low to proceed. Understanding not only provides the environment for strategization; it profoundly affects the calculation of strategic interest itself. One must immediately add, however, that this interactive effect works both ways: To some degree interpretation is itself a strategic phenomenon. We do not try to "understand" every impression that enters our consciousness. Considerations of nearness and farness, time, energy, and the extent of possible knowledge all come forcefully into play. They push typification and invention in this direction or that. What is understood, moreover, will not be equally valued. Our ranking of conceived impressions, I believe, is partly affected by which will be easier to act upon—that is, which segment of reality is more likely to be institutionalized in the future environments of contingent acts.

I have now presented a model—schematic as it must remain at this point—of action in the empirical sense of individual activity. This meets half the obligation I incurred in my hermeneutical reconstruction of the micro/macro debate, for the model seeks to describe the nature of action *qua* action (action in its contingent mode) that was left as a black box by Parsons and filled polemically by his individualist critics. The obligation that remains concerns what microelements order this individual action. From the model I have presented, as from my earlier discussion of the diverse orientations of current microtheorizing, it is clear that the very description of contingent action implies the noncontingent environments within which it occurs. To understand contingency is to understand that it must be oriented to constraint, and to understand the dimensions of contingency is to understand the variation within such constraining environments. The collective environments of action simultaneously inspire and confine it. If I have conceptualized action correctly, these environments will be seen as its products; if I can conceptualize the environments correctly, action will be seen as their result.

4. A MICROEMPIRICAL MODEL OF ORDER

To produce a model of these environments I turn once again to Parsons. I will take up what I regard as his most important contribution: the three-system model of personality, society, and culture through which he reconceptualized the legacies of Weber, Durkheim, and Freud in "functional" terms. It is necessary, however, not simply to appropriate this vital distinction (which most of contemporary social science still has not done). One must also, given the theoretical resources now at hand, seek to develop it in more sophisticated ways than Parsons was able to do himself. I start, moreover, from a position Parsons did not share. I do not conceive this three-system model as a substitute for conceptualizing action in itself. Concrete action cannot be analytically broken down into its three systematic elements. These systems, rather, enter action as its more or less ordered environments. It is this very departure, of course, which allows us to conceive systemic order in a micro way. Only by conceptualizing contingent action in an explicit way can we learn how to present the "systems" of collective order as real environments.

The social system constitutes one major environment for action by providing actors with real objects. These can be physical or natural objects such as forests, fences, automobiles, and horses, which, because of their location in society, attain much more than purely nonhuman status. More often, or at least more significantly, these objects are human beings. The division of labor and institutions of political authority provide crucial settings for individual interpretation and strategization. The division of labor results from the historically specific mode of allocating and distributing personnel, whereas the authority system derives from the intersection of this allocative system with social control and integration. My concern here, however, is not with the macroscopic question of how these systems function in their own right but with their impact on action. Surgical residents in a university teaching hospital, for example, must typify, strategize, and invent within the confining limits of the authority and power of the staff surgeon directing their rotation (see Bosk 1979). Power, authority, and control are allocated to this staff director, not to the residents. It is the director who sets the standards that residents seek to typify in their patient conversations and surgical interventions; it is through the director and the facilities he or she controls that energy, time, and knowledge are distributed in such a way that the resident's strategizing will be more costly if it steps outside established medical and neophyte roles. Conversely, it is the same division of labor and authority that make the resident fairly inconsequential to the action of the staff surgeon in turn. The resident does not set significant standards for the staff surgeon's interpretive procedures, nor does he or she exercise significant control over the surgeon's costs and rewards. The residents, of course, stand as superordinates in relation to others. Surgical nurses and hospital orderlies do not significantly affect the residents' interpretive procedures, nor are they important objects for their strategic consideration.

Solidarity is another significant dimension through which the social system exercises its environing effects. Those with whom we stand in some community significantly affect our action. This community may be conceived both quantitatively, in terms of the number of its constituents, and qualitatively, in terms of the nature of the bonds that unite them. As Simmel (1955), Blau (1977), and modern-day conversation analysts (e.g., Sacks et al. 1974) have shown, we strategize and possibly even interpret differently depending on the size of the group with which we are interacting and according to whether the members in this group are defined consensually or conflictually. Similarly, whereas primordial ties lead the costs of conflict to be calculated in one direction, civil and impersonal ties allow social objects to enter strategic thinking about the consequences of action in quite another (Alexander 1980). Typification in a caste society extends the horizon of action in a persistently hierarchical way; cultural reproduction in a more egalitarian society leads, by contrast, to the extension of citizenship, to the reproduction of the salutation *citoyen*. Invention, too, is fundamentally affected by the experienced definitions of community that the social system provides (see Prager 1985).

In a relatively differentiated and fluid society, of course, actors can never be members of every solidary group at once. Even while they remain members of the national societal community, they move in and out of smaller communities whose boundaries are amorphous and in the end only interactionally defined. Changing community membership, however, means more than being "in" or "out." Actors rarely join a community with their whole selves; only certain parts of their character are engaged. Here is where Goffman's microsociology comes into play, for he supplied a kind of transformational grammar, a set of rules for the transformation from individual to group status. Goffman describes the action processes that link the individual to solidary groups. He views strategization as omnipresent (Goffman 1959). Actors make decisions about the costs of presenting different parts of themselves in open interaction; they also strategize simply about making themselves available as objects for others. Doing some things "backstage" and others "frontstage" makes certain individual actions rather than others available for interpretation and calculation. Rules about face-to-face interaction in public places—for example, understanding that direct eye contact implies (even a fleeting) familiarity (Goffman 1963)—direct typification in a manner that defines group membership. This status, in turn, has enormous strategic consequences.

Finally, one must not forget that the position of human elements in social systems must actually be understood in terms of social roles. Social objects take their position in the division of labor and the authority structure through the roles defined by that system. Roles are defined by complexes of sanctions and normative guidelines. Action orients itself to social system exigencies, then, by relating itself not simply to real objects but to objects as they participate in their social role, to sanction systems and specific norms. Both components of roles—norms and sanctions—alert typification, inspire strategization, and produce invention. Goode (1960) has demonstrated that role performance involves an elaborate microaccounting of social costs, for the complexity of institutional life makes it virtually impossible to fulfill the full complement of the roles in which one participates. The role strain that results from this situation is one of the most important triggers for strategization, and for typification and invention as well. Goode demonstrated that role performance is allocated according to implicit economic calculations about the cost, reward, and price of role compliance and evasion.

There are other environments for action, however, which are not so "real." Actors do not encounter the objects of social systems simply as external objects, even as objects that are normatively defined. They encounter those objects from within, as the referents of symbol systems, which means, for all practical purposes, as symbols themselves.[2] Symbols are signs that have a generalized status, that provide categories for understanding the elements of social, individual, and organic life. This understanding is the "meaning of life." Although symbols take as their referents the elements of other systems—the interactional objects of society, the cathected objects of unconscious life, the natural objects of the physical/organic world—they define and interrelate these elements in an arbitrary manner (that is, in a manner that cannot be deduced from specific exigencies at other system levels). These symbols, in other words, form a system of their own. This cultural system (Geertz 1973) has an independent internal organization whose principles of functioning have only recently begun to be explored.[3] This cultural functioning inspires and constrains interpretive action and strategization in complex ways.

Cultural systems are continually involved in two fundamental processes: constructing reality and evaluating it. Constructing reality can be understood in "structural" and semiotic terms. It involves naming, corresponding, and analogizing, each of which rests upon typification and invention (Lévi-Strauss 1966:172–216; Sahlins 1976:170–171; Leach 1976; Barthes 1967). Every object in the world is symbolized through its name. At some point every name is invented, it is new. Names are chosen because the new object is conceived as corresponding to some previous existing one—it seems "typical." Once a new object is symbolized, moreover, correspondence becomes quite intricate and complex. If I may illustrate this by drawing from some research I am doing on the Watergate crisis in the United States, the break-in to the Watergate Hotel in Washington, D.C. had first to be named (invented as) "Watergate" before "Watergate" could be called a crime (a typifying correspondence). This crime, in turn, was classified as either a third-rate burglary or the crime of the century (secondary correspondence and the beginning of analogy). The intricate web that cultures spin between binary correspondences is powered by analogy, a general term that covers diverse forms of theoretical comparison.[4] In the course of the Watergate crisis, for example, there developed an analogy between two correspondences: Watergate is to Gordon Liddy as the cover-up is to Richard Nixon. Cultural analogies eventually become extraordinarily complex, for their purpose is to relate each different plane of reality—nature, physical world, social world, moral world—to every other so that the actor senses the existence of a meaningful whole. See, for example, the cross-plane analogies implied by the following semantic equation developed during the Watergate crisis: Watergate = river = flood = dirty water = darkness = sin = pollution = Republican party = Nixon presidency. Whether the referent is an extraordinary public event like Watergate or the mundane routines of everyday life, the process of constructing reality through naming, corresponding, and analogizing fundamentally structures typification and invention and, indirectly, strategization. It informs every estimation of the typical and the new and every calculation of cost by providing an "arbitrary" definition of meaning for every encounter with the "reality" of social objects.

Cultural systems do still more than construct reality; they also evaluate it.[5] Though seamless, reality is not flat. It has centers that hold its meaningful order in place. These centers (Shils 1975) are the fulcrums of reality's various wholes. They mark its points of sacredness, points that are always strongly positively valued, sometimes awesomely so. In this sense, I believe, modern man is as archaic as Eliade's *homo religioso* (1959); he, too, orients himself to meaning by finding out how he stands in relation to the center of his world, the point that marks the origins of the existential order upon which, he feels, his very being depends. Typifying action often means reproducing one's relation to the sacred center, and invention is often a way of finding either a new relation to it or a new version of the center itself. Every strategic estimation of cost, of course, must take into account the distance between actors and centers.

The names, correspondences, and analogies that create symbolic reality are, then, differentially valued. Alongside the elements that are sacred, moreover, stands not only the world of routine but the highly charged negative world of the profane (Caillois [1939] 1959). Symbolic systems are more than cognitive classifications: They are emotional and moral mappings of good and bad.[6] These fiercely antagonistic worlds are privileged sources for analogies in their own right, but they are usually taken one step further than analogy into the realm of myth itself. Myth (Ricoeur 1969) elaborates valued antitheses by putting them into narrative form. It is this narration that allows the central symbols of culture to become persuasive models for social life, for within every human being there is a fundamental commitment to typifying meaningful experience in a chronological, dramatic form. Invention can create new stories and even new genres, but it can never erase the narrative form itself.

What I have described so far refers to symbol systems in themselves. Although signifiers in such systems all have noncultural referents, the meanings that are constructed from their arrangement—the codes they present—remain at one remove from the institutional processes of social life. They tell us the meaning of the elements of social systems, and they provide through their valuation the crucial references upon which economic, political, and integrative processes build. They do not, however, enter into the social system as socially embodied causal forces in their own right. One product of the cultural system does so; this is the element I will call "values." Values are produced (Parsons and Shils 1951) by the mediated encounter of social system relationships with symbolic worlds, the result of which is the differential valuation of specific social processes. By upholding capitalism or socialism, values (by directing typification, inspiring invention, or informing strategization) help to structure specific economic systems. By promoting equality or inequality, they affect stratification. By championing democracy or authority, values refer directly to crucial issues in political systems. By promoting inclusion or exclusion, they help create different societal communities; through asceticism or mysticism, they help effect different religious ones. Parsons's discussion of the "pattern variables" is an abstract, systematic delineation of values relating to the individual choice of, and commitment to, the objects with which one interacts. People may look at objects in terms of their universal or particular qualities and value them for their achieved or ascribed qualities. In defining their commitments to these objects people may value more direct affectivity or more neutral, and they will act toward these objects in a more diffuse or specific manner.

No matter what their proximity to the social system, classification, sacralization, and valuation embody what might be called the "statics" of cultural life. There is also a distinctive class of cultural processes that take a dynamic form. It is through them that the equilibrium problems of social systems become symbolically reconstructed. Conflicts inside social systems are culturally translated (typified) as threats to the sacred symbols of the center, threats that emanate from the powers of the symbolically profane. Social system threats, in other words, are often seen as polluting (Douglas 1966), for the profane, as cultural disorder or symbols "out of place," soils the purity and cleanliness of the sacred. Social disorder brings tabooed symbols into contact with symbols that are normally protected by the space that surrounds sacred things. This causalty can move in the other directions as well, from the threat of cultural pollution to social system disorder.

Pollution and purification, then, are endemically cultural components of social life; and if the threat of pollution is great enough, these purifying processes will take on a ritual form. If social processes threaten to undermine meaningful order, they must be separated from social structure and placed in a marginal or liminal position (Turner 1969). In this liminal form their meaning can be worked through in the simplified, stereotyped, traditionalized manner that is ritual process. Rituals generalize from the specificity of social structure; they shift the conscious attention of actors to the components of meaning itself, to the classifications and valorizations upon which the existence of culture depends. Rituals, however, are not simply typifications of cultural antinomies in a highly charged form; they are inventive processes that create new versions of old forms and sometimes even new forms themselves. This invention is, of course, all in the service of preserving "central" cultural concerns and proceeds under the wary eye of strategic calculations about the costs and benefits of invention and reinstitutionalization.

I have argued that interpretation and strategization are oriented toward external objects representing economic facilities, political authority, and ecological/solidary ties. These social system elements establish constraints and normative guidelines for typification; define the circumstances and allocate the resources for invention; and distribute time, energy, and knowledge in ways that set the costs for strategic behavior.

These objects or, more accurately, the exigencies they represent, are encountered from within as symbols, as units in the complex representational systems that define reality, distribute the sacred and profane, and establish the universe of potentially institutionalized social values. This symbolic system introduces the "arbitrary" into the meaning of social objects: Every object is simultaneously cultural form and social fact. Because social objects must be named, not just dominated or deferred to, typification and invention proceed not only within limits established by power and rules but also within the grid of cultural classification. Strategization affects action at both levels. It enters interpretation through the back door, so to speak, by making certain relationships more costly; it enters social interaction through the front by translating system exigencies into considerations of time, energy, and knowledge.

Social forms are not the only objects with which action deals, nor is culture its only reference from within. Actors have personalities. Indeed, more than either of the other two system references actors "are" personalities, their action proceeding entirely within the confines of this system alone. Yet personalities, in turn, represent a selection of objects introjected from social encounters, a selection dictated by the play of organic and developmental needs. Each acting "I" and his or her personality, moreover, changes decisively at different stages in his or her own life. Personalities supply differential capacities for interpretation and strategization. The actor qua social object rewards and sanctions; the actor qua personality cathects and rejects. The object cathexes, or affective charges, that emanate from the personality are guided by interpretation of and strategizing about the potential responsiveness of the social objects and the meaning they have. "Mother," for a young man, is a complexly defined cultural symbol; a role performer with effective sanctions and rewards; and also a cathected object representing opportunities for security, dependence, sexual fulfillment, and guilt.

Emotional demands and the shifting demands of organic life articulate with changing social objects and cultural grids to produce the complex structures of personality. Not just the superego but also the ego and the id represent unconscious object systems (Weinstein and Platt 1973), distillations from different stages and different modes of social interaction. Together, these objects form the third system with which action must contend. Given the relatively simple unconscious system of a two-year-old child, for example, adult criticism means "bad" and produces tears and conformity. For a four-year-old personality, however, the same criticism—interactionally parallel and symbolically analogous—may mean "unfair" and lead to resistance. At still a later point of development the criticism may not even be heard; the defense mechanisms of the ego may allow it to be completely rationalized away.

The active part of the ego responds to the fantasized threats and promises of internalized objects—to the anxieties of object loss and promises of recovery—by constructing defenses (Freud 1936) such as denial, neutralization, projection, and splitting. Because they are systematic distortions of cognition (in the service of unconscious emotional needs), these defenses enter typification as yet another determinant of its specific form. They are one frame of reference for constructing and valorizing reality, but they also provide an affective reference for interpreting symbols that already exist and for calculating the costs and benefits of interaction in society. The cultural need for sacralization and the centering of symbols can valorize reality only if the personality finds gratification in the organization of cathected objects into "good" and "bad." This emotional need develops, according to orthodox theory (Fenichel 1945:279–80, 286), with the anal drive for control and exclusion and, more significantly, with the growth of superego strictures in the first Oedipal phase. It might even be considered to have begun earlier, with the splitting of good and bad breasts that Melanie Klein (1957) believes to be part of the oral stage. Whatever its origins, however, it seems clear that this psychological capacity, which is as necessary for the social system construction of deviance and conformity as it is for cultural classification, must be continued as an "adapting" ego process even if it does not survive in pathological form. Vital social and cultural processes depend on it. Without the psychological inclination for this special kind of organization, action would not have the environmental support to carry it out.

Typification, invention, and strategization, then, are capacities of the personality, not merely modes by which epistemological categories come into play or avenues for social exchange and control. These capacities change historically. Elias ([1939] 1978) explained how social differentiation creates a "civilizing process" that is at once psychological and social. In the course of modernization authority becomes more rationalized and specific, whereas the societal community becomes more expansive, impersonal, and inclusive (Alexander 1980). New cultural codes arise that are more ascetic, more universalistic, more committed to world mastery and control. Personalities, too, must change if "civilization" is to occur, however. They must develop the capacity for depersonalization and control, for the repression, neutralization, and splitting upon which modern rationality depends. These affective changes are initiated when traditionally authoritative objects become compromised or withdraw (Weinstein and Platt 1969), but they also occur in more systematic, long-term ways. Childhood becomes elongated (Ariès 1962); there is an enormous lengthening of psychosocial training and, with it, a much more jarring transition between the site of early personality development and adult life (Keniston 1960). This simultaneously allows the modern adult personality to be created and the unconscious needs for dependency and immediate fulfillment that remain to be isolated in differentiated, private spheres (Slater 1963).

By a process of affective modernization, then, the personality comes to undergird interpretation and strategization in so-called civilized ways. In this long-term view equilibrium is assumed. With the uneven development that characterizes real modernization, the independent variable of personality throws a much more problematic element into play. The early emotional experience of German youth immediately following World War I vitally affected the unconscious object systems they brought into the later period of German instability (Loewenberg 1983). As a result, this cohort experienced the "same" national and international events in more paranoid and unstable ways than Germans in other generations. This emotional experience led them to typify these events in terms of more primordial streams of national culture, to respond to frustration by inventing more aggressive ideologies, to conceive political strategies by a different and more fateful calculation of costs and rewards. Nazism was created by contingent action; it was not the inevitable and determined result of collective forces. The microarena within which the structures of Nazism were created, however, was not simply an arena of action alone. Action occurs within systemic environments, the organization of unconscious emotional needs not the least among them.

5. THE "PROBLEM OF RATIONALITY"

Before concluding I would like to comment on the relevance of the preceding points for the prevailing image of contemporary action as consummately rational and endlessly creative, an image that is vital not only to modern common sense and to important traditions of microexplanation—as typified, for example, by Giddens's (1976) notion of "reflexivity"—but also to various utopian reconstructions of contemporary human capacity. First, I do not believe that creativity and rationality need be understood as contravening typifying action or, indeed, the constraints of action's environing systems. Because all action is contingent, typification and strategization make invention continuous. More to the point, social segmentation, which occurs in even the simplest societies, makes invention a fundamental "social need." Segmentation means that institutions are differentiated ecologically. Social objects defined as the same are not physically identical. An individual encounters not "the family," "the father," "the manager" but concrete and segmented versions of the same. This segmentation mediates and makes more inconsistent psychological internalizations, cultural understandings, and the process of sanctioning and rewards. Slightly different objects are constantly thrown up to the acting person. When inconsistency reaches a certain point, strong personalities act to simplify complexity by creative transformations of cultural forms. This "regression in service of the ego" (Kris 1937), however, still does not produce completely new inventions; it appears to the creative person and particularly to his or her appreciative audience in "typical" and strategically possible ways.

What about "rationality" in the modern sense of action carried out according to universalistic, verifiable standards, action that is thereby subject to constant, consciously directed change? This rationality, it seems to me, is not a question of a particular kind of action but of a particular structure of environments. The environments of action can be more or less open, a fact that allows us to conceive a continuum of action stretching from ritual to rationality. Ritual action and rational action both occur within meaningful, experienced worlds, worlds in which typification, cultural order, and "irrational" psychological interests come fully into play.[7] In ritual, however, the environments of action are relatively closed, structured in ways that are less open to change, whereas in rational action they are relatively open. Rituals are standardized and repeatable sequences of action. They more frequently define action in social situations in which the division of labor is rigid; in which authority for all practical purposes is unchallengeable; in which culture is fused with its social system referents in an anthropomorphic and particularistic way; in which the personality is cathected to objects through the familial modes of trust, deference, and charismatic domination. In this closed situation standardization follows naturally from interpretation and calculation.

Insofar as the environments of action are less rigid and more complex, depersonalizing capacities develop in the personality and more abstract and generalized classification systems develop in the culture. This separation of the self from its world and the differentiation of the actor's standards of evaluation do not eliminate the noncontingent element of action. Rather, rational action may be conceived as "fixed" above and "open" below. The social objects encountered are more complex and changing; the cultural referents defining them and the personality motivating them are more structured in ways that allow active adaptation and change. Typification is less standardized; strategization is more ramifying; invention is more dramatic. Because action is more rational, specialized institutions of social control are necessary to maintain psychological, social, and interpretive consistency over the life course. New media of exchange, such as money and influence, allow continuous strategic calculation and frequent changes in the direction and lines of action without abandoning the cultural classifications and social role definitions to which typification always returns. The continuum ritual-rationality operates within any given historical system, as I indicated earlier in my analysis of the dynamics of cultural life, but it may also be seen as a historical continuum with comparative scope. Medical practice, institutions of mass communications, and political structures and processes, for example, all may be seen as having moved from being embedded in ritual to being more contingent and rational, if we understand this rationality as implying neither utter contingency nor the removal from cultural and emotional controls.

6. CONCLUSION

I have argued in this essay against the micro/macro split. There need not be one in sociological theory; there certainly does not seem to be one in empirical reality. Why, then, the great divide in sociological discussion today? Because, I believe, theorists falsely generalize from a single variable to the immediate reconstruction of the whole. They have taken one particular system—the economy, the culture, the personality—as action's total environment; they have taken one action mode—invention, typification, or strategization—as encompassing action in itself. Moreover, by acknowledging only the kind of action presupposed by their conception of collective order, macrotheorists have prematurely closed the action-environment circle: Theories of economic systems have reasoned that action is strategic, cultural theorists have stressed typification, social movement theorists the inventive, and so forth. It seems perfectly appropriate that each of these different elements of microprocess and macroprocess can be viewed as the objects of independent scientific disciplines, as they are in the natural and physical sciences. It is unacceptable, however, for any one of these variables and disciplines to be considered privileged in relation to the others. Rather than being thought of as dependent and independent variables, these elements should be conceived as parameters and variables in an interactive system comprising different levels of different "size." This, of course, requires a common conceptual scheme, one the social sciences do not yet possess. The current revival of interest in theorizing about the micro-macro link may make such a conceptual scheme possible, a possibility to which the present essay has sought to make a contribution.

NOTES

1. The notion that perception—which for all practical purposes in the phenomenological tradition is action—involves a process of typification derived most directly from Schutz's (1967:139–214) recasting of Weber's "ideal-type" method in phenomenological form. This recasting goes far beyond anything Weber envisioned, the considerable deepening being due, I believe, to the real intention of Schutz, which is to use Weber to make Husserl's theory more social. Typification, then, can be traced back to the "intentionality" and "constitutive practices" Husserl noted ([1931] 1977); it is also related to the "indexicality" discussed by Garfinkel (1963, 1967).

2. This notion that all social objects are seen "from within"—indeed, the very phrase itself—is Garfinkel's, from the path-breaking early essay on trust (1963), which sought to introduce a phenomenological lining to Parsons's theory of internalization (see Alexander 1985*b*). That the same phrase can be used to describe not only action but one of its environments indicates what I earlier called the "principle of homology"—that is, the necessity for the theory of environments and the theory of action to be complementary.

3. It is precisely for this reason—the underdeveloped state of cultural analysis in the social sciences—that I will be spending more time analyzing the internal functioning of this environment than I spend on the other two. Only with a much more nuanced understanding of cultural systems than is currently available can the complex relationship between action and meaningful environment be seen.

4. Again, what I have called the rule of homology is demonstrated by the fact that although this great opponent of historicity and phenomenology, Lévi-Strauss, makes "analogy" basic to the structural analysis of cultural systems, Husserl ([1931] 1977), the great exponent of contingency and individuality, makes "analogizing" fundamental to consciousness. My point is that if either theorist is correct, then both must be. They are identifying different yet interdependent levels of reality.

5. Here I am moving back from a structuralist interest in classification to the earlier Durkheimian interest in the emotional charge attached to symbols and their moral meaning.

6. Caillois was the first theorist to notice the ambiguous definition of "profane" in Durkheim's work and to argue, in Durkheimian terms, for a theory of profane as evil. Again, it is unnecessary to separate such discussions from those of cognitive classification.

7. In what follows I am drawing on the implications of the present essay to elaborate criticisms I have made of Habermas's recent work (Alexander 1985*a*).

REFERENCES

Alexander, Jeffrey C. 1980. Core Solidarity, Ethnic Outgroup, and Social Differentiation: Towards a Multidimensional Model of Inclusion in Modern Societies, pp. 5–28 in Jacques Dofny and Akinsola Akiwowo, eds., National and Ethnic Movements. Beverly Hills and London: Sage.

———. 1982–1983. *Theoretical Logic in Sociology*. Vols. 1–4. Berkeley, Los Angeles, London: University of California Press.
———. 1984. Structural Analysis in Sociology: Some Notes on Its History and Prospects. *Sociological Quarterly* 25:5–26.
———. 1985*a*. Habermas' New Critical Theory: Prospects and Problems. *American Journal of Sociology* 91(2):400–424.
———. 1985*b*, The "Individualist Dilemma" in Phenomenology and Interactionism, pp. 25–57 in S. N. Eisenstadt and H. J. Helle, eds., *Perspectives on Sociological Theory*. Vol. 1. Beverly Hills, Calif.: Sage.
———. 1986. *Twenty Lectures: Sociological Theory Since World War II*. New York: Columbia University Press.
Ariès, Philippe. 1962. *Centuries of Childhood*. New York: Knopf.
Barthes, Roland. 1967. *Elements of Semiology*. New York: Hill and Wang.
Berger, Peter L., and Thomas Luckmann. 1966. *The Social Construction of Reality*. New York: Doubleday.
Blau, Peter. 1977. *Inequality and Heterogeneity*. New York: Free Press.
Blumer, Herbert. 1969. *Symbolic Interactionism*. Englewood Cliffs, N.J.: Prentice-Hall.
Bosk, Charles. 1979. *Forgive and Remember: Managing Medical Failure*. Chicago: University of Chicago Press.
Bourdieu, Pierre. 1977. *Outline of a Theory of Practice*. Cambridge: Cambridge University Press.
Caillois, Roger. 1959. *Man and the Sacred* (1939). New York: Free Press.
Collins, Randall. 1981. On the Micro-Foundations of Macro-Sociology. *American Journal of Sociology* 86 (March):984–1014.
Dilthey, Wilhelm. 1976. The Construction of the Historical World in the Human Studies, pp. 168–245 in H. P. Rickman, ed., *Dilthey: Selected Writings* (1910). Cambridge: Cambridge University Press.
Douglas, Mary. 1966. *Purity and Danger*. London: Penguin.
Durkheim, Emile. 1951. *Suicide* (1897). New York: Free Press.
———. 1965. *The Elementary Forms of Religious Life* (1911). New York: Free Press.
———. 1974. Individual and Collective Representations, in *Sociology and Philosophy* (1898). New York: Free Press.
Eliade, Mircea. 1959. *The Sacred and the Profane*. New York: Harcourt, Brace, and World.
Elias, Norbert. 1978. *The Civilizing Process* (1939). New York: Urizon Books.
Fenichel, Otto. 1945. *Psychoanalytic Theory of Neurosis*. New York: W.W. Norton.
Freud, Anna. 1936. *The Ego and the Mechanisms of Defense*. Vol. II. *The Writings of Anna Freud*. New York: International Universities Press.
Garfinkel, Harold. 1963. A Conception of and Experiments with "Trust" as a Condition of Concerted Stable Actions, pp. 187–238 in O. J. Harvey, ed., *Motivation and Social Interaction*. New York: Ronald Press.
———. 1967. *Studies in Ethnomethodology*. Englewood Cliffs, N.J.: Prentice-Hall.

Geertz, Clifford. 1973. Ideology as a Cultural System, pp. 193–233 in *The Interpretation of Cultures*. New York: Basic Books.
Giddens, Anthony. 1976. *New Rules of Sociological Method*. New York: Basic Books.
———. 1979. *Central Problems in Social Theory*. Berkeley and Los Angeles: University of California Press.
Goffman, Erving. 1959. *The Presentation of Self in Everyday Life*. New York: Doubleday.
———. 1963. *Behavior in Public Places*. New York: Free Press.
Goode, William J. 1960. A Theory of Role Strain. *American Sociological Review* 25:483–496.
Gouldner, Alvin W. 1970. *The Coming Crisis in Western Sociology*. New York: Equinox.
Habermas, Jürgen. 1984. *Reason and the Rationalization of Society*. Vol. I. *Theory of Communicative Action*. Boston: Beacon.
Homans, George C. 1961. *Social Behavior: Its Elementary Forms*. New York: Free Press.
Husserl, Edmund. 1977. *Cartesian Meditations* (1931). The Hague: Martin Nijhoff.
Keniston, Kenneth. 1960. *The Uncommitted*. New York: Harcourt, Brace, and World.
Keynes, John Maynard. 1965. *The General Theory of Employment, Interest, and Money* (1936). New York: Harcourt Brace Jovanovich.
———. 1973. *A Treatise on Probability*. Vol. 8. *The Collected Writings of John Maynard Keynes* (1921). New York: St. Martin's.
Klein, Melanie. 1957. *Envy and Gratitude*. New York: Basic Books.
Kris, Ernst. 1937. On Inspirations, pp. 291–302 in *Psychoanalytic Explorations in Art*. New York: International Universities Press.
Leach, Edmund. 1976. *Culture and Communication*. Cambridge: Cambridge University Press.
Lévi-Strauss, Claude. 1966. *The Savage Mind*. Chicago: University of Chicago Press.
Loewenberg, Peter. 1983. The Psychohistorical Origins of the Nazi Youth Cohort, pp. 240–283 in *Decoding the Past*. New York: Alfred A. Knopf.
Luhmann, Niklas. 1980. *Trust and Power*. New York: John Wiley.
Marx, Karl. 1962*a*. *Capital*. Vol. I (1867). Moscow: International Publishers.
———. 1962*b*. The Eighteenth Brumaire of Louis Bonparte, pp. 247–344 in Karl Marx and Frederick Engels, *Selected Works*. Vol. I (1852). Moscow: International Publishers.
———. 1965. Theses on Feuerbach (1845), in Nathan Rotenstreich, ed., *Basic Problems in Marx's Philosophy*. Indianapolis: Bobbs-Merrill.
Parsons, Talcott. 1937. *The Structure of Social Action*. New York: Free Press.
———. 1954. Certain Primary Sources and Patterns of Aggression in the Social Structure of the Western World, in *Essays in Sociological Theory*. New York: Free Press.
Parsons, Talcott, and Edward A. Shils. 1951. Values, Motives, and Systems of Action, in *Toward a General Theory of Action*. New York: Harper & Row.

Parsons, Talcott, and Gerald N. Platt. 1973. *The American University*. Cambridge, Mass.: Harvard University Press.
Prager, Jeffrey. 1985. *Building Democracy in Ireland: Political Order and Cultural Integration in a New Independent Nation*. New York: Cambridge University Press.
Ricoeur, Paul. 1969. *The Symbolism of Evil*. Boston: Beacon.
Sacks, Harvey, Emmanuel A. Schegloff, and Gail Jefferson. 1974. A Simplest Systematics for the Organization of Turn-Taking for Conversation. *Language* 50:697–735.
Sahlins, Marshall. 1976. *Culture and Practical Reason*. Chicago: University of Chicago Press.
Sartre, Jean-Paul. 1956. *Being and Nothingness*. New York: Philosophical Library.
———. 1963. *Search for a Method*. New York: Alfred A. Knopf.
———. 1976. *Critique of Dialectical Reason*. London: New Left Books.
Schutz, Alfred. 1967. *The Phenomenology of the Social World*. Evanston, Ill. Northwestern University Press.
———. 1978*a*. Phenomenology and Sociology (1940), in Thomas Luckmann, ed., *Phenomenology and the Social Sciences*. London: Penguin.
———. 1978*b*. Parsons' Theory of Action: A Critical Review by Schutz, pp. 8–70 in Richard Grathoff, ed., *The Theory of Action: The Correspondence of Alfred Schutz and Talcott Parsons*. Bloomington: Indiana University Press.
Shils, Edward A. 1975. *Center and Periphery: Essays in Macrosociology*. Chicago: University of Chicago Press.
Simmel, Georg. 1955. *Conflict and the Web of Group Affiliations*. New York: Free Press.
Slater, Philip. 1963. On Social Regression. *American Sociological Review* 28:339–364.
Touraine, Alain. 1977. *The Self-Reproduction of Society*. Chicago: University of Chicago Press.
Turner, Victor. 1969. *The Ritual Process*. Chicago: Aldine.
Weber, Max. 1946. The Social Psychology of World Religions (1916), in Hans Gerth and C. Wright Mills, eds., *From Max Weber: Essays in Sociology*. New York: Oxford University Press.
———. 1978. *Economy and Society*. Berkeley, Los Angeles, London: University of California Press.
Weinstein, Fred, and Gerald N. Platt. 1969. *The Wish to Be Free*. Berkeley and Los Angeles: University of California Press.

CHAPTER FOURTEEN

The Interpenetration of Microinteraction and Macrostructures in a Complex and Contingent Institutional Order

Richard Münch

INTRODUCTION

In a society in which markets and competition dominate in each societal sphere—from the economic to the political, communal, and cultural spheres—as much as they do in the United States, it is not surprising that models of social order propagated in sociology reflect this inclination toward the idea of market and competition. When models of social order formulated by exchange theory, conflict theory, symbolic interactionism, and ethnomethodology emphatically argue against the Parsonian normative and structuralistic concept of order that order is *created* in interaction, they imply that macrostructures are always created, re-created, and changed in microinteraction. At the same time they more or less unconsciously represent the American creed that everything can be changed by the individual and that society is indeed only the product of individual action. In this sense they are more typical representatives of American optimism than Parsons's approach, which is influenced more by European thought. Independent of Parsons's personal American optimism, Parsonian action theory is more receptive to *analytically* radical approaches to the problem of order and to the interrelation between microinteraction and macrostructures.

The typical approaches of American sociology converge in a concept of social order that overemphasizes the weight of microinteraction in general, sees the interrelation between micro and macro levels *primarily* as a spontaneous creation of macrostructures in microinteraction, and conceives of microinteraction mainly as market exchange. Exchange theory interprets interaction as economic exchange,[1] conflict theory as political bargaining,[2] symbolic interactionism as interpretative negotiation,[3] ethnomethodology as situational indexical interpretation of actions.[4]

Distinct from these biased and primarily *economic* approaches to the problem of interrelating microinteraction and macrostructures, the logic of Parsonian action theory allows us to conceive of interaction in a more comprehensive sense than economic exchange, political bargaining, symbolic negotiation, and situational indexical interpretation alone and to interpret the interrelation between microinteraction and macrostructures in a more complicated manner than purely in terms of the spontaneous creation of macrostructures in microinteraction. I would like to elaborate this thesis in five steps. In the first step an analytical scheme is introduced in order to distinguish different fields of action. This scheme is a new construction of the well-known four-function paradigm. The second step defines four types of interaction and related macrostructures according to the analytical scheme just introduced. The third step sketches how microinteraction and macrostructure of the same and of different types are interrelated in a complex web. The fourth step outlines in more detail for the four types how interaction creates related macrostructures and how these structures determine action and interaction. The fifth step completes the analysis in considering the linking of macrostructures and microinteraction of different types through intermediate interaction. The result is a complex and contingent order of microinteraction and macrostructures.

1. FIELDS AND PRINCIPLES OF ACTION AND INTERACTION

Action takes place in a space defined by the two variables of symbolic complexity and contingency of action. Human action is meaningful action and thus is controlled by symbols leaving a larger or smaller number of possible actions covered by the symbols—that is, leaving more or less *contingency of action*. The relevant symbols are meaning constructions, norms, expressions, or cognitions. The symbols guiding action vary in number and interdependence—that is, they vary in *complexity*. The action space of symbolic complexity and contingency of action can be subdivided into four fields of action by cross-tabulating the two basic

Action Fields and Structures

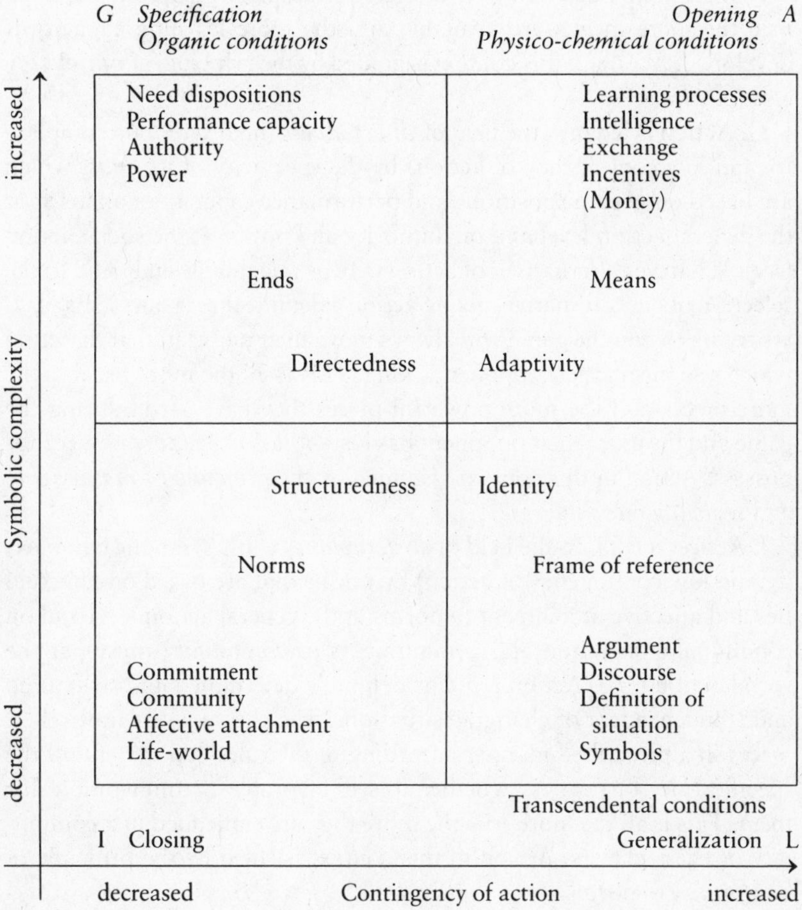
G Specification
Organic conditions
Opening A
Physico-chemical conditions
Need dispositions
Performance capacity
Authority
Power
Learning processes
Intelligence
Exchange
Incentives
(Money)
Ends
Means
Directedness
Adaptivity
Structuredness
Identity
Norms
Frame of reference
Commitment
Community
Affective attachment
Life-world
Argument
Discourse
Definition of situation
Symbols
Transcendental conditions
I Closing
Generalization L
decreased
Contingency of action
increased
Symbolic complexity
increased
decreased

FIG. 14.1

dimensions. Thus we can distinguish the fields and basic factors leading action into these fields[5] shown in figure 14.1.

A. Action is led into the field of *adaptivity* (high symbolic complexity and high contingency of action) by the availability of *means* based on learning processes and intelligence on the general action level and on exchange and incentives (money) on the social action level. There is a multiplicity of means that can be applied in a multiplicity of actions. Action varies here from situation to situation according to changing conditions and means. The chess players use one tactic or another and vary their action according to changing situations. This is all the more true the more means are available and the more learning capacity is developed. Action in this context is guided by the principle of *optimizing* a set of ends.

G. Action is led into the field of *directedness* (high symbolic complexity and low contingency of action) by the specificity of its *ends*, which are based on need dispositions and performance capacity of an actor at the general action level and on authority and power at the social action level. Whatever alternatives of action may be imaginable ends lead to the selection of one alternative, giving action a definite direction. Chess players trying to win the game will always move their pieces in that direction which endangers their opponent's king. This is all the more feasible the more pieces and the more powerful pieces they have saved during the game and the more their opponent has lost—that is, the more power they possess. Action in this context is guided by the principle of *maximizing* and *realizing* one single end.

I. Action is led into the field of *structuredness* (low symbolic complexity and low contingency of action) by norms that are based on affectual ties and affective attachment to norms at the general action level and on communal association and commitments to community norms at the social action level. Action remains definitely determined and structured and is independent of changing situations. The chess players move their pieces in a prescribed manner according to the rules and they fulfill the specific rules of fairness whether this is favorable or unfavorable for them. This is all the more true the more they are embedded in a community of chess players. Action in this context is ruled by the principle of *conformity* to norms.

L. Action is led into the field of *identity* (low symbolic complexity and high contingency of action) by the *generality* of its symbolic frame of reference based on symbolic constructions and definitions of situation on the general action level and on discourse and arguments on the social action level. Action maintains a general identity independent of its variation according to situations. Chess players play in a definite style (for example, in an offensive style), although every game is different. Both chess players play fairly, and the general value of fair play can be realized in the most different ways. This is all the more true the more broadly defined a symbolic frame of reference is, thus enabling action to maintain identity in variation. Action in this context follows the principle of *consistency* to a symbolic frame of reference.

We can sum up as follows: In a completely comprehensive view, action in its four qualities of directedness (d), adaptivity (a), structuredness (s), and identity (i) is respectively determined by ends (E), means (M), norms (N), and symbolic frames of reference (F) under given conditions (C):

$$A_{d,a,s,i} = f(E,M,N,F)\ C$$

There are specific approaches appropriate for each of the four fields of action, but they fail in their explanation of action if they claim validity for all four fields. This holds true for positivistic power and conflict theory the appropriate field of which is that of directedness; for positivistic economic theory the appropriate field of which is that of adaptivity; for idealistic normativism the appropriate field of which is that of structuredness; and for idealistic rationalism the appropriate field of which is that of identity. In the frame of reference of voluntaristic action theory we can specify the conditions of their validity and invalidity.

2. TYPES AND INTERRELATIONSHIPS BETWEEN MICROINTERACTION AND MACROSTRUCTURES

If we apply the scheme now constructed to interaction, we can distinguish four types of interaction.

A. Market exchange involves the use of incentives at the disposal of both actors in order mutually to motivate one another to action. Money is a general incentive which can be used by ego in order to motivate alter to offer concrete incentives (goods, services) for exchange. In exchange each actor, ego and alter, is completely free in his or her imagination of alternative wants, and no one is forced to take specific actions in order to satisfy the wants of other actors because it is completely open and voluntary who will satisfy the articulated wants. Mother may offer one dollar to her daughter for cleaning the bathroom.

G. Political decision making involves the use of power at the disposal of ego in order to impose a specific way of acting on alter independent of the alternatives alter may imagine. If a mother asks her daughter for help in cleaning the bathroom, she may threaten the child with the withdrawal of her love.

I. In communal interaction in solidarity, ego motivates alter to fulfill ego's expectations according to common norms using alter's commitment to the community to which both belong. Both the horizon of their imagination of expectations and the number of possible actions conforming to the expectations are narrowed to self-evident expectations and actions. In this case it is enough for the mother simply to ask her daughter if she could clean the bathroom. In this sense she has influence based on their common commitment to the family and to its norms.

L. In rational discourse ego motivates alter to accept a proposition, norm, expression, or meaning construction as valid by using arguments, thus demonstrating that a particular symbolic construction can be justified by a more general one the validity of which has been demonstrated. In this case the mother has to convince her child that the expectation of her cleaning the bathroom can be justified by universal norms such as equality and freedom and by their application to family life.

These different types of interaction start with presuppositions that lie temporally and spatially outside the interactive situation and have more or less lasting and far-reaching effects that exert influence on further interaction. *Inasmuch as presuppositions and results reach beyond the interactive situation, they have the character of givens and, in this sense, of macrostructures.* Thus macrostructures are givens for interacting parties and not changeable in the interactive situation because they have been created temporally and spatially outside the interactive situation. At the same time, they are changeable by interacting parties because their interaction exerts effects on macrostructures; but this change is effective only for *further* interaction and not for the interactive situation under consideration.

Each type of interaction has presuppositions and results related to its own character, as well as presuppositions and results stemming from different characters according to the other types of interaction.

In *market exchange* ego and alter start with a given distribution of money income, goods, and services that are the results of former exchange involving many other actors besides ego and alter. Their exchange has a result that contributes itself to the further distribution of money income, goods, and services. A given inequality of income may have increased or decreased, but their exchange also begins with contractual norms that were created not by ego and alter but by the community of market parties extending in time, space, and number of actors beyond their situational interaction. At the same time the exchange has effects on the contractual norms insofar as they are changed according to their practicality experienced in exchange and transmitted to the tradition of the community. Positive contractual laws are political presuppositions of exchange, whereas exchange may result in the change of positive contractual laws, again according to experienced practicality. Universal values are cultural presuppositions of exchange. They set a frame for legitimate forms of contracts—for example, measures of contractual justice. Exchange itself has dynamic effects on universal values because it confronts these values with new questions that have to be culturally answered.

Political decision making starts with given positive laws that have resulted from former decision making and contributes to the change of positive laws. It begins with normative rules anchored in a community, extending the situation of decision making in space, time, and number of actors and results in legal specifications of communal norms, thus contributing to the change of these norms. It presupposes universal values delimiting the scope for rationally justifiable positive laws and contributes to the specification of universal values, thus leading to shifts in the pattern of values. It commences with a given set of articulated market interests and accumulated economic problems and results in changes of these interests and problems.

Communal interaction starts with a given tradition and given norms and contributes to the creation of new norms. It presupposes a given pattern of universal values that set measures for justification of norms, and it influences the further interpretation of the universal values. It begins with articulated market interests and produces structurings of these interests as a result. It commences with given positive laws and determines the obligatory character of these laws.

Rational discourse presupposes existing universal values that serve as starting points for processes of rational justification. At the same time it has effects on the pattern of values by examining their validity. It begins with communal norms as given binding interpretations of values, and it changes them in the process of questioning their validity in light of universal values. It starts out with positive laws that confine the given selection of possible interpretations of values, and it results in changes of these laws because it broadens the scope for legitimate interpretations of values. It commences with a set of market interests and problems that have to be culturally interpreted, and in this way the interests are changed in the direction of legitimacy within a cultural frame of reference.

This sketch of macropresuppositions and macroresults of microinteraction demonstrates that the differentiation of micro and macro levels is a question of perspective. We may, for example, concentrate on economic exchange. In this case we treat all former results of economic exchange and also of political decision making, communal interaction, and rational discourse as macrostructures that, as givens, exert effects on the process of economic exchange. With a change of perspective, however, we may treat the result of this particular economic exchange as given macrostructures with effects on situational interaction in rational discourse, communal interaction, and political interaction. In reality macro and micro levels are always interwoven in concrete interaction. What we do in sociological analysis is to differentiate them analytically as sharply as possible in order to determine exactly the complicated nature of their interrelationship.

3. THE INTERPENETRATION OF MICROINTERACTION AND MACROSTRUCTURES

In an analytical sense we thus may distinguish four types of interaction and four types of macrostructures. In applying this scheme I want to outline the character of the complicated web of micro-macro interrelationships in concentrating on the *normative* aspect in every type of interaction and structure. I do this in the interest of analyzing the network of a complex and contingent normative institutional order, which I call a voluntaristic order. Thus in the following sections each type of interaction and macrostructure is specified to the normative dimension:

A. Economic interaction is *market exchange*. It presupposes and results in *situational regulations* as *macrostructures*. These types of interaction and structure give institutional orders *adaptivity* with regard to changing situations.

G. Political interaction is *decision making*. It presupposes and results in *positive laws*. These types of interaction and structure give institutional orders *directedness* independent of changing situations.

I. Communal interaction is *mutual help in solidarity*. It presupposes and results in *communal norms*. These types of interaction and structure give institutional orders *regularity* independent of changing situations.

L. Social-cultural interaction is *rational discourse*. It presupposes and results in *universal values*. These types of interaction and structure give institutional orders *identity* independent of situational change.

In elaborating the interrelation among these types of analytically distinguished interactions and macrostructures, the interactive creation and re-creation of macrostructures is given much more prominence than usually conceded to the Parsonian approach by its critics. At the same time, the effects of macrostructures on interaction is more often taken into account than is usually done in the individualistic and exchange-biased approaches of exchange theory, conflict theory, symbolic interactionism, and ethnomethodology. In the next step it will be shown how the different types of interaction create and re-create their own macrostructures and what specific effects these macrostructures exert on human action and interaction. After that the analysis will concentrate on the links between the different types of interaction and macrostructures, dealing with the question of how the macroresults of one type of interaction are linked to another type of interaction. These links are provided by specific intermediate types of interaction[6] (fig. 14.2).

L. Universal norms and values serve as measures of the justification of concrete norms. These universal norms and values result from *rational discourse* and form the general, enduring identity of an institution. Rational discourse is based on the general rule that every norm must withstand severe criticism by arguments in order to be valid.[7] In Kantian terms these arguments attempt to point out that the application of norms leads to contradictions and conflicts in social order. The function of norms is the ordering of social action. Insofar as this function is not fulfilled by norms they are falsified in the same way that cognitive propositions are rejected, if they do not fulfill the function of producing unity in the multiplicity of perceptions. Contradictions and conflicts in social order resulting from the *correct* application of a system of norms to concrete social action are falsifying instances (facts) for the system of norms. Rational discourse relies on the unlimited introduction of new test cases for norms (opening) and on the claim that concrete norms must be logically subsumed under universal norms (generalization). Compared to the functions of opening and generalization of the scope for action fulfilled by these aspects of interaction, the functions of closing and specification of the scope for action by the commitment to traditional norms shared in a community (closing), and by the forming of a concrete consensus in procedures at a specific place and time (specification), are of only secondary importance in rational discourse.

Concrete social orders in concrete historical situations must be continuously exposed to rational criticism in light of universal values and norms in order to be continuously changed and voluntaristic in this aspect. Change in this sense has a general direction: Concrete orders approach universality through interpenetration with rational discourse, but they never merge with the universal norms and always retain their particularity. This is more true the more there is mutual penetration rather than simply one-sided intellectual criticism of the concrete social order, or one-sided domination of intellectual life by communal con-

The Interpenetration of Microinteraction and Macrostructures in a Complex and Contingent Order

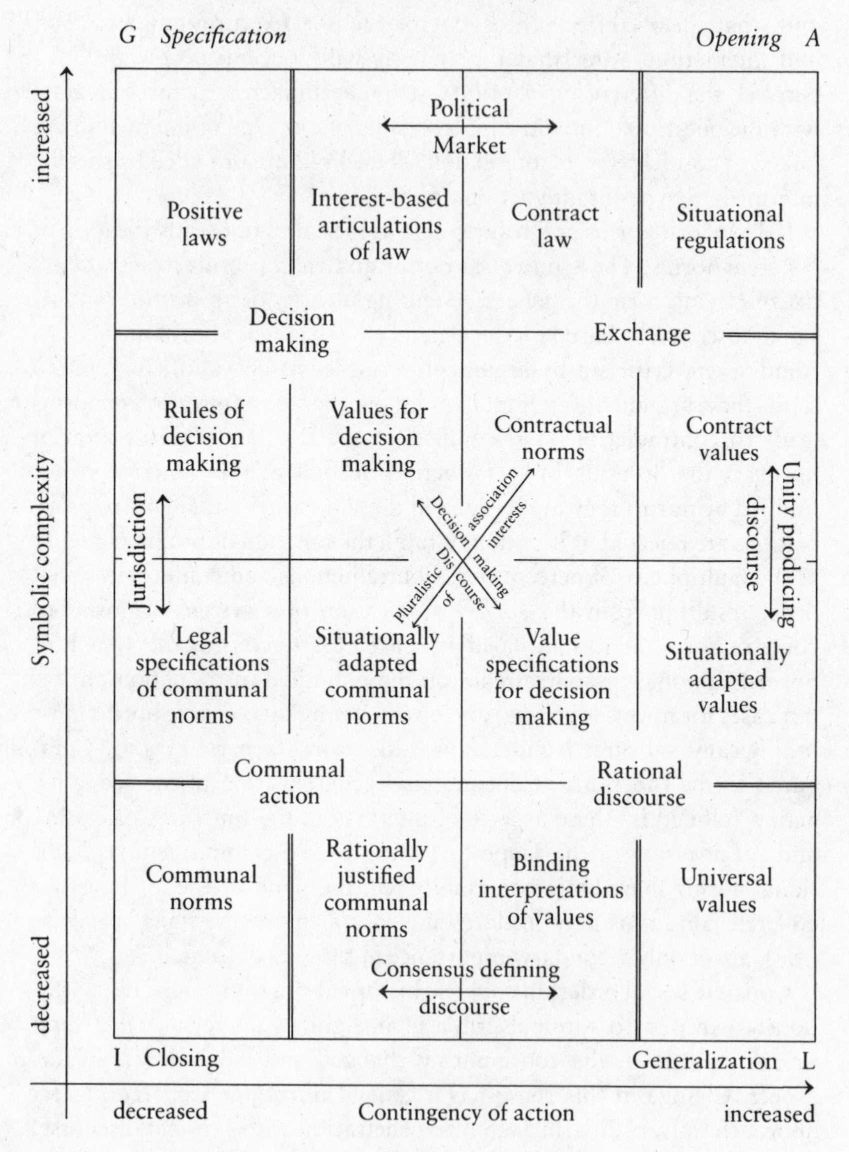

FIG. 14.2

straint. The independent existence of both sides is required; otherwise there would be cultural and societal stagnation. Only in this way can concrete societies maintain a particular identity in a universal culture.

Rational discourse and therewith a process of universalization of values and norms is based on the existence of an intellectual culture that is independent of commitments to particular communities, powers, and even societies. It has to be international and global in character. The more intellectual culture attains this independence, the more it exerts a universalizing effect on culture, thus producing a world culture that is a critical measure of every particular life-world and every politically enforced law in concrete existing societies. The international character of intellectual discourse implies the worldwide questioning of practices in particular societies contradicting universally valid values and norms. Neither the USSR nor Argentina—any clan-society, or any society at all—can uphold practices contradicting human rights as *justified practices* before the worldwide public of international intellectual culture, as represented by such institutions as Amnesty International. This does not imply that global intellectual criticism of inhuman practices in particular societies must be politically effective immediately. In this case rational discourse would merge with political enforcement and would lose its independence. What is needed, however, is the connection of rational discourse with particular societal life-worlds and with political decision making. Amnesty International is an institution that performs this task of introducing universal values and norms into the life-world and political practice of particular societies.

I. The universal validity of values and norms does not of itself render the norms obligatory for individuals. Universal values and norms do not prescribe action in concrete situations in a definite way. They leave a relatively wide scope for their interpretation and transformation into concrete rules. The individual can always imagine a large number of alternative interpretations and concretizations of universal values. This is particularly true of the modern values of rationality, equality, freedom, and active shaping of the world, which perform the functions of generalizing, closing, opening, and specifying the scope for action and which are combined in a pattern covering the total action space. The scope for interpretation of these values must be narrowed if norms subsumed under the general values are to be self-evident and obligatory—that is, without any alternative for the individual. This narrowing of the imagination of the individual is the function of communal interaction in solidarity embedded in a traditionally based and consensually borne life-world of a *community*.[8] To the extent that individuals feel committed to this community, their horizon of imagination is confined to the common life-world. This common life-world is always particularistic and historically concrete in character compared to the universal values. It consists in normatively binding meaning constructions, norms, expressions, and cognitions that are relatively concrete in character and prescribe action in a definite way. There is ideally a one-to-one relationship between life-world symbols and corresponding action.

A common life-world of a community can be maintained only if every individual and every group is included: in a social sense, in the solidarity of the community; in a cultural sense, in the consensual definition and redefinition of norms; in a political sense, by participating in decision making; and in an economic sense, by sharing the economic surplus. This demands the extension of social rights through universal social solidarity (security systems), of cultural rights through equal and universal higher education, of political rights through mass political participation, and of economic rights through universal equality of opportunity.

G. Neither universal values nor common norms of a life-world guide action definitely where action is oriented to specific goals and exceeds the confinements of the life-world. Here action must be controlled by rules that prescribe definite procedures and that are only selections from many alternatives subsumable under the wider frame of reference of the universal values. This field of action is dominated by the conflict between the alternatives: a conflict that must be settled by binding decisions. Thus interaction according to formal *procedures of decision making* fulfills the function of specifying action by imposing positive laws on actors even though a great many alternatives are conceivable. The necessary relationship in interaction is the authority relationship defining positions that have the right to impose decisions on actors. Legitimate power is the specific medium that enables those in positions of authority to enforce decisions in the face of conflicting alternatives.

This is the context in which institutional orders are dynamically developed in specific directions by the mobilizing force of social movements and charismatic leaders. These forces bind the affectual dynamics of individuals to concrete goals in decisive historical situations.[9]

A. Insofar as institutional orders should be variable according to the change of situations, interests, and information, however, there must be interaction in *markets* of ideas, associative affiliations, decisions, and interests in order to keep social order variable. In this context a great number of ideas, associative affiliations, decisions, and interests are conceivable, and each of these can be related to very different kinds of actions.[10] There is, for example, no limitation on choosing associations with others for action and also no limitation on the action goals of an individual served by an association. Markets exert a dynamic force on institutional norms, changing them from situation to situation but without a specific direction. The basic mediating links in markets are incentives for providing and exchanging goods and services—that is, ideas, associative affiliations, decisions, and material goods and services. Thus there must be a market for norms. That is, individuals choose associative affiliations that guide their everyday action according to their situational interests and the information they receive; equally, there is a market for such associations. Choosing one's neighborhood, one's friends, or one's religious, intellectual, or political association or economic organization means choosing norms for everyday action according to one's interests and according to the incentives they provide. Another market is the political market of collective decisions. In this instance political parties compete in order to gain the support of the public for specific decisions. Intellectuals compete in the ideas market in order to gain support expressed by having their work published, gaining research grants, or seeing an increased demand for education through student enrollment in departments of universities and colleges.

A complex and contingent order—which upholds a general identity, possesses an obligatory character in concrete norms, can be enforced in specific decisions, and remains variable with regard to changing situations—must combine universal norms evolving from rational discourse, concrete norms relying on communal interaction within a common lifeworld of a community, specific norms resulting from decision making according to authority relations, and situational norms related to the associational affiliations of the individual and to market exchange of ideas, affiliations, decisions, and individual goods and services. If they are to maintain their specific character and fulfill their specific functions, these structures must be based on their specific preconditions. If they are to constitute a unified pattern comprising the total action space, however, they have to be connected by mediating forms of interaction, thus securing their *interpenetration*.

Mediating interaction starts with the macroresults of two opposing fields of interaction in the space of interaction and mutually transmits them from one field to the other in a filtering process. The macrostructures that result from a specific field of interaction in this way become transformed into structures that are amalgamated with the qualities of the structures of an opposing field of interaction.[11]

L–I. Rational discourse must be linked to the common life-world of particular societal communities by *consensus-defining discourse*. In this way universal values are transformed into rationally justified communal norms and communal norms into binding interpretations of universal values. The universalization of higher education continuously exposes the common life-world to the rationality of intellectual discourse, thus breaking its particularism. The inclusion of intellectual opinion leaders in practical life and in mass education binds rational discourse to a minimal common sense that serves as a limit to the rational questioning of norms. The inclusion of professors in graduate and undergraduate education in universities performs this function to a considerable degree. The separation of the intellectual culture from common life, the sharp differentiation of higher education from mass education, and the separation of research, intellectual life, and teaching are contrary to the linking of rational discourse and the common life-world.

L–G. The linkage of rational discourse and authoritative decision making requires *decision-making discourse*. In this case universal values are transformed into values for decision making and positive laws into value specification for decision making. In this way specific decisions must be rationally subsumed under universal values and norms, thus securing their rational justification. The contingency of action left open by the generality of values and norms is reduced by formal procedures for finding consensus in concrete historical situations. Institutions such as the U.S. Supreme Court in particular perform this task of interconnecting rational discourse and authoritative decision making. Interpretation of the Constitution by the Supreme Court is a historically variable selection from a number of possible interpretations. In this sense it defines a historically concrete and specific consensus that is smaller in scope than the consensus on the Constitution itself. Only if it maintains independence and is at the same time involved in practical decision making can the Court truly connect rational discourse and political decision making.

L–A. Linking rational discourse to the market in ideas, associational affiliations, decisions, and material goods and services demands *unity–producing discourse*. Universal values are transformed into contract values and situational regulations into situationally adapted values. The multiplicity of normative regulations articulated on the market has to be integrated into a common frame of reference and into a consistent system of norms. This consistency is permanently questioned by the unlimited articulation of possible norms, thus leading to changes in the normative frame of reference in order to attain a new internal consistency. Insofar as intellectuals are involved in everyday questions of situational regulation of behavior through norms, this mutual interpenetration of rational discourse and practical regulation of behavior can be accomplished. This means, for example, that the behavioral regulations pursued by the plurality of associations must be discussed with regard to their consistency with universal norms involving intellectuals and common people. The theological compendia of religious associations, as studied, for example, by Weber in Baxter's compendium, are precisely this sort of interpenetration of universal meaning constructions and norms on one hand and practical situational needs on the other. In this instance it is important that this association of rational discourse and practical needs not rest in the hands of pure intellectuals, because this produces only the mutual alienation of pure religiousness and practical needs. Unifying discourse must associate intellectuals and the common human individual. This is more true the more intellectual life is decentralized and connected with the similarly decentralized life of the plurality of associations. This is clearly the associational structure of voluntarism, which is particularly apparent in the importance of voluntary associations in American life. The pluralism of voluntary associations provides a large field of experimentation for normative systems.

G–I. Authoritative decision making and the common life-world of the societal community are associated by *jurisdiction* within the legal system. In this instance communal norms are transformed into rules for decision making and positive laws into legal specifications of communal norms. In jurisdiction the decisions oriented toward specific goals and selected from a set of alternatives are transformed into binding law by shaping the decisions according to the rules of jurisdiction: predictability, consistency, formal correctness, and justice. The law emerging from jurisdiction forms a kind of secondary tradition between the common life-world and the decision-making process. It controls decision making by narrowing the range of alternative decisions according to the rules of jurisdiction. Only what conforms to the requirements of a predictable jurisdiction can become binding law. With regard to the life-world, jurisdiction specifies the conceptions of justice embedded in the life-world in concrete laws, thus selecting specific interpretations of justice as obligatory interpretations. Whereas the common-law tradition paradigmatically performs this function of mediating between the common norms of the life-world and goal-directed decision making, statute law is much less rooted in the common tradition and is much more a linkage between intellectual culture and political authority. The shaping of jurisdiction by a practical legal profession, as in the common-law tradition (contrary to a theoretical profession, as under statute law), is a fundamental precondition for increased interpenetration of the common life-world and decision making through jurisdiction.

G–A. *Political market exchange* links the plurality of possible normative regulations on each respective market to the collectively binding selection of specific norms in decision-making processes. Here situational regulations are transformed into interest-based articulations of positive laws and positive laws into contract law. Social movements and their charismatic leaders gather divergent interests in political market exchange and push them in a specific direction in the process of selecting collectively binding laws in the face of a wide range of conceivable alternatives and according to the need to regulate action uniformly and precisely. Political market exchange opens the decision on positive norms to the plurality of interests; social movements specify this plurality by transforming it into a specific program for decision making. The viability of social movements is a first precondition for the interpenetration of the pluralist market and decision making. Movements must gather interests on the level of voluntary associations and carry them into the field of political decision making via political parties and immediate participation. It is easier in the United States than in Europe for social movements to gather together interests dynamically and to incorporate them into the process of decision making, but the mechanism is frequently confined to particular local circumstances. Dynamic new movements have less easy access to political decision making in Europe, particularly because the decision-making process is in the hands of bureaucratically organized, nationwide, uniform parties. Thus they continue as more radical protest movements without a feeling of inclusion and remain alienated from the political system.

I–A. The *pluralist association of interests* is the mediating link between the multiplicity of interests articulated on the normative market and the common life-world of the societal community. Here situational regulations are transformed into situationally adapted communal norms and communal norms into contractual norms. There must be institutions that define the voluntariness of associational membership and the freedom of associations in regulating the behavior of their members as commonly binding norms. At the same time, the limitations of this freedom must be determined by common norms. The individual cannot form associations that contradict common norms, and associations cannot impose norms on their members which contradict these norms. The violation of human rights by associations is not allowed by the norms of modern societal communities. Federalism is a fundamental institution furthering this mutual penetration of common life-world and market pluralism, particularly in the United States. It is much less institutionalized in Europe; in West Germany can be found the most significant federal institutions. Pluralist associations of this kind regulate market pluralism on one hand and carry over the multiplicity of normative ideas and experimentation into the narrower area of the common life-world of the societal community on the other, thus exposing tradition to the change of situations, interests, and innovations.

CONCLUDING REMARKS

The linking of different subsystems and fields of interaction and macrostructures is by no means a naturally emerging quality of institutional orders. In reality the relations between interaction fields and macrostructures all too often consist of constraint, constriction, mutual isolation, dynamic overthrow, or anomic conflict. A differentiated system of fields of interaction that is integrated by intermediate zones of interaction can only be approached step by step. Only in such a system does interaction create and re-create macrostructures, at the same time being determined by these structures. It must be taken into account here that determination of interaction by macrostructures means not only constraint but also opening, as is always the case when a more closed type of interaction is influenced by more open macrostructures such as the determination of communal interaction by universal values, situational regulations, and positive laws. An institutional order involving complicated interrelations of this kind between micro and macro levels is a complex and contingent order. The relationship between microinteraction and macrostructures is that of interpenetration.

NOTES

1. G. C. Homans, *Social Behavior. Its Elementary Forms* (New York: Harcourt, Brace, 1961); G. S. Becker, *The Economic Approach to Human Behavior* (Chicago: University of Chicago Press, 1976); J. M. Buchanan, *The Limits of Liberty—Between Anarchy and Leviathan* (Chicago: University of Chicago Press, 1975); J. S. Coleman, "Collective Deci-

sions," in H. Turk and R. L. Simpson, eds., *Institutions and Social Exchange* (Indianapolis: Bobbs-Merrill, 1971), pp. 272–286.

2. R. Collins, *Conflict Sociology: Toward an Explanatory Science* (New York: Academic Press, 1975).

3. H. Blumer, *Symbolic Interactionism* (Englewood Cliffs, N.J.: Prentice-Hall, 1969).

4. H. Garfinkel, *Studies in Ethnomethodology* (Englewood Cliffs, N.J.: Prentice-Hall, 1967).

5. Cf. T. Parsons, R. F. Bales, and E. Shils, *Working Papers in the Theory of Action* (New York: Free Press, 1953), pp. 63–109; R. Münch, *Theorie des Handelns. Zur Rekonstruktion der Beiträge von Talcott Parsons, Emile Durkheim und Max Weber* (Frankfurt: Suhrkamp, 1982), pp. 233–280.

6. This model is further elaborated for different institutional spheres in R. Münch, *Die Struktur der Moderne. Grundmuster und differentielle Gestaltung des institutionellen Aufbaus der modernen Gesellschaften* (Frankfurt: Suhrkamp, 1984). More historical and comparative details are provided in R. Münch, *Die Entwicklung der Moderne. Evolution und Institutionalisierung des kulturellen Codes der modernen Gesellschaften in England, USA, Deutschland und Frankreich* (Frankfurt: Suhrkamp, 1985).

7. This view of the social-cultural sphere tries to elaborate Parsonian action theory with some insights of Habermas's theory of discourse, but in distinction to Habermas in line with Kant's universalism and Popper's criticism. J. Habermas, *Theorie des kommunikativen Handelns*, 2 vols. (Frankfurt: Suhrkamp, 1981), vol. 1, ch. I.; I. Kant, *Kritik der praktischen Vernunft* (1797; reprint, Hamburg: Meiner, 1967); K. R. Popper, *Objective Knowledge* (Oxford: Clarendon Press, 1972).

8. Here I combine Durkheim's concept of "conscience collectif" and the phenomenological concept of *Lebenswelt*. E. Durkheim, *Les formes élémentaires de la vie religieuse* (1912; reprint, Paris: Presses Universitaires de France, 1968); E. Husserl, *Logische Untersuchungen* (1900–1901; reprint, Halle: M. Niemeyer, 1928).

9. This is the appropriate place for a conflict theoretical interpretation of Max Weber. M. Weber, *Wirtschaft und Gesellschaft* (1922; reprint, Tübingen: Mohr Siebeck, 1976), pp. 140–148, 654–637; R. Collins, "A Comparative Approach to Political Sociology," in R. Bendix, ed., *State and Society: A Reader in Comparative Political Sociology* (Berkeley and Los Angeles: University of California Press, 1968), pp. 42–67.

10. Here we can apply the insights of theories of economic exchange, political bargaining, and symbolic negotiation in the appropriate place. G. C. Homans, *Social Behavior*; J. S. Coleman, "Collective Decisions"; H. Blumer, *Symbolic Interactionism*.

11. The linking of the contributions of the approaches thus far applied—namely, discourse theory, normative and life-world theory, conflict theory, economic and symbolic negotiation theories—to form an integrated framework has not been accomplished by these approaches in and of themselves. The forging of a link can be approached only in a more comprehensive framework as provided by Parsonian action theory. R. Münch, *Theorie des Handelns*, chaps. 1–3.

CHAPTER FIFTEEN

Beyond Reductionism: Four Models Relating Micro and Macro Levels

Bernhard Giesen

1. INTRODUCTION: BEYOND REDUCTIONISM

Ranking the issue of the German-American conference on the micro-macro link among the classics of sociology seems to be an obvious starting point for our discussion. A closer look at the past debates, however, raises some doubts about this positioning of the problem among the monuments of the sociological tradition. Until the 1970s the micro-macro theme was less a field of sociological theory construction than an object of vigorous controversy among philosophers of science and social philosophers. The problem was focused not on the relation of micro and macro levels or of structure and action but on the unresolvable opposition of different reductionisms (Brodbeck 1968; Nagel 1961; Mandelbaum 1973; Lukes 1970; Eberlein and Kondratowitz 1977). Particularly called into question was if and by which methodological or social-ontological reasons so-called collectivistic theories could and should be reduced to individualistic theories of action or behavior (Hayek 1952; Popper 1961; Watkins 1959; Goldstein 1973; Gellner 1959; Scott 1961; Agassi 1960; O'Neill 1973; Giesen and Schmid 1977; Opp 1979). Like many other grand problems, this issue, too, has progressed from a violent philosophical feud to a sober research program.

There is no longer any demand for rigorous strategies of reduction. On the contrary; those theoretical paradigms under suspicion of a pronounced individualistic or collectivistic social ontology, such as neoutilitarianism, are particularly eager to deal with the relation between the micro and macro levels (Wippler 1978; Lindenberg 1977). In general these paradigms assume that the aim of theory construction does not consist in reductive operations—micro to macro or vice versa—but in explaining or classifying the relations and connections between two levels of social reality viewed by a theory program. The type of connection that is produced by a sociological theory program, however, shows some fundamental differences that hint at past philosophical debates. I shall try to reconstruct four models of such connections and look at their implicit metatheoretical assumptions.

2. THE PROBLEM: DESCRIPTIVE, PRACTICAL, AND EXPLANATORY EMERGENCE

If we assume that the program of reductionism aimed at decomposing the micro/macro dichotomy has been succeeded by new theoretical models stressing the distinction between the macro and the micro level and requiring some *connection* of both levels, these models should deal with the following questions:

1. Does the model in question assume a fundamental difference between micro and macro level, or is the connection between these levels produced by a simple aggregative procedure conceiving the macroproperties essentially as a common property of many microunits? I shall call this the problem of *descriptive emergence*. It is closely related to the classical debates on reductionism (Brodbeck 1968) and is resolved by the four models in different ways.

2. The difference between micro and macro levels of a social system appears to be not only a problem of scientific description of reality but also a *practical* problem for the individuals acting in this system. If the macrostructural properties of a social system no longer correspond to the internalized rules and intentions of the individual actors, these actors tend to experience practical inconsistency between the micro and the macro level. This "falling out" of the micro and macro levels can be considered a well-known experience of everyday life; the four models differ in the degree to which they account accurately for this problem of *practical emergence*. In particular they should deal with the question as to whether the formation of practical emergence or paradox effects (Boudon 1979; Wippler 1978), contradictions, and dissynchronous development viewed by sociological observers must be conceived as an "error" of societal development or as a kind of "dead end" of history that in principle can be avoided, or whether it can be explained as a complemen-

tary relation. This being the case, the tension or discrepancy between macrostructures and individual interests or intentions could provide the solution for a crisis of the interaction process.

3. The drifting apart of the micro and macro levels will result not only in problems of scientific *description* for the sociological observer or in practical difficulties for the actors concerned but also in problems of *explaining* the processes of change at the micro and macro levels. To be more accurate, macro and micro levels are described in different terms and experienced as different realms of reality; in addition, the processes of change on the macrostructural and interaction levels can become mutually independent to a certain extent. Such independence remains unproblematic if it merely means that interaction processes relying on the creativity of individuals can "rush ahead" of the corresponding structures of the macro level and represent the origin of processes of change. Far more controversial, however, is the idea of an *explanatory emergence* (Brodbeck 1968) of macroprocesses; macrostructures are viewed here as a source of innovations that are independent of interaction processes in a certain way. Given such explanatory emergence, the macrostructure becomes more complex and has greater problem-solving capacity than an individual actor. Although the idea of explanatory emergence is met with skepticism and by no means can be regarded as universally accepted, some of our everyday experiences seem to provide evidence in favor of it. The acceleration of scientific and technological change or the fast-growing system of complex administrative regulations supports the idea of a macroprocess that takes place quasi-automatically without any corresponding changes in interaction patterns. I shall discuss whether this idea of explanatory emergence fits the conceptual architecture of the different models. Possible answers consist, on one hand, in rejecting the idea as misleading and, on the other, in giving some evidence of a process leading to autonomous dynamics of structures.

3. FOUR MODELS RELATING MICRO AND MACRO LEVELS

As indicated earlier, all of the current theoretical paradigms provide some solution to the problem of relating the micro and macro levels. From the standpoint of a post-Kuhnian philosophy of science, we should expect nothing else: Whether a theoretical paradigm will provide a solution for a given problem will depend on the creativity of its advocates, the scope and quality of research activities, and the amount of additional assumptions, ad hoc hypotheses, and inferences that are accepted. With regard to this last point, however, there exist some obvious differences. What is decisive for the heuristic power of a theory program (Lakatos 1970) confronted with a problem situation is whether a conceptual differentiation or a hypothesis is contained by some additional interpretations, ad hoc explications and refinements, by the "parasitic" process of importing formerly external pieces of theory, and, finally, by additional endeavors of scientists. In dealing with the solution the different models provide for the problems of emergence, I will refer to this heuristic power of the theory core that is considered to be the self-evident starting point of analysis by scientific adherents of the program concerned.

3.1. THE MODEL OF COORDINATION: INDIVIDUAL ACTIONS AND MACROSOCIAL EFFECTS

The first model conceives the relation established between the micro and the macro levels as a *causal* relation between different events or empirical states of reality. This model of causal relation can be found mainly in the so-called individualistic theory programs guided by utility theory and represented by Boudon (Chapter 1), Coleman (Chapter 6), and Wippler and Lindenberg (Chapter 5). The starting point and paradigm of this theory program are the rational actions of many individuals, which produce—mediated by social mechanism of coordination—some macrosocial effects (Boudon 1979; Coleman 1975; Homans 1974; Opp 1979; Lindenberg and Wippler 1978; Vanberg 1975, 1978; Raub and Voss 1981). These effects need not coincide with the intended aims of the actors but can become "effets perverses" (Boudon) or unintended consequences of purposeful actions. The model focuses on research on the empirical relations among (1) the self-interested actions of individuals; (2) the structural and institutional conditions coordinating these actions (e.g., voting procedures, markets, hierarchies); and (3) the macrosocial effects resulting from these conditions. Special attention is paid to those effects that can be considered *social contracts* between the individual participants and that serve as the mechanism for coordinating further actions.

Although the behavioristic ancestors (Opp 1979) of this theory program maintain an extreme and rigorous reductionism (which simply denies the possibility of distinguishing empirically between macrostructures and behavioral properties), its current advocates have abandoned these restrictions in many ways and have paid considerable attention to the problem of macrosocial effects of self-interested individual actions. Coleman, who originally accounted only for markets and organizations as social mechanisms of coordinating, proposed in an interesting paper presented at a Chicago conference that even social movements and mass hysterias should be considered a kind of structural mechanism coordinating individual actions (Coleman forthcoming). Even the focus on the process of rational action itself seems slowly to give way to concentration on the institutional conditions and consequences of instrumental or strategic action. The practical problem of obtaining a large amount of data on individuals in an organization or society led to increased attention on structural and institutional conditions resulting in individual rankings of preferences. Although the research program was considerably enlarged and refined, its theoretical core remained individualistic: The core heuristic is represented by the RREEMM model of instrumental action (Resourceful, Restricted, Evaluating, Expedient, Maximizing Man; see Lindenberg 1983; Meckling 1976). Institutionalized social obligations are regarded not as a categorial a priori of social action but as the result of *contracts* between free and self-interested individuals, a contract in need of some explanation. This Lockean idea of contract shapes and limits solutions to the problem of emergence suggested by the coordination model.

The difference between the micro and macro levels corresponds to the empirical distinction between *performing* an action and the *results* of actions. Both are empirically distinguishable events that can be described by the same set of categories. The terms "law" and "norms" mean nothing other than the common expectations of the majority of individuals: a systematically induced coorientation of these individuals with reference to a situation or, in the constitutionalistic version of this problem, a contractual agreement between individuals. These macroproperties are mainly represented by legal norms that determine the control over certain resources (Coleman 1983). The distinction between micro and macro can be characterized on one hand by its empirical connection as action and action effect and on the other by the fact that macroproperties refer not to a person but to an aggregate of individuals. Consequently the most important characteristic of macrostructures is represented, first, by the actions producing this structure and, second, by the scope of its factual validity. The description of a law as a macroproperty correspondingly requires some explication of the procedure legitimizing the law and of the group of individuals observing the law. In this context the individualistic social theory exhibits some interesting parallels with the inductivist program of the growth of knowledge: Both deal with inferences from *single* events—empirical observations or individual actions—to *general* structures—theories or contracts.

In contrast to this, the claim on validity that is implied by theories or contracts and the meaning of this claim remain in the background. This concentration on the empirical constitution of macrostructures reaches its limits if the objects of analysis are worldviews, languages, or religions; that is, general orientations that are not purposefully produced and whose instrumental value cannot be properly realized by individual actors. Though not paying much attention to problems of *descriptive emergence*, individualistic theories about the unintentional consequences and paradox effects of social action offer elegant solutions for the problem of *practical emergence*. Starting from the model of the prisoner's dilemma, theoreticians such as Boudon show that the particular interdependencies of social actions produce some unexpected results on the macro level in an unintentional way. In this case the change of macrostructures is no longer tied to simple procedures of contracting and is explained as the intentional product of action of social collectivities. This accounts for the superior heuristic power of this model compared to other conceptions. The core of the individualistic theory of actions, however, cannot be overlooked: The appearance of paradox effects is the unavoidable result of rational individual actions that are considered to be a kind of side effect, difficult to calculate and contradictory to the purpose of the action.

These side effects are commonly the result of insufficient information about the intentions and action alternatives available to other actors. Objective properties of structure (e.g., the size of the collectivity, the network of interaction, or the distribution of resources) to some extent are taken into account by the individualistic model of coordination but are considered contingent background conditions.

It is difficult to fit the assumption of explanatory emergence into the model of coordination. Individual actors are the generators of change—even of macrostructures. The idea of macrostructures that dispose of a complexity and problem-solving capacity higher than the individual actors producing them opposes the very core of the individualistic ontology. In addition, the conception of a fast macrochange disconnected from individual actions is difficult to explain on the basis of the individualistic model of coordination. From an individualistic point of view this idea of an autonomous macrodynamics comes close to "Frankenstein monsters" dominating their human creators: Both ideas are collectivistic nightmares that will quickly dissolve in the clear light of the coordination model.

3.2. THE CATEGORIAL-ANALYTIC MODEL: LANGUAGE AND SPEECH ACT

The second model, which I call "categorial analytic," differs considerably from this. It is not the idea of producing macrostructures by individual actions that forms the core of the relation between the micro and the macro level but the relation between *language* and *speech act* (Austin 1962; Searle 1969; Habermas 1981). Macrostructures are conceived in analogy to a common language that represents the "categorial prerequisites" or the "constitutive rules" for "individual" speech acts. They are not the intended or unintended result of social actions but the indispensable prerequisites of these actions. In consequence the relation between action and categorial structure, between language and speech act, is viewed not as an empirical relationship of causation but as an analytical relationship of constitution (Münch 1982; Alexander 1982). When social actions are analyzed within the categorial framework of a law system, of a religious worldview, or of a subcultural orientation, this categorial framework on one hand and actions on the other do not represent two different events or states of reality the empirical connections of which can be subject to investigation. A categorial frame or a language never comes about as a particular event except in the speech acts incorporating them. Conversely, the event of a speech act cannot be identified as such without referring to the language the speaker uses. Categorizing the rules of language (that is, the constitutive rules) as macrostructure and the speech act as microevent is based on a special difference between rules and actions: Rules are applicable not only to particular actions or interaction situations but in principle to an infinite number of possible situations, whereas the temporal, the spatial, or the social scope of an action is always limited. In the background of this categorial-analytic relation between the micro and macro levels a Kantian theory of knowledge can easily be detected (Münch 1979, 1982). (At this conference I suspect that the categorial-analytic model underlies the presentations of Münch, Alexander, and Habermas.)

This categorial-analytic model centers on the problem of *descriptive emergence*. Its solution is obvious and simple: Structures and actions refer to each other, but in each case they can be distinguished as clearly as Kant's categories of perception and the act of recognition, as general theories and singular perception, as the rules of language and speech acts. The descriptive emergence of normative structures in relation to individual actions can be illustrated by the logical problem of induction. Practical inductive reasoning takes place when theories are psychologically generated from certain individual observations; the claim on validity and meaning, however, that is implied by general theories cannot be inductively based. Just as theories surpass a finite number of single observations, general normative structures are logically and descriptively emergent toward a consensus of a great but finite number of individuals.

Although the categorial-analytic model conceptualizes the descriptive emergence of macrostructures in an elegant and convincing manner, its answer to the question of practical emergence (that is, the inconsistency of micro and macro levels) is unsatisfactory and requires further qualification. If we consider the macro level as the milieu of normative and cognitive structures and the micro level as normative structured acts, then at a first glance the inconsistency between micro and macro level cannot be thought of as anything but a deviance from the rules. An act or a communication that does not follow the rules and does not account for the norms cannot be understood. On the basis of the simple categorial-analytic model, the adequacy of an act to a situation and the rationality of action cannot be conceived but as adherence to the rules. Just as a speaker, ignoring the rules of language, cannot be understood, so individuals, neglecting any constitutive rules of action, can find no basis of social interaction. The discrepancy between structure and action appears to be a kind of irrational mistake or a pathological distortion of rule-guided communication. Within the framework of a categorial-analytic model we can take practical emergence into account only if we replace the rule system under consideration by *two* mutually inconsistent rule systems or languages representing the micro or macro level. This inconsistency is conceptualized as the impossibility of translating one language into another. Certain actions that are meaningful and understandable when referring to the microlanguage seem to be irrational and without meaning when referring to the macrolanguage, and vice versa.

I suppose that this kind of inconsistency between micro- and macrostructures can be associated with Habermas's theory of modern society: Media-controlled systems (that is, the macrostructures) are not able to account for the variety of life-worlds and interaction processes in an adequate and satisfactory manner (Habermas 1981). The solution of the inconsistency between life-world and system in favor of the structures of the life-world—as suggested by Habermas—is by no means the only solution to this inconsistency provided by the categorial-analytic concept. There is no reason supporting an a priori decision that the micro level must be regarded as a stronghold of rationality and the source of any change. In addition, the categorial-analytic heuristic fails to give a satisfactory account of the genesis of practical emergence (that is, of inconsistencies and paradoxical relations between the micro and the macro level). The concept of "*praxis*," of "life form," or of the "situation" to which speech acts refer could offer a clue as to the origin of change. Within the scope of the categorial-analytic model these concepts remain, however, remarkably vague; they have a marginal position similar to the "initial conditions" in the individualistic model of coordination.

The general weakness of the categorial-analytic heuristic with respect to "genetic" explanations has a bearing on the problem of *explanatory emergence*. Certainly the categorial-analytic heuristic does not deny explanatory emergence, but it does not specify the mechanisms promoting the change of macrostructures except by stipulating a transcendental subject who directs the structural change on the macro level as a kind of growth in rationality. Framed by this growth in rationality on the macro level, the idea of explanatory emergence indeed becomes particularly evident. Whereas the interactional processes are embedded in a relatively stable anthropologically universal structure of the life-world, the evolution of macrostructure outpaces the acting individuals. The accelerated tempo of scientific and technological change, which is only partially understood and grasped by individuals, or the erratic oscillations of market processes contrasted to relatively stable working and consumer behavior, seems to provide some evidence for these autonomous dynamics of macroprocesses. There is considerable skepticism, however, as to whether the autonomous dynamics of macrostructures can be conceptualized as *progress* or improvement without stipulating the existence of some individuals aiming at this improvement (Giesen and Schmid 1976). The individualistic model of coordination takes a rather skeptical view of this prospect: If the actual effect of cooperation departs from the goal, in the majority of cases this deviation results in a change for the worse. From the point of view of the categorial-analytic model, however, this unintended progress is indeed possible. Every new cognitive and normative structure contains objective excess meaning and gives rise to new possibilities of application that are unknown to their inventors. The application of these symbolic structures to yet unknown or new situations can, of course, result in improvements. Although the individualistic model of coordination views macrostructures (for example, laws or distributions of scarce resources) mainly as restrictions and impediments to individual autonomy, the categorial-analytic model stresses the opening of the action field made possible by macrostructural innovations such as new morals or worldviews.

3.3. THE MODEL OF ANTAGONISM: SOCIAL REPRESSION AND INDIVIDUAL AUTONOMY

I shall call the third model of the micro-macro relationship the *model of antagonism*. In contrast to the categorial-analytic scheme, it has undergone a rapid rise in popularity in everyday life. This model views the relation between micro and macro level as an antagonistic relation between social actors. The core paradigm is the relation of domination between two social collectivities or groups. The macro level appears as a powerful and repressive authority that attempts to restrict the actions of individuals at the micro level. Opposed to this authority is the position of the individual: relatively powerless, trying to defend and enlarge his or her autonomy and to achieve emancipation from social repression.

Both descriptions—the macro level as a repressive structure and the micro level as individuals with restricted autonomy—are seen as meaningful only by referring mutually to each other. Only if there are autonomous individuals can repression result in restrictions of opportunities, and only if there is some repressive structure can the actor experience lack of autonomy. This idea provides a plausible solution to the problem of descriptive emergence and to that of the practical inconsistency between micro and macro levels: That the societal repression sets limits to practical acting is, from the point of view of the model of antagonism, as obvious as the fundamental and insurmountable difference between master and slave, between dominant and dominated. Even the problem of explanatory emergence, the idea of an autonomous dynamics of macrostructures, has its place in the model of antagonism. If the micro-macro relation is seen as a conflict between a dominant class and the individuals who are excluded from participating in the process of structure formation, then the macrostructural changes produced by an innovation-prone elite can indeed rush ahead of the traditional life-styles on the side of the repressed classes. In this case explanatory emergence is the result of actions of an elite as powerful as it is innovation-prone.

Unfortunately, the model of antagonism assumes a social structure that holds true only in exceptional cases. In particular, for modern societies there is no evidence for the assumption of an almighty collective subject who produces macrostructures voluntaristically and against the resistance of the repressed. If a structure-producing dominant class or some other subject of social repression is lacking, it seems difficult to meet the conditions necessary for applying the model of antagonism. Speaking of antagonism makes sense only if there is interaction between two subjects. Transfer of the antagonism into the personalities of the actors seems to solve the problem: In the *psychoanalytical* scenario societal repression has cut its ties with an external subject and has become an internal element of personalities. Thereby psychoanalysis becomes, as indicated by Marcuse, a sociological method.

This elegant twist by which the model of antagonism retains its analytical power without any external subject of repression demands a price, however. The idea of an *explanatory* emergence that can be explained by the actions of a macroscopic subject becomes unclear. In addition, the psychoanalytical interpretation of the model of antagonism in no way hints at the conditions and direction of macrosocial change. Indeed, dialectical analysis does not deal at all with exact predictions about the process of change. Antagonistic structures induce conflict-acting, which finally results in dissolution of this structural relation and gives birth to something new. The conditions shaping this process remain out of the analytical scope of the dialectical heuristic. Here, too, a particular vacancy of the theoretical model is laid open.

3.4. AN EVOLUTION-THEORETICAL ALTERNATIVE: SYMBOLIC, PRACTICAL, AND MATERIAL STRUCTURES

I believe the three models previously discussed represent the most influential and elaborate models of the relation between the micro and macro levels in sociological theorizing. Their conceptions of macrostructures and their ideas of the relation between both levels differ so fundamentally that a combination of their respective virtues seems to be impossible. The categorial-analytic model conceives the macro level mainly as a *symbolic-categorial reality* and deals with worldviews, morals, religions, and the claims on validity involved in propositions or symbolic utterances. In contrast, the individualistic model of coordination sees macrostructures as distributions of resources and rights of control, as the *empirical reality* of norms and social contracts. Finally, the model of antagonism views the relation between the macro and micro levels not as a categorial or an empirical relation but as a kind of *social relation* between *actors*. This last model presupposes relatively restrictive initial conditions.

In spite of the apparent incompatibility of the three models, I would like to outline a fourth model, which tries to retain the virtues of the categorial-analytic model with respect to the problem of descriptive emergence and which makes use of the advantages of the individualistic model with respect to the explanation of paradox effects, and which, finally, does not fail to give a satisfactory account of explanatory emergence. In two respects, this model enlarges the simple opposition of macrostructure and interaction process which previously underlay the reconstruction of the micro-macro relation. First, situations are introduced into the model as a kind of linkage between macrostructures and interaction processes. These situations contain the symbolic knowledge that is the basis of a rational interpretation of the situation, the acknowledged rules and differentiations of positions, and the material circumstances of actions. These properties of the situation manifest the macrostructure at the micro level. The knowledge relevant to a given situation, for example, is only a section of the total worldview of society, and the norms and rights of control valid in a situation represent only a part of the system of institutions and structures of a society. The number of power positions in an organization is usually greater than the positions that are present in a special situation of interaction. If this were not the case and thus the whole system of institutions were manifested in a particular interaction situation, phenomena of practical emergence would occur only rarely.

The second point enlarging the previous models cuts across the distinction of interaction process, situation, and structure. It results from a simultaneous analysis of symbolic, practical-conventional, and material aspects of social reality and can be used to clarify the problems of descriptive and explanatory emergence. As already mentioned, the model of coordination and the categorial-analytic model differ fundamentally with regard to the idea of macrostructures: On one hand the focus is on the social contracts in operation, the acknowledged institutional regulations, and the social distribution of control rights; on the other hand the focus is on *symbolic* rule systems with objective meanings, which are not always realized by the actors, and with implicit claims on validity, which are not acknowledged and observed in every process of social interaction. Symbolic structures such as worldviews, morals, or ideals of a good life involve an unrestricted claim on validity that should be distinguished strictly from the factual-practical validity of norms and institutions. Finally, there has to be a differentiation between the reality of norms and conventions that exist only in and through acting and the material-organic reality that manifests itself in organic and material-technical be-

TABLE 15.1

	Process	Situation	Structure
Symbolic Reality	Rational interpretation of the situation	Symbolic core structure, relevant pattern of conceiving	Worldviews, morals
Practical Reality	Action	Practical core structure, valid rules and norms, interests induced by social positions	Valid institutions and structures of differentiation
Material Reality	Organic behavior	Material core structure, material resources, and techniques available in a situation	Material resources, size of collectivity, technostructure

havior. This distinction between the symbolic "reality" of objective meaning and claims on validity, the practical reality of action and social rules in operation, and the material reality of technical adaptation to nature refers to the three-world ontology of Karl Popper (Popper 1972; Popper and Eccles 1977). Taking this in conjunction with the differentiations among microprocess, situation, and macrostructure, the scheme shown in table 15.1 will result. According to this scheme, social action occurs within the framework of rules and differentiations of positions that are universally acknowledged by all participants of an interaction process as the constitutive basis of their actions (Giesen 1983). In principle, the practical core structure of the situation can be changed, as can contracts and conventions, but only if some other practical core structure is presupposed.

At the level of the symbolic system, the relevant patterns of conceiving the situation correspond to the practical core structures. They present the basis of rational interpretations and problem solutions. Whether the actors are aware of all these relevant patterns of conceiving and whether their practical acts correspond to a rational interpretation of the situation will depend on contingent-practical conditions. Not in every case is practical acting rational; it can miss its mark, it can fail to be understood, and it can give rise to a crisis of interaction.

Symbolic macrostructures such as worldviews, morals, or, in general, symbolic codes open fields of possible processes of interaction. Practical structures such as the differentiation of positions restrict these fields of interaction. This opposition of categorial, symbolic, and practical structures cannot be adequately conceived by the Humean idea of causality, the analytical relationship of rule and rule-guided action, or even by the dialectics of master and slave. A more adequate formulation is provided by the Darwinian model of evolutionary processes by which living organisms reproduce themselves in different environments (Campbell 1965; Giesen 1980; Giesen and Lau 1981; Schmid 1983). If a symbolically codified action fits the selective factors operative in a situation, the interaction process proceeds smoothly. If the action fails to fit the selective factors, however, the processes of exchange are deadlocked, understanding will tend to be blocked, and the levels of communication will be subject to frequent change. Whether or not this will be the case can be known in advance from the point of view of the actor only to a very limited degree: The actor neither disposes of complete knowledge about the practical structure of the situation nor is he or she able to control the selective results of practical structures sufficiently. This unpredictability of selective processes will often result in phenomena of practical emergence. The effects of intentional actions are biased by the selective factors of the situation in a way that counteracts the aims and intentions of the actors. Therefore the model of situational selection will center on the unintended consequences of purposeful actions.

Phenomena of practical emergence can be the consequence of unavoidable practical deviations from the ideal of a rational interpretation of the situation. Actors construct their actions according to a symbolic pattern of conceiving that is not always perfectly adequate to their situation. This is the case, for example, when spouses attempt to control actions in the family by the monetary code or when the egos of the individuals present in a situation are rigorously questioned by a certain action. Unintended effects of purposeful actions, however, may even occur if the action in question is rational and perfectly adequate to the practical core structure of the situation. In this case the distorting selective factors are situated outside the practical core structure: in other sectors of society influencing the effect of action or in previously unknown material scarcities. The basis of the paradoxical effects can be found in the interdependencies of actions in modern society which have been brilliantly analyzed by Boudon. The factors that determine the success of an action are positioned beyond the scope of an interaction situation. This gradual separation of the practical core structure and the societal macrosystem, which cannot be controlled or even predicted, forms the background of the practical emergence of macrostructures.

The distinction between symbolic system and practical structures sets the stage for a plausible answer to the question of explanatory emergence of macrosocial processes, without assuming a transcendental subject entering the stage as a generator of historical change. Practical structures, such as distributions of income or hierarchies of power, are the result of many individual actions and cannot vary without corresponding microactivities preceding or accompanying this variation. In contrast to this, symbolic systems can indeed undergo change without corresponding changes at the level of social microstructures. Let me illustrate this through reference to a well-known action field. The forms of social interaction between scientists, their social relations, and the organization of their research activities within scientific institutions can remain completely unchanged although their scientific ideas and acknowledged theories undergo rapid and far-reaching evolution. Conversely, we can hardly imagine that a fundamental change of the practical organization of research or of the distribution of resources takes place without any corresponding development on the level of interaction processes. My thesis is that *symbolic macrostructures can have explanatory emergence in relation to microsocial processes of interaction, whereas practical macrostructures cannot.* This thesis involves the recognition that explanatory emergence is not regarded as a relation between micro- and macroprocesses on one level of reality but that emergence will not arise until a change of level from the material to the social-practical or from the social-practical to symbolic processes and structures has taken place.

Most important for an evolutionary model of emergence is the possibility of structural variation at the emergent level without the necessity of corresponding changes at the lower level and the acceleration of reproduction that results from this. The evolution of organisms, for example, produced a great variation of species without any significant change in the organic attitudes of actors. This "decoupling" of organic attributes and social behavior was not possible until the brain processes of human beings met the conditions of consciousness, social learning, and social conventions in varying norms. On the basis of an organic evolution largely neutralized, a social and historical change could start and accelerate. In a similar fashion changes in the valid norms and institutions on one hand and in the symbolic systems on the other can be decoupled in the course of the sociocultural evolution. In this case as well, a normative structure is presupposed which gives way to an autonomous change of symbolic systems in a manner similar to that in which the brain system opens the way for processes of consciousness. This is achieved largely through the historical differentiation between the cultural subsystem and other subsystems of society. This differentiation sets the stage for an evolution of autonomous science, art, and morality. Thereby some clues as to the historical limits of phenomena of explanatory emergence are given. Societies that tie the evolution of symbolic systems to social change (e.g., by the dogmatic prohibition of new ideas) will only rarely exhibit phenomena of explanatory emergence. Every symbolic innovation is tightly bound to a corresponding institutional or structural change, leading in extreme cases even to the death of the adherents of the old ideas. Popper's challenge, "Let theories die instead of men," aims at such a decoupling of symbolic evolution and organic evolution.

The distinctions among symbolic, practical, and material structures also can be utilized for the problem of descriptive emergence. Descriptive emergence refers to the shift from symbolic to practical attributes and from practical to material attributes. The categorial claim on validity of a norm cannot be reduced to the practical decision of observing this norm, and this practical decision is not equivalent to similarities in organic behavior. Conversely, the validity of institutions is not descriptively emergent for the practical decision of individuals to acknowledge the institution and to behave accordingly. From the standpoint of the outlined model of evolution theory, the difference between categorial-analytic and individualistic models need not lead to contradictory conclusions, for the following reasons.

1. The individualistic model of coordination deals with the micro-macro relationship only at the level of practical structures and factual behavior. Because the realm of symbolic systems remains hidden, descriptive and explanatory emergence appear not as a problem but as a kind of collectivistic chimera. In contrast to this, the model centers on the problem of practical emergence and the selective pressures that are raised by incomplete knowledge and the lack of coordination possibilities with respect to the success of action.

2. The categorial-analytic model tends to neglect the difference between symbolic and practical processes; it deals with interaction and acting as *practical* processes, but it considers macrostructures mainly as *symbolic* systems. This simultaneous change from micro to macro and from the practical to the symbolic level directs attention to the problem of descriptive and explanatory emergence, but it obscures the development of paradoxical effects. Categorial structures cannot simply be purposefully produced by individual actions and consequently cannot be considered as an unintentional effect of such actions. The missing distinction between practical and symbolic processes tends to give rise to a view of history as a kind of growth of rationality or as progress. This

continuous growth of complexity characterizes only symbolic systems, and not the social change of institutions and structures of differentiation. In historical change differentiation can indeed be lost and some regressive developments can take place.

3. The model of antagonism generalizes the practical relation between master and slave to a model of micro and macro relations, of interaction and structure. It overlooks the point that this generalization holds true only in exceptional cases: that is, if an omnipotent elite voluntaristically produces macrostructures against the interests of an oppressed majority. If this assumption holds true, the model of antagonism provides plausible answers to the question of descriptive, practical, and explanatory emergence. The psychoanalytical interpretation of this model certainly enlarges its scope, but in exchange for this it trades an analytical loss with regard to the problem of practical and explanatory emergence. Its merits consist mainly in applying an everyday concept to the description of micro-macro relations, not in discovering a previously unknown process that gives rise to a relation of emergence.

Even if the evolution-theoretical model is able to show some connections among the three models discussed, and even if it has given us some clues as to their respective faults and virtues, at the moment it represents only a promising but still elliptical scheme for sociological analysis, a scheme that joins the countless efforts to integrate sociological theorizing and (a kind of paradoxical effect indeed) perhaps only increases the scattering of the theoretical field.

REFERENCES

Agassi, J. 1960. Methodological Individualism. *British Journal of Sociology* 11:244–270.

Austin, J. L. 1962. *How to Do Things with Words*. Oxford: Oxford University Press.

Alexander, Jeffrey C. 1982. *Theoretical Logic in Sociology*. Vol. 1. *Positivism, Presuppositions and Current Controversies*. London: Routledge & Kegan Paul.

Boudon, Raymond. 1979. *Widersprüche sozialen Handelns*. Neuwied: Luchterhand.

Brodbeck, M. 1968. Methodological Individualism—Definition and Reduction, pp. 280–303 in M. Brodbeck, ed., *Readings in the Philosophy of the Social Sciences*. London: Collier-Macmillan.

Campbell, Donald T. 1965. Variation and Selective Retention in Socio-Cultural Evolution, pp. 19–49 in H. R. Barringer, G. J. Blankstein, and R. W. Mauck, eds., *Social Change in Developing Areas*. Cambridge, Mass.: Schenkman.

Coleman, James S. 1975. Social Structure and a Theory of Action, pp. 76–93 in P. M. Blau, ed., *Approaches to the Study of Social Structure*. London: Free Press.

———. forthcoming. Micro Foundations and Macrosocial Theory, in James S. Coleman, S. Lindenberg, and S. Nowak, eds., *Approaches to Social Theory*. Chicago: University of Chicago Press.

Eberlein, G., and H.-J. Kondratowitz. 1977. *Psychologie statt Soziologie? Zur Reduzierbarkeit sozialer Strukturen auf Verhalten*. Frankfurt: Campus.

Gellner, H. 1959. Holism versus Individualism in History and Sociology, pp. 488–502 in P. Gardiner, ed., *Theories of History*. New York–London: Free Press.

Giesen, Bernhard. 1980. *Makrosoziologie*. Hamburg: Hoffmann und Campe.

———. 1986. Media and Markets, in M. Schmid, ed., *Evolution Theory in the Social Sciences*. Dordrecht: Reidel.

Giesen, Bernhard, and C. Lau. 1981. Zur Anwendung darwinistischer Erklärungsstrategien in der Soziologie. *Kölner Zeitschrift für Soziologie und Sozialpsychologie* 33, 2:229–256.

Giesen, Bernhard, and M. Schmid. 1976. *Erklärung und Geschichte*. Gersthofen: Maro.

———. 1977. Methodologischer Individualismus und Reduktionismus, pp. 24–47 in E. Eberlein and H. J. Kondratowitz, eds., *Psychologie statt Soziologie*. Frankfurt: Campus.

Goldstein, L. 1973. The Two Theses of Methodological Individualism, pp. 272–286 in J. O'Neill, ed., *Modes of Individualism and Collectivism*. London: Heinemann.

Habermas, Jürgen. 1981. *Theorie des kommunikativen Handelns*. Vol. 1. Frankfurt: Suhrkamp.

Hayek, F. 1952. *The Counter-Revolution of Science: Studies on the Abuse of Reason*. Glencoe, Ill.: Free Press.

Homans, George C. 1974. *Social Behavior: Its Elementary Forms*. London: Routledge & Kegan Paul.

Lakatos, I. 1970. Falsification and the Methodology of Scientific Research Programs, pp. 191–196 in I. Lakatos and A. Musgrave, eds., *Criticism and the Growth of Knowledge*. Cambridge: Cambridge University Press.

Lakatos, I., and A. Musgrave, eds. 1970. *Criticism and the Growth of Knowledge*. Cambridge: Cambridge University Press.

Lindenberg, Siegwart. 1977. Individuelle Effekte. Kollektive Phänomene und das Problem der Transformation, pp. 46–84 in K. Eichner and W. Habermehl, eds., *Probleme der Erklärung sozialen Verhaltens*. Meisenheim/Glan: Hain.

S. Lindenberg. 1983. The New Political Economy: Its Potential and Limitations for the Social Sciences in General and for Sociology in Particular, pp. 7–66 in W. Sudeur, ed., *Ökonomische Erklärung sozialen Verhaltens*. Duisburg: Sozialwissenschaftliche Kooperative.

Lindenberg, Siegwart, and Reinhard Wippler. 1978. Theorievergleich: Elemente der Rekonstruktion, pp. 219–230 in K. O. Hondrich and J. Matthes, eds., *Theorienvergleich in den Sozialwissenschaften*. Neuwied: Luchterhand.

Luhmann, Niklas. 1980. *Gesellschaftsstruktur und Semantik. Studien zur Wissenssoziologie der modernen Gesellschaft.* Vol. 1. Frankfurt: Suhrkamp.
Lukes, Stephen. 1970. Methodological Individualism Reconsidered, pp. 76–88 in D. Emmert and A. MacIntyre, eds., *Sociological Theory and Philosophical Analysis*. New York: Macmillan.
Mandelbaum, Maurice. 1973. Societal Facts, pp. 221–234 in J. O'Neill, ed., *Modes of Individualism and Collectivism*. London: Heinemann.
Meckling, W.H. 1976. Values and the Choice of the Individual in the Social Sciences. *Schweizerische Zeitschrift für Volkswirtschaft und Statistik* 112:545–559.
Münch, Richard. 1979. Talcott Parsons und die Theorie des Handelns I. Die Konstitution des Kantschen Kerns. *Soziale Welt* 30, 4:384–409.
———. 1982. *Theorie des Handelns*. Frankfurt: Suhrkamp.
Nagel, Einert. 1961. *The Structure of Science*. London: Routledge & Kegan Paul.
O'Neill, John. 1973. *Modes of Individualism and Collectivism*. London: Heinemann.
Opp, Karl–Dieter. 1979. *Individualistische Sozialwissenschaft*. Stuttgart: Enke.
Popper, Karl R. 1961. *The Poverty of Historicism*. London: Routledge & Kegan Paul.
———. 1972. *Objective Knowledge: An Evolutionary Approach*. Oxford: Clarendon. German translation: 1973. *Objektive Erkenntnis*. Hamburg: Hoffman und Campe.
Popper, Karl R., and J.C. Eccles. 1977. *The Self and Its Brain*. New York: Springer.
Raub, Werner, and Thomas Voss. 1981. *Individuelles Handeln und Gesellschaftliche Folgen*. Neuwied: Luchterhand.
Searle, J.R. 1969. *Speech Acts*. Cambridge: Cambridge University Press. German translation: 1973. *Sprechakte*. Frankfurt: Suhrkamp.
Schmid, Michael. 1983. *Basale Soziologie: Theorie sozialen Wandels*. Opladen: Westdeutscher Verlag.
Scott, K.J. 1961. Methodological and Epistemological Individualism. *British Journal for the Philosophy of Science* 11.
Vanberg, Viktor. 1975. *Die zwei Soziologen*. Tübingen: Mohr und Siebeck.
———. 1978. Markets and Organization. *Mens en maatschappij* 53:259–289.
Watkins, W.W. 1959. Historical Explanation in the Social Sciences, pp. 503–514 in P. Gardiner, ed., *Theories of History*. New York: Free Press.
Wippler, Reinhard. 1978. Nichtintendierte soziale Folgen individueller Handlungen. *Soziale Welt* 29, 2:155–179.

CONCLUSION

Relating the Micro and Macro

Richard Münch and Neil J. Smelser

Our objective in this concluding chapter is to take an overview of the major issues raised at the Schloss Rauischholzhausen conference, issues that are also represented in the chapters of this volume, the precipitate of that conference. We cannot be exhaustive, of course. The essays are too discursive and rich to permit systematic cataloguing of issues; only a highlight of the major ones is possible. In attempting to carry out our objective we will proceed by three steps: First, we will say a few words about the definition of the micro and macro levels. Second, we will present a few outstanding examples of micro (individualistic) and macro (structural-cultural) traditions. Third, we will make an effort to identify the ways in which microtheorists have attempted to make the transition to the macro level and macrotheorists to the micro level, indicating some of the problems that are encountered in each effort.

DEFINITIONS

In perusing the chapters of this volume a number of possible meanings have been mentioned, though not necessarily advocated, by different authors:

- Micro as dealing with individuals and macro as dealing with populations (Blau and Haferkamp)
- Micro as the focus on small social units and macro as dealing with large social units (Alexander)

- Micro as individual interactions with limited scope and macro, with societal scope (e.g., value-systems) (Wippler and Lindenberg)
- Micro as interaction (encounters and exchanges) and macro as repeated experiences of large numbers of persons in time and space (Collins)
- Micro as empirical indicators of observable units (individuals) and macro as constructed from the behavior and statements of individuals (Wippler and Lindenberg)
- Micro as psychological propositions, on the basis of which statements and laws about larger-scale social processes and structures (macro) are made (Wippler and Lindenberg)
- Micro as social processes that engender relations among individuals and macro as the structure of different positions in a population and their constraints on interaction (Blau)

It is apparent from these selected definitions that the terms "micro" and "macro" have been assigned a number of diverse meanings in the sociological literature and that these meanings are not always consistent with one another. Furthermore, in our estimation some of these definitional efforts cause fewer analytic problems and therefore have more analytic promise than others. Our own preferred definition is probably closest to the last on the list. We see the micro level as involving encounters and patterned interaction among individuals (which would include communication, exchange, cooperation, and conflict) and the macro level as referring to those structures in society (groups, organizations, institutions, and cultural productions) that are sustained (however imperfectly) by mechanisms of social control and that constitute both opportunities and constraints on individual behavior and interactions. Moreover, following Alexander's admonition, we regard this distinction as analytic rather than as concrete with respect to the usual phenomena that sociologists take as their focus of study. The institution of the family, for instance, can be studied from the standpoint of the patterns of cooperation, competition, domination, and subordination among members of the family (micro), or as a structure that is shaped by other institutional forces (religious or legal tradition, occupational structure) and that constitutes both opportunity (for example, for sexual gratification) and constraint (for example, sexual constraint, as in taboos against adultery and incest) on the members of the family and their interactions. The same point can be made for economic, political, and medical institutions, as well as others.

We turn now to the second item on the agenda, the identification of a representative number of micro- and macrotraditions in sociology (and, to a limited extent, in other behavioral and social sciences). Before beginning, however, a qualifying note is in order. Even though it is convenient and in many ways accurate to label a given tradition as micro or macro because of its conceptual starting points and its basic units of analysis, we will see that the distinction loses force because microtheories invariably involve definite assumptions about the macrocontext in which interactional processes are embedded (and therefore have a macrocomponent) and that macrotheories invariably involve assumptions about individual motivation and interaction (and therefore have a microcomponent).

SOME MICROTRADITIONS

NEOCLASSICAL ECONOMIC THEORY

We begin with a tradition outside sociology, partly because of its clarity of formulation and partly because, as Coleman argues, it represents a creative but restricted solution to the micro-macro problem. Initially it seems an error to classify the neoclassical tradition as micro in character, because the phenomena that economists in this tradition strove to explain were macro in character: They wished to explain the level and pattern of *production* of different commodities (goods and services) in a society, the pattern of application of *resources* (factors of production) in the economy, and the pattern of *distribution* of commodities on one hand and the shares of income on the other. All of these can be characterized as macroeconomic in character and appear to fall within the general definition of macro that we have proposed. The apparent error disappears, however, when we observe that the analytic apparatus constructed by neoclassical economists is clearly microeconomic in character, by virtue of the following emphases.

The basic units of analysis in neoclassical economics are individual buyers and sellers of resources and products. Wippler and Lindenberg argue that this is not strictly the case, as households and firms—which are social organizations, not individuals—are the main actors in neoclassical markets. Their point is correct, but insofar as internal differences of interest and orientation within the household and firm were not taken into account in the neoclassical economics—and they were not—

they can be regarded analytically as corporate actors who act like individuals.

Certain assumptions are made about the motivation of the individual actors by classical economists. The most evident is the assumption, bred in the utilitarian tradition, that the individual actor will behave in such a way as to maximize his or her material well-being, or utility, in economic transactions. An additional assumption is that both buyers and sellers possess full knowledge about the availability and prices of products, job opportunities, and other market conditions. These first two assumptions are linked by a third, a postulate of rationality, whereby it is assumed that buyers and sellers, possessing preferences and full information, will act rationally on the basis of these. They will not make errors, they will not forget what they know, and they will not act irrationally (that is, on bases counter to their interests and information).

Certain assumptions are made about the interaction between buyer and seller. It is assumed that they will meet in a peaceful setting in which it is understood that neither will engage in transactions other than economic exchange (e.g., coercion, violence), that the terms of exchange are understood (labor for wages, commodities for money), that each will make offers on the basis of his or her own preferences (supply schedule and demand schedule), and that on this basis an equilibrium price point will be reached. It is also assumed that the exchange will not be negotiated (haggled over) but will be a more or less automatic intersection of the schedules of each.

On the basis of these kinds of microassumptions, neoclassical economists reached back toward the macro, as it were, by the simple mode of aggregation of the thousands of microsolutions in the market, which would yield solutions to the questions of the structure of production, the allocation of resources, and the distribution of shares. We only take note of this at the moment, reserving a more substantial discussion of this mode of transition for a later section.

There is another sense in which neoclassical economic theory took cognizance of the macro, and that has to do with another set of special assumptions explicitly or implicitly built into the theory. Among these is the special assumption of the "frictionless" market, in which is assumed perfect mobility of resources and commodities upon demand. Another is the assumption of the incapacity of either firms or consumers to exercise control over others with respect to output and prices; this is the assumption of the independence of actors and virtually rules out power and influence that might affect economic transactions. Still another—this one completely implicit—is that it is in the nature of culture (information) to be equally and fully available to everyone. Certain further assumptions have to do with the givens of institutions, such as a credit or banking system, a political system to guarantee conditions of peace and stability in processes of exchange, and so on. At this moment we do not concern ourselves with the realism or unrealism of these kinds of assumptions (most seem unreal); rather, we stress that the operation of the microprocesses at the market level calls for the systematic availability of opportunities and the systematic constraining of other, possibly disruptive activities.

In his economic sociology Max Weber took note of these kinds of macrosociological givens, although he described them as ideal-type *empirical* conditions (as contrasted with simplifying *assumptions*) that were the institutional conditions of what he called "maximum formal rationality of capital accounting." Among these were the appropriation of all nonhuman means of production by owners; the complete absence of all formal appropriation of opportunities for profit (the independence assumption); the complete absence of appropriation of jobs by workers (the "frictionless" assumption); the complete absence of the regulation of consumption, production, and prices (the independence assumption again); and a legal and administrative order that guaranteed the validity of formal contractual exchanges (Weber [1922] 1976).

All these simplifying assumptions, both at the individual psychological level and at the institutional level, may be regarded as parameters in the sense that they are unvarying but, if varied, would make a decisive difference in the kinds of equilibrium resulting in the market. It is worth noting, furthermore, that whole new schools of economics have been formed by the systematic modification of one or more simplifying assumptions (as contrasted with the nature of microprocesses in the market itself). To posit a backward-bending supply curve, for instance, so that labor will prefer leisure to higher wages at a certain point, changes the equilibrium solution for the allocation of labor; to acknowledge the power of firms, consumers, and government to influence output and production permits a whole line of theorizing known as "imperfect competition"; and much of the alteration of neoclassical economics achieved by Keynes rested on his modification of assumptions about consumption (the marginal propensity to consume), labor supply (the stickiness of money wages), and the availability of credit (the liquidity preference function).

To summarize, the neoclassical tradition in economics is a thoroughgoing microtheory in that individuals and individual interaction are at the core of its analytic framework, but it is also macro in character in terms of solutions sought and simplifying assumptions made. Changes in the latter would reverberate to the micro level and, by modifying processes at that level would produce a different pattern of macro-output solutions.

MICRO CONFLICT THEORY

Micro conflict theory shares with the economic tradition in social theory the concentration on actors in situations as its unit of analysis—either individual actors or corporate, collective, group actors. Society and the institutions of society are conceived as momentary results of a never-ending history of conflict settlement between competing historical actors (Collins 1975).

Both individualistic economic theories and conflict theories apply their assumptions to individual and collective actors, between which there is no difference in principle. A social group is a corporate actor insofar as its members make group decisions (e.g., the decisions of its leaders, or of a group meeting, as binding). Collective actors are closer to the macro level than individual actors, however. The actions of an individual worker in a workplace normally have less far-reaching consequences than the actions of trade union leaders when they negotiate with the employers' organizations on a national level. Nevertheless, the actions of the trade union leader can be explained by the same action theory as the actions of the individual workers. For both we can ask how much power the group or individual has compared to other groups and individuals. We need no special device for translating micro into macro in this instance; it is a matter of the size of territory and population affected by actions.

The difference between economic and conflict theory occurs in the assumptions made about the determination of actions, interactions, and outcomes. In economic terms actors have a set of preferences (ends) and seek to attain optimum realization of these in applying the most efficient means. The economic actor maximizes utility. The economic actor changes his or her preferences if they turn out to be costlier than other possible preferences. An economic actor never persists in useless or costly actions. The conflict actor differs from the economic actor in that he or she has a more predetermined and much smaller set of preferences. The conflict actor is less flexible than the economic actor, for example, in working toward abolishing racial discrimination, stopping air pollution, or reintroducing school prayer. The conflict actor normally does not replace these ends with ends that are easier to attain, as the purely economic actor would do. He or she seeks the realization of a predetermined set of ends.

As a result the conflict actor becomes involved in a type of interaction different from that of the economic actor in the market. The economic actor cannot exercise power to maximize his or her utility. This forces the economic actor to *exchange* something of value for something else of value. The conflict actor is committed to some specific ends and normally does not want or is not able to exchange anything to attain those ends. He or she is in a situation in which the realization ends conflicts with the realization of the ends of other actors.

In order to realize their own and prevent others' goal realization, conflict actors need *power* over other actors. A win for one athletic team automatically means a loss for the other. A winning team has to attack and defend effectively, and this means the exercise of power over the losing team. In the conflict perspective interaction takes place in such a situation of scarcity. All actors cannot realize their goals fully; to realize their ends they must apply power to overcome the obstacles set by the other actors. At this point we also arrive at the macro level: The more power actors have at their disposal, the more they can enforce goals and impose ways of acting on others. The union leader has more power than the average union member, and his or her decisions are more far-reaching at the macro level.

In most situations actors do not have the power to overcome all obstacles. Thus they must compromise and thereby reduce the degree to which they realize their goals. Imagine ten party guests, each of whom wishes to monopolize the time of an eleventh, very prominent guest, but with none of them having the power to prevent the others from talking to that guest. The distribution of talk at the party will depend on the ability (power) of the different guests to attract the attention of the prominent one with some interesting remark. The guests with the highest speaking ability have the most power. The power distribution determines the distribution of talking time. Gaining talking time means more resources for the talkers. Accordingly the more powerful actors emerge from a conflict settlement with even more power. Such is the case, however, if power is the only determinant of talking time. Intelligent tactics, the norm of equality, and the congruence of ideas may yield more talking time to low-power persons. This complication indicates the limits on conflict theory in explaining interaction and its outcomes, as follows.

All conflict takes place within structures that have not been created by the actors involved. For this reason individualistic conflict theories at least implicitly must presuppose the existence of macrostructures. The first such structure is the existing distribution of power itself. The conflict between a son and his father or between an opposition and a government is prestructured by the distribution of power between them. This power distribution applies to their roles in general and not merely to the incumbents of those roles. Nor is this distribution of power solely a result of earlier conflicts. Traditional norms, cultural ideals, and economic calculations also enter into the institutional framework of conflict settlement. These are the nonconflictual foundations of conflict and conflict settlement. Without being able to presuppose the rules of the game, the sports team cannot act in a rational way in order to attain its goal of winning the game. The degree to which conflict is indeed structured by these nonconflictual foundations is, of course, variable.

The logic of individualistic conflict theory is found in Collins's chapter. His units of analysis are the actions of individuals in situations. The goals of the actors in these situations conflict with those of other actors. In Collins's model, negotiating actors make use of their resources by negotiating. Conflict settlement is combined with a kind of economic calculation. Collins conceives macrostructures as composed of aggregations of microencounters. He also transcends the pure microapproach, however, by acknowledging that every microencounter takes place within macrostructures, which have emerged from previous aggregations of microencounters. Collins singles out the distribution of property (seen as a means to act) and power as the most salient macrostructures.

Haferkamp's essay also makes reference to the conflict model. Some macrostructures result from planned actions carried out by actors (e.g., political entrepreneurs, social groups, social movements) who act on the societal scene. This process inevitably involves processes of conflict, negotiation, and conflict settlement. In addition, macrostructures result from actions of large-scale actors without explicit intentions. Structures that are advantageous for large numbers of actors are subject to selection in an evolutionary process. Conflict theory enters into this process secondarily, in that powerful groups exercise greater influence as selective forces than do weak ones. Haferkamp is aware, however, that both micro- and macroprocesses that create macrostructures themselves occur within preexisting structures.

ETHNOMETHODOLOGY

In contrast to the positivistic, individualistic economic, and conflict theories, ethnomethodology is an interpretive (idealistic) version of individualism in sociological theory (Garfinkel 1967). Harold Garfinkel, countering macrostructuralist sociology such as Durkheimian and Parsonian sociology, has emphasized that human actors are not "cultural dopes" who act out what is prescribed by objective social facts and cultural patterns. Rather, he argues that social life is an ongoing process in which order is created in situations by the "concerted action" of individuals. Actors give "accounts" of their social world, and these accounts determine how they act in this world.

The analysis of "accounting" emphasizes the contingency of interactional situations by pointing to the indexical nature of expressions. Not only expressions such as "here," "he," or "she" are comprehensible solely within the situations in which they are used; the indexical rule applies to language in general. This implies a complete self-referential character of every situation of action. Even in situations in which actors seemingly apply general norms, they must define their meaning in the situation of action itself. There is no one-to-one transmission of the meaning of norms from one situation to another. The scheme for coding types of death as used in the Suicide Prevention Center studied by Garfinkel has been defined at time t_1, the students apply this scheme at time t_2, and they must establish the concrete meaning of the scheme at this time in applying ad hoc definitions. These ad hoc definitions of suicide types are not predetermined by the coding scheme that might be treated as a macrostructure. Thus what becomes the really effective coding scheme is created in every new situation of coding.

What makes ethnomethodology a unique individualistic approach is its view of action itself. Action is seen as an order-producing activity in the process of accounting. Individuals are seen as free from macroconstraints but as permanently engaged in the creation of an ordered social world, but it is an ordered world only for the situation itself and not beyond the situation. The "preference schedule" for the ethnomethodological actor appears mainly to create momentary stability and order through creation of the situational rules. The type of interaction on which ethnomethodology focuses its interests is the coordination of the actions of actors. Interaction is seen as "concerted action" of individuals (Zimmermann and Pollner 1971).

A major question is whether this spontaneous creation of order in situations of interaction is presuppositionless with respect to the preexistence of macrostructures. With regard to the students who fill out the death coding scheme of the Suicide Prevention Center work alone, they do not have to coordinate their actions. What happens when several students discuss each case, however, and must find a common interpretation? The general meaning of death sets limits for their interpretation; there may be an authority relationship between doctors and students which gives doctors greater power to define the meaning of certain types of death; there may also be some common rules that restrict individual freedom of interpretation. For example, it may be a rule that every student must hand over ambiguous cases to a central clearing committee. Without any such predetermined structures the students would not be able to predict the actions of others and thus would have no foundation for the spontaneous creation of situational order. These are the nonspontaneous foundations of the spontaneous situational ordering of action. Order does not come from chaos; it always presupposes some other order.

Schegloff puts forward the argument of ethnomethodology. He demonstrates how certain situations of conversation—"repair," "interruption," "doctor-patient interaction," and "turn-taking"—call for some ordering (see also Schegloff 1980; Schegloff and Sacks 1973; Schegloff, Jefferson, and Sacks 1977). He discovers a remarkable similarity of solutions established in different cultures. In the radical individualistic version of ethnomethodology it could be argued that the actors in these situations apparently are able to coordinate and order their interactions with no guidance from preexisting macrocultural norms. Otherwise we would discover more cultural variation. A major question arises, however: What explains the fact that they come to a certain order and with such uniformity? In this case the structure of the situation seems to enter. The situation (e.g., repair) and the problem of the actors involved (they want to understand each other) determines what type of order can provide a solution to the problem. Because this structure is the same, we arrive at similar solutions in different cultural contexts. Thus ethnomethodology that began by denying any cultural predetermination of individuals' actions ends up with a technical predetermination of their actions. This result again confirms that order does not emerge from chaos but only from some preexisting order. Because the preexisting cultural order is closed from the analysis of order creation, only physical and technical structures are left.

SYMBOLIC INTERACTIONISM

In his formulation of symbolic interactionism as a unique sociological paradigm, Herbert Blumer (1969) repeatedly rejects the view that institutions, social structures, human group life, and society can be analyzed separately from the actions of human individuals. Rather, these entities are compositions of interwoven individual actions. Therefore we must study these actions of individuals and their characteristics if we want to know something about what we think of as macrostructures. This position denies even the analytic independence of macroentities. Everything is micro, if studied closely enough.

Symbolic interactionism is thus as individualistic as economic and conflict theory, but it differs from both in how it conceives individual action and motivation. In this approach human action always involves interpretation of the *meaning* of objects (physical, social, and cultural). This assumption is for symbolic interactionism what economic calculation is for economic theory, what goal realization is for conflict theory, and what ordering action is for ethnomethodology. To find a certain meaning in an object is to see it in the context of a certain idea or symbolic construction. For example, we interpret an action as an attack because we see it in consistency with the general idea of what one does when one attacks.

The process of interpreting the meaning of objects takes place in social interaction between two or more actors. Moreover, interaction itself is basically shaped by the interpretations actors reveal to one another. The fact that interaction implies mutually conveying and interpreting the meaning of actions gives social interaction a specific character. To put it another way, interaction is always communication, not mere exchange or realistic conflict strategy. How actors act is determined by the meaning they attribute to each others' actions. If a first actor interprets a second's action as an attack, though the second actor did not intend it as such, the first will react with a defense or a counterattack, which may be interpreted by the second as unfriendly, thus initiating a counter-counterattack. In this way their mutual interpretations possibly generate interaction and possibly a lasting conflict.

Blumer emphasizes that macrostructures are not external forces that "play upon" the individual actors. They enter the situation of action only through processes of interpreting their meaning. The constitution of the university may assign professors a position of authority over students.

This structure, however, does not affect students' and professors' actions immediately but only through the meaning they give it in a situation of interaction. Thus a professor may or may not allow students the right to intervene during lectures.

Nevertheless, we argue that communication is impossible and that actors cannot understand one another if everything were open to interpretation in concrete situations. Mutual understanding depends on the predictability of others' interpretations beyond particular situations. Thus when we enter a situation of interaction, the interpretational process is shaped by the language we share, by authority relationships that assign rights of interpretation, by norms of communication, and by means of communication. These are noninterpretational foundations of interpretation in social interaction. They must be presupposed at least implicitly.

Elements of symbolic interactionism are found in both Collins's and Haferkamp's essays. Both combine conflict theory and symbolic interactionism. They conceive of microencounters not only as conflict settlement involving power relations but also as communication, as conversations involving processes of interpretation of meaning. For them, however, the definition of a situation and of interpretations of meaning is primarily determined by the power relations among actors. Neither author deals with the meaning conditions set by large-scale meaning systems (as, for example, religions), but they concentrate on the distribution of property and power in society.

SOME MACROSCOPIC TRADITIONS

Macroscopic approaches start with the assumption that macrophenomena are emergent entities with distinctive qualities that make them qualitatively different from the mere aggregation of individual actors or actions. In this view macrophenomena—the economic, political, or social structure and the culture of whole societies and their development—are worthy of study at their own analytic levels, without reference to the actions of individuals, and certainly are not reducible to these actions.

The macroscopic paradigms can be analyzed according to four basic features: (1) how they emphasize the macroscopic as a level of analysis, (2) what they conceive as the central macroscopic aspect of society, (3) how they see the macroscopic forces spreading through society on the macroscopic level, and (4) how they view macroscopic processes sustained by individual and group actions.

A MACROTHEORY OF ECONOMIC STRUCTURES AND PROCESSES: MARX'S THEORY OF CAPITALISM

According to Marxist theory, history develops in dialectical spirals from primitive communism to slaveholder society, to feudalism, to capitalism, and finally to communism. This is a necessary development and transcends individual and group actions in particular historical situations. These may influence minor variations, but they cannot change the overall macroscopic development (Marx and Engels 1959).

What produces the developmental logic in history is the fact that the human being must *work* in order to maintain existence. Out of the work process arise the forces of production. Labor also means that the human being necessarily enters into certain relations with nature and with fellow human beings (relations of production), and also develops human culture, the political and ideal superstructure. In the historical process development of the forces of production (e.g., technology) proceeds more rapidly than development of the relations of production and of the superstructure; the latter then come to be fetters on the development of the forces of production. This contradiction leads to a revolutionary period in which the relations of production and the political and ideal superstructure are transformed (Marx 1961). Whether this macroscopic dynamic leaves any room for the actions of individuals and groups in historical situations has long been debated in Marxist theory. Marx's more historical writing stresses group actions and group coalitions in historical situations, thus modifying and possibly contradicting the macroscopic developmental logic of his theory of history (Marx 1960).

In a macroscopic system of commodity production, human action is determined by the laws of the system that develop independent of individual motivation and that exert external power on human individuals and are unmodifiable by them. This is what Marx calls the *self-alienation* of the human individual in commodity production, a notion that explicitly states the independence of commodity production as a macroscopic system from individual action and its impact on this action.

In Marx's view the laws of commodity production spread on the macroscopic level throughout society, because they are the basic determining forces. The dynamic of the capitalist system necessitates political crisis management and welfare politics in order to balance antagonism in the system. Ideological systems develop to maintain the legitimacy of the capitalist system. If one considers Marxist explanations of these relationships between the capitalist economy and other societal systems, one discovers mainly functionalist explanations. The political and sociocultural systems generally support the economic system, and in times of crisis the economic crisis precipitates political, motivational, and legitimation crises.

Although his theory is mainly concerned with macroscopic laws, Marx cannot avoid referring to the actions of individuals and groups, particularly when it comes to explaining revolutionary change. In this case the organized classes and parties enter the scene as political actors, acting at least in the role of accelerating or retarding historical necessity. In addition, Marxist theory moves in the direction of taking microprocesses into account.

A MACROTHEORY OF CONFLICT: THE ANTAGONISM OF DOMINATING AND DOMINATED GROUPS

In developing his argument Marx proceeds from economic macroprocesses of capitalism to the antagonism of classes. In this way he adds elements of a political macrotheory of conflict to his economic macrotheory of capitalism. Ralph Dahrendorf (1958) generalized the conflict elements in Marx's theory to form a macro conflict theory.

The predominant macrostructure for macro conflict theory is the division of every society into dominating and dominated groups. These groups form according to their access to positions of power. Those who have access can enforce binding decisions throughout society. The incumbents of both dominating and dominated positions form quasigroups with latent common interests and stand in adversary relation to one another. The dominating group is interested in maintaining the status quo; the dominated group wants to change the existing order according to its own interests.

As quasi-groups become organized they feel a common belongingness; they have material means, an ideology, and a leadership; they form overt interest groups as collective actors; and the conflict becomes manifest. This conflict is the potential for change. The more the dominated group can overcome the capacity of the ruling group to stay in power, the more likely is societal change to occur according to its goals, change accompanied by greater access to power accruing to the previously dominated group. After the new group has come to power, a new, opposing dominated group also emerges. This is the dynamic for continuous change.

According to macro conflict theory, heated conflicts between the politically dominating and the politically dominated group spread to every sphere of society. In present-day Western societies the conflict between men as the dominating group and women as the dominated group seems to be such a conflict, one that is not limited to the political field. Women fight not only for access to political power positions but also for economic, academic, family, and community positions. Religion, the arts, and science come under attack from the women's movement for being structured predominantly according to men's way of thinking.

The further macro conflict theory moves from the explanation of latent conflicts to the explanation of change, the more it must take into account the actions of individuals and groups in historical situations. The conflict logic must be complemented by a conflict dynamic. Thus macro conflict theory, like Marxist theory, relies on microprocesses to the extent that it wishes to explain concrete historical processes of change.

A MACROTHEORY OF NORMATIVE ORDER: DURKHEIM AND FUNCTIONALISM

No one has stated the case for the macroscopic as a reality in itself as emphatically as Durkheim did in his programmatic treatment of the social fact in his *Rules of the Sociological Method*. What Durkheim ([1895] 1973*b*) refers to as social facts are macroscopic phenomena: the legal system, the system of currency, the language in a society. These institutions extend into both past and future and endure longer than the lives of their individual incumbents. As Durkheim insists, social facts are things in themselves, external to individuals, universal, and exert an external constraint on individuals.

The legal system of a society is a reality that determines both individual action and societal development. For example, the fact that West Germany has a system of codified general laws is a reality that insists that any institutional innovation must be formulated in keeping with and integrated into the existing system of laws. Insofar as the realization of rights to freedom at the workplace, in schools, in universities, or in families necessitates new laws, this leads to growing juridification of life. This legal system is independent of the will and motivations of individuals, is external to them, is universal because it affects every member of society, and is constraining on individuals.

The center of the social fact as a reality in itself is, for Durkheim, the collective constituted by all members of the society and sustained by their solidarity and commonly shared norms and beliefs, which in turn build the collective conscience and consciousness. The association of individuals to constitute a society is for Durkheim what the laws of commodity production are for Marx and what the antagonism of groups is for conflict theory. When Durkheim studied the division of labor, the state, education, religion, or science, he sought to discover how the moral forces spread over these different spheres of society. The moral forces must extend to the spheres to create order in society.

Durkheim could not formulate his insights, however, without reference to acting individuals and, by definition, to the microscopic level. When he argued that collective representations arise from an immense cooperation spreading out in time and space, when he referred to the association of members of society in ritual practice and the collective effervescence emanating from them as a form of the maintenance and recreation of collective solidarity, he pointed to the fact that macroscopic phenomena are created and sustained through individual and group actions. It is a certain type of action, however: the association of individuals as members of the same group or society and their cooperation in which they reaffirm their belongingness and sharing of basic beliefs. In this way cooperation and ritual practice for Durkheim are actions necessary for the creation of (macroscopic) collective solidarity and common beliefs, just as for Marx the political action of groups is necessary in order to sustain revolutionary change in society.

Functionalist sociology, as developed especially in the 1950s, also identified society as a unit of analysis independent of individual action. This approach seeks to explain certain structures and institutions in a society by identifying the functions they fulfill in maintaining the working of society as a whole. For example, the functionalist theory of stratification explains a system of stratification not as resulting from conflict and its resolution among rival groups, as would conflict theory, but by the function it fulfills for the working and maintenance of society. In terms of Davis and Moore's (1945) theory, every society must allocate positions to its members, according to the importance of their contribution to society and the scarcity of people qualified for the positions. Without a grading scale that defines the importance of positions, there could be no uniform system of stratification in society. For this reason the central macroscopic unit for functionalists is the central societal value system that defines what is more and what is less important for society. Furthermore, the central value system permeates society, defining the functions to be fulfilled and setting the criteria for the institutions that fulfill those functions (Parsons 1951). Thus a value system that stresses mastery of the world, as the traditional American system does, would also stress strong economic institutions and an advancement of technology and would rank individuals in those areas highly. The high rank of individualism in this value system would also discourage a very strong government. The opposite is true in Germany, where the Protestant emphasis on the mastery of the world has been allied with the responsibility of a strong state for society and a high place in the ranking system for governmental and administrative positions. These examples show how, in terms of functionalist sociology, the values of society spread throughout society to shape those institutions that contribute to the maintenance and working of society.

Is such a functionalist sociology possible without any reference to the actions of individuals and groups? We believe not. The value system itself is the outcome of processes of defining what is valuable. This involves priests, theologians, intellectuals, writers, lawyers, and politicians, who contribute to defining the valuable and thereby legitimizing and delegitimizing ideas, values, and norms. This process of defining the value system involves the association of groups, conflict among groups, domination of some groups by others, and the settlement of conflicts among rival societal groups. The same holds when considering the interpretation and application of values to create and sustain concrete institutions. It is not an automatic process of functional fit between institutions and a value system but concrete historical action in which the norms are defined for institutions through a process of competition.

Niklas Luhmann (1970, 1984) formulated a radical version of functionalism. He abandoned the premise of a common value system, making the system and its environment the only basic elements. For Luhmann systems have no internal standards for coping with their environment apart from the abstract survival of systems as such. Luhmann then introduces the concept of growing world complexity, which sets the problem of reducing complexity for the human being. Systems are always reductions of complexity in the context of the higher complexity of their environment. The general device for this accommodation to environmental complexity is through internal differentiation of subsystems that are specialized in the function of translating areas of environmental complexity into internal terms of the system itself. The system is Luhmann's unit of macroanalysis. The basic macroprocess is the differentiation of systems. It spreads throughout society, leading to more specialized units in society. Luhmann develops this line of argument without reference to historical situations and actions of individuals and groups. In applying his theory to concrete historical developments he interprets changes in politics, law, economics, community, literature, and religion as processes of growing societal differentiation.

Giesen's discussion of the evolutionary paradigm in this volume resembles Luhmann's approach. According to this approach, ideas, norms, institutions, and actions undergo a process of selection as conditioned by prevailing factors in their environment. This process of selection takes place without human intention. Haferkamp formulates this view in discussing one type of development of macrostructures. Luhmann's theory can be interpreted in such a way that growing environmental complexity sets the external selective conditions for systems that can survive only if they become more differentiated functionally.

Blau's macrotheory of the structural influence on aggregated action presented in this volume can also be interpreted in light of a theory of structural selection (see also Blau 1977). He states that societal structures leave open certain options for action and close off others. Thus in an environment of heterogeneity—for example, with greater inequality and greater intersection of social groups, social strata, and social spheres—we may expect more intergroup, interstrata, and intersphere relations.

In recent years the tradition of functionalist thought has evolved significantly. Alexander (1983), for example, in his contribution to this volume and elsewhere, combines functionalist macrotheory with positivist and interpretive microtheory. Other contributions to this innovation in functionalism from a more distinctively German theoretical perspective have been formulated by Münch (1982). A major point is the emphasis on the foundations of Parsons's work in action theory. Münch's contribution to this volume breaks down the working of social subsystems with their specific effects on the confirmation, continuity, enforcement, and change of social order into different types of social action. Social order is seen as an outcome of the interpenetration of preexisting symbolic, normative, authoritative, and economic macrostructures and discursive, associational, political, and economic microaction. Gerstein elaborates in his essay on Durkheim's theory of suicide in terms of Parsonian action theory, moving from a "macrodeterminist" approach toward a model of macro-micro interdependencies.

A MACROTHEORY OF CULTURAL SYMBOLISM: EVOLVING REASON FROM HEGEL TO HABERMAS

In his essay in this volume Giesen draws attention to the "categorial-analytic model" as an approach to the macro-micro relation. The roots of this approach lie in the tradition of German idealism. This tradition stresses in macroterms the explanation of the development of culture. Hegel (1970, 1976) provided the classical formulation. His philosophy of history seeks to demonstrate that history has meaning and proceeds in stages of realization of basic ideas; it is the development of an objective spirit. Culture transcends all subjective human thinking and develops according to an internal logic.

In this approach systems of ideas are the basic units of macroscopic analysis. The structure, consistency, contradictions, and development of these systems can be studied without regard to the individual subjects involved in their formulation. The natural sciences, for example, have evolved as a system of ideas that can be studied without reference to key personalities such as Kepler, Newton, and Einstein. The same can be said of the development of thought in the humanities, social sciences, literature, religion, and morals. The system of ideas is an emergent phenomenon that has a structure and internal logic of development. This is the message of the German term *Geisteswissenschaft* (Dilthey 1970).

The basic process of culture according to the premises of idealism is rationalization. For religion this means approaching ever more consistent systems of meaning; for morals it means approaching ever more universally valid moral norms; for the arts it means approaching ever more valid systems in which the feelings of human individuals can be expressed; and for science it means approaching ever truer and more inclusive propositions concerning the world. The process of rationalization is not, however, confined to culture but can affect society itself, leading to the rationalization of the economy, politics, law, education, the family, and so on. In Hegel's terms this is a dialectical process. Insofar as primitive perception becomes replaced by conscious understanding and the family-organized tribal society by civil society, there is a contradiction between thought and world, family and civil society. The progress of thought to universal reason, however, and integration of the family and civil society by the state that is committed to the idea of *Sittlichkeit* (the synthesis of morality and legality) leads to a higher-order reconciliation of thought and reality. In this way reason finds its realization in the world. Cultural rationalization succeeds in a complete societal rationalization.

The question concerns how these processes of rationalization can be explained without reference to individual and group actors in historical situations. On the macro level of ideas the theory formulates only a logic of development, but the theory does not show what really happens in history because it does not address the actions of individuals in historical situations. The more these actions enter the explanatory framework, the more room there is for aberrations from the path of rationalization: Group formation; solidarity relationships; conflict among intellectuals, scientists, politicians, classes, and groups; economic calculations; and rational criticism and discourse between equals together determine the fate of ideas.

The difference between developmental logic and the historical dynamics of development has given rise to a great deal of historical debate. Hegel's developmental logic of ideas has been opposed by Marx's emphasis on the economic forces and the antagonism of classes. Marx's paradoxical transmission of the developmental logic of ideas to a developmental logic of economic forces, which nevertheless ultimately leads to realization of the idea of humanity in communism, has been criticized by more historically oriented Marxists. In the philosophy of science Popper's (1972) developmental logic of the progress of scientific knowledge has been attacked by Kuhn (1965) in his psychology and sociology of the historical dynamics of science. Weber's ([1920] 1972) theory of religious and subsequent societal rationalization has as its starting point a developmental logic of religious rationalization, the emergence of ever more internally consistent systems of theodicy providing meaning and explaining the contradiction between the conception of a perfect God or godly principle and an imperfect world. Weber ([1922] 1976), however, himself combined this developmental logic of ideas with a microtheory of historical actors who carry forward and apply ideas. In this way the developmental logic of ideas is complemented by the historical dynamics of the actions of individuals and groups.

Habermas (1981) conceives of societal evolution as a developmental logic of cultural rationalization that becomes transformed into societal rationalization. In his view historical development has resulted in incomplete cultural rationalization because it remained confined to purely cognitive instrumental rationalization. This, in turn, led to the differentiation of instrumentally rationalized systems from their cultural origin, which is conceived of as the "life-world." The more the systems of the economy, administration, and law progressed in their development, the more they actually came to dominate (colonize) the original life-world. Habermas's intention is to explain in this way the growing economization, bureaucratization, and juridification of society, even of life-world spheres such as the family, school, the arts, science, and public discussion.

What Habermas provides with regard to the underlying microprocesses of the macro-level development of ideas is his theory of rational discourse. We can assume that ideas approach validity in proportion to actors' greater involvement in procedures of rational discourse, in which everyone has the same right to propose and criticize ideas and only the best argument is relevant to the acceptance of ideas. In this instance Habermas gives a microprocessual foundation for the macrodevelopment of ideas that was not formulated in the tradition of German idealism. He calls this the failure of the philosophy of consciousness in German idealism, which he remedies with his procedural theory of consensus formation. Habermas gives the German macrodevelopmental logic an Anglo-Saxon microprocessual foundation.

Habermas's microsociological supplement to his developmental logic of ideas, however, remains confined to communication as a type of interaction. Because he is primarily devoted to studying history as a process of the realization of ideas, he is more interested in sustaining the developmental logic of ideas than in explaining historical dynamics. Such an explanation would also have to refer to the conflict between involved groups, to the formation of relationships of solidarity in association, and to economic calculation.

MOVING FROM THE MICRO TO THE MACRO: ATTEMPTED SOLUTIONS

In many respects the central theme of this volume of theoretical essays can be represented as struggling with problems and dilemmas that arise in attempting to move from the micro to the macro level, and vice versa, in an effort to generate more comprehensive and adequate accounts of variations in individual behavior, interactions, and structures. Most of the rest of this concluding essay will be dedicated to exploring attempted solutions to these problems and dilemmas. We begin by considering modes of moving from the small to the large.

AGGREGATION

We have already mentioned this simplest of modes of moving from micro to macro, which is built on the assumption that the whole (the macro) is equal to the sum of its parts. We mentioned also that this was the primary solution for neoclassical economics, to aggregate discrete market transactions into measures that constituted ingredients of the structure of an economy. It might also be mentioned that Durkheim's characterization of a suicide rate, which he regarded as something we would call macro (a social fact), was also constituted by aggregating individual suicides as discovered in the public records. At least one contributor (Collins) seems to accept the aggregative transition as legitimate, in his characterization of the macro as "only . . . the repeated experiences of large numbers of persons in time and space."

It strikes us that the aggregative mode is appropriately applied only when the investigator represents this aggregation as some kind of social *rate*, such as purchases, votes, or suicides. Even this has its problems, for, as Wippler and Lindenberg point out, it rests on the assumption that $\text{individual}_1 = \text{individual}_2 = \text{individual}_n$, a criticism that rests on Weber's insistence that a statistic cannot be interpreted without knowing the meaning or context in which the events constituting that statistic were generated. More serious objections to the use of aggregation arise when we take note of the fact that sociologists are interested in arriving at and explaining other kinds of macrophenomena than rates alone. They often wish to characterize and explain discrete events (such as a major decision, a revolution, the passage of a law), organizational behavior, changes in social structure, and value systems. Here the limits of aggregation are apparent, as revealed by efforts to describe culture by adding up responses to surveys, to characterize political stability by adding up accounts of riots in newspapers and periodicals. More often investigators, at least implicitly sensitive to the limitations of aggregation, tend to rely on some other, more complex kind of combinatorial method.

COMBINATION OF MICROINTERACTIONS WITH OTHER FACTORS

The logic of combination differs from that of aggregation in that whatever factors are combined are done so not by addition but by attempting to assess variables that are qualitatively different in character but, when combined, give a more adequate explanation of some macrophenomenon. In his efforts to refine the aggregative method, Coleman cites examples of introducing institutional, organizational, leadership, and collective process variables into the refinement of explanations of macroevents and macrostructures. This same combinatorial logic is evidenced in Boudon's characterization of Tocqueville's explanation of the onset of the French Revolution and Weber's characterization of the Protestant sects, both of which relied on micro (individual behaviors and interactions by actors) but which interacted with existing historical situations and the confluence of events. The evident difficulty in the combinatorial logic is in assigning weight to the factors to be combined; but if they themselves can be represented as rates, a variety of multivariate statistical techniques are available to attempt to weigh their respective influences.

It might be noted in passing that Weber's conception of the ideal type was not only a means for moving from the micro to the macro but also constituted a kind of mixture of an aggregative and a combinatorial logic. Weber's starting point for sociological study was subjectively meaningful action and interaction. The problem created by this starting point might be called the *ideographic dilemma*: If all actors attach different subjective meanings to their situations, how is it possible to arrive at any kind of generalization (macrostatement) about them? Weber presumed that for any historical group sufficient numbers assigned sufficiently common meanings to their situation that generalizations could be made, and these took the form of ideal types such as religious belief systems. The ideal types were not arrived at by aggregation, however, but by the investigator's imaginative extraction of common elements and by combining them into coherent ideal-type concepts that represented no individual's belief exactly but that captured the essence of many. This represented Weber's solution to the difficulty of moving from the micro to the macro.

EXTERNALIZATION

Later we will mention the phenomenon of internalization of societal and cultural elements as one means of solving the transition from macro to micro. There is a cognate version moving in the other direction. This is found in the psychoanalytic tradition, most notably in Freud's *Totem and Taboo* ([1913] 1955), in which a wide range of religious beliefs, structures, and rituals are represented as institutional solutions to basically psychodynamic conflicts. This tradition extended into the anthropological tradition of culture and personality, exemplified in Kardiner's *The Psychological Frontiers of Society* (1945), in which a variety of "secondary" institutions, such as folk and religious traditions, were represented as projections of psychological conflicts generated in the early phases of childhood socialization. The same kind of relationship is envisioned as a possibility in Smelser's essay, in which it is pointed out that cultural elements (adages, ideologies, folk tales, religious beliefs) may be sustained as legitimately available defenses against both internal conflicts and external threats. The logic of explanation in this case is that the persistence of such cultural elements (macro) cannot be understood without reference to the processes of intrapsychic and external coping processes of individuals (micro).

CREATING, SUSTAINING, OR REPRODUCING THE MACRO

At the beginning of his chapter Schegloff states that a conversational sequence, with its pauses, intonations, turn-taking, and the like, "effects a form of social organization." The kind of social organization produced does not appear to be very macro in its reference, but the principle is clear. A kind of "speech-exchange system"—a bit of culture, if you will—constitutes the building block, which in turn is a "substantial proportion of the conduct of which all the other major social institutions is composed." It is this kind of building through interaction that we have in mind in this section. It is clearly identified with different strands of the phenomenological tradition, considered broadly. Garfinkel, for example, in his original exposition of the ethnomethodological perspective, rejected those role theorists who explain regularities of behavior in terms of compliance with standardized expectancies, regards the control of behavior as a continuously negotiated or monitored process, in which those in interaction bargain over the meanings and terms of exchange. Blumer, too, rejects the idea that the repetitious character of most of social action is the result of "adherence to sets of rules, norms, values, and sanctions that specify to people how they are to act in their different situations" (Blumer 1969:18). Rather, repeated actions are as dependent upon interpretation as are novel types of interaction, and orderliness in a society is a function of a multitude of continuously interpreted interactions that may yield macrouniformities. The stress on the "social construction of reality" falls into the same genre of theories (Berger and Luckmann 1966). The view of society arising from this perspective is, of course, symbolic in character, and exponents of the perspective have as a polemic target what they regard as the tendency for many social scientists to reify structures and to seek regularities among them at their own level (Boudon's nomological paradigm). Certainly within this perspective the macro appears to lose much of its independent status.

CONFORMITY

To complete the picture of types of transition from micro to macro, we refer to that polemic target—the conformity model—of the school of thought to which we have just referred. Associated with role theory and the social action (or system) theory of Parsons (1951), this kind of transitional model actually begins with a macro set of assumptions—namely, that there is a kind of social reality (norms, expectations, institutions) that exists in a kind of independent if not transcendent level, separate from individual persons. The key question associated with this approach concerns whether individual persons are socialized to conform to these expectations or whether the socialization system "misfires" or fails in some way and deviant behavior occurs, in which case an ancillary set of mechanisms, usually categorized under the heading of "social control," is called into play. The micro side of the theory is the degree of conforming or deviating behavior on the part of the individual, either on his or her own or in interaction with others, and the macro outcomes usually are phrased in terms of social order in general, institutional behavior, and rates of various kinds of deviance. It is noteworthy that this particular transitional model, which still informs the work of many sociologists in the field, even though it has been eclipsed to some degree by other models of the transition from micro to macro, scarcely figures in the pages of this volume.

MOVING FROM MACRO TO MICRO: ATTEMPTED SOLUTIONS

If we can say that the dilemma for the individualistic approaches is how to attain the level of macrophenomena from the analysis of situations of action, then we can also say that the distinctive dilemma for the macroscopic approaches is, first, how they can demonstrate the relevance of macrophenomena for individual action and, second, how they can sustain their propositions on the macro level by reference to the actions of individuals and groups.

THE MACRO AS INTERNALIZED

One mode of moving macro to micro has to do with asserting that elements of the macro *penetrate* individuals in some way, and that these elements (moral standards, rules of conduct, language) operate to govern, in either general or detailed ways, personal conduct and personal interaction. The most evident example is found in Kurzweil's account of Parsons's discussion of the superego, in which Parsons attempts to synthesize both Freudian and Durkheimian positions by arguing that the superego is the locus of internalized culture and society and, as such, constitutes society's regulatory presence in the individual. The mechanism of internalization is rooted, of course, in the socialization process. Consideration of Giesen's discussion of the constitutive rules of language as macrostructure and speech acts as microinteraction at least implies some kind of internalization of the constitutive rules (in socialization). No one has argued that these constitutive rules are invented or negotiated in every interactive situation; rather, they seem to stand as "categorical prerequisites" for interaction. They are evidently learned in the process of acquiring language and "knowledge" about societal macrostructures through language. The same observation can be made with respect to Schegloff's discussion of "repair" of conversation, which appears to presuppose some kind of understood rules to which the repair is directed. These rules, too, are not manufactured on the spot in every interaction but have been made the constitutive grounds for both recognizing "trouble" and "repairing." The general perspective that emerges here is that there is some kind of internalized cultural component, the integrity of which is continuously monitored in the communicative process. Even in cases in which the individual and his or her interactions break down in some pathological way, one makes use of the assumption of penetration. Hondrich's discussion, for example, of "contradiction between regulative principles"—referring to a diversification and contradiction of values via the avenue of structural differentiation—implies that in order for these to constitute a contradiction *for the individual*, they must have been internalized and positively connected in some way, or else there could be no contradiction.

THE MACRO AS SETTING LIMITS

A common solution to the question of the relevance of macrophenomena for the actions and interactions of individuals and groups in situations is to conceive of macrophenomena as limiting frames of reference that set the agenda for microprocesses. Examples are law, markets, and property.

The law of a society is a set of rules covering a whole range of types of action throughout space and time. For example, the law of contract can be applied to any concrete contractual relationship independent of time, place, and the persons involved. The law defines how a contract can be concluded and defines the rights and duties of the contracting parties; it lays down rules for concluding a contract; and these rules determine an agenda for what the contracting parties can and cannot do. The contracting parties must take into account these laws insofar as they are institutionalized and backed by binding sanctions. The existence of contract law controls the actions of contracting parties and makes it possible to predict the actions of various actors, including third parties.

In a similar way a competitive market sets limits and agendas for the actions of individuals. The fact that there is a market for the exchange of goods forces the individuals who want to satisfy their needs to buy and sell goods and services according to the prices resulting from market competition. A seller who always sells below market prices may endanger his or her survival on the market in the long run. Only the possession of sizable reserves allows some sellers to sell below market price in order to drive competitors from the market. Similarly, buyers are forced to buy goods at the market price. All participants are limited in their actions by the laws of the market, and these laws also set the agenda for the economic actors in that setting.

The institutionalization and distribution of property represent other factors that limit action and set agendas for actors. Insofar as private property is the institutionalized form, individual actors are allowed to satisfy needs only by acquiring property or rights in property owned by other people, by a corporation, or by the state. If one wants to get from Los Angeles to San Diego, one either needs to own a car (which must be bought), rent a car, or buy a train or airplane ticket. If one steals a car or tries to travel without a ticket, one will be punished for misuse of others' property. In this case the existing system of property structures is a determining environmental constraint; and the distribution of property means that such a constraint is structured differently for different individuals according to what they do or do not possess.

In one respect Alexander's synthetic essay in this volume represents a statement of how macroelements such as the division of labor, authority systems, solidarity, and culture set limits on individuals' typifying and inventing of empirical reality and on the avenues of action (strategies) available to the individual. At the same time, however, he regards these limits not as fixed parameters but as constantly being reproduced, interpreted, and modified by these same processes of typification, invention, and strategization. By stressing this constant two-way flow of action—with neither direction capable of being grasped without simultaneous reference to the other—Alexander comes as close as anyone to making the micro/macro distinction a purely analytical one.

To follow these general lines of discussion, we now move to a more detailed consideration of some special problems distinctive to the specific paradigms.

The Macrotheory of Capitalism: The Macro as Repressive, and Triggering Microprocesses

For Marx (1970) contract law, the market, and property are macrostructures that force individuals into relationships that are determined by external laws they cannot control. This implies the estrangement of the individual from other human beings, of the social community from the external world of the economy and politics that governs people's lives, and of the human being from the world in general. Another consequence is the class antagonism resulting from capitalist accumulation.

The more the autonomous macroprocesses sharpen alienation and antagonisms, the more the classes involved become conscious of their position in the system and organize themselves as active parties in the historical process. It was at this point that Marx not only formulated a radical version of the macrostructural setting of limits and agenda for action but also touched on the problem of how the microprocesses themselves generate changes on the macrostructural level.

The Macrotheory of Conflict: Repressive Macrostructures Precipitating Opposition and Counteraction

In a way similar to Marx's macrotheory of capitalist development, macro conflict theory conceives of macrostructures as involving basic antagonisms that initiate microprocesses in order to change the macrostructure (Dahrendorf 1958). The antagonism between the dominating and the dominated group leaves room only for opposition and struggle for change, which brings the dominated group into conflict with the dominating group. Both groups become involved in a growing struggle, which ends with some settlement of the conflict and the emergence of a new macrostructure. It is through this repeated struggle that processes of social change are generated. Both Collins and Giesen, in the discussion of the model of antagonism, provide insights into these processes.

The Macrotheory of Normative Order: The Macro as Constraining, Producing Microresponses and Macro-Aggregated Rates

Durkheim ([1893] 1973*a*) provided the classical formulation of the conception of macrostructure as setting the limits and agenda for the actions of individuals by emphasizing the noncontractual foundations of contract. In his criticism of Spencer's utilitarianism he pointed to the fact that no individual would be able to predict how contracting parties would act or, therefore, to act rationally if there were not rules of contract transcending any individual contract. Contract rules are social facts that exert an external constraint on the actions of individual contracting parties.

In his study of suicide Durkheim paid special attention to the ways in which macrophenomena produce certain responses in the individual which aggregate to form a macrophenomenon ([1897] 1973*c*). The organization of the Protestant religion, for example, gives the individual more freedom of inquiry—which implies greater opportunity to question the meaning of life—than in the Catholic religion. This explains the higher rate of suicide among Protestants than among Catholics. Durkheim established a relationship between a macrostructure (the degree of collective control of belief in a religion) and aggregated individual action in a collective (the suicide rate of members of a particular religion). The two are linked by mediating assumptions about individual reactions to the macrostructural phenomena.

In this volume Smelser's contribution elaborates Durkheim's attempt to relate constraining macrostructures to microresponses that aggregate to form another macrophenomenon. Applying psychoanalytic theory, Smelser points out different ways in which the individual personality can cope with macrosocial constraints: through different types of defensive strategies. These modes of defense again can be related to external social conditions in order to explain their probability of selection and then can be aggregated to form macro rates of behavior.

The Macrotheory of Cultural Symbolism: The Realization of Ideas

The macrotheory of cultural symbolism sees systems of cultural ideas evolving according to their internal logic of rationalization. In its Hegelian version the development of the objective spirit becomes completely translated into the development of the subjective spirit of the human individual (Hegel 1970, 1976). The more actors become "enlightened" by the diffusion of the objective spirit, the more they will realize the valid ideas in their action. In practical terms this means, for example, that education has the task of leading the human individual to the light of universal reason. *Bildung durch Wissenschaft* (approximately, "Education through humanities and sciences") has been propagated as the basic task of the German university since its reform in 1810. Thus the organization of education—for example, the integration of research and teaching, learning in research, the fiduciary responsibility of the teacher for the education of the student—has been of central interest for German idealism in addressing the problem of transforming the development of reason into concrete human action. The educational process is the typical microprocess that corresponds to the evolution of universal reason. In Habermas's (1981) version of this approach it is the institutionalization of procedures of rational discourse which must provide the microprocessual foundations for the spread of universal reason.

The relation of the macrodevelopment of reason to microinteraction is seen as a process of realization of reason that only has to overcome the obstacles set by reality. What is neglected in this view is the question as to whether there are, in principle, obstacles to value realization such as those expressed in paradoxes of value realization, as discussed in this volume in Hondrich's essay on "Micropathology and Macronormality." What (according to Weber) can be called "the paradox of rationalization" is another problem for the idealist theory of value realization (see Schluchter 1981; Schluchter and Roth 1979).

A CONCLUDING NOTE

In bringing this chapter and this volume to a close, we would like to strike a note that ran through the original conference, that runs throughout this volume, and, we believe, has come to characterize theoretical discourse in this decade: Both microscopic processes that constitute the web of interactions in society and the macroscopic frameworks that result from and condition those processes are essential levels for understanding and explaining social life. Moreover, those who have argued polemically that one level is more fundamental than the other (in some kind of zero-sum way), or who have argued for the complete independence of the two levels, must be regarded as in error. Virtually every contributor to this volume has correctly insisted on the mutual interrelations between micro and macro levels, and on the necessity of characterizing transitional and emergent processes moving in both directions. It seems to us that to strive for the better theoretical and empirical understanding of these processes constitutes a proper agenda for the coming years.

REFERENCES

Alexander, Jeffrey H. 1983. *Theoretical Logic in Sociology*. Vol. 4. Berkeley, Los Angeles, London: University of California Press.

Berger, P. L., and T. Luckmann. 1966. *The Social Construction of Reality*. New York: Doubleday.

Blau, Peter M. 1977. *Inequality and Heterogeneity*. New York: Free Press.

Blumer, Herbert. 1969. *Symbolic Interactionism*. Englewood Cliffs, N.J.: Prentice-Hall.

Collins, Randall. 1975. *Conflict Sociology: Toward an Explanatory Paradigm*. New York: Academic Press.

Dahrendorf, R. 1958. Toward a Theory of Social Conflict. *Journal of Conflict Resolution* 2:170–183.

Davis, K., and W. E. Moore. 1945. Some Principles of Stratification. *American Sociological Review* 10:242–249.

Dilthey, W. 1970. *Der Aufbau der Geschichtlichen Welt in den Geisteswissenschaften*. Frankfurt: Suhrkamp.

Durkheim, Emile. 1973*a*. *De la Division du Travail Social* (1893). Paris: Presses Universitaires de France.

———. 1973*b*. *Les règles de la Méthode Sociologique* (1895). Paris: Presses Universitaires de France.

———.1973*c*. *Le Suicide* (1897). Paris: Presses Universitaires de France.

Freud, Sigmund. 1955. *Totem and Taboo* (1913). The Standard Edition of the Complete Psychological Works of Sigmund Freud. London: Hogarth.

Garfinkel, Harold. 1967. *Studies in Ethnomethodology*. Englewood Cliffs, N.J.: Prentice-Hall.

Habermas, Jürgen. 1981. *Theorie des kommunikativen Handelns*. Frankfurt: Suhrkamp.

Hegel, G. W. F. 1970. *Grundlinien der Philosophie des Rechts*, in E. Moldenhauer and K. M. Michel, eds., *Werke*. Vol. 7. Frankfurt: Suhrkamp.

———.1976. *Phänomenologie des Geistes*, in E. Moldenhauer and K. M. Michel, eds., *Werke*. Vol. 3. Frankfurt: Suhrkamp.

Kardiner, Abraham. 1945. *The Psychological Frontiers of Society*. New York: Columbia University Press.

Kuhn, Thomas. 1965. *The Structure of Scientific Revolutions*. Chicago: University of Chicago Press.

Luhmann, Niklas. 1970. *Soziologische Aufklärung*. Vol. 1. Opladen: Westdeutscher Verlag.

———.1984. *Soziale Systeme*. Frankfurt: Suhrkamp.

Marx, Karl. 1960. Der achtzehnte Brumaire de Louis Bonaparte, pp. 111–207 in *Marx-Engels Werke*. Vol. 8. Berlin: Dietz.

———.1961. Zur kritik der politisichen ökonomie, pp. 3–160 in *Marx-Engels Werke*. Vol. 13. Berlin: Dietz.

———.1970. *Das Kapital* (3 vols.), in *Marx-Engels Werke*. Vols. 23–25. Berlin: Dietz.

Marx, Karl, and F. Engels. 1959. Manifest der kommunistischen partei, pp. 459–493 in *Marx-Engels Werke*. Vol. 4. Berlin: Dietz.

Münch, Richard. 1982. *Theorie des Handelns*. Frankfurt: Suhrkamp.
Parsons, Talcott. 1951. *The Social System*. New York: Free Press.
Popper, Karl R. 1972. *Objective Knowledge*. Oxford: Clarendon.
Schegloff, Emanuel A. 1980. Preliminaries to Preliminaries: "Can I Ask You a Question?" *Sociological Inquiry* 50:104–152.
Schegloff, Emanuel A., and H. Sacks. 1973. Opening up Closings. *Semiotica* 8:289–327.
Schegloff, Emanuel A., G. Jefferson, and H. Sacks. 1977. The Preference for Self-Correction in the Organization of Repair in Conversation. *Language* 53:361–382.
Schluchter, W. 1981. *The Rise of Western Rationalism*. Berkeley, Los Angeles, London: University of California Press.
Schluchter, W., and G. Roth. 1979. *Max Weber's Vision of History*. Berkeley, Los Angeles, London. University of California Press.
Weber, Max. 1972. *Gesammelte Aufsätze zur Religionssoziologie* (1920). Vol. I. Tübingen: Mohr Siebeck.
———.1976. *Wirtschaft und Gesellschaft* (1922). Tübingen: Mohr Siebeck.
Zimmerman, D. H., and M. Pollner. 1971. The Everyday World as a Phenomenon, pp. 80–123 in J. D. Douglas, ed., *Understanding Everyday Life*. London: Routledge.

Index